POWER AND PROGRESS
ON THE PRAIRIE

Power and Progress on the Prairie

Governing People on Rosebud Reservation

THOMAS BIOLSI

UNIVERSITY OF MINNESOTA PRESS

MINNEAPOLIS • LONDON

The University of Minnesota Press gratefully acknowledges the generous assistance provided for the publication of this book by the University of California, Berkeley.

The author's royalties are assigned to the Sicangu Heritage Center, Sinte Gleska University.

Published by the University of Minnesota Press
111 Third Avenue South, Suite 290
Minneapolis, MN 55401-2520
http://www.upress.umn.edu

Printed in the United States of America on acid-free paper

The University of Minnesota is an equal-opportunity educator and employer.

24 23 22 21 20 19 18   10 9 8 7 6 5 4 3 2 1

Library of Congress Cataloging-in-Publication Data

Names: Biolsi, Thomas, author.
Title: Power and progress on the prairie : governing people on Rosebud Reservation / Thomas Biolsi.
Description: Minneapolis : University of Minnesota Press, [2018] | Includes bibliographical references and index. |
Identifiers: LCCN 2017056062 (print) | ISBN 978-1-5179-0082-3 (hc) | ISBN 978-1-5179-0083-0 (pb)
Subjects: LCSH: Rosebud Indian Reservation (S.D.)—Politics and government. | Rosebud Indian Reservation (S.D.)—History. | Rosebud Sioux Tribe of the Rosebud Indian Reservation, South Dakota—Politics and government. | Rosebud Sioux Tribe of the Rosebud Indian Reservation, South Dakota—Government relations. | Liberalism—United States—History—20th century—Case studies. | New Deal, 1933–1939—South Dakota. | Todd County (S.D.)—Politics and government. | South Dakota—Economic conditions—20th century.
Classification: LCC E99.D1 B565 2018 (print) | DDC 978.3/62—dc23
LC record available at https://lccn.loc.gov/2017056062

To Rose, and to Noah

CONTENTS

ABBREVIATIONS

AAA   Agricultural Adjustment Act
BAE   Bureau of Agricultural Economics
BIA   Bureau of Indian Affairs
CIA   Central Intelligence Agency
CNO   Chief of Naval Operations
DGXB   designated ground burst
DGZ   designated ground zero
FEMA   Federal Emergency Management Agency
FOIA   Freedom of Information Act
FY   fiscal year
IIM   individual Indian money
IR   intermediate range
IRA   Indian Reorganization Act
IRBM   intermediate range ballistic missile
JCS   Joint Chiefs of Staff
JSTPS   Joint Strategic Target Planning Staffs
KT   kiloton
MAD   mutually assured destruction
MALOA   Missile Area Land Owners Association
MRBM   medium range ballistic missile
MT   megaton
NGO   nongovernmental organization

NRA	National Recovery Act
NSC	National Security Council
NSDM	National Security Decision Memorandum
PD	presidential directive
SAC	Strategic Air Command
SCS	Soil Conservation Service
SIOP	Single Integrated Operational Plan
TLE	Tribal Land Enterprise
USAID	United States Agency for International Development
USDA	U.S. Department of Agriculture
USSR	Union of Soviet Socialist Republics
VRA	Voting Rights Act
WSEG	Weapons Systems Evaluation Group

INTRODUCTION

This book is about governing and government, but its primary object is not "the government," understood as legislatures, executive agencies, or courts. The actions of such constituted federal, state, and local entities are part of the subject matter of this book, but my central theoretical concern is the processes and practices of governing that are "beyond the state," in the sense of being both different from and more foundational than the state.[1] This does not mean that the state is insignificant or that it does not govern as I use that term here, but that the *practices and processes of governing have a relative autonomy from the state* and are what enables the state to exercise much of what power it deploys. They colonize state agencies and are taken up by state officials and other actors in historically specific ways, but they cannot be explained by reference to the state as an institution. "The state" does not have an inherent way of "seeing" or acting, although how state agencies and civil society "see" and act is very much at the core of this book.[2]

What, then, do I mean by "processes of governing beyond the state," or by "governing" or "government"? Michel Foucault offered a preliminary answer in a 1978 lecture at the Collège de France in which he defined government as "the right disposition of things that one arranges so as to lead them to a suitable end."[3] Foucault argued that modern power originates less in formal institutions such as the modern state or its agencies than in the kind of governing directed at the getting the right disposition

of things. Mitchell Dean and Barry Hindess provide a more concrete description of government as an assemblage of strategies, not one of political
institutions (legislatures, executives, courts). Government in Foucault's
framing can be understood, as it will be in this book, as

> an inventive, strategic, technical and artful set of "assemblages" fashioned
> from diverse elements, put together in novel and specific ways, and [aimed
> at] specific governmental objectives and goals. These assemblages com-
> prise a whole host of mundane and humble practices, techniques, and
> forms of practical knowledge which are often overlooked in analyses that
> concentrate on either political institutions or political thought. These
> might include: forms of practical know-how, from managerial doctrines to
> "total quality management" to recipe books for "entrepreneurial govern-
> ment"; intellectual tools, such as the flow-chart, the map, and the architec-
> tural or engineering plan; calculative technologies, from the budget and the
> statistical table to sophisticated forms of audit and cost accounting; modes
> of evaluating human, natural and financial resources, in terms of such
> entities as risks, profit, probability and danger; ways of knowing, training
> and regulating various agents, from those in positions of authority, such
> as politicians and bureaucrats, to those whose own self-government is
> thought to pose problems for the exercise of authority, such as the gay
> community, Aboriginal populations or even the long-term unemployed.[4]

It is this kind of governing, commonly called *governmentality* by Foucault
and by scholars influenced by him, that will be the focus of this book.
Although neither state institutions nor political and economic theory
will be ignored, the emphasis will be on the mundane and humble practices deployed in projects of governing.

To study governmentality is not to assume that projects of governing
are necessarily successful, or that those who govern achieve mastery over
the disposition of the people and things they mean to work on. Indeed, it
may well be the case that governing *congenitally fails*,[5] as Foucault argued
regarding disciplinary power in the prison,[6] but that does not mean that
governing does not have concrete effects that we must examine. Relatedly,
one should not assume that would-be governors—the actors who actively
plan, design, and implement programs of government—are consciously
aware of all the consequences of their governing. Mitchell Dean makes

this clear when he explains the significance of *mentality* in the concept of governmentality: "A mentality might be described as a *condition of forms of thought and is thus not readily amenable to be comprehended within its own perspective.*" In other words, in our examination of government, we want to include the "taken for granted" and thus a level of organization or systematicity "not usually open to questioning by its practitioners."[7]

In this vein, I take "progress" seriously as an intended goal of the governors, or as a "native category" in the terminology of anthropology. In this book, both Progress with initial capitalization and more humble progress, as in "making progress" on a problem, will be important explicit goals of the governors. Both forms of progress might also be called "improvement," as they are by Tanya Murray Li, and I follow her lead in assuming that "the will to improve can be taken at its word." But as Li's (and James Ferguson's) work clearly demonstrate, we need to follow this up with careful attention to the *actual power effects* of governing.[8]

Before describing the geographic focus of this book, I will briefly itemize the main concepts for the analysis of governing and government that will be used. These concepts are *not* mutually exclusive and have a good degree of overlap as they were used by Foucault (something that is often a frustration and challenge in reading Foucault's iterative corpus), but each concept refers to a distinct conceptual emphasis.

DISCIPLINE

This is a system of power, originating in the seventeenth and eighteenth centuries in which individuals are coerced and enticed to internalize a specific set of behaviors, or behavioral tendencies, intended by the disciplinary authorities. The classic example for Foucault is the prison, but the same system is at work in armies, factories, schools, corporate and other organizational offices, as well as in modern public space. The main disciplinary practices used to shape individual behavior are surveillance, examinations, the use of case files (reflecting specific kinds of disciplinary knowledge), and normalization (tracking the distribution of individuals relative to a prescriptive behavioral norm).

LIBERALISM

Foucault saw liberalism, which emerged in the second half of the eighteenth century, to some extent as replacing or reformatting discipline.

For him, liberalism is less a political-economic theory (although he recognizes the importance of political economy in its birth) than a concrete practice or habit of mind in governing where the central watchword is "how not to govern too much" (or, "let sleeping dogs lie"). The paradigmatic example for Foucault is the liberal market in which the economy is understood as a "natural" process with its own, inherent logic, that when protected from intervention will effectively govern without a governor.

GOVERNMENTALITY

This term is commonly used in a *generic* sense to refer to forms of power of all kinds as studied by Foucault and scholars influenced by him (hence the field of "governmentality studies"). But governmentality also has a *specific* meaning that overlaps with the concept of liberalism. For Foucault, governmentality refers to forms of power that take the population as the target of governing, that identify various kinds of "natural" processes requiring judicious regulation—birth, death, suicide, illness, accident, poverty, crime, pollution, and carbon emission and sequestration rates, for example. In other words, laissez-faire may be the watchword in a liberal regime of governing the economy but there are other natural phenomena that require wise intervention or attention to appropriately manage the disposition of things and people. The term also refers, as we saw, to specific programs to "responsibilize" individuals, as Nikolas Rose aptly describes it, such that they can and will take an active place in a liberal regime.[9]

SOCIAL GOVERNING

The concept of governmentality thus requires us to complicate the definition of liberalism in order to recognize its inevitably hybrid character in terms of actual practices. Alongside protection of the free market and privacy, liberalism encompasses, in its full development, interventions by both state agencies and civil-society organizations that move in the direction of what we commonly call the welfare state. Such interventions can be seen as brakes on the excesses (or myopia) *of liberalism*—or social corrections for the effects of free markets on human populations—that take the form of collective "security mechanisms," by which Foucault meant security as in "social security" in the United States. Here we find such practices as social insurance, worker protection, antitrust regulation, environmental protection, economic "stimuli," and others. However much classical liberals denounce such interventions, they are in terms of practices of modern power of a piece with laissez-faire in asking how best to regulate natural processes in the interest of caring for the population.[10]

BIOPOWER

This concept overlaps with governmentality and liberalism in that it refers, for Foucault, to the forms of power that emerged in the modern era and aim at the welfare and flourishing of the population, but it emphasizes governing that is close to biology or to human life itself—for example, public hygiene and public health. Biopower is "the power to make live,"[11] and the struggle over its exercise is biopolitics.

SUBJECTION

This is the process of individuals forming themselves into subjects with specific identities, drives, desires, and habits of mind—but under conditions not of their own choosing nor under their complete *or sovereign control* (this is why Foucault is sometimes called a "posthumanist"). Foucault described subjection as the process

> which categorizes the individual, marks him by his own individuality, attaches him to his own identity, imposes a law of trust on him, which he must recognize and which others have to recognize in him. It is a form of power which makes individuals subjects. There are two meanings of the word "subject": subject to someone else by control and dependence; and tied to his own identity by a conscience or self-knowledge. Both meanings suggest a form of power which subjugates and makes subject to.[12]

Subjection thus entails laying down the conditions of possibility for self-making, or the array of available technologies of the self (and how they are made available). Discipline, liberalism, governmentality, and biopower all entail subjection, or *attempts* by governors to frame the conditions under which individuals make themselves into acting subjects (acting in their "own" self-interest, as the process of subjection defines them). Just as we should make no assumptions about the success of programs of governing at reaching intended goals, we should not assume that programs to make "new" kinds of conscious individuals are effective in the ways governors, or would-be governors, mean to be effective.

Rural South Dakota is the setting for this book in part because of my abiding scholarly interest in the place, but also because it is a promising case for exploring a history of governing for progress in the countryside.[13] My focus is on the Rosebud country, four counties in the south-central part of the state, west of the Missouri River (see Maps 1.2 and 1.3). This was part of the aboriginal homeland of the Rosebud Sioux or Sičaŋǧu Lakota.[14] The Rosebud Sioux were horse-mounted, nomadic buffalo hunters in the nineteenth century, organized into flexible bands (tiošpaye) that coalesced and dispersed in synchrony with the availability of the game and grass on which they and their horses depended.[15] The larger homeland of what was to become the Rosebud country was recognized by the United States as "[t]he territory of the Sioux or Dahcotah Nation" in the Fort Laramie Treaty of 1851,[16] and was included in the Great Sioux Reservation established by the Fort Laramie Treaty of 1868.[17] Rosebud Reservation was established by the Great Sioux Act of 1889.[18] Beginning in the 1890s, the reservation was subdivided into allotments of land that were assigned to individual Indian people. Allotments, to be initially held in trust by the United States, were meant to "civilize" Indian people by vesting them with the (eventual) private property that was to ground their "interest" as private individuals, and would also provide for their support as they became farmers and farm wives, living on family farmsteads. At the same time, once all Lakota people were allotted land, a "surplus" of reservation land would remain, and this would be opened to homesteading by non-Indians, who became the majority population of the Rosebud country during the first two decades of the twentieth century. While the geographic size of the reservation decreased as a consequence of this settlement by non-Indians, the population size of the Rosebud Sioux Tribe has grown, as has the size and complexity of the tribal government (established in 1936). The Lakota language, elements of traditional Lakota culture (especially pertaining to sharing, generosity, and the obligations of relatives), and sacred ceremonies (for example, the sun dance, sweat lodge, pipe-loading ceremony, and *hunka* or making of relatives) and traditional spiritual practices have all survived, and the tribe, its members, and its communities are engaged in an ongoing struggle to revitalize and preserve all of this, which is considered key to their sovereignty and self-determination. Today the population of the area is estimated at approximately 21,650, half Indian and half non-Indian.[19] The reservation includes both Todd County and outlying Indian trust land in the other three counties. The Rosebud Sioux Tribe, with headquarters in Rosebud, South Dakota, exercises criminal and civil jurisdiction over these lands under tribal and federal law. As will be seen, there has been a fraught history between the tribal government and the subdivisions of state government (counties and municipalities) in the Rosebud country.

The Rosebud country is an apt place to examine the history of schemes for governing. It was first subjected to modern forms of government rather late in American history. Lakota people were not "pacified" until the 1880s (or even later), and the white settlement of the area began only in 1904. In part because the frontier disappeared only in the twentieth century in the Rosebud country, the archival sources are rich, offering a concrete sense of how governing grew in power and mutated in its targets over the course of the century from the 1880s to the 1980s. We will examine how the Lakota people were effectively pacified at the end of the Indian wars, how they were concentrated on reservations in order to open up a new "public domain" that could be settled in as systematic a way as possible, and in a way that fostered economic growth and political development. Once the territory was generally stabilized, Indians needed to be "civilized" in order to take their place as citizens alongside their (mostly white) neighbors, and these white farmers themselves needed to be guided into being progressive farm families so that they would not become a problem akin to Indians stuck in the past. During the Depression and drought of the 1930s, new ways needed to be found to take action on economic and environmental crises, and a major reform of the practices of government took place. During the Cold War rural South Dakota took on an unprecedented significance in nuclear strategy as the possibility of using the countryside in new ways to make nuclear war more "rational" gained currency. And in the wake of the civil-rights movement, South Dakota was also targeted in a new way as a place where racial discrimination against minority voters needed correction and surveillance.

The history of these challenges or problems could be narrated in terms of formal policy or acts of Congress, and these are not ignored here. But the emphasis in this book will be about how these challenges or problems were *made into problems* or *problematized*—the emerging practices and habits of mind by which a prevailing disposition of things appeared as a problem to be worked on, and the practices by which solutions, or at least mitigation of the problem, were pursued.[20]

Chapter 1, "The Birth of Liberalism on the Prairie, or How Not to Govern Too Much," reviews the history of settlement of the Rosebud country, beginning with the process by which the Lakota were concentrated on the reservation and "surplus" land deemed not needed by them was made available to white homesteaders in an early-twentieth-century land boom. Particular attention is given to how the U.S. public land survey turned formerly Indian land into "empty space" safe for the investment of labor and capital. Also examined is the (Jeffersonian) political vision of democracy and nationhood grounded in the ownership of farmland—a vision at the core of both the homestead policy for whites and the allotment policy for Indians. Finally, the chapter describes the commitment to growth and progress that was enabled by the liberal framework inherent in the conversion of Indian land into private property.

Chapter 2, "Discipline and Governmentality: Civilizing Indians and Making Farmers Progressive," focuses on the plans to improve Indians and white farmers, drawing on Foucault's concepts of discipline and governmentality. The Bureau of Indian Affairs (BIA) embarked on a policy of civilizing Indians as soon as they had been pacified and confined to the reservation. Illiberal (disciplinary) means—based on the BIA's authority over Indians and over the resources they needed to survive—were deemed necessary to make Indians into proper liberal subjects. But the BIA also found that authoritarian discipline was too blunt an instrument to reach its goals, and that more liberal forms of governmentality would be necessary. For white farmers, there was also much room for improvement, and the improvers in the extension service and the U.S. Department of Agriculture set about to teach farmers to be good businessmen and businesswomen. Although extension agents and government staff had no authority to impose their views on white farmers, as did the BIA with Indians, the attempt to secure improvement of rural people and communities was nonetheless a remarkable case of governmentality.

Chapter 3, "New Deal Practices: How Not to Govern Too Little," concerns the radical—in comparison to sod-busting liberalism—attempt to redefine the "problems" of rural Indians and whites. The chapter brings to light the key governmental practices of the New Deal as they played out in rural South Dakota. These practices of social governing, as distinct from liberalism, included a new attention to scale and to practices of scaling up, new ways of "seeing" that brought into focus "natural" patterns and processes that were not visible in the liberal grid (for example, soil erosion, which was never limited by property lines, and Lakota communities that were invisible on an allotment map), and devising methods to manage the natural patterns and processes by introducing countervailing or countercyclical corrections (for example, removing Indians from the assimilative Jeffersonian model of national space and democratic government in order to recognize their *exception* to national space and government).

Chapter 4, "Making New Deal Subjects," analyzes the attempts of the New Dealers to responsibilize proper New Deal subjects among the rural population who would think and act in terms of the new schematics described in chapter 3. The New Dealers were convinced that if reform was not "democratic"—actively participated in by those who were the targets of improvement—it would fail. They believed that grassroots participation was necessary both to secure political legitimation for reform programs and to benefit from the local knowledge of "the natural" that local people were in a unique position to provide. While there were certainly some people in South Dakota who embraced the New Deal (and some local agrarian thinkers had a leading role in the New Deal agricultural plans), most South Dakotans accepted the material benefits of the New Deal while either not understanding or not agreeing with the New Dealers' rationale. Indeed, for good reasons, many South Dakotans contested and were scandalized by the theories behind the reforms, which some even saw as totalitarian.

Chapter 5, "Planning Who Shall Die So Others May Live: Biopower and Cold War National Security," moves a little beyond the Rosebud country to trace the history of U.S. nuclear security policy and the placement of Minuteman missile silos in western South Dakota, just to the west-northwest of the Rosebud country (part of the Rosebud country was potentially in the thermonuclear blast and "fast" radiation zones if the missile silos were attacked by the Soviet Union). The aim to secure national security deployed an old (since the New Deal) practice of devaluing rural South Dakota in order to make "rational" the emplacement of strategic weapons there (and thus making it a primary enemy strategic target). Using Foucault's ideas about biopower and biopolitics, I trace the emergence of the theory of "limited war" that was developed by "defense intellectuals" and military planners in the late 1950s and early 1960s, and that was renewed as espoused policy in the 1970s and 1980s—indeed, until the time that the missiles stood down after the collapse of the USSR in 1991. I show how limited war, or a "counterforce" policy of strategic nuclear readiness, was attractive to policy makers because it promised that "populated" or "urban" (more "civilized"?) areas of the nation would be better protected by drawing a potential enemy's intercontinental ballistic missiles to strategic targets located in rural (less "civilized"?) places. I ask how it came to be that the consequences of such a spatial dividing practice could be countenanced—or suppressed—without comment on, much less concern about, the "target areas." How did a place once the target of New Deal pastoral power to help "the forgotten man," as Roosevelt put it, become a place to be sacrificed for "national" security, and what does that tell us about *subjection*?

Chapter 6, "Voting Rights, or How a Regulatory Assemblage Governs," traces the history of a Voting Rights Act case that concerned Todd County (the last remaining reservation county of the original Rosebud Reservation). Because of the scarcity of non-Indians and non-Indian land in Todd County (Indian trust land, even in individual allotments, is not taxable), it was originally "attached" to neighboring Tripp County for the provision of state and local services to both whites and Indians in Todd. By the 1970s, however, because Todd County residents could not vote for Tripp County officials, the legal question of the right of Indians to vote for "the officials who govern them" was raised, and the voting-rights section of the civil-rights division in the U.S. Justice Department insisted, along with the U.S. Eighth Circuit Court of Appeals, that people in Todd

County had the right to vote in Tripp County elections. The chapter unpacks how this administrative-legal schematic of racial discrimination in voting was at odds with the treaty-based and federal Indian-law-based understanding of an Indian reservation. In the end, both the Indian people and the white people living in Todd County got precisely what they did not want—an organized county government.

We turn first to how a good part of the Rosebud country was transformed from Indian country (a legal term of art dating from the English Proclamation of 1763) into private property where capitalism and economic growth would be at home. It is often—perhaps tritely—said that it was the Winchester rifle (model 1873) that won the West. As a symbol of the violence and coercion that were necessary to bring about the concentration of Native peoples on reservations, the Winchester works fine. But for "winning the peace," for taming the frontier (or "wilderness") into a pacified agrarian world, it was liberalism that did the work. Liberalism laid the groundwork for both settlement and property, and framed the productive activity that would civilize Indians and develop the West.

1

The Birth of Liberalism on the Prairie, or How Not to Govern Too Much

This chapter asks how liberalism made its appearance in the Rose-bud country. In liberalism's own accounting for itself—in John Locke, for example—it is the *natural* legal outgrowth of the elementary encounter between the individual and nature. The first (natural–legal) arrangement to flow from this is the right of the individual to his property—the land and other natural resources with which he (and the gender is clear in the birth of liberalism) has mixed his labor. The second (civil–legal) arrangement follows when such property owners consent in an *"original Compact"* to "joyn and unite into a Community, for their comfortable, safe, and peaceable living one amongst another, in a secure Enjoyment of their Properties." Such a "Body Politick" is inevitably to be governed by the consent of the majority.[1] Put differently, and closer to home, "the frontier is productive of individualism," Frederick Jackson Turner famously wrote in 1893. "It produces antipathy to control, and particularly to any direct control."[2]

Liberalism, in other words, presents itself as the pragmatic principle of leaving individual property and productive activity alone. Turner called the individual family the "primitive organization" of the frontier, not in the sense of being backward, but as fundamental or foundational.[3] Everything that comes after, though it may be progress, is derivative of the individual and his family. Foucault usefully describes liberalism as the perennial application of the question "how not to govern too much," and he sees much in an eighteenth-century English nobleman's aphorism for liberal rule: "Let sleeping dogs lie."[4] Closer to home, Foucault also quoted Benjamin Franklin: "It is said . . . that he is well advanced in the Science of Politics, who knows the full Force of [the] Maxim . . . : Not to govern too strictly."[5] Indeed, Foucault argued that the strength of liberalism's internal limitation on the state's exercise of power was even greater in the case in the United States, where, because of its birth in revolution, "[t]he demand for liberalism founds the state, rather than the state [passed down from a European absolutist era] limiting itself through liberalism," as in most of Europe.[6] The American state's function, given its revolutionary origins, is "simply to guarantee freedom."[7] The consequences follow seamlessly: "Liberalism in America is a whole way of being and thinking. It is a type of relation between the governors and the governed much more than a technique of governors with regard to the governed." Liberalism is not understood as a "political alternative," but as the ground of American democracy itself.[8]

But *is* liberalism best understood as simply the theory and practice of allowing "elementary," "foundational," "natural," or "autonomous" processes—such as work and the creation of value and wealth—to take their own course with a minimum of "interference"? This chapter will offer an alternative examination of the birth of liberalism in the Rosebud country by focusing on two very *productive* (in the sense to producing new arrangements of people and things) and decidedly *interventionist* forms of power that made the West both safe and organized for liberalism. One, which we will examine in the next section, was the primitive accumulation, as Marx would have called it, by which Lakota people were rounded up and concentrated on reservations in order to make way for a "public domain" predominantly free from Indians (or at least Indian tribes; some individuals had allotments on the public domain) that would be settled by white, and some African American, homesteaders. Accumulation by dispossession, as geographer David Harvey calls it, continued to open formerly Lakota land to white settlers well into the twentieth century. The other mode of power that was deployed to foster the birth of liberalism was the spatiolegal framework of the public land grid. Foucault called what was a similar arrangement in northern Europe a form of discipline, by which subjects were caught up in a spatial arrangement in obligatory entanglement, even if it went largely unnoticed consciously. In the second section of the chapter, we will examine how the grid disciplined settlement, Indians, and whites, and how it created not only the framework for private property and agrarian economic growth, but also the spatial imaginary that was part of making the nation thinkable, even if that had not been one of the goals of the Enlightenment thinkers who conceived of the public land system for settlement. Both these forms of power were anything but about letting sleeping dogs lie, and they represent the pre-history of liberalism in the Rosebud country.

In the third section of the chapter, we will examine the process of economic growth that took off—I use the phrase advisedly—immediately after land cleared of Indians was opened to white settlers. Boomtowns appeared, followed by remarkable growth curves, both of which were stunningly visible in high contrast as the prairie seemed to turn almost overnight from "wilderness" to "civilization." We will examine how this unregulated, sod-busting liberalism progressed, and how its temporality was understood in vernacular evolutionary terms.

MAP 1.1. The Great Sioux Reservation. Map by Alicia Cowart.

Primitive Accumulation and Accumulation by Dispossession

In the beginning, the countryside needed to be made safe for liberalism. In 1868, the Sioux Nation (Očeti Šakowiŋ, Seven Council Fires, which included the Lakota and others) and the United States negotiated the Fort Laramie Treaty, which guaranteed peace between the two parties and established the Great Sioux Reservation for the "the absolute and undisturbed use and occupation" by the Lakota; the Great Sioux included the western half of present-day South Dakota (see Map 1.1).[9] The language in this treaty is a stunning example of the recognition of indigenous people as a *nation* by the United States, and the treaty remains a critical document guaranteeing the quasi-national status of the Lakota. For Lakota people the treaty sits on the level of organic documents, along with modern tribal constitutions, or even "higher"; and by the terms of the U.S. Constitution the treaty is the law of the land, taking priority even over the Constitution itself. Yet, in recognizing the Sioux Nation with a permanent reservation, the treaty was deeply at odds with the project of opening the West to national incorporation. The treaty, in its stunning contradiction, represented the birth of the "Indian question," in Dakota Territory at least. Now that the Lakota people had been provided a reservation, and their off-reservation movements effectively limited, what was to become of them?[10] The idea that they would continue as a "nation" was, to say the least, inconsistent with the underlying assumption in liberalism that the wealth of the nation was necessarily both fungible and continuous within territorial units bounded by a national border. The 1868 treaty mentioned "the civilization of the Indians," and provided for schools, voluntary establishment of individual land allotments out of the common reservation (or even the equivalent of homesteads on the public domain outside of the reservation), seeds and agricultural implements, agricultural training, and cash "presents" to "the ten persons of said tribe who in the judgment of the agent may grow the most valuable crops."[11] But the Indian question in Lakota country was most dramatically answered by Congress when it adopted the Great Sioux Act in 1889. Although not technically a treaty—the United States stopped making treaties with Indian nations in 1871—the act was based on negotiations in Washington with Lakota delegations, and on negotiations by a treaty commission on the Great Sioux Reservation.[12] The act established five reservations to be carved out of the Great Sioux,[13] including Rosebud, as well as a sixth reservation, east of what had been the Great Sioux (see Map 1.2). One of the critical provisions applied the Dawes Act, or General Allotment Act, of 1887 to the South Dakota reservations. The president was "authorized and required" when he saw possibilities for the agricultural development of a reservation to "cause said reservation . . . to be surveyed . . . to allot the lands in said reservation in severalty to the Indians located thereon."[14] Each head of family was to receive 320 acres, each single adult 160 acres, and each child 80 acres.[15] These allotments were to be held in trust for the allottees by the government for twenty-five years (because of assumed Indian incompetence to manage personal business affairs). Allotment— the first step toward private property for the Lakota—was to be the great civilizing tool, as Theodore Roosevelt called it, "a mighty pulverizing engine to break up the tribal mass. It acts directly upon the family and the individual."[16] It would reform Indian subjects—uplift them—by making them into liberal (and, literally, sod-busting) individuals (eventually, citizens) rather than supposedly inert subjects in a tribal mass.

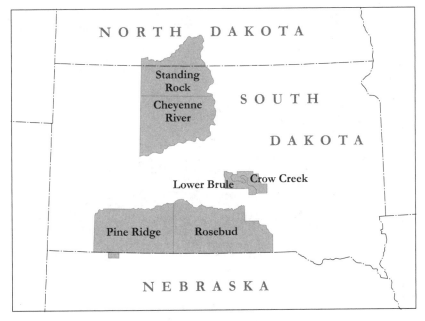

MAP 1.2. The 1889 Reservations. Map by Alicia Cowart.

If allotment was to be the solution to the Indian problem, it also was meant to lay the groundwork for the settlement of South Dakota, which became a state in 1889, the same year as the Great Sioux Act. The establishment of the six reservations—which were but fragments of the original Great Sioux Reservation—left 9 million acres of land, originally part of the Great Sioux Reservation. The 1889 act "restored"—as if the land had originally been allocated to the Lakota by the U.S. government rather than reserved by the Lakota out of their original homeland—these 9 million acres to the public domain and opened this land to homesteading by non-Indians.[17] Furthermore, the Great Sioux Act provided for the president to authorize the secretary of the interior to negotiate with the Indians for the sale of unallotted land within the six reservations for the purpose of opening the reservations to homesteading. The surveying and allotment of tribal land to individual tribal members in severalty began on Rosebud Reservation in 1892, and what became known as "surplus" land on the reservation was opened to non-Indian homesteaders by acts of Congress in 1904, 1907, and 1910—in each case after negotiation with the Rosebud Sioux Tribe (see Map 1.3).[18]

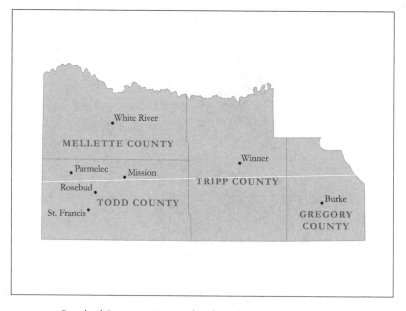

MAP 1.3. Rosebud Reservation. Map by Alicia Cowart.

It would be easy enough to read the texts of the various treaties and agreements by which land was ceded by the Lakota people for non-Indian settlement and presume a lawful process, even a process in which what is now called the "trust" obligations of the federal government toward Indians—the responsibility to act in the best interests of Indians—were given due diligence. But a more accurate depiction of this history would take a page from Marx's analysis of the enclosures at the birth of capitalism in England, where "the rule of law" took the concrete form of "bloody legislation against the expropriated."[19] The primitive accumulation that made capitalism possible was based not on "the market" but on political and even physical coercion that created the "free labor" (peasants stripped of their access to land) and the market in labor power and commodities, and explains the origin of the first stocks of "capital" that purchased the (newly available) labor power and raw materials to produce commodities for sale. As David Harvey has shown so compellingly, such nonproductive ("precapitalist") forms of capital accumulation—enrichment on the one side, dispossession on the other—were not only present at the origin of capitalism, but continue to operate as basic processes within capitalism, which Harvey calls accumulation by dispossession.[20] For example, despite the "permanent" reservation established in the bilateral negotiation of the Fort Laramie Treaty of 1868, the Lakota lost a wide swath of the Great Sioux Reservation, including the Black Hills, in 1877 by essentially unilateral, punitive, and illegal—according to the U.S. Supreme Court—action by Congress.[21]

Although 1,455 of the 1,476 men on Rosebud signed the 1889 Great Sioux Agreement, it is important to recognize the historical context in which these individual decisions were made.[22] General George Crook headed the commissioners who negotiated with the Lakota, and at his open meetings at Rosebud he emphasized not the land cession but the provisions for allotment in severalty, emphasizing that land allotted to individuals would be better protected against unilateral action by Congress than would tribal land held in common.[23] Add to this the fact that the Lakota people were now totally dependent on the Bureau of Indian Affairs (BIA) for rations and some wages, and it is not difficult to imagine the reasons why an overwhelming majority signed—but did so under coercion.[24] The 1889 agreement was not based on a negotiation between equally situated parties, and implied threat was present, as it had been in the cession of the Black Hills in 1877, although perhaps not as blatantly.

In the aftermath of the Ghost Dance and the Wounded Knee Massacre on neighboring Pine Ridge Reservation in 1890, Commissioner of Indian Affairs Thomas J. Morgan attributed "the Messiah craze" and "troubles among the Sioux" to, among other things, bitterness and second thoughts over the lands ceded via the Great Sioux Agreement, as well as to ration cuts that the Lakota had been promised would not happen.[25] Indeed, the signing of the Great Sioux Agreement had been a troubling event on Rosebud. Although, as we have seen, the overwhelming majority of men signed the agreement in assent, there had been an underlying struggle between those Lakota who saw the question of signing the document as purely an individual decision—each man signed, or declined to sign, as an individual (as the government presented it and insisted upon)—and those who believed that negotiations should be led by a handful of Lakota representatives from all six BIA agencies (which would become separate reservations via the agreement in question). Some Lakota leaders sought to hold out for a higher price for the land to be ceded to the United States and wanted additional time to be sure that they were not being "cheated." Tensions were high, and when one prominent man signed the agreement, "some of the Indians in the hall called out to kill him."[26] In the end, there would be no negotiation—the government's offer was "as written," in contrast to previous treaties and agreements that were negotiated between U.S. commissioners and the Lakota. On top of this, "delayed and reduced appropriations" resulted in "short rations . . . just after the Sioux commission had negotiated the agreement" and after it had "assured the Indians that their rations would be continued unchanged" in conformity with 1868 and 1877 treaties.[27]

The BIA agent at the Rosebud Agency reported that Lakota people had learned of the Ghost Dance from the Oglala Lakota Short Bull from the Pine Ridge Reservation (who had visited the Messiah) and that the dance had caused "a general demoralization among them, attracting Indians from all parts, interfering with schools, and causing a total neglect of stock and all belongings to partake in the wild excitement, until completely exhausted physically, morally, and intellectually."[28] When troops appeared on the reservation, 1,800 people fled for Pine Ridge: "They committed depredations en route, first destroying property in their own houses before going, being wild with excitement."[29] After the Wounded Knee Massacre, seven hundred people were returned to Rosebud under armed troops, and troops were stationed at the reservation after their return. The real show of force, however, was the massacre itself in December 1890, when the U.S. Army mowed down perhaps as many as three hundred men, women, and children at Wounded Knee Creek on Pine Ridge Reservation. The Rosebud agent succinctly summarized its effects: "[T]he collision at Wounded Knee, while to be regretted and unfortunate in many respects, will not soon be forgotten. *Indians have learned that it is dangerous to oppose by force, the law of the Great Father.*[30]

It was in the wake of terrorism at Wounded Knee, and in the face of total dependence on the BIA for daily subsistence, that the Lakota people lived in the early days of the reservation. When the BIA sought an agreement to open "surplus" lands in Gregory County to homesteading by non-Indians in 1904, the colonial carrot and stick must have been forefront in the minds of the Lakota people who listened to the deal offered by the BIA. We can never know precisely how much the threat of overwhelming legal, administrative, and military and police power influenced the "agreement" of the Lakota people (a majority, but not a "three-fourths" majority, of the men signed the agreement), that is to say, how much *primitive accumulation* and not an "agreement between nations" (which remains a legal fiction in federal Indian law) was at the center of this land cession. But there were plenty of complaints from Indian people and their allies that the offer was significantly below the market value.[31]

A notorious (in Native American history) process of what amounts to accumulation by dispossession of American Indians generally and of the Lakota in particular was rooted in the loss of trust status from individual allotments. As already mentioned, allotments under the Great Sioux Act were originally to be held in trust for twenty-five years, and the allottee was to be granted citizenship at the time of allotment. In 1906, however, Congress amended the process of allotment though the Burke Act (introduced by Senator Charles H. Burke, Republican from Pierre, South Dakota, who later became commissioner of Indian affairs) by postponing citizenship to the point at which the trust status of the allotment was removed, but also granting to the secretary of the interior the authority to remove the trust status from the allotment by issuing a fee patent "whenever he shall be satisfied that any Indian allottee is competent and capable of managing his or her affairs."[32] Fee patenting meant that the allotment became subject to local property taxes, and that the owner in fee simple had complete authority to sell or mortgage her or his land. The BIA aggressively pursued a policy of fee patenting. On Rosebud, individual applications from allottees for fee patents were liberally approved, and in 1917 the secretary of the interior declared all Indians in the United States of less than one-half Indian blood to be competent and fee patents were issued to all applicable allottees.[33] The vast majority of allottees who received fee patents lost their land quickly through sale (often, if not usually, at below-market value), defaulted mortgages, and tax delinquency.[34] It was widely recognized that non-Indian merchants—from sellers of magazine subscriptions to used-car salesmen—preyed upon Indians with assets or cash. Had political, military, and administrative power not been present, and had discounting of Lakota resources in coerced or pressured sales not taken place, none of what follows in this chapter would have been possible.

Space for Liberalism

As mentioned, survey and allotment work began on Rosebud Reservation in 1892. Figure 1.1. reproduces a detailed township plat drawn in 1896, consistent with the U.S. public land survey system established in 1785. The land survey literally inscribed upon the earth—with surveyors' corner markers—a rectilinear grid of six-mile-square townships, each comprised of twenty-four square-mile sections (most allotments on Rosebud were composed of one or two quarter sections; a quarter section is 160 acres). Critically, the survey and its subdivision of the reservation into square Euclidean allotments was meant to effect, as David Blomley puts it, "a conceptual emptying of space," a conception, of course, made into a social fact by the violence and primitive accumulation just described.[35] Marking and enforcing the grid constituted space as an "empty container,"[36] an imagined but also socially reliable (in the sense of people predictably respecting the boundaries) abstracted space on which new social and political projects would take place—specifically, the civilizing of Indians and the settlement of "public lands" on a twentieth-century frontier. The grid of the U.S. public land survey thus parallels the legal discourse of *terra nullius* and other racist, primitivizing fictions under-girding the larger European "doctrine of discovery" in making Native lands "legally" available for colonization in settler colonialisms.[37] The extent to which this history of instituting the grid was a *reterritorializa-tion,* or, more concretely, a moment of *creative destruction,* is made clear by paying attention to what would henceforth *not* be indicated in land-ownership plats and would quickly disappear physically. Clearly delin-eated by the surveyor in Figure 1.1 are clusters of dwellings (probably log houses)—from north to south in the center of the plat, Hollow Horn Bear's Village, Trade Dog Village—that represent Lakota bands *(tiośpaye)* that settled as units on the reservation, as well as an intricate system of pre-grid trails (later called "angle roads") that followed the most direct route between locations. Also elided in the new cadastral gaze were places used by Lakota people such as dance houses and sites for *hanbleceyapi* (vision quest). Although dance houses lasted into the allotment period, and sacred places have survived into the present, the open range in which all livestock ran at large and indiscriminately across the reserva-tion, with the occasional home fenced out from cattle grazing at large, disappeared with the eventual fencing of allotments with barbed wire.[38]

The new space of the grid was "abstract, homogenous, and universal,"[39] and provided a practical, measurable, linear, simplifying overlay for the commodification of land and the geographic extension of private prop-erty and capitalism into newly cleansed "virgin" territories. It also enabled the penetration of the state's capacity for surveillance and regulation of land titling, assessment and taxation, and other state projects.[40] Matthew Edney's description of the panoptical possibilities for the colonial state of British survey maps of India is applicable to the Rosebud country:

[M]aps of India—particularly those hung on council-chamber walls—presented to each British official a single and coherent view of South Asia. At one uniform scale, all portions of India became directly comparable and normalized. Knowledge of India was homogenized; particular varia-tions and contingencies were subsumed with a "house of certainty." Each town and district was identified and assigned its own particular location with the fixed and immobile mesh of meridians and parallels.... The maps of India form a disciplinary mechanism, a technology of vision and control which was integral to British control in South Asia.[41]

Nothing is more obvious than that the U.S. public land survey is a panoptical apparatus, with a centralized eye of power, represented graphically by the fixed-point perspective of state sovereignty.[42] Although Foucault did not discuss the U.S. system, he did describe the northern European "architectural module," revived from the Romans, of "the square or the rectangle, which is in turn subdivided into other squares or rectangles," as "a fundamental instrument of discipline."[43] This spatial discipline in the United States entailed government centers of calculation[44]—the BIA, the Department of Agriculture, the General Land Office, county assessors and registrars of property, and other agencies—that generated concrete knowledge/power that allowed formidable control across political space and over human activity. This may sound "statist," but it was the necessary precondition for *liberalism* as we know it. Without some cadastral registration and the application and enforcement of property law, private property itself could not be a social or practical fact.

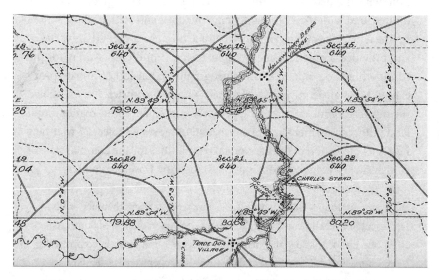

FIGURE 1.1. Detail from a U.S. General Land Office Plat, T38N, R32W (Sixth Principal Meridian), 1896. General Land Office Records, electronic document accessed November 1, 2016, http://www.glorecords.blm.gov.

The grid also went beyond the centralized, panoptical moment of discipline. It was not only a *hierarchal* apparatus of power. The public land survey was designed from the beginning to promote *liberal transparency*. Thomas Jefferson, for example, one of the visionaries who helped invent the system, intended that all settlers should understand the public land survey and that "everyone, who has a rule in his pocket" should be able to check his property lines (and implicitly everyone else's).[45] The public land survey was truly a democratizing discipline. This also was necessary for private property in land to exist as a naturalized social fact.

But there was more going on than the generation of discipline by the public land survey, and here we need to recognize that whatever the *programmers* (as uplifters, improvers, and modernizers of all kinds are usefully glossed in governmentality studies) of the grid had in mind, the grid has had effects *beyond anyone's intentions*. As in the case of the arcades, department stores, and museums examined by Tony Bennett, through the "scopic reciprocity" of the national grid "a public displayed itself to itself in an affirmative celebration of its own orderliness."[46] And that orderliness was part of the cultural basis that made it possible to think the nation. Like the space of the English nation as described by Mary Poovey, the space of the U.S. rectilinear grid was horizontally "continuous and uniform in all directions."[47] This was, in other words, the spatial counterpart to the temporality that Walter Benjamin called "homogenous, empty time" and that Benedict Anderson has argued made the nation thinkable.[48] If homogeneous, empty time makes possible the temporal simultaneity that renders the nation culturally imaginable, as Anderson describes, homogeneous, empty space grounds both the geographic continuity and the limits of the nation. Each owner of a quarter section could see how he or she—and a significant number of the homesteaders in western South Dakota were women—fitted into a larger spatial order in which the geographic and the political were made to appear seamless and naturally concentric. Both white homesteaders and Indian allottees knew the basics about reading a plat—how the plat (usually only a grid annotated with the names of property owners) corresponded to concrete landscape.[49] If one were sufficiently familiar with the public land survey, the owner of the quarter section in Todd County legally described as "SW ¼ Section 36, T. 38 N., R. 25 W., Sixth P.M." (the southwest one-quarter of section 36 in township 38 north, range 25 west, of the sixth principal meridian) could have easily recognized by referring to the appropriate survey maps that "SW ¼ Section 36, T. 1 N. R. 25 W., Sixth P.M." is the quarter section "exactly" 204 miles, and "directly" south of her, and she would probably have recognized that it is in Nebraska.

What is more, it was understood that all land encompassed in this system was—or should be—interchangeable legally and politically. In his analysis of government aerial photography during the New Deal, Jason Weems writes of a fundamental change in optics that applies equally to the grid of the public land survey: "In contrast to the sightlines and spatial recession of horizontal perspective, the aerial image depicted the land as everywhere equal and without a specified focus. The particularity of place gives way to the uniformity of a static and seemingly *a priori* pattern. [T]he images [the survey] produced gave an overall effect that dispersed focus and erased the ground-level experience of subjective passage and narration, replacing them with [an] unanchored, flat gaze that suggested disinterest and inaction."[50] The grid made landscape and concrete places invisible. And the same for denizens or land owners— *where* one lived, or *who* one was could make no conceptual (or legal) difference in this Enlightenment vision of inert (except for the "friction" of movement through it) space (Indian trust land complicated the picture but did not endanger it because trust land was to "graduate" to deeded or fee-patented land). The grid was the spatial expression of equality before the law, and it was logically parallel to the abstract labor Marx discovered at the core of capitalism. Abstract space meant that the particularities of place were formally irrelevant (this helps explain why the 1889 act was said to "return" part of the Great Sioux Reservation to the public domain—the history of place was replaced with the temporality of abstract legal fictions grounded in formally empty national space). Even the market value of a tract could be formally irrelevant (although not to a tax assessor, of course), because it was a quantitative and not qualitative characteristic. Thus, under both the 1862 Homestead Act and the 1887 General Allotment Act, homesteads and allotments are defined only in terms of the modular form of rectilinear boundaries and acreages: each homestead or allotment is the "same," legally speaking, as any other, regardless of what was actually contained within the tract. In the same way that "standardized and interchangeable parts brought with them a reconceptualization of the labor process" that led to Ford's assembly line, standardized and interchangeable space enabled a particular organization of territory and politics.[51]

This is abundantly clear in Thomas Jefferson's plan for possible states that would be incorporated into the United States. States, in this vision of political incorporation, are interchangeable, not a matter of history or place, but simply a matter of a more or less equivalent swaths of territory, for example, "two degrees of latitude," as described in the Ordinance of April 23, 1874.[52] The placelessness of this political space also anticipated and enabled a formal "racelessness" (although more on that later). Even Indian reservations were—or were to become—interchangeable with space in general within this economy of fungible American space. It was understood by legislators and federal and state government officials and bureaucrats, and by Lakota allottees and their white neighbors too, that once the trust restrictions were removed from an allotment, that tract of land became indistinguishable from homesteads or other tracts of privately owned land within the state.

Jefferson's plan also brings out how the horizontal system of space production was closely linked with the scalar or "vertical" nesting of graduated spatial units at the root of what is commonly called American federalism.[53] The Northwest Ordinance of 1787 established a three-stage plan for the incorporation of the Northwest Territory (including what was to become Ohio, Indiana, Illinois, Wisconsin, and part of Minnesota) into the United States on an "equal footing with the [thirteen] original States": (1) a temporary territorial administration headed by a congressionally appointed governor; (2) a general assembly composed of representatives elected by counties or townships—when a specified threshold of population was reached; and (3) statehood upon reaching a further population threshold.[54] The precedence established by these laws and reproduced in later acts of Congress constituted "a continental land system" that "helped create a single nation from the original thirteen states and all of the new country to the west."[55] Bare space is easily stackable in abstract thought, and each tier—from the individual farm, through the organized township and county, through the state, to the national level—of progressively inclusive spatial containers is understood to nest neatly both geometrically (because of the rectilinear boundaries of the "container" at each scale) and politically (because each "container" is founded as both a citizenry and an organized representative government with clear jurisdictional boundaries).[56] This was a "fee simple empire," both in the sense that the yeoman—white or Indian—on his quarter section of freehold land was, in the Jeffersonian–Lockean model, a sovereign writ small and because this sovereignty emerging out of a bounded spatial unit was replicated at successive scales.[57]

But it is critically important to recognize that this complex culture of homogeneous, empty space did not float in thin air, as a mere abstraction, shared though it was. As we have seen, it was useful for purposes of nation making, both ideologically in terms of visualizing the space of "the nation" and in terms of administrative processes, including the most basic of all state administrative processes, taxation. It was also, of course, practically useful for mapmaking and map reading (orienting oneself in space). But it was also a very pragmatic framework for addressing one of the concrete processes of capitalism, its necessity to expand geographically. Spatial expansion in capitalism is not simply an unanchored "search for wealth" understood as a motive on the same ontological level as "greed" or "acquisitiveness." As Marx showed long ago, capitalism's spatial expansiveness is systemic and driven by a crisis tendency at the core of the capitalism itself: *the tendency of the rate of profit to fall.* This is reflected in what is commonly called "the business cycle," but which Marx saw as recurring crises that amounted not to "corrections," but threats to the reproduction of the overall system, stemming from the inner workings of the system itself. These crises take the form of overaccumulation in which capital and labor power cannot be put to productive (profitable) use, and both are idled and devalued in the market, with all the disruptions—economic and political—entailed for the capitalist social formation.[58] The perennial response to recurrent crises or devaluations brought on by overaccumulation is geographic expansion and long-term borrowing that David Harvey has called the "spatio-temporal fix." We will focus on the *spatial fix* here, where "surpluses of capital and labor are sent elsewhere to set capital accumulation in motion in [a] new regional space."[59] Overseas colonialism was the historical outcome of the process of responding to capitalist crisis in Europe; in the United States, it was, of course, the westward-moving frontier. The grid of the public land survey and the system for incorporating territory and entitling individual property in land was the spatial grammar for the geographic expansion of capitalism. As with all enclosures, which Neil Smith reminds us, includes all boundary making from property lines to national borders, we witness in the case of the Rosebud country the "creation of absolute space" *for the absorption of capital and labor.*[60] The "conquering of the frontier" prior to World War I was the (pre-Fordist) "extensive" regime of capital accumulation in U.S. agriculture, a continental—as opposed to overseas—spatial fix.[61] This is the underlying stimulus to the processes of primitive accumulation, accumulation by dispossession, reterritorialization, and creative destruction that we have described.

The Temporality of Liberalism: Growth and Progress

The "opening" of the Rosebud country created a definite *boom,* humble though it may have been compared to other times and places, in terms of the absorption of capital and—especially, given the labor-intensive nature of agriculture at the time—labor. Competition for a chance to file as a homestead entryman on the opened reservation lands was intense, with 106,308 individuals applying for 2,412 available homesteads in Gregory County in 1904, and 114,769 applying for 4,000 homesteads in Tripp County in 1908, some 800,000 acres, "the size of the state of Rhode Island," as the *Wall Street Journal* reported on its front page.[62] Lotteries were held to pick registrants who would be allowed to file on homesteads.[63] Edith Kohl, a "girl homesteader," said of the opening of Tripp County: "The name Rosebud was emblazoned across the nation . . . in newspapers, in railroad pamphlets, on public buildings."[64] Figure 1.2 captures the lottery registration crowd for homesteads in Tripp County in 1911. In the background is the Corn Palace in Gregory, a town founded after the opening of Indian lands to homesteading in Gregory County.

By 1913, four years after its platting, Winner in Tripp County had become a major trade center with a railroad terminal, "[f]ive big general stores, two hardwares and two gents furnishing stores and five big lumber yards," three banks, seven hotels, three livery services, three automobile garages, four churches, and fifteen lawyers.[65] The non-Indian population of Tripp County increased from zero to 8,323 between 1905 and 1910.[66]

FIGURE 1.2. Registering for homesteads, Gregory, South Dakota, 1911.
Postcard owned by author.

White River, in Mellette County, had a population of 300 within ninety
days of its lot sale, and 500 in less than a year. The county seat, it had a
courthouse, "three general stores, an exclusive grocery store, meat market, furniture store, two banks, [and] garage."[67] The non-Indian population of Mellette County jumped from essentially 0 to 1,700 between 1905
and 1910.[68] By 1913, "[t]he combined capital stock of the banks in [Greg-
ory, Mellette, and Tripp] counties ... [was] $418,000; the combined
deposits [were] $1,944,838; with combined loans of $1,310,982."[69]

As the boom in the Rosebud country makes clear, empty space is anything but inert space, because it has the potential to absorb labor power
and capital when surpluses in those factors exist.[70] But the initial settlement and boom were only the first phase of growth in the process of place
making. Once land was privately owned and fixed capital was tied to
specific places, local and regional constituencies emerged with powerful
interests in growth within these new spatial containers (neighborhoods,
townships, towns, counties)—growth of population, "industry" (the production of wealth), tax bases, commercial infrastructure and built environment (public and private), and local government services, in a word,

progress. The "regional growth coalition" in the Rosebud country was reflected in intense promotionalism.[71] In 1913, the *Burke Gazette* published *A Rosebud Review*, a booster book meant to entice settlers to the Rosebud country, which was, the publication assured readers, "absolutely in the corn belt" (the Gregory Corn Palace also advertised the claims).[72] The growth in the acreage in corn production, the book told potential migrants, was "phenominal" *(sic)*.[73] The Dallas Real Estate Co. urged readers to "[s]ell the old Iowa or Illinois home and come here and quadriple *[sic]* your holdings for the benefit of your children."[74] The editors of local newspapers in the Rosebud country also boosted their counties, because they recognized that local papers were read by out-of-staters who might move to or invest in the area. The *Todd County Tribune* also assured readers that the county "is in the corn belt"[75] (a less credible claim than that of Gregory to the east) and published verse meant to allay any fears prospective settlers might have about local Indians:

> ... You will be surprised to
> See how many of
> Our Indians ride in
> Upholstered automobiles and
> That they live in
> Homes elegantly furnished,
> Doing their work
> And taking care of their
> Kids just like
> Other folks. . . .[76]

The *Tribune* succinctly described the logic of demographic and economic growth: "Everybody in our county is interested in getting more good farmers into our county. Every new family coming in means new business for one or more of our merchants and it means more and better schools and schools nearer together for our farmers who are already here. It also adds to the value of every adjoining tract of land when a farmer settles [and] begins to cultivate his land."[77]

The regional growth coalition was not just local, but also statewide. South Dakota's commissioner of immigration mounted exhibits at the

United States Land and Irrigation Exposition in Chicago and the Northwestern Land Products Exposition in St. Paul in 1911, and at the Panama-
Pacific International Exposition in San Francisco in 1915; staffed an exhi-
bition railway car that plied its way east as far as New York, Philadelphia,
and Washington; advertised in more than six hundred newspapers or
farm journals in eastern states (in Bohemian Czech, German, Norwe-
gian, and Polish, as well as English); mailed advertising (again, in multiple languages); distributed silent film segments and lantern slides on
the state's resources for showing to out-of-state audiences; and sent lists
of out-of-state prospects to "real estate dealers, commercial clubs, bankers" and others within the state.[78]

Growth in the Rosebud country *was* phenomenal in that it was so
visible on the landscape in the form of new fields, more and larger farms,
and growing towns with buildings and amenities. Figure 1.3 graphs the
growth in farm acreage in the three Rosebud country counties opened to
homesteading. Figure 1.4 depicts the growth in the value of farms in the
three counties.

Given all of this, it comes as no surprise that local people saw progress
as natural, inevitable, or unstoppable (just as more urban and more
wealthy Americans saw the stock market). Local organic intellectuals
articulated deep, evolutionary convictions about progress. Edith Eudora
Kohl was an emigrant from St. Louis who homesteaded in Lyman
County, South Dakota (just north of the Rosebud country), with her sister in 1907. She recorded her experiences in a 1938 book, *Land of the
Burnt Thigh*. What is remarkable about the book, besides the power of
the story of homesteading itself—by two young women, in this case—is
its evocative evolutionary narrative. She describes the prairie that she
and her sister encountered at the end of their first day of travel, sitting
on the claim locator's wagon: "At sunset we came up out of the draw to
the crest of the ridge. Perched on the high seat of an old spring wagon,
we looked into a desolate land which reached to the horizon on every
side. Prairie which had lain untouched since the Creation save for buffalo and roving bands of Indians."[79] For Kohl and perhaps many homesteaders, "[t]he buffalo and the Indian had each had his day on this land,
and each had gone without leaving a trace."[80] Here she clearly was referring to the fact that the Lakota appeared to have created no recognizable

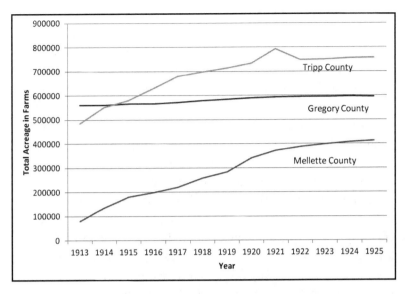

FIGURE 1.3. Growth in total farm acreage. Source of data: U.S. Census, Agriculture.

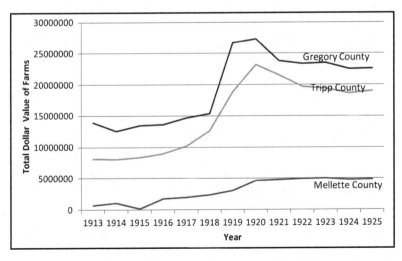

FIGURE 1.4. Growth in total farm value. Source of data: U.S. Census, Agriculture.

development; she could not have meant that there were no Indians left, because she had Indian neighbors. "[O]ne had to begin at the beginning," in this "desolate, forgotten land," this "wasteland."[81] "It would take slow, back-breaking labor, and time . . . to make the prairie bloom."[82] Kohl may well have been thinking along the lines of John Locke's observation that "in the beginning all the World was *America*," by which he meant that American Indians represented human beings in a state of nature.[83] While they had the rudiments of property in the resources they appropriated from Nature, they had yet to tame her or to enclose the commons (Locke was, of course, incorrect about the lack of farming or enclosure in the New World). In Locke's labor theory of value, an acre of land in America generates only one-one thousandth of the value generated by an acre of land in England. This is what made "in-land" America *vacant* or *waste*.[84] Even if Kohl had not read Locke, the essentials of his theory were already deeply imbricated in settler common sense in the United States. In one of the foundational cases of U.S. Indian law, Chief Justice John Marshall articulated, if he only reluctantly acknowledged, the presumption of mere hunters in a wasteland in 1823: "the tribes of Indians inhabiting this country were fierce savages, whose occupation was war, and whose subsistence was drawn chiefly from the forest. To leave them in possession of their country, was to leave the country a wilderness."[85]

Thus, Kohl, predictably, marvels at what the settlers did with the wasteland. Within a mere year,

[t]he plains, which had stretched to the horizon that spring untouched by a plow, unoccupied by white men, were now unrecognizable. A hundred thousand acres of fertile waste land had been haltered. Hundreds of settlers had transplanted their roots into this soil and had made it a thriving dominion. Fall rains filled the dams and creeks. There were potatoes and other vegetables in abundance. Think of it! Caves full of melons, small but sweet. [The local newspaper Kohl edited] told of one small field that yielded twenty bushels of wheat, another twenty-two bushels of oats, to the acre. There was fall plowing of more ground, schools being established, Sunday schools. . . . Never had a raw primitive land seen such progress in so short a time.[86]

Writing three decades after homesteading, Kohl appeared to have no regrets about her steam tractors "chug-chugging over the dark plain, turning under the bluebells and anemones as they went, and the tall grass where the buffalo had ranged."[87] The land was something to be "conquered," the "virgin earth" to be "broke[n]" into fields.[88]

An equally compelling progress narrative was written by Oscar Micheaux, an African American who homesteaded near Gregory. His 1913 novel *The Conquest: The Story of a Negro Pioneer,* was an account of homesteading in the Rosebud country with local towns easily identifiable even with the name changes meant to suggest that they were fictional. He made his 1917 novel *The Homesteader* into a film in 1919, shot in the Rosebud country (Micheaux is now noted as an early African American filmmaker). Micheaux wrote in *The Conquest,* "as I gazed over the miles of [brown grass] lying like a mighty carpet I could seem to feel the magnitude of the development and industry that would some day replace this state of wilderness."[89]

Sod busting's general theme of progress, civilization, and agriculture is, of course, an old and a deep one. Agriculture, as Frieda Knobloch tells us, implies "a whole system of domestication—that is, the transformation and improvement of nature—that is as much about structuring social and political life as it is about raising cattle or wheat."[90] The part of this "theory of social and agricultural evolution"[91] that is of particular relevance for the Rosebud country was laid out clearly by Frederick Jackson Turner in *The Significance of the Frontier in American History* (which Kohl and Micheaux had almost surely read, or at least been familiar with). Turner described the frontier as temporalized by what we would now call a process of evolutionary succession: first, hunters and traders (and Indians), followed by ranchers, in turn followed by farmers. Each successive stage represents an increasing density of population, industry, and wealth upon the landscape, in fact transforming the landscape, and materializing a clearly (unilineal) progressive teleology. Turner quotes John Mason Peck's 1848 *A New Guide to the West* regarding the farmers, who

> purchase the lands, add field to field, clear out the roads, throw rough
> bridges over the streams, put up hewn log houses with glass windows and

brick or stone chimneys, occasionally plant orchards, build mills, school-houses, court-houses, etc., and exhibit the picture and forms of plain frugal, civilized life. . . . Another wave rolls on. . . . The small village rises to a spacious town or city; substantial edifices of brick, extensive fields, orchards, gardens, colleges, and churches are seen. Broadcloths, silks, leghorns, crapes, and all the refinements, luxuries, elegancies, frivolities, and fashions are in vogue.[92]

We can trace the progress of social evolution, Turner argued, by scanning the continental space of the United States:

The United States lies like a huge page in the history of society. Line by line as we read this continental page from west to east we find the record of social evolution. It begins with the Indian and the hunter; it goes on to tell of the disintegration of savagery by the entrance of the trader, the pathfinder of civilization; we read the annals of the pastoral stage in ranch life; the exploitation of the soil by the raising of unrotated crops of corn and wheat in sparsely settled farming communities; the intensive cultivation of the denser farm settlement; and finally the manufacturing organization with city and factory system.[93]

The motor of this evolutionary process, at least on the frontier, is the rugged individual: "Turner always alluded to the frontiersman in the singular."[94] South Dakota homesteaders of Kohl's and Micheaux's generation not only had an intuitive sense of Turner's evolutionary theory, but believed they saw its materialization before their eyes, and as a product of their sweat. And their *material investments*—work, money, their future—were at stake in ways that made the evolutionary theory seem not just natural but *necessary*. At a minimum, the settlers hoped for—often faithfully, and usually desperately—"a new Iowa on the Plains,"[95] perhaps even a "little Chicago"[96] in the state. A 1939 sketch by Georgia Reed, an art student at Augustana College in Sioux Falls, is telling in its vision of a well-developed state (Figure 1.5). Although the South Dakota countryside and its cities might not actually have matched this image at the height of the Great Depression in 1939, the commonsense evolutionary narrative and the vision of a future that bested the past are clear enough.

FIGURE 1.5. *Roads to Progress.* Illustration by Georgia Reed in *South Dakota: Fifty Years of Progress, 1889–1939,* ed. York Sampson (Sioux Falls: South Dakota Golden Anniversary Book Company, 1939), 42.

Although there might appear to have been no place in formal liberal frameworks for racism, we would be remiss if we did not recognize the obvious openings for racist imaginaries based on the idea of Indians as standing in the way of progress, wittingly or otherwise. There is little doubt that the idea of "Indian" conjured up for many if not most settlers images of what they meant to surpass, and that there were not just evolutionary but moral valuations involved. For many years, Lakota people complained about a mural in the governor's office that, they believed, reflected a "frontier mentality." *The Spirit of the West* (Figure 1.6) was painted by New York artist Edwin Blashfield in 1910.[97] State historian Doane Robinson described it at the time: "South Dakota is represented as a beautiful woman, in the spot light, with the figure of hope floating over her and pointing forward. Trappers and settlers are beating back and overcoming the Indians who are clinging to her garments, attempting to impede her progress. Outlawry, represented by a dark and hooded figure is scuttling away into the darkness. In the back ground the prairie schooners of the early settlers are to be seen making their way across the prairie."[98] Although we cannot know how many white settlers even saw

FIGURE 1.6. Edwin Blashfield, *The Spirit of the West*, 1910. South Dakota Historical Society.

the mural much less felt "inspired" by it, the existence of a "savage slot" seems a very possible, if not probable, effect of the evolutionary narrative just described. Indeed, it may well be an important *national* settler-state imaginary.

Before moving on to the next chapter, we need to examine three additional—and complicating—characteristics of liberalism in rural South Dakota. We will deal only briefly with these matters here, since they will be taken up in more detail in subsequent chapters. First, we need to understand the thinking of settlers in economic context. They clearly needed, wanted, and celebrated what would be called, in contemporary terms, unregulated growth. The source of that commitment is not best seen, however, as a function of "ideology." While they might seem "acquisitive" or "possessive," those aspects of their thinking and acting were an effect of the financial pressures they faced. Mortgage payments had to be made, taxes had to be paid, and supplies and equipment had to be purchased. And, of course, one had to figure out how to plan for one's elder years when one could no longer farm (before Social Security most farmers hoped to rely on the appreciation of the value of their farmland, or their children's generosity, for their "retirement"). By 1921, in the wake of the postwar agricultural depression, the costs farmers faced could barely be met, when they could be met at all, by the prices they received for their products. The loss in the value of land equity was more than 50 percent, as the average value of farms in the state dropped from $33,625 in 1920 to $15,862 in 1930.[99] Farmers were, thus, *compelled* to be "maximizers."

Second, it is likely that sod-busting liberalism was itself one of the sources of the problem just mentioned—the cost–price squeeze encountered by farmers after 1921. At least that was the diagnosis of both Washington officials and agricultural economists during the New Deal. They developed the theory that farmers had saturated the market with their products, thus driving down prices. Because family farms were domestic units first and businesses second, no farm family could afford to stop producing until prices rose. It was, in other words, precisely the unregulated growth (more farmers, more agricultural products) and the investment in individual property rights to use one's land as one sees fit that at least partly drove the price deflation. Furthermore, when the drought appeared in the 1930s, the maximum use of land to produce cash crops was blamed by officials and agricultural experts for the environmental disaster of the dust bowl. Cleary, a policy of not governing too much had a very high price, at least according to the reformers, as we will see in chapter 4.

Finally, while Turner, for example, was not incorrect to argue that settling the frontier had fostered "individualism," he painted much too drastic a picture in claiming that the "tendency is anti-social."[100] Midwestern historian Jon Lauck has compellingly shown that the kind of liberalism that was embraced by rural South Dakotans—particularly the pioneer generation, but inherited by its progeny—was a more complex assemblage. Rugged individualism and faith in the free market and commerce there was aplenty, without doubt, but *liberalism was alloyed with republicanism*: "True republican citizens would overcome simple self-interest and an attraction to extravagance and luxury and instead promote the 'common good' and the interests of the 'commonwealth.'" The "duties of republican citizenship . . . required pursuing the best interest of the commonwealth and serving the public good, not simply following one's personal ambition."[101] Indeed, this was at the core of rural thinking about patriotism. In other words, the sod-busting version of liberalism was far removed from the Wall Street version.

These three qualifications mean that sod-busting liberalism in the Rosebud country will require a thicker description than the one laid out in this chapter, and we will return to these matters in later chapters.

For now, we will turn in the next chapter to focus on what uplifters and modernizers in the BIA and the South Dakota Extension Service targeted for their attention among South Dakotans, Indian and white. Although there is no question that both groups adopted aspects of liberalism—particularly ideas about growth and private property—the *programmers* had plans for making liberal subjects *better*. Much work needed to be done before rural South Dakotans would be truly good farmers and good democratic citizens.

2

Discipline and Governmentality

Civilizing Indians and Making Farmers Progressive

Liberalism's grid of individualism, private property, and economic growth was the initial project for governing the countryside. As we saw in chapter 1, it took a great deal of disciplinary power and discursive work to put into place what came to seem simply natural or inevitable in terms of private property, democratic political bodies, and progress. But by its own design, once established, liberalism was avowedly *minimalist,* seeking only to produce subjects sharing characteristics at the level of the least common denominator necessary for economic actors in a capitalist economy and citizens in a liberal democracy. Liberalism was not, by its own terms, concerned to improve people or society beyond a basic level. And, as we will see in chapter 3, liberalism as a noninterventionary rationality of government actually created problems that it was not, on its own terms, able to solve or even to recognize.

This chapter is concerned with how liberalism's minimalism set the stage for new forms of government to be invented and deployed—forms of government directed at the "Indian problem" and the "country life problem." Those actors—in and out of government—who theorized these problems and developed corrective policies and techniques to solve them, of course, would tell us that these were *real* problems that *required* intervention once recognized—for the good of all concerned. This necessity, however, deserves our historical skepticism. If Foucault's work tells us anything, it is to beware the rationalizations of the agents of government about the "necessity" or "inevitability" of their interventions. Foucault saw governing and the power entailed in it, not as a stage of human mastery, but as the outcome of practices of power flowing, morphing, seeping into new niches for its exercise. If something can be problematized and targeted for correction, improvement, or another rationale of government, individual actors may well do that. Perhaps we might even say, if it can be problematized, it will be governed. Sometimes these interventions seem to work, but as Foucault insisted, they seldom or ever work as anticipated. The point is that we not approach the history of governing in terms of how preexisting problems were managed, but ask how problems were invented by those who would govern them. What can we learn if we take forms of government not as fixes for "real problems," but instead see them as opportunistic programs driven by human actors bent on managing, regulating, improving, and solving in and of themselves as satisfying expression of human agency, as ways of exercising the power of agency? Human subjects—both the would-be programmers and those they would program—become subjects only by deploying the power of agency.

In more concrete terms, what this means is that any program of government always leaves other "problems" to be creatively "recognized" simply because no program is total, and any program creates new, unintended outcomes that may themselves come to be recognized as problems by other programs. *Problems* do not so much "arise" or "become recognized" in a realist sense, as get *invented,* and both problems and their "solutions" have an arbitrary—as anthropologists say of the symbolic realm—relationship to necessity or reality. This is not at all a cynicism about those who govern, but a theoretical position on the open-endedness and relative autonomy of all forms of systematic "improvement," as Tania Murray Li glosses it.[1] The point is not that governing, policy, and expert practice cannot be practically evaluated against real outcomes, but that it is a mistake to evaluate them in their own discursive terms, because any apparatus of governing, policy, and expert practice is, from the start, self-reinforcing and self-justifying. This is because any governing apparatus must necessarily take some background factors for granted. There was nothing inevitable about the "Indian problem" or the "country life problem" as these were defined, or about the "solutions" sought, by the BIA and the extension service.

This chapter will examine two governing projects meant to improve people beyond the level of minimal liberal subjects. These projects were developed by self-appointed, as Li aptly describes them, *trustees* who "claim[ed] to know how others should live, to know what is best for them, to know what they need. . . . The objective of trusteeship [was] not to dominate others—it [was] to enhance their capacity for action, and to direct it. . . . [T]he list of trustees include[d] colonial officials and missionaries, politicians and bureaucrats, . . . specialists in agriculture, hygiene, . . . and conservation, and [nonstate] organizations. . . . Their intentions [were] benevolent, even utopian. They desire[d] to make the world better than it [was]."[2] Li urges us to take "the will to improve . . . at its word," if we are to understand power and domination.[3] She means by this not that the improvers are politically innocent any more than the targets of improvement are politically naive. Rather, she means that we should not presume that the stated goals of improvement projects are mere ideological cover for the "real" goals that are supposedly hidden from view and rooted—in prevailing critical scholarly narratives of colonialism and neocolonialism—in the underlying system of capitalist domination. Li does not, by any means, suggest that capitalism is not a critical context for power.[4] But she insists that if we are to understand how power saturates improvement projects, we need to look for the source of both "problems" and "solutions" in places other than simple "domination" or "exploitation."

But taking the trustees at their word does not mean that we see their projects in the same terms that they do. In other words, even when the trustees speak in realist and utilitarian terms about problems "out there" and solutions, we need to keep the anthropologist's notion of the arbitrariness of shared meanings (or symbolic systems) in mind. Foucault often seems to describe governing in utilitarian terms—for example, the practical value of surveillance, of docile or disciplined bodies for prisons, schools, armies, and factories.[5] But one of his central ideas, the *productivity* of power, entails the recognition that the deployment of power in governmental projects, rather than rationally or correctively addressing practical problems that already exist, in fact creates the very "problems" that it claims merely to observe and seek to correct or manage. The classic examples of this (arbitrary) productivity for Foucault were the tendency of the prison to *produce delinquency* rather than correct it, and the tendency of the psychoanalytic "repressive hypothesis" to *positively generate talk about sex.*[6] Foucault's most original thinking about government viewed it not as a utilitarian response to actual "problems," but as the effect of the *opportunistic* nature of power. In other words, *government is about power being exercised where it can be, by whom it can be, under specific conditions of possibility* (and the same goes for *resistance* to government). Paul Rabinow aptly summarizes Foucault's insight on this point: "The end of good government is the correct disposition of things—even when these things have to be *invented* so as to be well governed."[7] This may well be driven by the desire of trustees to find authority or employment for themselves, but the Foucauldian lesson is not the self-interestedness of "Man." Rather, the lesson is to look for how things become problems to be worked on.

Civilizing Indians

It is not surprising that the evolutionary narrative of liberalism examined in chapter 1 was imbricated with, if it did not necessarily determine, policy directed toward Native peoples. Allotment of Indian lands—or em-propertying Indians—was an ingenious technique for civilizing Indians.[8] The commissioner of Indian affairs described the policy in 1921 as having "the aim of inducing . . . a departure from old communal traits and customs to self-dependent conditions and to a democratic conception of the civilization with which the Indian must be assimilated if he is to survive."[9] Allotment on Rosebud Reservation began in 1892 and was completed for all tribal members willing to accept allotments (seventy-nine would not) in 1905, although children continued to be allotted as they were born until 1919 when there was no more tribal land available for allotment. The reterritorialization intended is graphically depicted by comparing Figure 2.1 with Figure 1.1.

This process of reterritorialization was not done by the stroke of a pen, and the plat remained something (only) on paper for decades. The original reservation landscape probably survived, at least in parts of the Rosebud country, until the mid-1910s. Prior to that time, allotments and homesteads in Todd and Mellette counties, at least, were not fenced, and Indian and non-Indian cattle roamed at large—individual ownership was

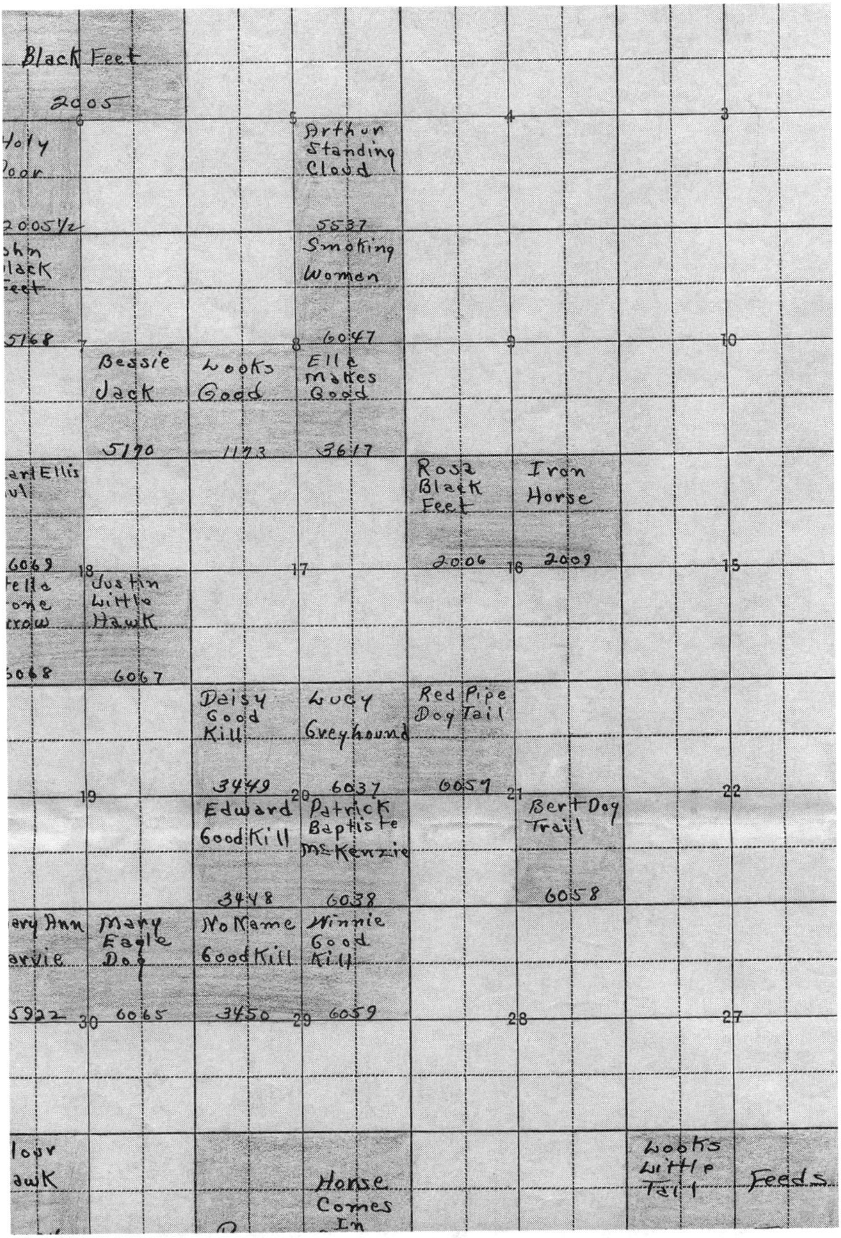

FIGURE 2.1. Allotment plat map. Rosebud Agency Records, Records of the Bureau of Indian Affairs. Kansas City, Missouri: National Archives and Records Administration.

FIGURE 2.2. Peter Big Turkey choosing an allotment. Courtesy of St. Francis Mission and Marquette University. St. Francis Mission Records, ID 6–6 0015.

identified during roundups through brands.[10] Angle roads, formed by riders and teams repeatedly taking the most direct route across the territory to their destination, established a trail system, some of which was improved into roads. "It was all open country after leaving Nebraska"—without fences—a settler in Mellette County recalled.[11] In 1917, however, the Rosebud superintendent reported that "[i]n the last few years a large portion of the land has been fenced up with the result that these old roads are cut off and travel forced on the Section lines."[12] Because World War I had driven up the price of wheat, reservation land that had remained in native grass was put into wheat production and fenced by both Indian allottees and non-Indian landowners and renters. The landscape was coming to *look like* the plat.

Prior to the war, Lakota people had not been reorganized into property-owning liberal subjects by the process of allotting them on paper. Some Lakota seemed uninterested in allotments and did not cooperate with the allotting agents (the process required visiting the land, or at least coming in to the BIA agency office and locating the allotment on a plat; see Figure 2.2).[13] What induced many, if not most, Lakota people who did want allotments was almost certainly not the prospect of a farmstead but of "Sioux benefits." The 1889 Great Sioux Act provided that each individual who has "take[en] his or her allotment of land in severalty, shall be provided with two mil[k] cows, one pair of oxens, with yoke and chain, or two mares and one set of harness . . . one plow, one wagon, one harrow, one hoe, one axe, and one pitchfork . . . and fifty dollars in cash."[14] Sioux benefits were paid as cash (the market value of the physical goods itemized in the act) deposited into individual Indian money accounts held in trust by the BIA. This cash (or a purchase order) could be requested by individuals to purchase the actual items or to pay for alternative items that in theory were equally justified in the spirit of the 1889 act, such as health care and education. Sioux benefits were in great demand, and the only way to get them was to take an allotment. In 1893 the allotting agent reported that "no better inducement could be affected to [Lakota who had not yet accepted allotments] to scatter out and take allotments [than] articles guaranteed be furnished as allotments are made." In 1900 he reported that many families were not bringing in their children to take their allotments because there were temporarily no funds left for

Sioux benefits.[15] In 1894, Lakota people in the Butte Creek District of Rosebud Reservation (Mellette County) sent a petition in Lakota to the BIA asking for their Sioux benefits after they had taken their allotments.[16]

Allotments were not generally chosen by Indian people with a live-lihood in farming or a rise in land values in mind; this differentiated them from their non-Indian neighbors who saw land in precisely the latter terms, and who had often invested money in acquiring their land. As a new allotting agent explained in 1905, "[a]s a rule the head of a family would select his own allotment and that of his wife where there was wood and water and then select for the children apparently at ran-dom, without any regard to the present or future value of the land. . . . The bulk of the allotments generally do not constitute, by any means, the best land on the reservation. They have apparently selected them on account of their nearness to the [Rosebud BIA] Agency, to some princi-pal stream, as the White River, or to some favorite camping ground in-stead of selecting them with regard to the character of the surface soil."[17] Some Lakota people, called "the kickers" by the allotting agent, refused to take allotments other than along the Little White River where they were already living (in *tioŝpaye*, or band, camps) in a zone that the BIA wanted to exempt from allotment as a tribal timber reserve. Their con-cern was most likely not opposition to allotment in principle but fear that they would be moved away from their existing homes and the exist-ing village composed of *tioŝpaye* members. In 1903 the allotment survey crew encountered this opposition in the form of "a war party in war paint, dress, mounted and armed of some sixty or ninety young braves . . . ordering the party to quit work and clear out or they should all be killed."[18] The BIA acceded to "the kickers'" demands because, as the allotting agent reported, "[t]hese people have been living here because the river affords the only water supply in the vicinity and will, in all prob-ability continue to do so whether allotted or not."[19] Today the tribal tim-ber reserve is still checkerboarded with individual allotments along the Little White River.

While the assignment of allotments to individuals on a cadastral map with a trust patent was considered a success by the BIA, getting Lakota people to take private property in land seriously in ways appropriate to liberal subjectivity was quite a different matter. Initially, the BIA bent to the reality of the Lakota *tiośpaye* and built day schools and even plowed communal gardens in each of the villages. Dispersing nuclear families to scattered allotments presented a number of practical problems, including increasing distance to day schools, construction of new housing, fencing (to protect homes and gardens from open-range cattle), and wells.[20] Indeed, it was only in 1920 that the BIA superintendent could report that "90 per cent. of the adult males of this reservation have comfortable, sanitary houses in which to live, and their allotments fenced and are living on them."[21] That was a quarter-century after allotment had begun on the reservation.

Converting Lakota families into self-supporting farm families was even more difficult. While the Rosebud superintendents (called agents before) often blamed that failure of Indians to become agriculturally self-supporting on their character, some superintendents admitted that other factors were to blame. In 1911 the superintendent explained how, since he assumed his post in 1909, he had, "by dint of much moral encouragement and the assistance of the farmers and police" increased the acreage plowed to crops 100 percent in 1910 over 1909, and increased the 1911 plowed acreage over 1910.[22] In the end, however, writing during the 1911 drought, the superintendent admitted that "[t]his is not an agricultural district. The seasons are very uncertain on account of lack of rain. Crops for the season of 1910 were poor and crops for the season of 1911 are a total failure and it will be very difficult to get the Indians to take any interest another year after having experienced two successive failures."[23] Some of the superintendents recognized that ranching could be a profitable business in the area, but they realized that such a land-extensive industry would be able to make only a limited number of families agriculturally self-supporting ("surplus" reservation land had clearly been miscalculated). When one adds to these climatic and physical limitations the general economic problems of farmers especially after World War I, it is not difficult to understand why Indian families were not self-supporting, and could not see their way—quite *rationally*—to invest labor and income substantially in farming. Indian families had gardens, milk cows, chickens, perhaps a few hogs and cattle, and they raised small acreages of corn. During the war, a larger number of them raised wheat. Some of this—especially wheat—was sold locally and produced cash income that varied in amount from year to year, but that was appreciated by Indian families because it was not subject to trust restrictions as were funds from land sales, and could thus be spent on goods the BIA considered frivolous. But few Indian families had cash incomes sufficient for household reproduction (they continued to depend on cash from individual or tribal land sales, renting land to non-Indian neighbors, and rations issued by the BIA).

In other words, although some BIA superintendents believed the Indians would not farm or engage in commercial ranching because they were simply not yet "far enough from the old buffalo days,"[24] the real source of Indian resistance to full-scale commercial agriculture is to be found in the material constraints of their *class position* (or "class fraction"). To start with, Indian allottees did not have sufficient land to make a living at commercial agriculture or ranching; this was a direct result of the ill-advised opening of their "surplus" lands to homesteading in the settler-colonial "primitive accumulation" described in chapter 1. Had sufficient land been available, the reservation economy would have turned out very differently. On the other hand, because of the trust status of what land they did have, Indian allottees, unlike their non-Indian neighbors, did not have mortgage or tax bills to keep them in the game of commercial agriculture, which was a business with very narrow margins in this landscape and climate. Lakota allottees *did* come to value their allotments as sources of money, but through rental income rather than primarily through farming. Allotments were very commonly rented to non-Indian farmers and ranchers, who combined the Indian land with their deeded holdings.[25] As mentioned in chapter 1, when trust restrictions were removed from allotments in the wake of the 1906 Burke Act, the vast majority of these fee-patented lands were quickly sold or lost to defaulted mortgages or tax liens. While this was explained at the time as a result of Indian "incompetence" (scholars and other specialists who presently write about historic Indian land loss use a more polite description of the same imputed character trait: Indians did not know how to handle money, land, or other assets), the reality, again, was a *class* situation (understood as a particular niche in the economy, often the result of compulsion or other forces beyond one's control that are often more "political" than "economic") in which land is not a source of money except by converting it directly into cash through lease, mortgage, or sale. By using the term "class" here, I am referring to the concrete set of strategies that a group of people develop to make ends meet, given a particular structure of concrete opportunity and constraint. Given the constraints and opportunities Indian people faced on the reservation— as an effect of federal law, BIA policy, the prices paid for agricultural and other goods, the forms of income or strategic resources (for example, rations) actually available—the pressure on Indian families was to rent out their land or liquidate it rather than work it.

Nevertheless, the trustees in this case, BIA officials in Washington and field personnel, continued to see the problem in terms of Indian *character*—an apt example of the propensity of regimes of governing to find problems and solutions that have a *questionable, to say the least, relationship to actuality.* For example, the Rosebud superintendent reported in 1914 that "[t]he lack of husbandry [not just of livestock but of resources generally] is innate in the Indian character, and particularly so among the former buffalo-eating Sioux, and as a consequence they feast heavily when food is to be had" and fast at length when they have none."[26] The source of this fiction, I would suggest, is to be sought in the history of the discourse itself—which has a relatively autonomous, perhaps even "closed," logic of development. In other words, the project of civilizing Indians had more to do with a long history of debates on "the Indian problem"—located not only in the BIA, but in the quasi-public Board of Indian Commissioners and a host of nongovernment organizations such as the Lake Mohonk Conference of Friends of the Indian and the Indian Rights Association.[27] A rich "public sphere" or "thought collective" (limited to privileged, white interlocutors) had come to a general agreement about "the Indian problem," and debated only over the details of how to solve it—all the while, spectacularly missing the material (class) basis of the relationship of Indian people to farming, ranching, and "self-support."[28]

By the opening of the twentieth century, Lakota families were settled around day schools on the reservation, so that their children were within commuting distance of schools (either by foot or by horseback). Usually, these schools had been built in the neighborhoods of the *tiošpaye* villages, and although Lakota land had been allotted, almost no one lived

on her or his allotment. Extended families lived in log houses and survived on the basis of subsistence gardens, cash annuities from land
cessions, cash from leasing allotments to non-Indian ranchers and farmers, and rations provided by the BIA (they pooled resources, and a band
had no fixed "membership" or limits on families coming and going).
One of the primary concerns of the BIA was the goal of making Indians
"self-supporting."

In his annual report for 1901, Commissioner of Indian Affairs W. A.
Jones (head of the BIA) argued that "the indiscriminate issue of rations
was an effectual barrier to civilization; that the periodical distribution
of large sums of money [from tribal land cessions] was demoralizing in
the extreme; and that the general leasing of allotments instead of bene-
fitting Indians, as originally intended [for farmsteads], only contributed
to their demoralization."[29] "What, then," he asked, "is the function of
the state?"

> Briefly this: To see that the Indian has the opportunity for self-support,
> and that he is afforded the same protection of his person and property
> as is given to others. That being done, he should be thrown entirely upon
> his own resources to become a useful member of the community in which
> he lives, or not, according as he exerts himself or fails to make an effort. . . .
> He must be made to realize that in the sweat of his face he shall eat his
> bread. He must be brought to recognize the dignity of labor and the
> importance of building and maintaining a home. . . . It is there he must
> find the incentive to work, and from it must come the uplifting of his race.

Commissioner Jones admitted "[t]hat there will be many failures and
much suffering," but this was "inevitable in the very nature of things, for
it is only by sacrifice and suffering that the heights of civilization are
reached." In the end, Jones actually eased the evolutionary transition
he had in mind by replacing rations for able-bodied men on the Sioux
reservations with per diem wage work for the BIA.[30] Jones's successor,
Francis Leupp, had a similar view of the necessary lesson of hunger:

> A great deal has been said and written about the "racial tendency" of the
> Indian to squander whatever comes into his hands. This is no more "racial"

than his tendency to eat and drink to excess or to prefer pleasure to work: it is simply the asserting of a primitive instinct common to all mankind in the lower stages of social development. What we call thrift is nothing but the forecasting sense which recognizes the probability of a to-morrow; the idea of a to-morrow is the boundary between barbarism and civilization, and the only way in which the Indian can be carried across that line is by letting him learn from experience that the stomach filled to-day will go empty to-morrow unless something of to-day's surplus is saved overnight to meet to-morrow's deficit.[31]

What is the significance of this carrot-and-stick approach to civilizing Indians?

As Mitchell Dean aptly describes it, liberalism's minimalism makes inevitable certain "non-liberal and explicitly authoritarian types of rule that seek to operate through obedient rather than free subjects":

> Within liberal forms of government . . . there is a long history of people who, for one reason or another, are deemed not to possess or to display the attributes (e.g. autonomy, responsibility) required of the juridical and political subject of [liberal] rights and who are therefore subjected to all sorts of disciplinary, bio-political and even sovereign [that is, overriding state power] interventions. The list of those so subjected would include at various times those . . . with the status of the indigent, the degenerate, the feeble-minded, the aboriginal, the homosexual, the delinquent, the dangerous or even, and much more generally, the minor.[32]

Indeed, we might fruitfully set the reservation alongside the prison and the asylum as part of the disciplinary archipelago that liberalism was forced to countenance because of the "problem" subjects who could or would not bend to its grid.

Besides cutting off "free" food—a classic technique for regulating the poor, if there ever was one, and still very much alive today—the BIA used its legal position as trustee over individual and tribal property as the basis for disciplinary control of Indian use of allotments and income derived from tribal and individual land sales, and sometimes from leasing allotments, which was deposited into individual Indian money (IIM) accounts.[33] Requests for funds from IIM accounts were generally super-vised by the BIA "farmer" for the reservation district. The farmer was in theory to act as the equivalent of an agricultural extension agent, but he was also tasked with other supervisory duties by the reservation super-intendent, including acting on requests for funds. The BIA's aim was to prevent "improvident" use of funds, such as using them rather than working for subsistence, but the degree of actual, "successful" supervi-sion was, at best, variable. A BIA inspector reported in 1926 that "every scheme possible is used to obtain [Sioux benefits] for the slightest illness, under the guise of furthering their education, to purchase horses, wag-ons, harnesses and agricultural implements, and in nearly every case the real object is to obtain a 'meal ticket.' Agricultural implements, horses and harnesses are purchased and other articles to assist in making a home and start farming, but in many instances the articles are sold for a small sum and proceeds used for personal use."[34] A BIA inspector report in 1930 was even more critical of the system; he stated that he had encountered automobile traffic on the reservation such as he had never experienced before—all from the purchase of cars with IIM funds. Deal-ers of new and used cars were flocking to the reservation, competing to make sales to Indians. In addition, Indians were buying monthly grocer-ies and clothing (which, presumably, women were expected to make for their families).[35]

In fact, the reservation system under the BIA amounted to—*at least formally*—a system of administrative "micro-penality" in which the "whole indefinite domain of noncompliance is punishable."[36] In 1883, the secretary of the interior called the attention of the commissioner of Indian affairs "to what I regard as a great hindrance to the civilization of the Indians, viz, the continuance of the old heathenish dances, such as the sun-dance, scalp-dance &c." He was also exercised about "[t]he marriage relation," and wanted "[t]he Indian [to] be instructed that he is under obligations to care for and support, not only his wife, but his children. . . ." "Another great hindrance to the civilization of Indians," the secretary went on, "is the influence of the medicine men, who are always found with the anti-progressive party." Then there was the problem of "the very general custom of destroying or distributing his property on the death of a member of his family." "The Government having attempted to support the Indians until such time as they shall become self-supporting, the interest of the Government as well as that of the Indians demands that every possible effort should be made to induce them to become self-supporting at as early a day as possible. I therefore suggest whether it is not practicable to formulate certain rules . . . that shall restrict and ultimately abolish the practices I have mentioned." Rules enabling the establishment of a BIA court on a reservation, along with a list of offenses, was promulgated by the commissioner of Indian affairs and approved by the secretary.[37] There was no statute law behind the list of "Indian offenses" and their punishments, other than the general power of the president to "prescribe such regulations as he may think fit for carrying into effect the various provisions of any act relating to Indian affairs and for the settlement of Indian affairs."[38] The 1904 edition of *Regulations of the Indian Office* listed as Indian offenses the "'sun-dance,' and all other similar dances and so-called religious ceremonies"; plural marriages other than those already in existence; and the "usual practices of so-called 'medicine men.'" Penalties ranged from withholding rations to "incarceration in the agency prison." The code also subjected misdemeanors in general to the reservation courts of Indians offenses.[39]

The significance of "Indian offenses" for disciplinary power was less in the specific crimes listed or specific punishments meted out than in the general understanding that the BIA had legitimate administrative authority to intervene in many areas of daily life on the reservation. This understanding was formalized in an 1888 U.S. District Court holding in Oregon that sustained the power of the BIA to arrest and punish Indians for a "misdemeanor"—in this case a woman's adulterous cohabitation—even if the misdemeanor in question is not listed as a crime in any state or federal penal statute or in the Code of Indian Offenses itself. Because the reservation courts were in essence "educational and disciplinary instrumentalities," the district court reasoned, they could not be expected to operate as do "the constitutional courts." "[T]he reservation itself is in the nature of a school," and the court cleared the way for BIA agents to, in essence, make up the law as they went along in the project of civilizing Indians.[40] Thus, BIA agents commonly issued "orders" to Indian people. In 1910, for example, the Rosebud agent directed his farmer in the Cut Meat District to investigate reports of a giveaway (a traditional Lakota social practice) at a dance hall. The farmer reported that the culprits admitted to circling the hall and shaking hands as they gave away. One man said he realized that they were not allowed by the BIA to give away horses, cattle, wagons, or hoses but that it was possible to give away small gifts, so when he shook hands, he would tell the recipient to come to his house later to receive, say, a pair of moccasins. The culprits were ordered to the agent's office.[41]

But it would take more than reservation discipline and even "sovereign" power—as in BIA "orders"—to make Indians "self-supporting," and even Commissioner Jones recognized that it would require changing their "moral character."[42] Disciplinary and sovereign power would not be ignored when they could be used to advantage, but the limits of authoritarian remaking of the (supposed) Indian character that was the goal here would require a new form of making subjects that is best distinguished as a (liberal) governmentality of improvement—a program (or set of programs) for producing subjects who would be self-governing, prudent, and industrious. Although the term "governmentality" can have different emphases, we are concerned here with how it operates to shape subjects in ways distinct from both sovereignty and discipline, which may be thought of as more coercive techniques. While sovereignty seeks to create minimally obedient subjects through force or its threat, and discipline aims at docile and "trained" subjects through surveillance, micro-penality, and normalization—there is clearly a great deal of overlap between sovereign and disciplinary power and it is often difficult to untangle them—governmentality works on the "souls" (or, in this case, the *character*) of individuals, and recruits them to work on their own characters, by offering "technologies of the self" that to be effective must ultimately be "freely" taken up by individuals as they are guided to see the value of work on the self.[43] They reform their own characters, in other words, if properly guided, effectively taught. Graham Burchell aptly describes governmentality in the way it is used here: "the promotion . . . of specific techniques of the self around which questions as, for example, saving and providentialism, the acquisition of ways of performing rules like father or mother, the development of habits of cleanliness, sobriety, fidelity, self-improvement, responsibility, and so on."[44] Complex forms of responsibilization cannot be *drilled* or *forced* into individuals; they must be *implanted* and *nurtured*. In the case at hand, the trustees recognized that Indians would, in the end, have to *freely choose* "civilization," by recognizing what they have to gain by taking on new responsibilities, by seeing their interests in a radically new light, to be shone by the trustees, some already "civilized" Indians among them. Getting Indians to willingly accept "industry" and "thrift" would have more in common with what we call "consciousness raising," "enlightenment," or simply "teaching" than with discipline or control, and the teacher–student game—as paternalistic as it obviously can be—is a critical form of governmentality.

It is common to find mention of what we are calling governmentality amid the tougher talk of the trustees about getting Indians to be self-supporting. We can see this in the BIA's and missionaries' concern with the Omaha dance among the Lakota.[45] The Omaha (so named because it was learned by the Lakota from the Omaha people), or grass dance, was a secular dance (which is why it was tolerated by the BIA) that spread on Plains reservations in the early twentieth century and that was the forerunner of the contemporary "powwow."[46] In 1913, an Episcopal missionary in Rosebud complained to the bishop in Sioux Falls: "Once a series of these night dances begin a large number of the people care nothing for work or home duties of any sort but scheme to spend their time largely in visiting from district to district, sponging on their neighbors and hoping for a portion of the proceeds of the 'give-away' with which to replenish their stock,—or, perhaps, to enable them after a while to cut a great figure in such a 'give-away' at their home dance-house."[47] In 1921, Commissioner of Indian Affairs (and South Dakotan) Charles H. Burke issued an order to superintendents on dancing. Although "dance *per se* is not condemned," "frequent or prolonged periods of celebrations which bring the Indians together from remote points to the neglect of their crops, livestock, and home interests," and "shiftless indifference to family welfare," constituted punishable offenses under the Code of Indian Offenses.[48] The commissioner hoped that through cooperation with the missionaries, it would be possible to instill in Indians "a higher conception of home and family life, and . . . the dignity and satisfaction of his personal labor and attainments. [T]here should be no perversion of those industrial and economic essentials which underlie all civilization."[49] The Rosebud superintendent reported that Commissioner Burke's order would have allowed the agency to limit dancing, but the "elite East" and "uplift-ers" had interfered. Dancing was difficult to control because the Indians knew that even if they went hungry from lack of industry, they would get relief thanks to the friends of the Indians.[50]

At a conference called by Commissioner Burke in Pierre, South Dakota, in 1922 to discuss dancing, the assembled missionaries and BIA superintendents seemed to be in general agreement that the (Omaha) dance in itself was not detrimental, but that the attendant waste of time and resources needed to be addressed. The bishop of the Episcopal dio-cese argued that "the greatest count against these dances is its economic loss. These people go away for a week and leave their people. This hap-pens time after time during the year. . . . The welfare of the Indians, just as the welfare of the white man, depends upon their effort and their application, and we must always keep before them the things that they have in life, and it is bound up with agriculture."[51] Furthermore, "[t]he give-away is one of the most detrimental features of these dances"; "it is a form of gambling in that it is founded on the hope of getting more back than they give away."[52] It also was remarked that local towns near the reservations eagerly sought Indian participation in fairs, where Indians both performed dances and spent their money. As a result of this confer-ence, Commissioner Burke dispatched another circular on dancing to his superintendents urging that they

> persistently encourage and emphasize the Indian's attention to those prac-tical, useful, thrifty, and orderly activities that are indispensable to his well-being and that underlie the preservation of his race in the midst of complex and highly competitive conditions. The instinct of individual enterprise and devotion to the prosperity and elevation of family life should in some way be made paramount in every Indian household to the exclusion of idleness, waste of time at frequent gatherings of whatever nature,[53] and the neglect of physical resources upon which depend food, clothing, shelter and the very beginnings of progress.[54]

Striking a less punitive tone than in his 1921 circular, Burke continued: "Of course, we must give tact, persuasion, and appeal to the Indian's good sense a chance to win ahead of preemptory orders because our success must often follow a change of honest conviction. . . . We must go about this work with some patience and charity and do it in a way that will convince the Indian of our fidelity to his best welfare."[55] Included with the circular was a letter "to all Indians" in which the commissioner made an appeal: "[S]omething must be done to stop the neglect of stock, crops, gardens and home interests caused by these dances or by celebrations, pow-wows, and gatherings of any kind that take the time of the Indians for many days." The commissioner sought to draw the attention of Indian people to the distinction between work and leisure:

> Now, what I want you to think about very seriously is that you must first of all try to make your own living, which you cannot do unless you work faithfully and take care of what comes from your labor, and go to dances or other meetings only when your home work will not suffer by it. . . . No good comes from your "give-away" custom at dances and it should be stopped. You do yourselves and your families great injustice when at dances you give away money or other property, perhaps clothing, a cow, a horse or a team and wagon, and then after an absence of several days go home to find everything going to waste and yourselves with less to work with than you had before. . . . I urge you to come to an agreement with your superintendent to hold no gatherings in the months when the seed-time, cultivation of crops and the harvest need your attention, and at other times to meet for only a short period.[56]

The superintendent reported in 1925 that the dances were under control.[57]

We can gain another glimpse into the rationale of the BIA civilization program—a wider one—by examining a standardized BIA survey conducted on Rosebud Reservation in 1907. The men were surveyed by the local day-school teacher, and the women by the local housekeeper, who was usually the teacher's wife. None of the goals reflected in this assessment could be brought about by "orders" or other compulsion; it would require remaking subjects at the moral level of self-understanding.

Age of patron
Wear citizen clothes?
School attended

No. of years at school

Progressive?

Hair long or short.

No. days worked.

Patronize church?

Member of church?

Patronize dance?

Draws rations?

Married legally?

Takes interest in school?

No. of times visited school

No. of times visited school for medication, advice, etc.

Read and write?

Working knowledge of English?

Name of physician called on

No. of cattle owned

No. of horses

No. of domestic fowls owned

No. of cows milked

Tons of hay harvested

Acres fenced

Employed by a show?

Gives personal attention to cattle

No. of school entertainments attended

Distance from school

No. of wives

Sufficient food?

Sufficient clothing?

No. of visits made to each home[58]

The BIA and the missionaries were thus keenly aware that compulsion alone would not bring about Indian progress, and that it was not possible for administrators to "legislate upward"—"You can't build character by an order," someone put it at a meeting with BIA personnel in 1922.[59] Although "orders" and punitive enforcement would sometimes be necessary in view of the Indians' own interests (in the trustees' view), the

BIA at all levels understood that the way to Indian civilization was through a *pedagogical* process based on a teacher–student game. This was a key Progressive Era contribution to Indian affairs—although it has obvious parallels with missionary work—and it was perhaps most clear in the work of the BIA farmers, who worked along the lines of agricultural extension agents, teaching and encouraging farming among Indian men (as well as doing general administrative work as local representatives of the reservation superintendent).

BIA records suggest that by 1914, "farmer meetings [were] organized and conducted during the winter" to encourage and perhaps train Indian families to expand their gardens and small plots of tilled land.[60] In 1923, the Rosebud Agency conducted a survey of every family on the reservation, part of a nationwide industrial survey of reservations meant both to collect data that would show the degree of progress in Indians becoming self-supporting and to provide a pedagogical opportunity to encourage thrift and industry. At the time of the survey, Commissioner Burke instructed BIA superintendents in a circular:

> It is important for Indians to do better every year. They can not stand still. If they do not move forward they go backward. All Indians who do not respond will ultimately be left behind in the march of progress. Impress this thought upon each individual Indian. . . . A five-year program has been worked out with certain definite things to be done, having a view in the self-support of every Indian family. Every Indian should have a definite program for the year and decide just what he expects to do. . . . We shall expect the reports next year to show improved conditions among the Indians, and especially a substantial increase in the acreage cultivated by them. We shall expect you to make this industrial campaign a success.[61]

Every family was to have a garden and root cellar to provide food for the winter, and also chickens, hogs, and milk cows, if possible. While the commitment of the agency to reaching Indian men with the five-year plans varied over the years, it is likely that subsistence gardens and some commercial products resulted from the plans. By 1931 the farm program had been reorganized to follow the general lines of the cooperative extension service for non-Indians. The BIA agricultural extension agent reported that twenty-one farm chapters had been organized in local Lakota communities, and that meetings were devoted to seed testing, potato growing, control of insect pests and diseases, preparation for the annual Rosebud Fair, corn cultivation methods, 4-H Club work, and other topics typical of agricultural extension nationally at the time.[62] This is an apt example of the noncoercive teacher–student game at the heart of liberal governmentality.

Running through all of the BIA work to civilize Indians was the assumption that men and women needed to be responsibilized differently into gendered subjects, as reflected in the criteria used to assess women in a standardized 1907 survey:

Age of patron
School attended
No. of years at school
Wear citizen clothes?
Cleanliness of home
Cleanliness of beds
Cleanliness of children
Cleanliness of women
No. of rooms in home
Kind of home (log, etc.)
No. windows in home
Ventilation of home
No. of occupants
No. times visited school
No. times visited school for medicine, advice, etc.
Belong to sewing society?
Name of physician called upon
Children had vermin?
Took interest in school?
Progressive?
Member of any church?
Attend church?
Attend dance?

No. of children born
No. of children living
No. of children attending school
No. of children excused from school
No. of beds
Use tables?
Use chairs?
Have sewing machine?
Have cupboard, etc.?
No. of visits made to each home[63]

As the male day-school teachers and BIA farmers worked with Lakota men, "housekeepers" (usually the day-school teacher's wife) and field matrons were detailed to work with women. By 1911, the Rosebud Agency employed five "female industrial teachers," or matrons, under the direction of the agency physician, each having a case load of 160 families in a sixteen-mile radius.[64] Their pedagogical mission was clearly spelled out:

Your duties . . . are to visit Indian women in their homes and to give them counsel, encouragement and help in the following lines:

1. Care of a house, keeping it clean and in order, properly warmed (not over-heated), ventilated and suitably furnished.
2. Cleanliness and hygienic conditions generally, including disposition of all refuse.
3. Preparation and serving of food and regularity in meals.
4. Sewing, including cutting, making and mending garments.
5. Laundry work.
6. Adorning the home, both inside and out, with pictures, curtains, home-made rugs, flowers, grass plots and trees, construction and repair of walks, fences and drains. . . .
7. Keeping and care of domestic animals, such as cows, poultry and swine; care and use of milk, making of butter, etc.
8. Care of sick.
9. Care of little children, and introducing among them the games and sports of white children.

The goal was not simply to develop practical skills among women but to work on the Indian woman's character: "In general you should instruct them in civilized home life, stimulating their intelligence, arousing ambition and cultivating refinement."[65] Women's programs eventually took the form of a home extension service, and Rosebud had a home extension agent by 1932. She organized a competitive yard-improvement project with financial assistance from the local Winner, South Dakota, branch of the General Federation of Women's Clubs, and offered magazine subscriptions as prizes. The "white women" of the Winner club "were anxious to be of service and helpful to our sisters of another race."[66] The federation's Department of Public Welfare had an Indian Welfare Division that asked humanely regarding "the Indian": "[w]hy should we expect him to transform his primitive condition into the complex civilized life of today within a few generations, when this same process of change has taken the whites thousands of years?" The federation urged the expanded formation of "Indian women's clubs . . . , eventually to become affiliated with the Federation, [which] are increasingly producing far-reaching beneficial results. And year by year there are fewer Indian families huddled in improperly ventilated houses, with earth floors and with such a lack of sanitation as to encourage transmission of communicable diseases from one member of the family to another."[67] Women's clubs were, in fact, organized on Rosebud during the 1930s.

There is no doubt that at least some, and possibly a good deal, of these uplift projects were welcomed by Indian people, some of whom were enthusiastic about gardens, small acreages of cash crops, improving their homes and yards, sewing projects, and so on. But "self-support" must have seemed to anyone who thought seriously about it an increasingly distant, if not impossible, goal. Despite decades of attempting to get Indian people to plan for tomorrow, Commissioner Burke wrote to his superintendents in 1927 that not enough progress had been made on the problem of Indian time orientation. The problem was still, at least for Burke, located in the Indian character:

> far too many [Indians] fail to look ahead and heed the necessity to provide for themselves the things essential to keep them in comfort and health. They may engage in farming or other activity during the summer, and

during that season live fairly well, but they ignore the fact that winter always follows summer, and that their needs are actually greater in winter than in any other season. [The] conception of the needs of the future is lacking in the minds of many Indians largely because of the fact that providing for the future requires so much more work and self denial than simply drifting, with the government in the background to call upon when any particular day or season fails.

Burke distributed copies of a letter signed by him and meant "to awaken in the mind of the Indian who is below average a desire to place himself in the class which is above average. The plan of distribution contemplates the filling in of the name and address of any Indian to whom you deem it advisable to send the letter and then either mailing or handing it to him personally." Burke's letter included the following:

[T]here still remain many individual Indians who show little or no evidence of progress, but who are just where they were years ago. [T]hey are still living in miserable shacks, not worthy of the name of houses, their allotments are either uncultivated or are leased to some more ambitious Indian or white person in the community. They have no gardens, no milk cows, pigs, or chickens; indeed, if it is summer you will probably not find them at home,—they are visiting somewhere, attending some celebration or wild west show, or living with some relative or friend,—anywhere but home. The children of the family are poorly clad and probably under nourished because they have no milk or eggs or other articles of diet which they should have to make them keep well and grow up to be healthy men and women. When winter comes on they are found clamoring for rations. . . . The old saying, "The Lord helps those who help themselves" is just as true of the red man as it is of the white.[68]

Burke and other BIA personnel were to a certain extent correct when they recognized that Indian people were in a position to make light of "thrift" and "industry" because of the "government in the background to call upon when any particular day or season fails." This is not a "culture-of-poverty" explanation, however, but a recognition of the material basis for the reproduction of domestic units on the reservation—a material basis that differed significantly from that of non-Indians, not because of "character differences" but because of distinct class (or fractional class) positions. Non-Indian farm families in the Rosebud country were dependent on the soil to produce their subsistence, of course, but, more important, they were dependent on the soil and their toil to yield marketable farm products that brought in cash through sale. This cash was necessary for covering mortgage and loan payments, real-estate taxes, the cost of agricultural inputs (seeds, livestock, transportation, equipment), and, of course, any necessities that could not be provided on the farm. Without a cash income sufficient to cover these inescapable costs, farms went broke and farm families left the area, a common enough outcome, especially in the wake of the postwar recession of 1920–21. Non-Indian families thus faced directly what Marx called the "silent compulsion of economic relations";[69] the reproduction of the family farm—the (fragile) continuity of its basic sources of income, food, and other necessities—meant the necessity of staying in the game of commodity production (production of products for sale on the market). Under such conditions of reproduction, "thrift" and "industry" were virtues made out of necessities (but, as we will see shortly, many "trustees" of the welfare of the countryside deemed non-Indian farm families in need of improvement too).

Indian families, at least on Rosebud Reservation, on the other hand, were never *yeomanized* or *proletarianized*—never made dependent on the market for the reproduction of domestic units. This was partly owing to the trust status of allotments that exempted them from real-estate taxes and protected them from alienation through the market (with the notorious exception of fee patenting). It was also owing in part to the fact that the BIA did indeed provide rations that, along with cash payments from tribal land sales and leasing of allotments, played a critical role in supporting Indian families. Indian families *did* do some farming and some wage work. They gardened and kept some stock, including beef and milk cows, chickens, pigs, and horses, and they raised feed crops for their livestock, especially corn; some also raised wheat for sale when prices were high. Fixed-term or seasonal wage work was also common, either for the BIA agency or for farmers or ranchers. All of this activity contributed to subsistence directly, and the petty cash was probably used for what were, by reservation standards, luxuries. The price that Lakota people paid for their "freedom" from the market was living in poverty, or at best, on the edge of poverty. The only way that families and communities survived—and this is still the case today—was by pooling scarce resources or otherwise sharing. In other words, the forms of "improvidence" that seemed to the administrators to be the root of Indian backwardness—resources and time devoted to dances, giveaways, and church convocations; sharing, pooling, and generosity—were precisely the forms of social insurance that allowed Indian people to survive reservation life. As anthropologist Haviland Scudder Mekeel reported on a Lakota community on neighboring Pine Ridge Reservation, "[w]hatever money [comes] into the community is quite evenly divided by the functioning of many customs, which, in their totality, virtually prescribe a state of socialism. . . . Teton Dakota society . . . has founded its cardinal values on the release of wealth. . . . [T]his attitude toward wealth is one of the most outstanding characteristics of a Teton Dakota community and has proven to be one of the foremost stumbling blocks to missionary and administrator alike."[70] The project to "civilize" Indians failed not only spectacularly but *positively,* precisely as Foucault argued that the prison fails—by *maintaining and even creating and intensifying precisely the problem that it claims to solve.*[71] The lesson here is that the trustees systemically misrecognized (or ignored) what they were actually doing in the realm of the economic organization of the reservation. While they spoke in abstract terms about improving the moral character of Indian people and took seemingly pragmatic measures to accomplish their goal, the general arrangements meant to civilize Indians produced the very conditions under which supposed Indian "character flaws"—for example, generosity and sharing—were reproduced. It is difficult to imagine a more circular formation of discourse on, and practices of, government. The likely *inefficacy* of Burke's letters to Indian people, given their material situation, is stunning.

Modernizing Farmers

It was not only Indians who needed improvement. The Progressive Era witnessed the emergence of new of trustee actors who did not believe that the market or liberalism was sufficient to bring about the progress that was needed among white citizens in the countryside. These trustees invented specific forms of *moral* improvement. Non-Indian farmers and their wives were certainly liberal subjects disciplined by the market—in ways that Indians were not, as I have argued—but they were not *perfected* liberal subjects from the point of view of the progressives, and they were in need of uplift beyond the *limited realm* of liberalism and market discipline. Furthermore, liberalism might need adjustments, these trustees reasoned, and capitalism itself might need disciplining.

In 1908, in the wake of the Populist revolt of the 1890s, President Theodore Roosevelt appointed a Country Life Commission to study and make recommendations on the matter of the "social and economic institutions of the open country . . . not keeping pace with the development of the nation as a whole."[72] In his charge letter Roosevelt wrote that it was not enough for national policy to aim merely at the maximization of agricultural production:

> [R]ural interests are human interests, and good crops are of little value to the farmer unless they open the door to a good kind of life on the farm. . . . How can the life of the farm family be made less solitary, fuller of opportunity, freer from drudgery, more comfortable, happier, and more attractive? . . . How can life on the farm be kept on the highest level, and, where it is not already on that level, be so improved, dignified, and brightened as to awaken and keep alive the pride and loyalty of the farmer's boys and girls, of the farmer's wife, and of the farmer himself? . . . All these questions are of vital importance not only to the farmer but to the whole nation. (23)

Among others, the commission included Henry C. Wallace, publisher of *Wallace's Farmer* and who would serve as secretary of agriculture from 1921 to 1924, and Gifford Pinchot of the U.S. Department of Agriculture's Forest Service, who developed the regime of sustained-yield management (see chapter 3).

The commissioners delved deeply and broadly into farming and rural life. Among the problems identified was public health, where what was at stake was not only a "humanitarian" concern for farmers themselves, but also the health of the nation, because "infection may spread from farms to cities in the streams and also in the milk, meat, and other farm products." Part of the problem was simply providing more doctors and seeing to the organization of effective rural boards of health and "federal or other rigid sanitary control" over slaughterhouses. More interestingly for present purposes, the knowledge (or lack thereof) and behavior of rural people were targeted for improvement:

> [T]here are numberless . . . farmhouses . . . and even rural schoolhouses, that do not have the rudiments of sanitary arrangement. . . . [T]oo much visiting in the case of contagious diseases; patent medicines, advertising quacks, and intemperance; . . . unwholesome and poorly prepared and monotonous diet; lack of recreation; too long hours of work. . . . There is great need for the teaching of the simplest and commonest laws of hygiene and sanitation in all the schools. The people need knowledge, and no traditions should prevent them from having it. How and what to eat, the nature of disease, the importance of fresh air, the necessity of physical training even on the farm, the ineffectiveness or even the danger of nostrums, the physical evils of intemperance, all should be known in some useful degree to every body and girl on leaving school. (45–46)

The parallel with civilizing Indians is more than a little apparent, at least at this general level of problematization.

The commission was also concerned with the condition of women on the farm. In some areas, a "lack of prosperity and of ideals" meant that men's work is "likely to have precedence over . . . household work" in terms of the expenditure of resources and attention. In other words, "whatever general hardships, such as poverty, isolation, lack of labor-saving devices, may exist on any given farm, the burden of these hardships falls more heavily on the farmer's wife than on the farmer himself. In general, her life is more monotonous and . . . more isolated, no matter what the wealth or the poverty of the family may be." The solutions were clear:

> Development of a cooperative spirit in the home, simplification of the diet in many cases, the building of convenient and sanitary houses, providing running water in the house and also more mechanical help, good

and convenient gardens, a less exclusive ideal of money getting on the part of the farmer, providing better means of communication, as telephones, roads, and reading circles, and developing of women's organizations. . . . The farm woman should have sufficient free time and strength so that she may serve the community by participating in its vital affairs. . . . It is important also that all rural organizations that are attended chiefly by men should discuss the home-making subjects, for the whole difficulty often lies with the attitude of the men. (47)

Thus, physical improvements would be necessary, but so would newly gendered subjects—farm women who saw clearly their role in rural life beyond the family and work, and men who would see and support women in ways supporting that vision. The commission urged no less than making the personal political in the thinking of rural people.

The commission also wanted rural people more generally to become politically engaged in pursuing their own interests, and those interests had been made apparent by Populism and subsequent farm advocates. "Agriculture is not commercially as profitable as it is entitled to be for the labor and energy that the farmer expends and the risks that he assumes," the commission wrote, and the main reason for this was not difficult to find: the farmer "usually stands alone against organized interests." "The disadvantage or handicap of the farmer as against the established business systems and interests [prevents] him from securing adequate returns for his products" (14). "[T]here is," the commission noted, "a widespread disregard of the rights of the men who own and work the land. . . . The organized and corporate interests represented in mining, manufacturing, merchandising, transportation, and the like seem often to hold the idea that their business may be developed and exploited without regard to the farmers." This discriminatory arrangement was deeply structured not only in the economy but in law and politics. For example, the farmer's "visible and stationary property [is] taxed freely," while corporate "invisible and changeable property tend[s] to evade taxation" (29). More directly, "railway companies, by their rates, may decide where the centers of distribution shall be, what areas shall develop manufactures, and other special industries. To the extent that they do this they exercise a purely public function, and for this reason alone, if for no other, the Government should exercise a wise supervision over the making and publication of rates. Favoritism to large shippers has been one of the principal abuses of the transportation business and has contributed to the growth of monopolies of trade" (35). Then, of course, there was the matter of marketing: "certain middlemen consume a share of agricultural sales out of all proportion to the services they render, either to the consumer or the producer, making a larger profit—often without risk—in the selling of the product than the farmer makes in producing it." "There must be a vast enlargement of voluntary organized effort among the farmers themselves," the commission concluded, implying cooperative buying and selling. More broadly, farmers needed to organize politically, because they "do not influence legislation as they should" (36, 18).[73]

It is clear that the common thread in addressing all these problems was the creation of new agrarian subjects who would actively and voluntarily take the reins regarding their own destiny:

> [I]n the last analysis the country life problem is a moral problem. . . . The great spiritual needs of the country community . . . are higher personal and community ideals. Rural people need to have an aspiration for the highest possible development of the community. There must be an ambition on the part of the people themselves constantly to progress in all of those things that make the community life wholesome, satisfying, educative, and complete. . . . As a pure matter of education, the countryman must learn to love the country and to have an intellectual appreciation of it. More than this, the spiritual nature of the individual must be kept thoroughly alive. His personal ideas of conduct and ambition must be cultivated. (60)

While it was necessary that a certain basic financial stability be maintained for the countryside, "money hunger" among farmers needed to be overcome (64).

The family, the school, and the church—with appropriate reorganization—would obviously be indispensable here, but the commission recognized that a national social movement was necessary. The task of this movement would be to cultivate, through "a broad campaign of publicity,"

> a quickened sense of responsibility in all country people to the community and to the State, in the conserving of soil fertility, and in the necessity of diversifying farming in order to conserve this fertility and to develop a

better rural society, and also in the better safe guarding of the strength and
happiness of the farm women; a more widespread conviction of the necessity for organization, not only for economic but for social purposes, this
organization to be more or less cooperative, so that all the people may
share equally in the benefits and have voice in the essential affairs of the
community; . . . and a realization on the part of all the people of the obligation to protect and develop the natural scenery and attractiveness of the
open country. (14)

What was called for was a "reconstruction," a "rebuilding"—both economically and socially—of "a new agriculture and new rural life." Part of
this would involve new public-school curricula to provide education con-
ducive to farmer citizens, as well as government surveys and provision of
information to farmers on "the exact conditions underlying farming in
every locality" (17). The commission went so far as to plead for the development of rural "spiritual forces": "The forces and institutions that make
for morality and spiritual ideals among rural people must be energized.
We miss the heart of the problem if we neglect to foster personal character and neighborhood righteousness" (18). "The entire people need to
be roused," the commission said, with the goal of "preserv[ing] a race of
men in the open country that, in the future as in the past, will be the stay
and strength of the nation in time of war and its guiding and controlling
spirit in time of peace" (19, 20).

As William L. Bowers explains, the Country Life Commission was
part of a larger, and dispersed, movement for "country-life reform." Who
were the reformers?

Support for efforts to improve country life came primarily from an emerging professional rural leadership and from urban elements with either a
definite stake in agricultural matters or strong humanitarian, philanthropic,
or "social gospel" notions. Among the first to diagnose and offer remedies
for country-life problems were rural leaders such as the staffs of the land-
grant colleges, bureaucrats in the Department of Agriculture, members of
the new twentieth-century farm organizations, and editors and publishers
of prominent farm journals. Bankers, retail merchants, farm implement
manufacturers, mail-order houses, railroads, transportation companies,

chambers of commerce, and boards of trade were some of the urban groups which recognized the connection between their prosperity, and the farmers' and therefore took an active interest in rural welfare. Teachers, ministers, social workers, charitable institutions, and civil betterment leagues were representative of groups which joined from more altruistic motives.[74]

Many of the country-life reformers itemized in Bowers's list "were convinced that most farmers were not using scientific techniques and that extension education would eliminate this rural ignorance and indifference and replace it with agricultural efficiency, larger profits, and greater possibilities for country life."[75] Notwithstanding the desire of the Country Life Commission to focus on the spiritual and moral character of farmers, it was the technical practices of farmers that would receive the most attention.

In one of the dramatic successes of the reform movement, the cooperative extension service, a joint program of the U.S. Department of Agriculture (USDA) and the state agricultural colleges, was established by the federal Smith-Lever Act of 1914, and acts of the South Dakota legislature in 1915 and 1917 enabled any county to organize a farm bureau and hire a county agent, the salary partly defrayed by state and federal funding. The county agent in South Dakota, according to the service's first circular in 1917,

> endeavors through farm demonstrations to bring before the community agricultural facts that relate to the local problems; to make available to the people the results of experiments from the Experiment Stations of the country and the U.S. Department of Agriculture; to search for the best there is in the farm practices of successful farmers and give the widest publicity to their work; to inspire local leadership and develop interest among the farm boys and girls; in short, to assist in all lines of agricultural endeavor, so that the work of the Farm Bureau and other local agricultural associations develop a permanent and profitable agriculture with a high standard of community ideals.[76]

The key lesson that needed to be imparted to farmers—the lesson on which all the other lessons hinged—was the necessity for good farm management. Farming needed to "pay as a business proposition. . . . In other words, it should pay a reasonable return upon the capital and labor used in the actual farming operations." Simple enough, but "[b]efore a farmer can hope to give any intelligent study to means of increasing his profits, he must know what his profit or loss is and have some knowledge of its sources."[77] This would all depend on the keeping of farm account books, which were distributed by the extension service and by banks. By 1918, more than 3,300 books had been distributed in South Dakota by the extension service.[78] The extension service also provided a "farm management school" held over a period of one to two years, which was found to be the best method of training farmers to use the account books.[79]

Analysis of a farmer's account book would allow the extension service, and in theory the farmer, to identify ways to reduce costs and increase revenue by "[g]etting farmers to care about the numbers," as Deborah Fitzgerald aptly describes it.[80] The farm records thus allowed for extension service entrée into almost every dimension of farm improvement, through the key metrics of profit and loss. For example, a farmer might be relying on only one or two enterprises, and thus unnecessarily exposing his farm to the vagaries of price changes and weather conditions, both of which could be smoothed out by greater diversification.[81] Diversification would also make possible a more efficient use of human and horse labor:

> The total number of days or hours each horse works per year is an important factor. For example, suppose it costs $75 to keep a farm work horse for a year. If he works fifty 10-hour days or 500 hours per year, his labor costs 15 cents per hour. On the other hand, if the same horse works 110 days or 1100 hours the cost of keeping it will be very nearly the same, but the cost per hour for its work will be less than half as much, or 6.8 cents per hour. This gives a difference of 8.2 cents per hour in the cost of horse labor, depending upon the number of days' work the horse performs in a year. In growing an acre of corn, which requires about 45 hours of horse labor, this would make a difference of $3.69.[82]

The new farm accounting category of labor—both human and horse, and we can assume mule—income had been, as Fitzgerald says, *invented.*

More important, because farm revenue was heavily dependent on the number of days of labor at productive enterprises per year, labor (including that of the horse) "should be used most efficiently and every effort made to so organize the business as to provide the most possible days of productive work each year."[83] Here is a compelling example of how accounting practices produce subjects by changing the way individuals think about their interests. "Making people write things down and count them," Nikolas Rose and Peter Miller observe, "is itself a kind of government of them, an incitement to individuals to construe their lives according to such norms."[84] The farmer could also see through his account book how his productivity stacked up against that of the most productive farmers in the county and the state, and he could seek advice from these men if he fell significantly below their standard. This is an apt example of what Foucault called normalization—getting the subject to recognize and care about how he or she fares on the normal curve of the population. "If dairy cows are kept on the farm . . . it will pay to look into production per cow," via the records kept in the account book. "If this is low," relative to the statewide average, "the remedy probably lies in better breeding or better feeding, or more probably both."[85] The farmer was also assured that he would be "well repaid for time spent in studying markets and price trends," being very careful about expanding his production of a given commodity when the price is high, a tactic that seemed natural enough but that neglected the theoretically predictable—through the dynamics of supply and demand—odds that the high price would fall in the near future.[86]

Clearly, what the department of farm management (in the extension service at South Dakota State College in Brookings) had in mind was a comprehensive agrarian governmentality in which farmers would be made into new, enterprising subjects (we generally associate that term with contemporary neoliberalism, not the liberalism or progressive agrarianism of the early twentieth century) by coming to think in terms of the line items and bottom line of the farm account books, as well as about how to improve these numbers by new agricultural techniques and enterprises and better farm organization. More than that, this farm management technology may have represented the first time many farmers became aware of whether they were in the red or in the black, for the bottom line of "net farm profit," as defined in Brookings, was a complicated calculation (and perhaps an abstract one, given the relentless daily routine of making ends meet on the farm):

> Net Farm Profit = Gross Farm Income [(closing inventory + total sales) – opening inventory + value of livestock purchased during the year)] – (feed purchased + labor hired + repairs on permanent improvements + repairs on machinery + other farm expenses [taxes, insurance, rent, interest, and miscellaneous expenses not otherwise charged] + depreciation on farm property and farm machinery).[87]

Seat-of-the-pants farm management—Can we pay our taxes, mortgages, and other loans? Do we have the seeds, feed, livestock, and implements we need? Do we have enough to eat and sufficient clothing and shelter? (the same kinds of questions most Lakota families must have routinely asked, except for taxes and loans)—was hopelessly *backward* in the new vision of the farm business urged on farmers, and qualitative assessments of how the family was doing at farming were meant to be shunted aside by thinking like an accountant, or at least a bookkeeper.

The extent to which the farmer was urged to think in accounting terms was formidable. In analyzing an account book kept by a particular farmer during 1917–18 and published as a case study in a circular, the extension service wrote: "To strengthen his business [the farmer] had to know the part each department played in making or losing money for him." The recommendation was that the farmer estimate on a weekly basis "the amount of time he spent on taking care of the horses, cattle, etc." For estimating feed use, the extension service recommended that the farmer separate his feed—for example, oats—into different bins for hogs, chickens, calves, or horses. Thus, when he refills the bin for horses, "he charges it up to the horses" in the account book. "If the farmer is also keeping a weekly work record of his [hired] man and his [own] labor, this and his feed record kept on a cost account supplement will let him figure the exact cost of production on any crop or class of livestock."[88] Deborah Fitzgerald succinctly describes the model farmer that the extension agents and agricultural economists sought to foster: "In exhorting the farmer to 'think of his farms as a business unit,' the expert was telling farmers something negative and something positive. Farmers should not think of their farms as just the place where they lived. . . . They should think of their farms as places of business, perhaps as factories for producing things like pork and wheat, as places where productive activity was all business."[89] How many farmers took this enterprising way of thinking seriously, much less practiced it in a deliberate way, is impossible to know from the archives.

Understandably, some farmers had their doubts not only about specific extension service advice, but about the value of extension agents and the service as a whole: "A few farmers seem to feel that the county agent is a young college educated, theorist farmer without practical experience, who is employed to 'show them how to farm.'"[90] While the extension service insisted that the agency was merely providing the most current scientific information and pointed out that the agent would be under the supervision of the local county farm bureau, not all counties in South Dakota saw fit to organize a farm bureau and hire an agent. No doubt many counties saw the benefits of having an extension agent as not worth the average annual cost to the county of $1,500.[91] Gregory, Mellette, and Tripp counties in the Rosebud country received their first extension agents not on the basis of county appropriations but as emergency demonstration agents made available by the federal government because of its food-production goals during World War I.[92] When the emergency funding ended with the war, the Rosebud country lost its emergency agents (except for Mellette, which organized a farm bureau and retained an extension agent, though that position was later abolished) and extension agents did not reappear in the Rosebud country until the economic and environmental emergency warranted them in 1933, when agents were again provided to counties by the government cost free (see chapter 3). While the extension service also worked in counties without organized farm bureaus and agents (through short courses and distribution of circulars and bulletins), it is unlikely that extension had much impact in the Rosebud country prior to the New Deal.[93] In fact, it seems likely that farmers in the Rosebud country put about as much stock in "farm management" as Lakota people put in the project to "civilize" them. Farmers must have planted crops and raised livestock that they guessed would bring the most money at market, no doubt taking relative

costs into consideration as a rule of thumb, but not in the vast majority
of cases to analyze accounts beyond that—especially if they owned land
that had significantly appreciated in value. They likely made ends meet
as best they could from month to month, season to season, and year to
year, receiving what cash they could from sales and making what expen-
ditures they thought necessary or warranted by the seat of their pants.
For these farmers, thrift and hard work were survival strategies as well
as "character traits" one would organize the self around and be proud of;
accounting must have had much less moral weight.

Another attempt to make farmers more businesslike in their decisions
was the Outlook Program, a cooperative venture between the USDA and
the state extension services. The aim was to provide farmers with reliable and useful information on crop estimates (including foreign crop
yields in wheat), weather conditions, and market price trends so that
they could rationally plan production. *The Agricultural Outlook,* published since 1913 (prior to that the USDA Bureau of Statistics published a
Crop Reporter), was relocated in 1922 to the new Bureau of Agricultural
Economics (BAE), headed by Henry C. Taylor, previously an agricultural
economist at the University of Wisconsin.[94] A new Outlook Program was
rolled out in 1923, aimed at "forecasting trends in agricultural production and demand with the hope of providing in advance of the seeding
period information which will give guidance to the thinking farmer who
is looking for facts," as described by Taylor. The plan was "to draw a picture of the conditions with respect to the probable supply and demand
through the competing area. . . . The farmers were not to be told what to
do but given the facts they needed in order to act intelligently."[95] The new
Agricultural Outlook was based on "farmers' intentions to plant [from
forty-three thousand responses to inquiries] . . . together with a review of
the general agricultural outlook. . . . The purpose of this combined report
is to furnish information which will enable farmers to make such adjustments to their planting plans . . . as may seem desirable in order to prevent the over or underplanting of particular crops."[96]

The main innovation in the new *Agricultural Outlook* was a more
direct attempt to steer farmers toward keeping a keen eye on probable
demand relative to probable supply, as well as on the economic, social,
political, climatic, and other factors that went into determining supply

Very Unfavorable Price Outlook	Unfavorable Price Outlook	Slightly Unfavorable Price Outlook	Slightly Favorable Price Outlook	Favorable Price Outlook	Very Favorable Price Outlook
Potatoes Hay	Wheat Oats	Barley	Certified seed Potatoes Corn	Flax	Alfalfa seeds
		Lambs	Hogs Poultry Eggs	Beef Cattle Dairying Wool Work Horses	

FIGURE 2.3. Advice on agricultural production, 1928. Adapted from "Outlook as to Desirability of Expansion of Various Crop and Livestock Enterprises," *South Dakota Monthly Farm Outlook,* January 14, 1928 (Brookings: Extension Service, South Dakota State College), 7.

and demand. The *Outlook* was extremely thorough (in terms of the range of factors considered), highly technical, and more descriptive of the complexity of factors potentially affecting supply and demand than practically predictive of price changes. In fact, it is fair to say that it was not of practical use in predicting prices at all. Not surprisingly, BAE Chief Henry C. Taylor did not expect that individual farmers would make sense of the *Outlook* reports themselves, but that the reports would serve "as a splendid method of giving to the farmers through the press and through the extension agencies the best available information at the beginning of the crop year."[97] In South Dakota, it was the extension service that took on the job of translating the *Outlook* for "dirt farmers," and it began publishing mimeographed monthly and annual outlook reports in 1925. The most challenging guidance for the extension service to produce was identifying which commodities farmers should produce more or less of.[98] Figure 2.3 appeared in the January 1928 issue of the *South Dakota Monthly Farm Outlook,* and it would obviously have been of great interest, and practical use, to farmers in its explicit recommendations for farmers. The extension service also published an annual *Agricultural Outlook* that compared prices over the previous five years (see Table 2.1). Of course, these data were not *easily* used by farmers for production decisions.

TABLE 2.1. Index of price levels of South Dakota farm products. The index baseline of 100 equals the average price for the period of July 1910 to June 1915, based on prices received by South Dakota farmers. Adapted from "Price Level of South Dakota Farm Products," *South Dakota's Agricultural Outlook for 1930* (Brookings: Extension Service, South Dakota State College), 19.

Commodity	Year-to-Year Variation 1925–1930	Average January Price Level 1925–1930	Price Level January 1929	Price Level December 1929	Price Level January 1930
Hogs	up 6	135	118	121	125
Cattle	up 4	143	177	168	172
Chickens	up 6	184	206	159	170
Sheep	up 17	186	189	131	147
Corn	up 3	135	134	124	124
Wheat	up 6	142	101	120	114
Oats	up 5	108	100	95	95
Flax	up 3	130	127	172	167
Barley	no change	97	81	74	74
Hay	down 7	121	103	106	106
Potatoes	up 9	153	67	168	167
Rye	up 5	117	108	104	101
Butter	down 7	187	198	177	151
Eggs	down 41	206	150	146	198
Wool	down 2	214	211	164	164

Current prices might have meant *something*, but how did one interpret it against the average of the last five years? What were the costs of producing different commodities? And what about the relative prices *between* different commodities? How would one weigh a higher price for a low-priced commodity against a lower price for a high-priced commodity?

There was also, from the standpoint of the extension services and other farm advocates, the perennial problem of overproduction. Overall agricultural production was on the upswing, while agricultural demand was "inelastic." This meant that the fundamentals of the market model of supply and demand could not be counted on to serve the interests of individual farmers. "Some improvement in agriculture is expected for 1928 if farmers avoid expansion of production and continue their efforts to balance production with demand," the *South Dakota Monthly Farm Outlook* declared in February 1928. In other words, prices would rise compared to 1927, "provided agricultural production is maintained at its present volume and farmers continue to make further adjustments toward a more balanced production. Expansion, especially in cash crops is to be guarded against." Of course, *expanded production in cash crops is precisely what the market model would predict among farmers if they have good reason to expect a rise in price.* The *Outlook*'s message was that "[t]he experience of recent years indicates that farmers should guard against expanding production to such a point that the consequences of increased supplies would more than offset any probable improvement in domestic demand."[99] The extension service was particularly concerned about expanded production resulting from higher prices brought on by a previous season of poor yields.[100] But no individual farmer could be expected to abide by this *collective* reasoning, and in fact limiting production in the face of higher prices would be a directly *perverse* (as economists say) response to price in the market model. In addition, the extension services were concerned about another perverse price response—the possibility that farmers would increase production of commodities as prices fell, in order to make up the gap between prices received and costs incurred by marketing more volume of lower-priced commodities. Even *South Dakota's Agricultural Outlook for 1930* pointed out that, barring poor yields, "increased production should be at least sufficient to offset the lower prices which may result from larger production in the United States."[101]

Former BIA Chief H. R. Tolley wrote in 1931 that "[e]qually as important as the actual information which an outlook report contains is the stimulus to thinking which it gives. . . . Farmers should know the forces that have caused things to be as they are, and the reasons for them."[102] Indeed, one lesson farmers who considered the *Outlook* reports in earnest would have learned was that the prices they received for their products were determined by a complex and formidable range of factors that affect supply (acres planted; yield as determined by soil fertility, range conditions, weather, and other variables; relative costs of transportation to market; agricultural imports entering the United States or affecting

supply in countries where U.S. surpluses are sold) and demand (the purchasing power of urban workers, the U.S. tariff on agricultural imports,
and import duties on U.S. agricultural sales to foreign countries). But
there was also a *political lesson,* because acting practically on those data
and predictions in a way that would make a difference in farm prices
could not be accomplished by individual farmer decision makers. The
BAE and extension services surely realized this, and no doubt they were
aware at some level in their thinking that what the data and predictions
really meant in terms of policy was the necessity for farmers to think
and act *collectively.* Only by collectively limiting production or otherwise managing supply (as manufacturers did with their products), or by
price setting by the state (which many farmers came to demand), could
the prices farmers received be raised. This was abundantly, if implicitly,
the clear lesson of the *Outlook* reports for any thoughtful reader, and the
Farmers Union and other farmer organizations were already committed
to organizing marketing and other cooperatives among farmers (more on
this in chapter 4). This is where liberal governmentality—and the eter-
nal return to the individual decision maker—reached one of its inherent
limits. *Agricultural economists had discovered macroeconomics,* even if
of a pre-Keynesian variety, and they understood that all their research
findings called for an interventionary, very visible hand in managing
agricultural supply and demand. This expanded scale of agricultural
rationality and lever pulling remained largely in the wings in the 1920s,
but it would come into its own and take center stage with New Deal
production control under the 1933 Agricultural Adjustment Act. This
necessitated a new program of governmentality—one based on collective measures—to which we turn in the next chapter.

South Dakotans, both Indian and non-Indian, were seen by their appointed and self-appointed trustees as in need of improvement during
the Progressive Era, and in the interwar years. As for Indians, it was clear
to those legally responsible for their welfare, or those who took it upon
themselves to be friends of the Indians, that disciplinary and pedagogical illiberalisms would be necessary to make them into civilized citizens
capable of self-support and self-government, although there was also a
less authoritarian, more *pedagogical* element in civilizing Indians. When

it came to whites, the "trustees" who sought to improve them realized that private property and private enterprise were not enough, and that farmers and their wives needed to be made into better citizens, better managers, and even better people. The parallels between improving Indians and improving whites are remarkable, bearing in mind that whites could, as they did in the Rosebud country, simply ignore the improvers by not hiring them to do their uplifting work locally. But things would change drastically as the New Deal dawned in 1933, as we will see in the next chapter.

3

New Deal Practices

How Not to Govern Too Little

W e saw in the previous chapter that liberalism, even at its height, did not monopolize government: forms of pastoral power—sometimes quite illiberal—accompanied it with the goal of making subjects who would thrive in liberalism. We also need to recognize that liberalism itself might be seen by historical actors to require interventions, or that its apparent effects might be understood as the excesses of liberalism in need of correction. This is precisely how New Deal reforms were understood by those who advocated and implemented them. In South Dakota, the deteriorating position of farmers in the agricultural market, the marginalization of Indian people on reservations, and what was understood as the environmental emergency of the drought were targeted as the negative consequences of liberalism's governing too little. These problems took their place in the 1930s and 1940s alongside the Depression's widespread unemployment, entrenched poverty (both rural and urban), the risks of illness and old age, and other targets in the well-known, if controversial, programs of the New Deal, some of which are very much alive, if still controversial, today.

How should we theorize the New Deal? Let us return to liberalism. Foucault saw political economy in its laissez-faire version as a key *practice* at the core of liberalism. For him, political economy is less significant as a theory than as a method (or we might think of it as a protocol) by which government would limit its activities (from a European standpoint, this was a very important invention, because it came in the wake of and in reaction to autocracy and the ancien régime). Political economy was, for Foucault, the leading edge in the "transformation of governmental reason" and in the "birth of a new governmental reason" in the eighteenth century.[1] But while this seems consistent with celebrating the Enlightenment and the birth of democracy, Foucault had a different perspective. His interest was in how political economy signaled government's new focus on *the population,* which entailed much beyond simply allowing the free market to work. In a series of lectures that foregrounded biopolitics as opposed to political economy specifically, Foucault described the new form of power as biopower, which focuses on

a set of processes such as the ratio of births to deaths, the rate of reproduction, the fertility of a population, and so on. It is these processes—the birth rate, the mortality rate, longevity, and so on—together with a whole series of related economic and political problems . . . which, in the second half of the eighteenth century, become biopolitics' first objects of knowledge and the targets its seeks to control. . . . We . . . see the beginnings of a natalist policy, plans to intervene in all phenomena relating to the birth rate. This biopolitics is not concerned with fertility alone. It deals with the problem of morbidity. . . . These are the phenomena that begin to be taken into account at the end of the eighteenth century, and they result in the development of a medicine whose main function will now be public hygiene. . . . Biopolitics' other field of intervention will be . . . the problem . . . of old age, . . . accidents, infirmities. . . . We see the introduction of . . . subtle, . . . rational mechanisms: insurance, individual and collective savings, safety measures, and so on.[2]

By the nineteenth century, biopower would be further extended to concern itself with "the direct effects of the geographical, climactic, or hydrographic environment" upon the population.[3]

The point to draw here is that Foucault understood modern power—which he (frustratingly) called variously, and with different emphases, "biopower,"[4] "security,"[5] and "governmentality"[6]—as rooted in the same practical impulse to govern the natural processes relevant to the flourishing of the population. More to the point: modern (Western) power inherently involves both what we know as laissez-faire or classical liberalism *and* forms of intervention that we associate with the "welfare state" (which Foucault called the "security state"—as in "Social Security" in the United States). Modern power inevitably involves *a judicious balance of leaving well enough alone and making needed interventions*. As Pat O'Malley aptly describes it, "'social' ways of governing" have "genealogical origins . . . in the heart of the classical liberal era." Noninterventionist and interventionist impulses are bound "together . . . in an uneasy mélange in which issues of freedom and compulsion are never far from the surface."[7] We have seen the role of pastoral interventions in chapter 2. Foucault went so far as to say that "socialism"—by which he meant social government, or practices of "welfare"—is *internal* to liberalism, or to the governmental assemblage that includes liberalism. Socialism's "forms of rationality function as counterweights, as a corrective, and a palliative to internal dangers" of liberalism.[8] Roberto Esposito similarly argues that liberalism "continually risks destroying what it says it wants to create," and government therefore needs "to construct and channel liberty in a nondestructive direction for all of society"—or at least that is how those who would govern understand their own activities.[9] This is a very useful description for the rationality at the center of New Deal reform.

This chapter considers the ways in which New Deal reform built on the impulse within modern power to intervene in a range of processes so as to act in the (supposed) interests of the population. The New Deal was not invented out of whole cloth. Many of the critical practices of the New Deal had been around since the nineteenth century, and others are arguably the legacy of Populism or progressivism.[10] But the New Deal conjuncture assembled these practices and rationalities in new ways, and on the basis of new metapractices that seemed—at least to the New Dealers and their supporters—to be called for by the crisis. This brings to mind another touchstone of the New Deal—the conviction that classical liberalism had governed too little and that precisely because of that, the nation now—during the Depression—found itself in a deadly crisis.

Complicating Liberalism in the Context of Emergency

South Dakota farmers—or, those who remained—had weathered repeated droughts and even the post–World War I agricultural depression without loss of faith in "growth" (even if people understood it as often deferred to "next year").[11] The sustained drought, insect pests, and price deflation (for farm products) of the 1930s were, however, unprecedented within the memory of people in the Rosebud country, not to mention those who made and implemented policy.

The first crisis was the collapse of agricultural prices because of the Depression. Figure 3.1 depicts an index of prices received for South Dakota agricultural products from 1909 through 1939. As is clear, prices plunged to unprecedented levels by 1931 (also clear is the stunning rise in prices received by farmers between 1915 and 1920, and the equally stunning precipitous plunge in prices in 1920–21). Added to this was the environmental catastrophe of the drought and grasshoppers. The emergency agricultural assistant for Tripp County (appointed with federal funds because of the Depression) reported the damage that had taken place in 1935 (and see Figure 3.2):

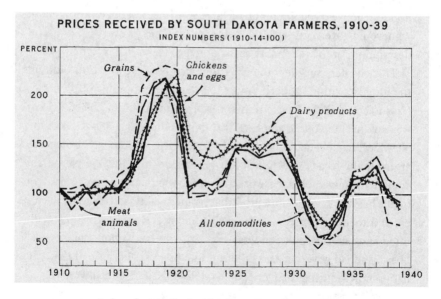

FIGURE 3.1. Index of prices for South Dakota farm products. From *Local Market Price Movements in South Dakota, 1909–1939* (Washington, D.C., and Pierre: U.S. Department of Agriculture and South Dakota Department of Agriculture, 1940).

[B]y January and February the moisture that had fallen was almost lost and the wind again took its toll of top soil, increased the heights of drifts and caused many blowouts or places that looked like small gravel pits. Every thistle in the field became a mound and every woven wire fence acted as a snow fence for the soil. Then when the spring of 1935 approached a more desolate, barren desert could not be conceived of. Not only was the land a desert but man's heart was dejected for the very soil that he had put so much faith in seemed to be lost. . . . Since in the previous year and the year before the crops had failed, farmers were at the end of their financial resources and the prospect for 1935 was anything but hopeful. . . . Because of his inability to raise crops in previous years, practically every farmer in the county has been placed on relief roll.[12]

The mayor of Winner, in Tripp County, issued a proclamation in March 1935: "Realizing as we do, the dire distress over climatic conditions, unprecedented drought and widespread threatened poverty which approaches famine, as Mayor of Winner . . . I . . . call upon our churches and our citizens to humble themselves before the Almighty and make supplications for deliverance."[13]

Mabelle Stewart Worsley, who lived in Witten in Tripp County, recalled in an interview:

One day I went with Tom to a place close to Witten. These people had been our neighbors, but they had gone. They had a beautiful four-bedroom, two-story home. He had raised cattle and sheep. There were low sheds on one side. . . . The barn was filling with blowing dust. Then we went looking for the sheds. We couldn't find them, they weren't there. The drifting soil completely covered them. There was just a mountain of dust and soil. They had an orchard. We went looking for it. It, too, was adrift of dirt, fourteen feet high, with a limb sticking out now and then. . . . Someone bought the house and moved it away.[14]

Dust bowl conditions in Dallas, near the border between Gregory and Tripp counties are depicted in Figure 3.2. Ollie Napesni, who grew up on her father's allotment in the Salt Camp community in Todd County, recalled in her memoir the dust storms and grasshoppers:

FIGURE 3.2. Dust storm in the Rosebud country, 1934. Reproduction Number LC-USZ62–95674, Library of Congress. Copyright by Rosebud Photo Company, Gregory, South Dakota.

Remember the Dust Bowl[?] How terrible the clouds were. Every morning we'd get up and couldn't see the sun. It was all red all over and a dark haze that was really low. When you looked straight up wherever the sun was supposed to be you could barely tell. . . . If you looked another way at a cloud underneath there was all grasshoppers or locusts. They were just thick like clouds. And then the hot dry wind came. I mentioned before that my folks always prepared for the winter and they always had plenty to eat. And here when the locusts came, no more garden! They just ate it up overnight.[15]

In 1934, the Tripp County emergency agricultural agent wrote with sincere feeling for the farmers in his county:

It seems that when things are at a decline every pest jumps in and sees if it can not put us down a little further. Four years ago grasshoppers started to invade this territory and each year made great inroads into the growing crops that thus added to the desolation the drought had wrought. Under normal conditions Tripp County is one of the best west [of the Missouri] river counties, not only for small grain but also for the production of cattle and hogs. Producers in this territory have made considerable money. . . . High hopes rest within the breast of every individual, hopes of a farm owned by himself with convenient and comfortable buildings and surroundings. The grasshoppers laid waste [to] the first of these possibilities four years ago.[16]

The effects of the drought and grasshoppers can be read in the drastic reductions in corn acreage harvested (see Figure 3.3). In 1929, before the drought and grasshoppers, Rosebud country farmers harvested 424,202 acres of corn. This figure dropped to 32,139 in 1934, a reduction of 92 percent. Because corn was primarily used to feed hogs, the commercial impact of the drought and grasshoppers was probably mostly felt in the loss of hogs for sale.

Such conditions of fewer units of farm products to sell at the same time when prices were low meant a drastic loss in the value of livestock and crops sold (see Figure 3.4). Under such conditions, farm families went

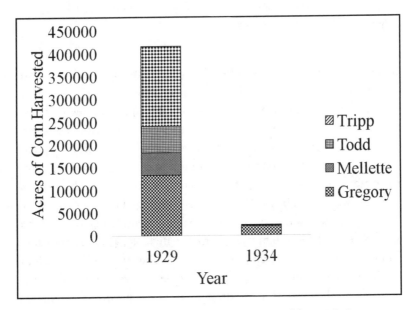

FIGURE 3.3. Collapse of corn acres harvested. Source of data: U.S. Census, Agriculture.

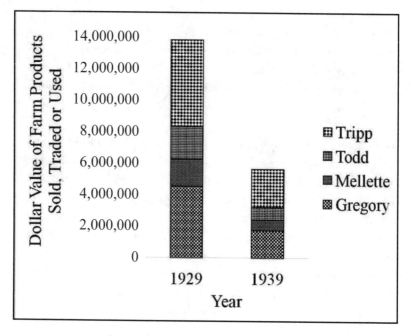

FIGURE 3.4. Collapse of the value of farm products sold, traded, or used. Source of data: U.S. Census, Agriculture.

broke or otherwise opted to find an alternative to making a living at farming in the Rosebud country. The emergency agricultural agent for Mellette and Todd counties reported in 1940 that the previous ten years had witnessed a reduction "from 320,000 acres of farm land with 1,800 farmers to 150,000 acres with 1,000 farmers and ranchers."[17] The total population of the Rosebud country was reduced from a high of 35,323 in 1930 to 29,312 in 1940, a decrease of 17 percent (see Figure 3.5). This population loss was driven by the loss of farms—through tax sales, defaults on mortgages, and "voluntary" sale and abandonment; farms were reduced in number in the Rosebud country from a high of 5,459 in 1930 to 4,032 in 1940, a loss of 26 percent (see Figure 3.6). The 1,427 farms that disappeared often left physical traces found by the survivors. Mabelle Stewart Worsley recalled: "During the drought and dust storms in the thirties, people just couldn't make a living, so they packed up the old car and left. They went wherever they had people to go to: Iowa, Illinois, anywhere.

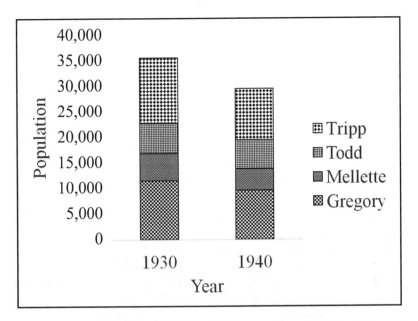

FIGURE 3.5. Population loss in the Rosebud country. Source of data: U.S. Census, Population.

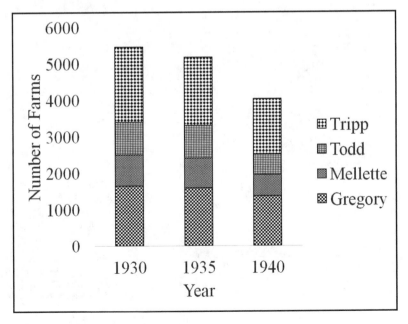

FIGURE 3.6. Loss of farms in the Rosebud country. Source of data: U.S. Census, Agriculture.

Those little homesteads, some nice little houses, sat there on the prairie with cattle carousing around, breaking windows, and letting the dust in."[18] While Dorothea Lange is most well known for her photographs of "Okies," she also shot portraits of migrants from South Dakota heading for the West Coast (Figure 3.7).

The Roosevelt administration, the U.S. Department of Agriculture (USDA), and the extension service were quick to diagnose the source of the problems in no uncertain terms: liberalism, particularly in its

FIGURE 3.7. South Dakota refugees in California, 1939. Photograph by Dorothea Lange. Print LC-DIG-fsa-8b34849, Farm Security Administration/Office of War Information Black-and-White Negatives, Library of Congress.

sod-busting variety based on unrestricted "growth"—and the unplanned and anarchic use of capital and of both human and natural resources in the framework of "rugged individualism." Although it was not possible to attribute natural events such as grasshopper infestation or drought to liberalism, both the erosion of the topsoil and the collapse of farm prices were laid at the doorstep of "overproduction" by farmers. This was part of the larger New Deal explanation of the Depression as the consequence of the market's failure to adequately balance supply and demand. *The problem with liberalism is that it governed too little,* in the thinking of the New Dealers. The absurdity of a lack of "plenty," "in the very sight of supply"—people going hungry, for example, while farmers produced more than they could sell—was cited by Roosevelt in his March 1933 inaugural address, and was meant to illustrate the utter exhaustion of laissez-faire. Roosevelt famously assured the nation that "the only thing we have to fear is fear itself," but he also insisted that "[o]nly a foolish optimist can deny the dark realities of the moment."[19]

The critique of liberal agricultural policy was not new, but the New Dealers refined it.[20] Rexford G. Tugwell, a Columbia University economist who became a member of Roosevelt's "brains trust" and who was appointed assistant secretary of agriculture under Secretary Henry A. Wallace, was especially clear about what he saw as exhaustion of liberalism—understood as the central dependence on private property and unregulated markets to direct production and distribution of goods and services. Regarding agriculture, he wrote in 1934, "[w]e have depended too long on the hope that private ownership and control would operate somehow for the benefit of the society as a whole. That hope has not been realized. Now we are coming to believe that our resources will best be utilized for the benefit of all if we give deliberate study to the needs of society and adjust our land uses to those needs."[21] In March 1929, on the eve of the emergency, he wrote that laissez-faire resulted in "an agriculture which is wasteful and backward and which continues to sacrifice social ends for meretricious individual ones." Liberalism as a framework for agriculture could make "no attempt to gauge the future or to penalize inefficiency or anti-social techniques." Farmers, "as good individualists, and believers in freedom of enterprise, would hold that they have rights, vested rights, with which even public authority ought not interfere. Among these may be the right to run furrows up and down a hill, thus facilitating as much as possible the flight of the soil to the sea or in other ways to exhaust fertility; and certainly the right to grow corn or cotton in any amount in the face of probably disastrous returns."[22]

In 1936, the Great Plains Committee appointed by Franklin Roosevelt to examine the crisis of the drought and recommend solutions directly targeted the privatization of the public domain and the free market in agriculture as the source of the environmental catastrophe on the Plains. The drought had led to soil erosion only because of the overuse of the land in crop production, in a viscous circle that was rooted in laissez-faire farming and that had spiraled out of control:

> After 1910 powerful new influences were felt. The tractor, the combine and other power machinery enabled an individual to plant and harvest a much larger acreage than before. At the same time the cost of buying and maintaining this expensive equipment obliged him to secure a cash crop. The World War and the following inflation pushed the price of wheat to new high levels and caused a remarkable extension of the area planted to this crop. When the price collapsed during the post-war period Great Plains farmers continued to plant large wheat acreages in a desperate endeavor to get money with which to pay debt charges, taxes, and other unavoidable expenses. They had no choice in the matter. Without money they could not remain solvent or continue to farm. Yet to get money they were obliged to extend farming practices which were collectively ruinous.[23]

The committee recommended, among other things, buying out crop farmers in regions suited only to grazing, a direct reversal of the homesteading policy. Such lands would be incorporated into federal grazing districts where they existed, or leased to grazing associations (more on this in the next section).[24] The committee did not have nice things to say about the rugged individualism of homesteaders: "The Plainsman cannot assume that whatever is for his immediate good is also good for everybody— ... in the short run there must often be sacrifices; he cannot assume the right always to do with his own property as he likes—he may ruin another man's property if he does; he cannot assume that the individual action he can take on his own land will be sufficient, even for the conservation and best use of that land." Such "attitudes of mind" were part of the problem and required "revision."[25]

It would be easy enough to see the argument here as a left-wing attack on private property, which we will see in chapter 4 was how opponents of the New Deal saw it (and still do). But, it is important to recognize that the New Dealers did not call for the abolition of private property, and were not, strictly speaking, socialists, except in Foucault's limited sense of the term mentioned earlier. A better genealogy of what was new about the New Deal comes into focus by examining the practices of New Deal schematic thinking, to which we now turn.

Attention to Scale

Assistant Secretary of Agriculture Rexford Tugwell hired Gardner Means as an economic adviser in 1933. Means was one of the "institutionalist" or "structuralist" economists, so named because they recognized that the modern market economy was constrained by patterns beyond the realm of individual actors because new institutions had evolved into place that structured the market.[26] He argued that the play of supply and demand as a process for setting prices and allocating labor and capital in production was fast being replaced by what he called administered prices characteristic of corporate concentration. Rather than accepting lower prices when faced with decreased demand (as farm families, for example, were forced to because they were in the end domestic units, not ultimately businesses), large corporations responded to decreased demand by lowering production, while maintaining prices. Large corporations "under the ultimate control of a handful of individuals" had to some extent escaped market forces, and "have passed far beyond the realm of private enterprise—they have become nearly social institutions."[27] A *new scale* had "evolved"[28] in the economy, and Means insisted that "*[t]he individualism of Adam Smith's private enterprise has in large measure given way to the collective activity of the modern corporation,* and economic theory must shift its emphasis from analysis in terms of competition to analysis in terms of control."[29] "[T]he farmer," Means wrote in 1938, after he had moved to the National Resources Committee, "is faced with a high degree of business combination."[30] But he argued that the analyst must "think of the whole national economy and envisage the role of the farmers and that of the big corporations in the setting of the whole national producing machine"[31] (see Figure 3.8). It was within this scale of optics that the problem of "inflexible administered prices" came into focus.[32] Big business was in a position to maintain prices when demand drops, making up the difference by laying off workers. Thus, business concentration undermined both the farmer (by maintaining price levels for manufactured goods even as the economy deflates) and the worker (by laying him off or undercutting his bargaining power). Secretary Wallace described the imbalance in blunt terms in

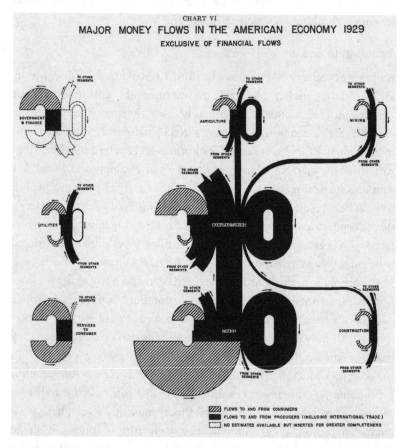

FIGURE 3.8. Gardner Means's visualization of the whole national economy. Chart VI in *The Structure of the American Economy*, Part I. Basic Characteristics, National Resources Committee (Washington, D.C.: U.S. Government Printing Office, 1939), 86.

a 1938 radio address: "The farmers are 6,000,000 competing units in a world of corporate organization and increasing industrial control."[33]

This offered a practical approach to the causes of the Depression, and what needed to be done about them: big business had appropriated the lion's share of "the national income" because of its scale of organization, while workers and farmers had lost income and were no longer able to buy the goods and services produced by big business; the national economy was structurally imbalanced. As Tugwell explained it in 1928, "[m]any of the larger industries at the present time are so articulated as to be able to effect a limitation of their own production to profitable amount. Farmers must buy their goods. But the nature of agriculture is such that no similar coordination is possible for farmers. The use of governmental machinery for such a purpose is not usual with us, but there would seem to be a quite reasonable excuse for it on these grounds."[34]

New Deal political-economic thinking called for a fundamental recognition of the *scalar nature of contemporary economic organization*. While the individual, private property, and private enterprise were by no means to be done away with as objects of governance—indeed, they came in for even more attention (as will be seen later in this chapter)— *emergent* (and, in Foucault's terms, *irreducible*) economic organization at scales above the level of the individual would be both visualized and managed.[35] Critically, the economists at the center of the "the first New Deal" were decidedly not within the antitrust tradition (they differed from many farmers on this score) and were opposed to any attempt to return to the "atomistic economy" of the laissez-faire market.[36] They insisted that new scales of economic organization had evolved into place and that other actors in the economy needed to be scaled up (through organized farmers and organized labor) to meet the structural power of big business. Scale was not to be reduced but *extended* to components of the national economy that had not been able to "evolve" on their own to the scale necessary for the market to function effectively.

This discovery of new scales of irreducible phenomena to be governed is a paradigmatic case of what Foucault was after in his analyses of liberalism, biopower, governmentality, and apparatuses of security. It will be recalled that Foucault saw modern power as self-consciously concerned with "respect" for "natural processes."[37] It is very important to recognize that in discussing modern power, he did not use terms such as "natural" or "reality" in their realist senses. Indeed, one of his genealogies of modern power traced the development of biopower's concern with the welfare of the population to the birth of Nazi racism and the Holocaust.[38] For Foucault, the genealogy of modern power was *anything but* governance developing a progressively more humane delivery or guarantee of ultimate human interests; Foucault did not believe in "progress," except as a (fictional) discourse. What is "natural" and "real" is, as anthropologists would put it, *arbitrary* for Foucault. His goal was not understanding how things get better and better, or how government becomes more and more rational, but rather "grasping the movement by which a field of truth with objects of knowledge was constituted through mobile technologies." The proper focus for Foucault concerned "the constitution of fields, domains, and objects of knowledge," how they came to have truth-value as understood by (and just as commonly, challenged by) actors, not their truth in an epistemological sense or by an empirically based yardstick. We could say that "the agricultural economy" did not exist, just as Foucault said that madness did not exist until it was "constituted" by the birth of a new way of conceptualizing power and governance.[39] With this proviso in mind, we can apply Foucault's description of modern power fruitfully to the New Deal horizon of governmental "problems." Those who govern must take the position of

> standing back sufficiently so that one can grasp the point at which things are taking place. . . . This means trying to grasp them at the level of their nature, or let's say . . . grasping them at the level of their effective reality. The mechanism of security [as in "Social Security"] works on the basis of this reality, by trying to use it as a support and make it function, make its components function in relation to each other. In other words, . . . the essential function of security . . . is to respond to a reality in such a way that this response cancels out the reality to which it responds—nullifies it, or limits, checks, or regulates it. . . . [S]ecurity . . . tries to work within reality, by getting the components of reality to work in relation to each other.[40]

In respecting newly discovered—or, more likely, *invented in context*— natural elements of reality, "[a]n entire domain of possible and necessary

interventions appears with the field thus delimited," and governance will
henceforth act "to ensure that the necessary and natural regulations [that
is, natural equilibria] work, or even to create regulations that enable natural regulations to work. Natural phenomena will have to be framed in
such a way that they do not veer off course."[41] That is the essence of security as a mode of governance.

One mobile technology that was central in the New Deal was the
recognition of scale, and the corrective measure of bringing autonomous elements operating at different scales into scalar balance with
one another, not by breaking up higher scales, but by raising "unorganized" processes to a higher scale by federal and state action.[42] Historian
Arthur M. Schlesinger aptly described the idea:

> The tenets of the First New Deal [prior to the recession of 1937–38 and
> the adoption of Keynesianism] were that the technological revolution had
> rendered bigness inevitable; that competition could no longer be relied on
> to protect social interests; that the large units were an opportunity to be
> seized rather than a danger to be fought; and that the formula for stability
> in the new society must be combination and cooperation under enlarged
> federal authority. This meant the creation of new institutions, public and
> private, to do what competition had once done (or was supposed to have
> done) in the way of balancing the economy—institutions which might
> well alter the existing pattern of individual economic decision, especially
> on investment, production, and price.[43]

Means recognized that it was precisely industrial concentration that
had "made possible a high standard of living."[44] The New Dealers were
convinced that "organization"—with its necessary implication of larger
scale, ultimately national and even international—was good because it
was more efficient (or could be).[45] The problem was not that some elements of the economy were centralized and corporately planned but that
others—agriculture, in particular, were not; the problem was the lack
of overall scalar "balance" in the national economy. One key technique
for correcting imbalance was government facilitation of "counterorga-
nization" or "countervailing" power, meant to correct imbalance caused
by sectors in the economy operating at different scales.[46] Those elements

of the national economy that were still unorganized and operating at the anarchic level of individual actors—such as farming—needed to be kicked upstairs, and the sovereign power of the federal government was to be the tool that would be used to bring about this rebalancing. As Tugwell explained, the role of the New Deal state was made inevitable simply by the scale of things: "Planning will necessarily become a function of the federal government," because "the agency which imposes its disinterested will on industry must equal, in the area of its jurisdiction, the spread of the industry."[47] Replacement of the anarchy of the market mechanism by rational central planning would yield "the smooth interchanging flow logically belonging to the system of industry."[48]

This rescaling was the key logic in the Agricultural Adjustment Act (AAA) of 1933, one of the central goals of which was to organize farmers throughout the United States to limit production. The key analysis at the core of this policy had widespread recognition among agricultural economists (in university departments and in the USDA), the institutionalist economists in Roosevelt's brains trust, and some farm leaders. The analysis ran as follows: the price of agricultural goods relative to manufactured goods had declined since the end of World War I as a result of two factors. First, despite antitrust regulation, manufacturing had benefited from concentration of industry (near monopoly), which allowed what amounted to price-fixing (Means's "administered prices"), even in the absence of outright collusion; this concentration and price-fixing worked in tandem with tariffs that protected U.S. manufacturers from foreign competition. Tariffs did not protect farmers (even though agricultural commodities were listed in for tariffs) who produced more than could be absorbed by the domestic market (in part because effective demand was "inelastic"[49]—it had an upper limit independent of price reduction). Thus, even high tariffs on foreign agricultural goods that competed with U.S. farmers would not raise the prices they received because they produced an expanding surplus (thanks to increasing productivity) relative to effective domestic demand. As brains trust member Adolf Berle put it in the *New York Times*, "We had the paradox that the more successful farming was [in terms of productivity], the more bankrupt was the farmer."[50]

As we saw in chapter 2, the USDA had sought to interrupt this growing overproduction and devaluation by disseminating information to farmers through its *Agricultural Outlook Report* produced by the Bureau of Agricultural Economics from 1923. The problem was that without collective organization among producers—including the ability to discipline producers within the collective—the provision of information in itself could not bring about changes in production. Without collective organization and organized discipline, the farmer who limited his production would, of course, lose out in a classic free-rider scenario.[51] It was only the national organization of farmers to limit production that could raise farm prices and bring about "parity" with manufacturing, which was benefiting from the concentration of corporate control over capital, production, and prices.

The concept of organized and directed production control originated from a range of individual thinkers in the context of policy discussions about agricultural overproduction and farm relief in the 1920s.[52] It was Tugwell who in 1928 (then professor of economics at Columbia) first suggested in the professional literature the idea of production control explicitly in relation to the agricultural surplus. In "Reflections on Farm Relief," published in *Political Science Quarterly,* he argued that "[t]he problem of immediate farm relief is . . . that of limiting production . . . to the buying capacity of the farmers' market," and he spelled out the "heroic means" of production control called for to meet the "emergency" (and that would later be at the center of the AAA): "(1) A survey of the amounts necessary to meet normal needs and which will command a profitable price. (2) Notice of limitation of planting, on a basis of ten-year averages, by local (probably county) agents of a Farm Board."[53] By 1932, Milburn Lincoln Wilson, who was head of the Department of Agricultural Economics at Montana State College, was advocating the marriage of domestic allotment and production control. Domestic allotment, which had been proposed by Harvard agricultural economist John D. Black, entailed allocating shares to individual farmers of the national supply of agricultural products necessary to meet domestic demand; the shares would be prorated on the basis of farmers' recent sales.[54] Wilson suggested that the government use its "taxing and spending powers to promote reductions in output. Each farmer would be free to refuse to participate in the program but would be encouraged to participate not merely by the promise of higher prices in the market but by payments to him from the government."[55]

South Dakota's own agrarian intellectuals were working on a domestic allotment plan at the same time.[56] Robert Lusk, editor of the *Evening Huronite* (Huron, South Dakota), wrote an editorial in favor of the plan in 1931, and his protégé, William Roy Ronald, editor of the *Evening Republican* (Mitchell, South Dakota), which was owned by the Lusk family, became "one of Wilson's most aggressive lieutenants in pushing the domestic allotment plan both in South Dakota and in Washington."[57] Ronald attended a conference on domestic allotment in Chicago in April 1932 chaired by Wilson that established a "Voluntary Domestic Allotment Committee" consisting of Wilson, Ronald, Henry A. Wallace (editor of *Wallace's Farmer* and soon to be Roosevelt's secretary of agriculture), Henry I. Harriman (who would become chairman of the United States Chamber of Commerce), and two representatives of the insurance industry, which had heavy investments in farm mortgages.[58] Ronald urged the plan on South Dakota Republican Senator Peter Norbeck, who introduced a bill to effect it, and Ronald ghostwrote an article for Norbeck's byline on the topic "The Domestic Allotment" published in the *Farm Journal.* The key provision was the payment to farmers of the equivalent of the tariffs for agricultural products for that portion of production destined for "domestic human consumption," the funds to be raised by an excise tax on processors. In return for the payment, each participating farmer "would agree to any horizontal reduction in production (in acres sown or pounds of hogs marketed) that might be ordered by the federal administrative agency, thereby to stabilize prices at a desired level."[59] Ronald convinced Wilson that the plan should be applied to corn and hogs, which Wilson recognized would bring support from farmers in the corn belt.[60] Early in 1933, the Senate Agriculture Committee asked Ronald to submit his redraft of a bill already passed by the House, as it deliberated on the legislation that eventually became the Agricultural Adjustment Act (AAA).[61]

The AAA was enacted in 1933 and provided for production control at multiple scales from the national to the county level (and even below, at the township or community scale). The USDA would carefully estimate the volume of critical agricultural products—in South Dakota these were wheat, corn, and hogs—necessary to meet projected demand in the national domestic market. Production quotas were then divided among

the states on the basis of the recent history of prorated state contribu-
tions to total national supplies. State quotas would then be divided into
county quotas by a state committee, and county production control committees in turn would divide county quotas into individual farm quotas.
Because the new quotas were designed to reduce or eliminate surplus—
so as to bring supply into line with effective demand and thus raise agricultural prices—they would generally be set lower than the recent history
of actual yields (except in the situation of years when, because of drought
or pests, crops failed). The key to the program that secured farmer compliance was that "cooperators" would be paid—originally from funds
raised by taxing processors of agricultural products—for reducing production from their historical yields.[62] Each cooperator entered into a
contract with the Department of Agriculture by which he agreed to limit
his production by a specified percent from previous years (translated
into acres for wheat and corn and numbers for hogs) in return for benefit payments. Farmers were free to decline the program and grow as much
as they wanted without agreeing with the government to limit production in return for cash benefits. The aims were to give farmers immediate
financial relief through benefit payments, raise the market price of agricultural commodities by reducing supply, and return farmer purchasing power to that during the period of 1909 to 1914, which the theorists
presumed was a period when agriculture and manufacturing had been
properly "balanced." The objective of the AAA (and of the National
Industrial Recovery Act [1933], which established the National Recovery
Administration to organize corporations and workers on industrywide
bases) was "the smooth functioning of the economic machine, the full
use of human and material interests, and a balance of interests among
individuals and groups." It was this "balance of interests" that was in the
"public interest."[63]

The wheat program was the first to be implemented in the Rosebud
country. Farmers signed contracts agreeing to reduce acres planted to
wheat by a specified percentage from previous years in return for a benefit payment proportional to the estimated bushel yield from the "contracted acres." Farmers marked their contracted acres with stakes or
posts at the corners. The corn-hog program was begun in 1934 and
worked similarly to the wheat program, except that in the case of hogs

the control was in the form of the number of hogs farrowed or purchased and fed for market, rather than acreage. As the county extension agents pointed out to farmers, the production control programs also constituted a form of crop insurance, because they would receive their benefit payments even if their *uncontracted* crops were a total failure.[64]

Precisely because of the national scale of its operation, the AAA was invalidated by the Supreme Court in January 1936. The arrogation of agricultural planning by the federal government justified by the supposed need to organize on a national scale—the scalar argument central to New Deal reform—was directly shot down by the Court's constitutional analysis of the AAA. Beyond any policy question, the Constitution expressly limits the powers of the federal government in the Tenth Amendment: "The powers not delegated to the United States by the Constitution, nor prohibited by it to the States, are reserved to the States respectively, or to the people." The government had argued that the taxing clause of the Constitution gave it the authority to act in "the general welfare," and that this was the authority that underwrote the AAA.[65] The Court, however, used the touchstone of the limited and delegated power of the federal government to arrive at the conclusion that "[t]he act invades the reserved rights of the states. It is a statutory plan to regulate and control agricultural production, a matter beyond the power delegated to the federal government." National production control—the precise logic of scaling up, as developed by the New Deal economists—was "an unconstitutional end."[66]

The USDA responded to the nullification of the AAA by securing passage of the Soil Conservation Act of 1935. Drafted under the supervision of the USDA, it "recognized that the wastage of soil and moisture resources on farm, grazing, and national forest lands of the Nation, resulting from soil erosion, is a menace to the national welfare, and that it is hereby declared to be the policy of Congress to provide permanently for the control and prevention of soil erosion and thereby to preserve natural resources, control floods, prevent impairment of reservoirs, and maintain the navigability of rivers and harbors, protect public health, public lands and relieve unemployment." It specified that "the Secretary of Agriculture, from now on, shall coordinate and direct all activities with relation to soil erosion." The secretary was authorized to "carry out preventative measures, including, but not limited to, engineering operations, methods of cultivation, the growing of vegetation, and changes in land use," and to "enter into agreements with, or to furnish financial or other aid to, . . . any person, subject to such conditions as he may deem necessary."[67] The Soil Conservation and Domestic Allotment Act of 1936 amended the 1935 law and added policy goals:

> (1) preservation and improvement of soil fertility; (2) promotion of the economic use and conservation of soil fertility; (3) diminution of exploitation and wasteful and unscientific use of national soil resources; (4) the protection of rivers and harbors against the results of soil erosion in aid of maintaining the navigability of water and water courses and in aid of flood control; and (5) reestablishment, at as rapid a rate as the Secretary of Agriculture determines to be practicable and in the general public interest, of the ratio between the purchasing power of the net income per person on farms and that of the income per person not on farms that prevailed during the five-year period August 1909–July 1914.[68]

The secretary was specifically authorized to make "payment or grants of other aid to agricultural producers" for "their treatment or use of their land, or a part thereof, for soil restoration, soil conservation, or the prevention of erosion" and for reducing their production to their *pro rata* share of production for national domestic consumption.[69]

For present purposes, the new act was not simply a replacement for the AAA that was expected to pass constitutional muster but the application of the technique of scaling up not only to raise farmer purchasing power to "parity," but also to address the real national emergency of soil erosion. As Richard Kirkendall argues in his *Social Scientists and Farm Politics in the Age of Roosevelt*, the Soil Conservation and Domestic Allotment Act allowed thinkers in the Department of Agriculture who saw the AAA as too narrow in its goals, such as Howard R. Tolley, to extend the technique of national domestic allotment to land-use planning and erosion control, as well as production control.[70] Scaling up was a "mobile technology" applicable to a range of substantively distinct matters of governance.[71] Farmers had already been encouraged under the old AAA to plant "soil building" crops—not for market—on their contracted acres. Under the new act, this became the goal (along with bringing production into line with the needs for domestic consumption in order to raise farm income to parity). "Systems of cropping which continually use up the organic and mineral matter in the soil without providing for replacement, can soon destroy what has required nature thousands of years to create," the farmers of Tripp County were informed on the front page of the *Winner Advocate* in April 1936.[72]

Under the Agricultural Adjustment Administration, Rosebud country farmers received payments for seeding former corn and wheat acreage to hay or rye for pasture (but without harvesting it for market), and even for wheat and oats, if they were plowed under without harvesting, and the acreage planted with legumes (because of the scarcity of forage crops attending the drought, plans were liberalized to allow some cover crops to be harvested for sale). Private range land was also brought under voluntary regulation by the Agricultural Adjustment Administration from 1937 on, through Range Conservation Program payment of cash benefits to ranchers for reducing cattle units per acre (in conformity with grazing capacity as determined by a trained, local range examiner), deferred grazing (dividing pasture into units that are grazed in rotation), reseeding with grass, contour furrowing and building terraces, constructing reservoirs and dams, and planting trees—all range-building or conservation practices.[73]

Rescaling and the harnessing of the powers of collectives was also at the core of reform of federal Indian policy during the New Deal. In 1933, a new commissioner of Indian affairs, John Collier, was appointed to reform the Bureau of Indian Affairs within the Department of the Interior. The centerpiece of the "Indian New Deal" was the Indian Reorganization Act (IRA) of 1934. The IRA halted the allotment of tribal lands, made the trust status of all Indian land—tribal and allotted—permanent, and provided for allotted land and inherited interests in allotted land to be put back into tribal ownership.[74] The IRA also provided for a tribe or a community of more than one tribe living on a reservation to "organize for its common welfare" and "adopt an appropriate constitution and bylaws." An organized tribe might also petition for a charter of incorporation in order to manage tribal property and enterprises.[75] The Rosebud Sioux Tribe organized under an IRA constitution in 1935 and received a corporate charter in 1937.[76]

Collier and the other New Deal reformers in the BIA (some of who were old hands in the BIA) were intent on reversing the previous policy of "individualizing" Indians for incorporation into the body politic—one of the touchstones of civilizing Indians, as we saw in chapter 2—and sought to organize Indian *collectives* with the power to compete in the modern world, the same kind of scaling up we just described regarding the AAA and the Soil Conservation and Domestic Allotment Act.[77] Collier laid out the importance of *organization*—scaling up—at a meeting for South Dakota Indians in Rapid City in 1934. In explaining the bill that would eventually become the IRA, Collier said (his words were translated into Lakota by interpreters from the reservations):

We take the position that it is very necessary for Indians to be permitted to organize, to organize for many different purposes. It is necessary for Indians to be allowed to organize to do business in a modern business world in competition with the modern white world. In the world at large, the white world, the unorganized people are powerless. They are victims. Only organized groups have power in the white world.

There are many kinds of organization in the modern world. For example, there are corporations; there are cattlemen's association and stock associations. There are co-operative societies to run, for example, creameries, to buy in quantities so as to cut out middlemen's profits; all kinds of co-operative economic organizations for mutual benefit. There are town governments which manage local affairs or towns.

Now I am going to say what is almost the heart of our plan . . . We are proposing that Indians shall be allowed and helped to organize for mutual benefit, for local self-government and for doing business in the modern, organized way. . . . We are proposing that when the Indians do organize . . . , then their organizations will be instrumentalities of the Federal Government. . . . The . . . Indian body organized under Federal law, organized as an Agency of the Federal Government, would be surrounded by the protective guardianship of the Federal Government and clothed with the authority of the Federal Government.

You can't govern yourselves, you can't do business, you can't protect yourself, unless you organize. That is true regarding everybody in the United States.

Collier also linked the bill to the larger New Deal goal of addressing the situation of Roosevelt's "forgotten man" by helping him to organize.[78]

Tribal government was not the only area where the BIA sought to collectivize Indians. Two "rehabilitation colonies" (funded by the Rural Rehabilitation division of the Resettlement Administration, under the direction of Rexford Tugwell) were established on Rosebud: the Grass Mountain and Two Kettle colonies. The goal was to provide physical facilities and organization to allow the *new* communities to become self-supporting through cooperative cattle enterprises and subsistence farming (Figure 3.9). Grass Mountain had nine families living in new houses, each with a poultry house; a cooperative, irrigated subsistence garden (with water drawn from the Little White River); a canning kitchen; and a dairy. Colony cattle were grazed on an adjacent tribal range unit. Colony members pledged on paper to "give full participation and cooperation in developing and producing a community garden, accepting remuneration for our labor in accordance with plans which may hereafter be agreed upon by members of the colony." Members also pledged to contribute to a "civic movement for beautifying and improving the physical aspects of the colony," and to "the development of livestock and other

FIGURE 3.9. The Grass Mountain Colony under construction, 1936. Rosebud Agency Records, Records of the Bureau of Indian Affairs (Kansas City, Missouri: National Archives and Records Administration).

industrial projects."[79] In at least one case, a colony member was removed on the basis of a petition from the other members because he "failed to cooperate and to live up to the conditions of his agreement," specifically "in the matter of taking care of the dairy," having worked only 40 days and 5 hours over the course of a year, when the colony average had been 73 days, 3 hours. This was, no doubt, understood by the BIA as a promising sign of Lakota "self-government." The culprit was also "asked about the complaint that he and his wife were in constant trouble and that he had been extremely abusive to his children."[80] The Two Kettle Colony had ten families, each starting with twenty acres of dry land for livestock forage and feed crops and twenty acres of land irrigated with water drawn from the White River. Range land for the cooperative cattle enterprise was provided, as in the case of Grass Mountain, by a nearby tribal range unit. Each family was supplied with livestock, machinery, and operating expenses for the first year. As the superintendent reported to Collier in 1940, in drawing up plans, the key was the selection of families "willing to work; able bodied; and a capacity to carry on consistently through an eight year program."[81]

The superintendent at Rosebud also devised an ingenious tribal corporate structure to rationalize both land use and even private interests in land on the reservation, the Tribal Land Enterprise (TLE).[82] Like most reservations that had been allotted, Rosebud was checkerboarded by interspersed tribally owned trust land, allotments still held by individual allottees, and allotments that were held by numerous heirs, none of whom had a controlling share. The TLE, formed in 1943 (and still in operation), was a stock certificate plan, which affirmatively provided for "the preservation and safeguarding of the values in individual ownership equities in land."[83] The TLE, a "subordinate organization under the Tribal Council," was authorized by the tribe's new IRA bylaws to accept the conveyance of individual inherited interests in allotments in exchange for stock certificates with a value equivalent to the assessed valuation of the interests conveyed.[84] These certificates were valuable because they yielded dividends from revenue generated from tribal land operations (grazing fees), could be deposited with the TLE in exchange for a land assignment for agricultural purposes (so, say, a family with fractionated interests in scattered allotments could deposit certificates for these in return for a consolidated tract of agricultural land), and could be sold to other tribal members or to the TLE.

Besides solving the heirship fractionation problem, the TLE was also meant to make the use of reservation land as a whole more rational and efficient by simplifying ownership through conveyance to the *tribe*. With large, continuous tracts of reservation land in tribal ownership, rather than individual allotments or allotments in heirship status, "natural" range units—obviously parallel to the "natural communities" examined in the next section—could be mapped out so as to make the best use of range and water resources at a reservationwide scale. This would both protect reservation land better against overgrazing and other destructive misuse and maximize revenues on reservation lands, increasing TLE dividends to shareholders above former individual lease incomes, and funding TLE purchases of land and inherited interests in estates. TLE purchases could—the hope was and remains so today—also correct the checkerboarding of the reservation with non-Indian fee land by buying out non-Indian landowners and putting that land back into trust status under tribal control (a process provided for in the IRA).[85] Even though individual equities of shareholders were preserved, the BIA found itself defending such policies against charges of "Communism." In 1934, for example, BIA land policy specialist Ward Shepard addressed a conference of the Women's International League for Peace and Freedom in Chicago by insisting that "[t]he new Indian land policy seeks to place the allotted grazing and forest lands back into tribal ownership. It does so, not because this is 'Communism,' but because long experience has shown that this is by all odds the best form of ownership for the intelligent management of such lands. . . . The allotment of the Indian grazing and forest lands was a costly blunder."[86]

Beyond the Grid: Bringing Other "Natural" Phenomena into Focus

Closely related to the technique of paying attention to scale—or, if necessary, inventing and instituting it—was the New Deal habit of looking for phenomena not ordinarily visible in the *resolution* of liberal, governmental optics. The New Dealers were mesmerized by the idea of bringing into focus phenomena that were not taken into consideration in the techniques of government that prevailed prior to the New Deal. This included both characteristics of land and climate that, they were convinced, needed to be recognized, managed, or otherwise adapted to, and social patterns such as the indebtedness of farmers, property tax burdens, and the existence of "natural" communities.

The Soil Conservation Service (SCS) in the Department of Agriculture offers a clear example of government bringing into focus natural processes as a way of organizing solutions to problems.[87] SCS director Hugh H. Bennett was a particularly strong advocate of the need to reframe farmers' habitual thought about farming and natural resources. He wrote in 1938 that "individual efforts to control erosion" could "never be anything but piecemeal," and that "[t]he one system of attack on erosion that promises success is the cooperative attack, beginning where erosion begins, at the crests for ridges, and working down, farm by farm and field by field, to the stream banks in the valleys below." Echoing John Wesley Powell's 1890 advocacy for the watershed as a natural unit of government in the arid West, Bennett called it a "natural land-use area" and envisioned self-governing soil conservation districts based on watersheds.[88] But Bennett and the SCS specialists were anxious to bring into focus not just natural units of common interest, but also natural processes that permeated all scales and all existing units of property and territorial jurisdiction. Bennett wrote in 1940 of the conviction of the new conservationists that

we would never get anywhere with permanent control of erosion unless the different kinds of land that make up the farms and ranches of the country could be treated in accordance with their individual needs and adaptabilities. In order to do this, it was recognized at once that it would be necessary to *study every farm and every ranch and actually to map every important, distinct body of soil, as well as the degree of slope occupied by these different kinds of soil, and the amount of soil that had be removed by cropping, overgrazing,* ... Having acquired this basic physical information, the detailed farm plans for conserving soil on a given farm were worked out in the field.[89]

Bennett insisted that there was "urgent need for a survey—the actual physical mapping—of the land resources of the country to determine accurately, as soon as possible, their capabilities and limitations in use."[90]

Bennett clearly and adamantly sought to replace what he must have thought of as "grid-think," if not in so many words, which imposed an arbitrary geometry upon the use of the land. Grid-think and its political imaginaries—the county, the township, the individual farm—did not just compete with thinking in terms of natural processes (such as erosion) and natural communities of interest (such as the watershed) but it actually caused damage directly. Here is Bennett on the grid in 1940:

> Most American farmers run their crop rows in straight lines regardless of slope. In doing this, it so happens that most of them are directed up and down the slope,[91] so that the furrows between rows of cotton, corn, potatoes, tobacco or any clean-tilled crops, serve as channelways for collecting rainfall and rushing it with maximum speed downhill, thus carrying away, in accordance with natural laws, the largest possible volume of soil. This practice predominates over the greater part of the United States. It probably originated with the division of public lands into sections— square miles with straight sides. Farmers began to plow parallel to the boundaries of these straight-sided sections, quarter sections, or half sections, and so got into the habit of thinking that straight rows are a part of good farming. So fixed has the habit become that it frequently takes technical assistance to get the farmers' operations properly realigned on the contour.[92]

"Slope maps" would be a key new technology, among others.

In 1935 the SCS launched a demonstration project on "49,280 acres of seriously eroded soil" in Tripp and Gregory counties, the Winner–Dixon project. Forty percent of the farmers had left the project area by 1929 because they could not make ends meet.[93] The project area was not a watershed or a preexisting community, but an expert-defined swath of agricultural property with both erosion and farm economic problems. Erosion and other environmental conditions were surveyed, and economic data on mortgages, ownership, and tax problems were inscribed by hand on gridded-outline maps (see Figures 3.10 and 3.11). While the

SCS admitted that the wisest course of action might have been to let "all this land . . . go back to grass," the agency recognized that this would depopulate the demonstration project area and not send the message it wanted to regarding the value of conservation practices.[94] Instead, the SCS entered into a limited number of agreements with farmers and ranchers to cooperate in instituting soil conservation measures, including wind strip cropping, contour strip cropping, pasture treatment, tree planting, and terracing (see Figures 3.12 and 3.13). The technique of bringing natural features into focus and adjusting farming practices to those features rather than to the grid alone is most clearly illustrated graphically in the planning for contour strip cropping (Figure 3.14) and in the landscape of contour cropping itself, one of the enduring icons of the New Deal and the SCS (Figure 3.15). We will return to examine the Winner–Dixon Project in more detail in chapter 4.

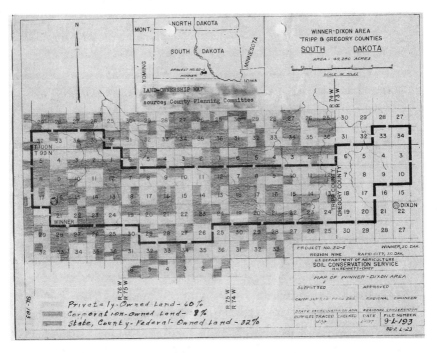

FIGURE 3.10. Land ownership map, Winner–Dixon Soil Conservation Project. Records of the Natural Resources Conservation Service (Kansas City, Missouri: National Archives and Records Administration).

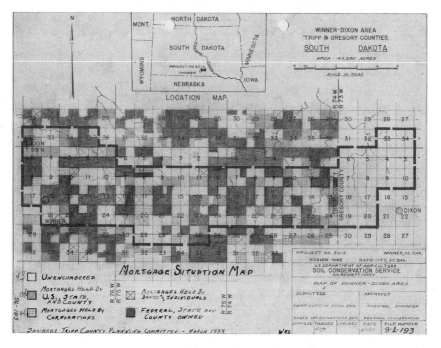

FIGURE 3.11. Mortgage situation map, Winner–Dixon Soil Conservation Project. Records of the Natural Resources Conservation Service (Kansas City, Missouri: National Archives and Records Administration).

The mapping of natural features of the landscape at the core of the thinking of the SCS comes through most graphically in the SCS maps produced for the Clearfield–Keyapaha Soil Conservation District, established in Tripp County in 1938. While, again, the boundaries of the district conformed to the property grid, not the watershed or a preexisting "community," the maps illustrate the investment in new forms of knowledge made by the SCS. Carefully plotted maps of soil erosion (Figure 3.16), slope (Figure 3.17), vegetation (Figure 3.18), and soil type (Figure 3.19) preceded the formulation of plans for field practices. These features were hand-drawn on gridded outline maps that were not published but survived in the office records of the SCS, now in the National Archives in Kansas City. We cannot know how much these particular maps circulated among SCS personnel, nor whether they were shared with farmers, but the detail depicted in brilliant color—the natural features visually

FIGURE 3.12. Strip cropping, Winner–Dixon Soil Conservation Project, 1939. Records of the Natural Resources Conservation Service (Kansas City, Missouri: National Archives and Records Administration).

eclipse the grid—at minimum served to concretize for SCS or other specialists who saw such maps the reality of the natural phenomena depicted. As we saw in chapter 1, maps can be "rhetorical," as Nikolas Rose puts it. A map, such as those depicted in Figures 3.16–3.18, "is a little machine for producing conviction in others," even if those others are like-minded specialists, but also for convincing oneself. The source of this rhetorical power flows from three sources. First, "salient features are identified and non-salient features rendered invisible," concretizing the disciplined thematic focus of the specialist. In this case, the property grid recedes to the background as, for lack of a better word, nature comes into focus. Second, a literate map reader or specialist recognizes in the finished product the concrete skilled labor that has gone into the product: "The construction of such a map is a complex technical achievement. It entails

FIGURE 3.13. Contour strip cropping, Winner–Dixon Soil Conservation Project, 1939. Records of the Natural Resources Conservation Service (Kansas City, Missouri: National Archives and Records Administration).

practices such as exploring, surveying, tramping . . . collecting statistics from far and wide . . . and so on. It involves the . . . uses of color, of symbols, . . . scales, keys and much more."[95] Finally, it is almost impossible to say that these maps do not have their own *aura*, humble though that may be—their inherent visual, material impact on the viewer. Although not a work of art, perhaps, it would be a mistake not to recognize how much there is an aesthetic element involved for the mapmaker and the viewer in bringing into living color the wondrous—if sometimes perilous— things that live off the grid in "nature." The SCS specialists were surely committed to the goal of halting soil erosion and making agriculture more, as we would now call it, sustainable, but they must also surely have found great dignity and satisfaction in their individual specialized craftsmanship, not least in its novelty, which can only have been experienced as exhilarating. New facts about the world were brought into focus, and

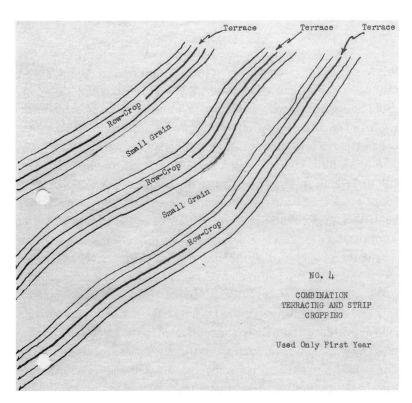

FIGURE 3.14. Plans for contour strip cropping on an individual farm. Records of the Natural Resources Conservation Service (Kansas City, Missouri: National Archives and Records Administration).

FIGURE 3.15. Close-up of contour strip cropping on a farm. Records of the Natural Resources Conservation Service (Kansas City, Missouri: National Archives and Records Administration).

this was in and of itself an *aesthetic* process quite beyond simple "empirical" or "scientific" collection of facts.[96] This is a good example of what I mean by urging that we remain open to the attractiveness (including the aesthetic) of governing to governors, beyond any will to power, and of course without assuming any simply utilitarian or financial motive.

A much more ambitious project to map natural conditions for agriculture and (creatively) adjust human use accordingly was cooperatively launched by the SCS and the BIA in Todd and Mellette counties. Individuals with agricultural expertise within the BIA had long recognized that range land on Rosebud and other reservations had not been used to maximum benefit for either the tribe or Indian allottees, or cattle operators (both Indian and non-Indian). As we saw, the TLE was established in part to gain the advantages of scale without leveling individual equities in land interests. The BIA recognized that both the Indian owners of rangeland and cattle operators could be considered boats that would be jointly lifted by a rising tide through rational range management. That rising tide would be initiated by cooperative grazing. Rangeland conditions and capacities—empirical metrics concerning natural facts—would be surveyed across as wide a space as possible without attention to ownership, and natural range units would be mapped out for optimal productivity.[97] Range units were first established on Rosebud Reservation in 1931 when a forester joined the staff. Familiar with concepts of sustained-yield management first developed in forestry in the 1890s, he set to work "dividing the reservation into grazing units, based on the topography of the country and the natural relations of the allotments offering the best facilities."[98] The IRA formalized the policy by providing that the secretary of the interior would promulgate rules for "sustained-yield management," for "restrict[ing] the number of livestock grazed on Indian range units to the estimated carrying capacity," and "to protect the range from deterioration, to prevent soil erosion, [and] to assure full utilization of the range."[99] But a systematic range management plan had to await completion of a detailed reconnaissance survey of Todd and Mellette counties (including land owned by non-Indians) conducted in 1937 by SCS personnel tasked with providing specialized services for BIA programs, known as Technical Assistance-BIA. The survey used aerial photographs and maps that were annotated with fieldworkers' observations on "types and subtypes of

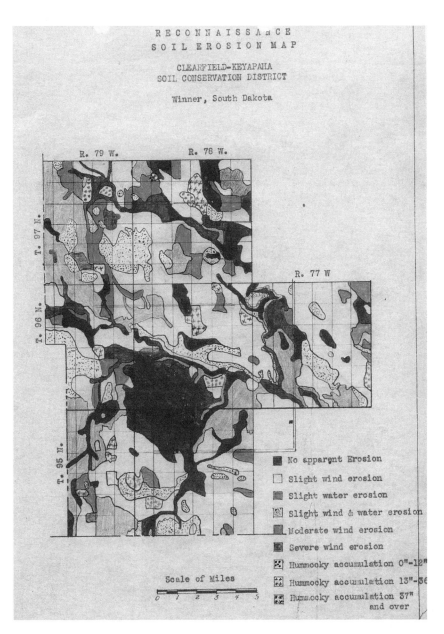

FIGURE 3.16. Soil erosion map, Clearfield–Keyapaha Soil Conservation District, Tripp County. Records of the Natural Resources Conservation Service (Kansas City, Missouri: National Archives and Records Administration).

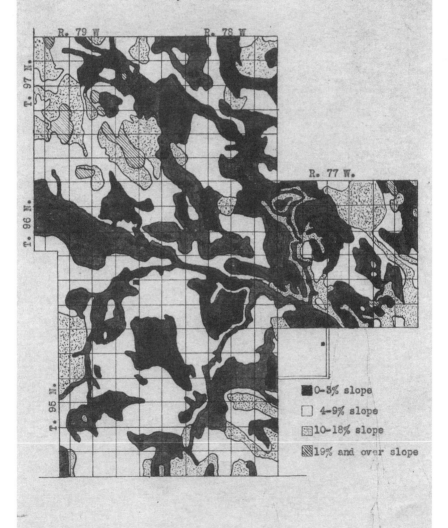

FIGURE 3.17. Slope map, Clearfield–Keyapaha Soil Conservation District, Tripp County. Records of the Natural Resources Conservation Service (Kansas City, Missouri: National Archives and Records Administration).

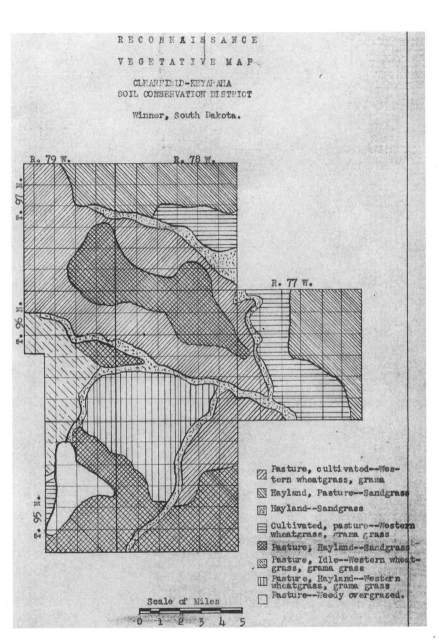

FIGURE 3.18. Vegetation map, Clearfield–Keyapaha Soil Conservation District, Tripp County. Records of the Natural Resources Conservation Service (Kansas City, Missouri: National Archives and Records Administration).

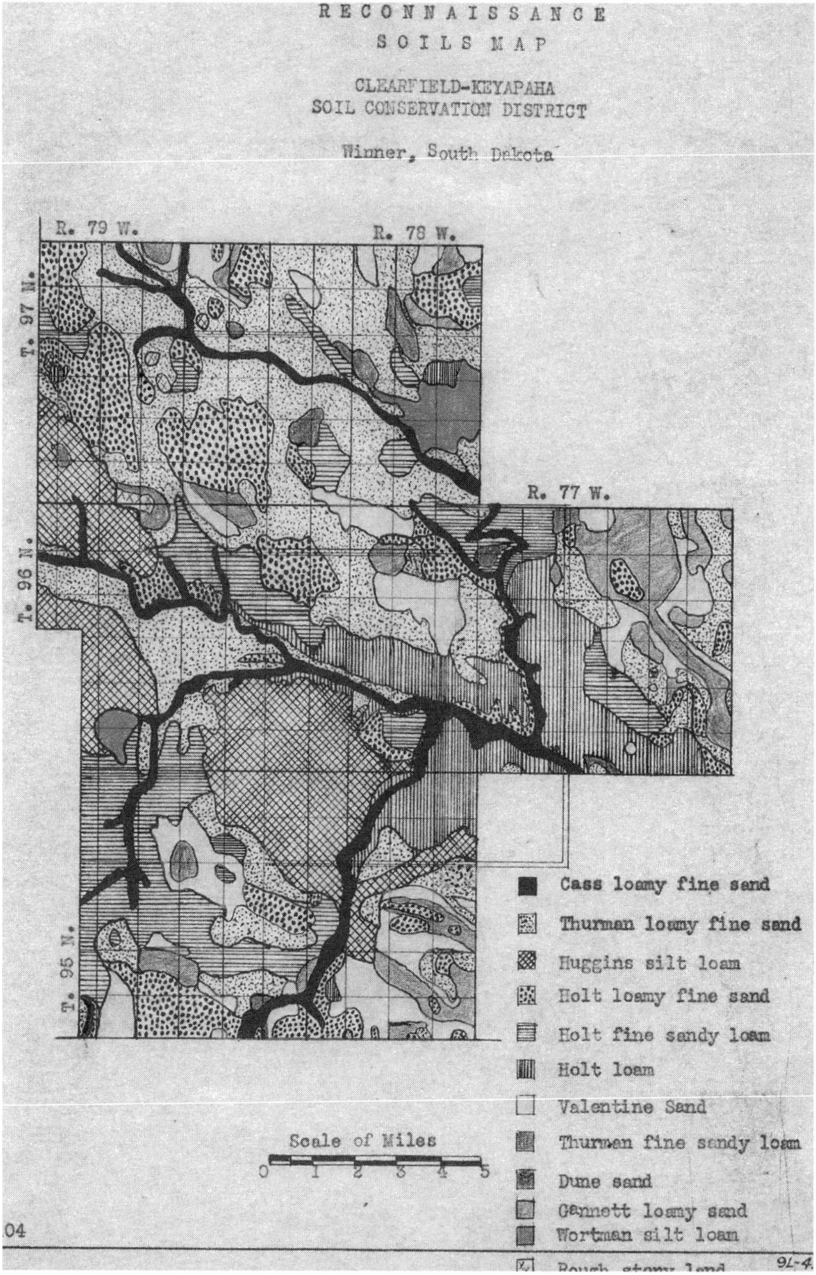

RECONNAISSANCE
SOILS MAP

CLEARFIELD–KEYAPAHA
SOIL CONSERVATION DISTRICT

Winner, South Dakota

Cass loamy fine sand
Thurman loamy fine sand
Huggins silt loam
Holt loamy fine sand
Holt fine sandy loam
Holt loam
Valentine Sand
Thurman fine sandy loam
Dune sand
Gannett loamy sand
Wortman silt loam
Rough stony land

Scale of Miles

FIGURE 3.19. Soil map, Clearfield–Keyapaha Soil Conservation District, Tripp County. Records of the Natural Resources Conservation Service (Kansas City, Missouri: National Archives and Records Administration).

vegetation," as well as on "fence lines, trails, water development, corrals, types and degrees of erosion, etc." Carrying capacities were ascertained by selecting representative pastures with multiyear records of stocking, with the ultimate aim of "blocking out and establishing . . . adequate livestock units with recommended plans."[100]

Once again, we see a new form of multiscalar governance optics, in which both fine-grained detail and larger aggregate patterns are brought into focus in a long-term temporal framework. At both the micro and the macro scales, private property and the grid are not completely ignored, but the emphasis is on recognizing and measuring natural patterns that could not be brought into resolution by organizing knowledge simply on the basis of bounded allotments or homesteads, or individual farms, much less undivided interests in allotments. The goal in the case of the range survey and planning range units was to optimize the use of range resources across the entire reservation, actually increasing the number of animal units at that level, while eliminating the overgrazing of areas around the limited number of existing water sources (additional water sources—wells and ponds—were to be constructed by Indian Civilian Conservation Corps crews). The ultimate aim was to establish natural range units encompassing a rationalized mix of forage, water, and shelter for livestock, all "designated entirely irrespective of land ownership and present land use."[101] But the complexity of checkerboarding and the challenge of securing the requisite power of attorney from the allottees and heirs proved daunting. The "heirship land problem" proved even "more insidious" than the "mixed ownership problem." In the end, range units were "delineated according to land tenure which disregards vegetative types, topography and soil conditions, a practice generally recognized as being contrary to sound land use." This "[g]reatly hinder[s]—often defeats—plans to treat natural units as such under a system of land-use adjustment. Thus it interferes with erosion control plans and range management plans, which work best where full control of natural units can be secured." Range units (Figure 3.20) were, in the end, composed primarily of allotments and tribal land, but not land in complex heirship status.[102]

New Deal experts had other kinds of natural processes in mind besides environmental ones. Under the liberal rationality described in chapter 1, it will be remembered, "Indian land" was understood as a temporary

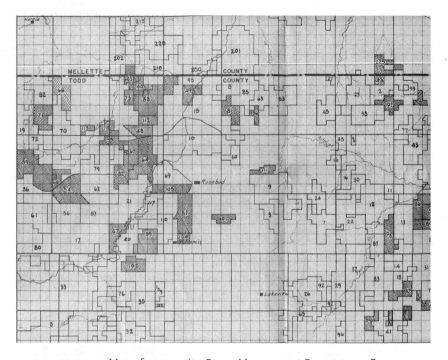

FIGURE 3.20. Map of range units. Range Management Report, 1939, Box 21, Records of the Soil Conservation Service, Region 7, Lincoln, Nebraska, Records of the Natural Resources Conservation Service (Kansas City, Missouri: National Archives and Records Administration).

artifice that would disappear as the trust status was removed as Indians became capable of managing their own affairs. Indeed, the process was well underway by the time that the New Deal arrived, and the checker-board pattern on interspersed non-Indian fee land and Indian trust had advanced significantly (at the time, this was viewed as "progress" in solving the "Indian problem"—moving toward the sunset of tribes, reservations, and even "Indians" as legal categories). The New Dealers advocated a very different theory of Indian land and Indian tribes, which was most clearly stated in a 1934 opinion of the solicitor of the Department of the Interior on tribal sovereignty and the powers of Indian tribes:

> Perhaps the most basic principle of all Indian law, supported by a host of decisions hereinafter analyzed, is the principle that *those powers which*

are lawfully vested in an Indian tribe are not, in general, delegated powers granted by express acts of Congress, but rather inherent powers of a limited sovereignty which has never been extinguished. Each Indian tribe begins its relationship with the Federal Government as a sovereign power, recognized as such in treaty and legislation. The powers of sovereignty have been limited from time to time by special treaties and laws designed to take from the Indian tribes control of matters which, in the judgment of Congress, these tribes could no longer be safely permitted to handle. The statutes of Congress, then, must be examined to determine the limitations of tribal sovereignty rather than to determine its sources or its positive content. What is not expressly limited remains within the domain of tribal sovereignty, and therefore properly falls within the statutory category, "powers vested in any Indian tribe or tribal council by existing law."[103]

Indian tribes, in other words, preexist the United States and hold inherent powers of self-government.

The implementation of the IRA thus amounted to a fundamental re-temporalization, rescaling, and respatialization of Indian country, indeed, of the national time and space of the United States. The IRA guaranteed that Indian reservations would remain extraterritorial with respect to state sovereignty, and remarkably, to some extent even with respect to the federal government. Ever since the 1896 Supreme Court case of *Talton v. Mayes*, it had been recognized that tribal "powers of local self government . . . existed prior to the [U.S.] Constitution" and thus are not subject to the limitations on government imposed by the U.S. Constitution.[104] Today this status is referred to as the "preconstitutional" and "extraconstitutional" nature of tribal sovereignty. But at the time of *Talton* the prevailing assumption was that the tribes would eventually disappear. The IRA froze in place the process of disappearing the reservations described in chapter 1 and made permanent under federal law the Rosebud Sioux Tribe as a corporate entity, as well as the new tribal council as the constituted government on a permanently protected land base. It halted the process of assimilating reservation lands into the homogenizing, national grid of state and local government and guaranteed a continuing, direct relationship between the tribe and the federal government, rather than aiming at an eventual off-loading of responsibility for

Indians to state and local government, as had been the stated goal in the regime of sod-busting liberalism. It also interrupted the empty homogeneous time of the nation and introduced what Partha Chatterjee calls heterogeneous time in which prenational collectivities are recognized as having political realities and legal claims outside of national time.[105] In this case, implementing the IRA required the Department of the Interior to specify the "inherent powers" of tribes that have "never been extinguished." These included, among others, tribal sovereignty over the form of government, membership, domestic relations, descent and distribution of property, taxation, and administration of justice.[106] This was a fundamental reversal of the Jeffersonian cookie-cutter approach to fungible, national political space examined in chapter 1. In fact, it would not be inaccurate to say that the New Deal was, in recognizing both nature and history, prepared to recognize *place* and its specificities in ways that Jeffersonian space making was not.

Natural communities were at the center of the government's new Indian policy, led by Commissioner John Collier. Collier and the New Dealers in the BIA believed that what they called "anthropological knowledge" could be useful in getting Indians to govern Indians, to foster collective self-government among them. The BIA superintendent at Rosebud had remarkable respect for both the discipline of anthropology and what he understood to be traditional Lakota culture (outside of which he seemed to believe the Lakota were not capable of thinking). Shortly before the IRA was enacted in 1934, and without knowledge of the form that self-government would take under the IRA, the Rosebud superintendent advised Collier that "a really self-governing capacity can be developed among the Sioux people," and that his "organization of self-governing communities in the Rosebud country has already . . . brought about a very distinct and noticeable result." On an accompanying plat map, the superintendent drew circles around "fourteen communities which have been organized" (see Figure 3.21, a partial view of the larger map with eleven communities circled):

> Briefly our plan of organization has consisted in bringing a community together, asking them to select three persons to act as a committee for the

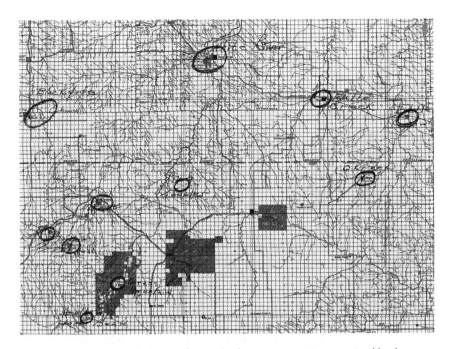

FIGURE 3.21. Detail of map of natural Lakota communities organized by the BIA superintendent, 1934. Under cover of Rosebud superintendent to Collier, April 25, 1934, File 20707–1934–066, Rosebud, Central Classified Files. Records of the Bureau of Indian Affairs (Washington, D.C.: National Archives and Records Administration).

general function of the community activities. This committee is empowered by the group to select one or more persons to act as a policeman, or, more exactly, a sort of "sergeant-at-arms" to keep order in the community. The community sets the dates for community activities, including Indian celebrations, Indian dances, business meetings of farm organizations, chapters, or groups; the committee cooperates in matters of general connection such as school, club work, and the like.

This arrangement had significantly lightened the load of the BIA agency police, and the superintendent argued that the community committees could function effectively in facilitating agricultural extension work. But even the map understated the complexity of these natural communities, which according to the superintendent were *not* simply local settlements, nor were they related to the location of members' allotted land. "[N]o hard and fast rules have been drawn around any community," the superintendent wrote to Collier. "Rather, it has been discovered that certain Indians, because of affiliations to past chiefs, or to the enterprise of present leadership, or through a religious significance, or for some other peculiar reason, will congregate at a certain community hall. By no means all the people within a reasonable distance will be there. If Grass Mountain is taken for example, it will be found that the descendants of Hollow Horn Bear make that their meeting place, even though there are two or three halls closer."[107]

This off-the-grid, fine-grained attention to local-level Indian collectivities, and the "anthropological knowledge" required to sustain it, was part of the rescaling and refocusing of governmental resolution that was at the core of the New Deal (we will see another illustrative case later regarding land and land use). The superintendent's analysis and plan for organizing the reservation on the basis of the "natural tendencies of the Indians" was cited approvingly by Felix Cohen of the Interior Department Solicitor's Office, who included it in his "Basic Memorandum on the Drafting of Tribal Constitutions" (1934).[108] When the IRA constitution for Rosebud Reservation was being drafted in 1935—mostly by the BIA's Organization Division and the Solicitor's Office of the Interior Department, with very little Lakota input—the Organization Division inserted what it called the "community plan," recognizing communities that were fixed, spatial versions of the fluid dance-hall communities the superintendent had outlined the preceding year and that he later referred to as traditional Lakota bands or *tiošpaye*. Representation on the tribal council was apportioned to these communities on the basis of population.[109] Collier was particularly impressed with this arrangement, and it clearly opened up for him the importance of natural communities in organizing tribes under the IRA. He wrote in a circular on "Group Organization" in 1935 of "the full utilization . . . of the 'natural' social group or actual community as the basic representation unit," rather than "artificial" districts or other "merely territorial" units as formerly established by the BIA (such as districts organized around ration issue stations). "Such 'natural' communities are usually based on older political groupings, on differing degrees of hybridization [of the Indian culture and the dominant culture], on remote kinship affiliations or, equally common today, on common economic activities such as farming groups in one portion of the reservation and stockraising groups in another. Religious differences in a number of cases must also be considered in the formation of such groupings." The necessity for careful study and analysis to get at these entities—which may not be obvious to the layperson—is consistent with the New Dealers' larger faith in a governmentality rooted in the blending of scientific knowledge and local knowledge of "the natural":

> The determination of these naturally cohesive social units or areas may only be determined by careful study of each of the various reservations. Often they exist in the consciousness of the people involved but are more or less completely masked by later administrative divisions which actually possess no such group sanction. Since this matter is of primary concern to those who are seeking stable and effective forms of tribal organization every effort should be made by the Indians concerned in cooperation with the field personnel to test the actual significance and social effectiveness of the basic political units decided upon. . . . On at least one reservation [Rosebud] excellent results along this line have been obtained by the Superintendent in cooperation with the Indians concerned. It is believed that tribal councils composed of delegates elected from socially significant districts will be more truly representative of the actual interests, economic or otherwise, present on the various reservations than would a council selected from purely artificial, territorial districts.[110]

The BIA was critically concerned with Indian resources, and the use of Indian land. In addition to the various forms of collective organization just described, the BIA embarked on a formidable land-use planning project on Rosebud Reservation that would replace the liberal model of allotment and individually owned farmsteads at the root of the earlier "civilization" policy. Indian allotment had, in fact, come to be systematically problematized in the 1920s, to some extent even within the BIA. The Brookings Institution's 1928 *The Problem of Indian Administration*, commissioned by the secretary of the interior, criticized the allotment policy for not having provided individuals with productive lands, and, when the allotment was productive, for allowing whites access to Indian land by purchase or lease: "[I]t is common to see the productive land that formerly belonged to the Indian owned or leased by whites and to find the Indians withdrawn to the remoter sections which afford comparatively little opportunity for development."[111] The National Resources Board published a study by the BIA in 1935, *Indian Land Tenure, Economic Status and Population Trends*. Among other issues, the report singled out heirship fractionation of allotments and checkerboarding of reservation lands as key problems. Heirship fractionation (still a challenge in Indian country today) refers to the tendency of individual allotments to be progressively divided into smaller interests through time as a result of the failure of most allottees and owners of interests in inherited allotments to execute wills limiting the number of heirs: "Partition of estates [dividing up an allotment and assigning the parcels to individual heirs] is a common procedure when the number of heirs is small; but small families are not the rule among Indians, and the very tardy process of probate in the Office of Indian Affairs causes long periods of time, often running into years, to elapse before the heirs are determined. In the meantime, new heirs may have been born, and the heirs of the original allottee may have died."[112] The original allotment thus "steadily subdivides into smaller and smaller equities as heirs, and heirs of heirs, increase. On the other hand, individual Indians accumulate increasingly more minute equities in increasing numbers of different estates."[113] The result was that increasingly more Indian land was becoming so subdivided by heirship status that it could not be practically divided into usable parcels and was either sold or leased, usually to white farmers and ranchers. The report illustrated the fractionation of an allotment in heirship with a case from Bad River Reservation in Wisconsin (Figure 3.22) and scattered, minute heirship holdings of individual families with a case from the Crow Reservation in Montana (Figure 3.23).

Planning: Panopticism and Governmentality

Many of the threads of New Deal reform, including the emerging multiscalar and long-term management optics, were pulled together after Secretary of the Interior Harold Ickes established a National Resources Planning Board in 1933 to manage relief spending on public works.

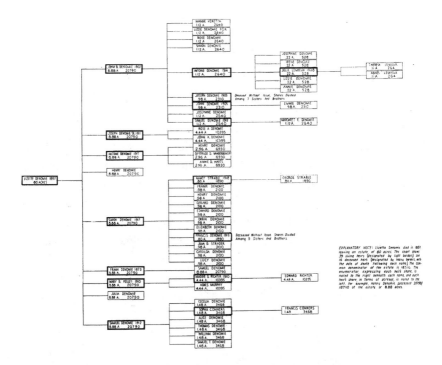

FIGURE 3.22. Heirship fractionation of an allotment. *Indian Land Tenure, Economic Status, and Population Trends,* Part X of the Supplementary Report of the Land Planning Committee to the National Resources Boards (Washington, D.C.: Government Printing Office, 1935), 16.

Pushed by the long-term planning ideas of Charles Merriam, the board quickly took on more formidable work and proposed to "stimulate the formulation of State, Regional and City plans" by providing funding for states to hire professional planners and other staff.[114] In June 1934, Roosevelt charged a reconstituted National Resources Board (with a professional advisory committee) to develop "a program and plan of procedure dealing with the physical, social, governmental, and economic aspects of public policies for the development and use of land, water and other national resources."[115] In its first report, the National Resources Board published "A Plan for Planning." The document argued that planning was nothing new or radical and had originated in the corporate sector and its systematic embrace of Frederick W. Taylor's scientific management, but it insisted that both government and civil society generally also needed to conduct planning. A new form of metaplanning was called for that would "align" the "plans of business, the plans of science and technology, the plans of social welfare, the plans of government . . . in such manner as to promote the general welfare in the highest degree attainable." "Planning," the board explained, "consists in the systematic, continuous, forward-looking application of the best intelligence available to programs of common affairs in the public field, as it does to private affairs in the domain of individual activity." Put differently, it is "based on control of certain strategic points in a working system—those points necessary to ensure order, justice, general welfare. It involves continuing reorganization of this system of control points from time to time. . . . The essence of successful planning is to find these strategic points as new situations

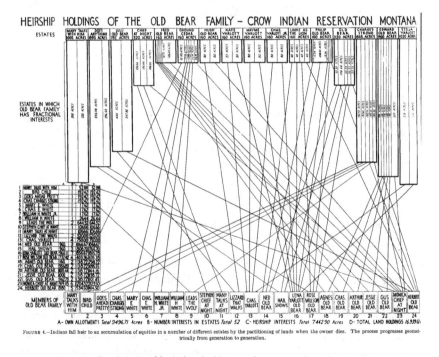

FIGURE 3.23. Fractionated heirship holdings of individuals. *Indian Land Tenure, Economic Status, and Population Trends,* Part X of the Supplementary Report of the Land Planning Committee to the National Resources Boards (Washington, D.C.: Government Printing Office, 1935), 18.

develop, without too great delay, and without seizing more points than are necessary for the purpose—or for longer time than is necessary for the purpose."[116]

Planning clearly had what we could call a panoptical, disciplinary side with a clear role for centralized authority at multiple scales (one inevitably thinks of a pyramid). But much more was involved than centralized discipline, and the board insisted that planning needed to be disseminated and distributed, "since planning is *an attitude and practice that must command the confidence and cooperation of wide groups of people . . . , must come from the bottom up as well as from the top down, from the circumference as well as the center.*"[117] Foucault himself suggested that disciplinary power in its full flower is "a network of relations from top to bottom, but also to a certain extent from the bottom to the top and laterally; this network 'holds' the whole together and traverses it in its entirety with effects of power that derive from one another."[118] Planning, which is "not an end, but a means," even "includes planning to preserve and, if necessary, create noncontrolled free areas of activity." Thus, planning might emerge in states and localities from "outside the governmental group altogether, from detached individuals and associations of individuals, industrial, scientific, or otherwise." Planning would not entail "a comprehensive blueprint to be clamped down like a steel frame on the soft flesh of the community, by the United States Government or by any government." Effective planning is based on "local self-government," albeit it "under a centralized supervision."[119] In other words, there are aspects of planning that are consistent with both discipline and what might better be called responsibilization within a regime of "planning" governmentality. Clearly, for the New Deal reformers, centralized control was simply not sufficient.

The South Dakota State Planning Board was appointed by the governor in 1934 and regularized by the state legislature in 1935, and quickly became an activist research and advocacy group under the chairmanship of W. R. Ronald, editor of the Mitchell *Daily Republic,* and who had a role in the origins of the AAA.[120] The board was assisted by professional planning consultants provided by the National Resources Board. In a brochure titled "The Planning Movement" distributed by the board at its booth at the state fair in 1935, it described its work as part of a national *movement* (again, we see the emphasis on the idea that planning cannot be a program of "the government" but must be taken up by individuals and communities) for "coordinated long-term planning," and explained that it was "*endeavoring to survey the entire field of human activities in the state* with the aim of formulating immediate and long time plans which will result *in the best type of civilization which can be secured within the limitation set by the environment.*" The breadth and depth of the plan must truly have been exhilarating for Ronald and his colleagues on the board; to others, it was scandalous and dangerous, as we will see in the next chapter. Planning would take place against the background presumption that agriculture, local government, and the built environment in South Dakota had been unwisely overextended: "[T]he spendthrift habits and impetuous expansion of the earlier days must give way to a more orderly and less wasteful development." This would require "readjustments."[121] In addition to publishing research reports and recommendations, the board, in conformity with the initiative of the National Resources Board, began fostering the organization of county planning boards in 1935. "[O]ur job is to work out a master plan for ten years for the development of the state and all its resources," Ronald told the assembled representatives of the county planning boards in 1935.[122]

Both the National Resources Board and the South Dakota State Planning Board were convinced of the necessity for county planning. These reformers understood planning as a new kind of public service and democratic process, separate from "politics" and from federal, state, and local government per se, but nonetheless necessary for wise democratic governance. In fact, because of their "short tenure of office, county officials cannot carry out long-range comprehensive planning no matter how competent they may be as they have no assurance that the program which they may initiate will be carried forward by succeeding administrations," the state board reasoned in 1935. "The business of operating a county for the profit and social benefit of its people requires periodic inventories and a long range program of planning just as does any industrial enterprise. County planning has a definite and distinct function to perform, the lack of which constitutes a missing link in the chain of planning activity which extends from the nation down to the village or neighborhood."[123] The board saw the county as a basic unit of land-use planning and recommended county land-use maps designating land appropriate for farming, grazing, and other uses. One of its most potentially radical recommendations was enforcement of land-use regulations by county zoning, and the blocking up of range land within each county through a rational system parallel to the range-unit system on Indian reservations.[124]

In 1935, the South Dakota Planning Board held meetings for county chairmen in Mitchell to discuss "the planning program of the National Resources Board and of the State Planning Board, and certain proposed planning problems for the county boards to work on." County boards had already been asked by Ronald to "submit reports on land use problems in their county [and] a practical water use report," based on outlines provided by the board.[125] The rural land-use outline (there was also a water conservation outline) requested county maps indicating:

1. Areas where erosion control work is needed. (Either water or wind— designate).
2. Areas where some of the farms are too small to provide an adequate living . . .
3. Areas suitable for extensive grazing only. That is[,] large blocks of land which are not adapted to farming or ranch headquarters and which should be in grazing districts (with no residences).
4. Areas suitable for a combination of stock ranching and limited farming.[126]

The planning board received the maps it requested from the county boards, and it is clear that it hoped they would become base maps not just for developing county land-use plans, but for enforcing them, in a cooperative endeavor between the county boards and the state board: "It is recommended that they be used as the basis of an official land use map to be developed as a result of further study. . . . A county zon[ing] enabling act should be enacted as an optional means of carrying out a land use program, with a crop land-grazing land ratio, and soil conservation practices, such as contour farming, included in the program. This contour farming should be required wherever necessary. . . . The grazing area in each county should be divided into ranges, each to be supplied with water from a central point with a maximum radius of 2½ miles."[127] As in the case of the range units on Rosebud Reservation, of course, this kind of systematic long-range agricultural planning would be most effective when natural agricultural and soil conditions were taken into consideration *irrespective of property titles or actual present land use, that is, the actual present interests of people living in the area.* This was the tacit assumption left unarticulated—no doubt to euphemize the radical nature of the proposal—by the planning board.

While the planning board had attempted to get county planning committees working on collecting and mapping facts from 1935, the start of local land-use planning was really instituted in the wake of the "Mt. Weather Agreement" (between the USDA and the Association of Land Grant Colleges and Universities; it was in the agricultural colleges that state extension services were located) in 1938, which initiated nested "Cooperative Land Use Planning" from the county level to the USDA in Washington.[128] In this arrangement, planning "extends down to all the small local communities in the county."[129] This planning process began in Tripp County in 1939–40 and, as it did nationally, started with the classification of land: "A total of 68 community meetings and four county land use meetings were held this year. At these meetings the committee mapped and classified the land into different agricultural areas based on land use, soil type and topography."[130] The ultimate aim—at least from the perspective of advocates—was that planning extend beyond simply land use to include "educational conditions, medical care, and a host of other things that are important in each community." The first order of business was for community committees composed of elected "farmers and farm women" to map the community and classify all lands into five possible categories, and submit a report "in which each area is described, the problems set forth and the committees' suggestion for the solutions to the problems are contained." The county land-use planning committee then started the job of "correlating" the community maps and reports in a county map and report.[131] "Cooperative" land-use planning—running from the grass roots to Washington—was meant to be "democracy in action": "The purpose of land use planning," the South Dakota state land-use specialist put in 1941, "is to pool the judgment of farm people with the knowledge of technicians and administrators of various local, state and federal agencies in working out the destiny of agriculture and rural living in the communities."[132]

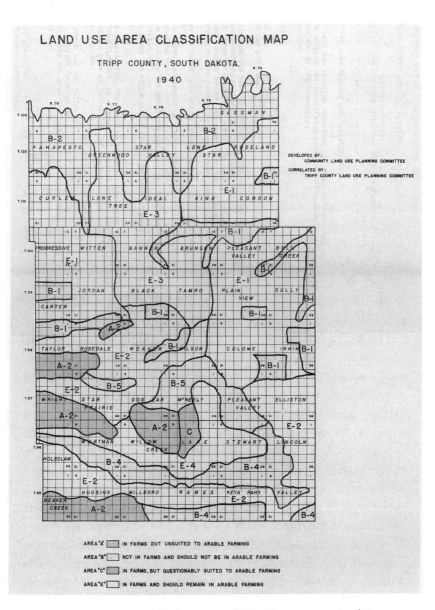

FIGURE 3.24. Prescriptive land-use map of Tripp County, 1940. *Land Use Planning in Tripp County*, Tripp County Land Use Planning Committee (1941).

The ultimate goal of the county land classification and mapping was to sustain a "unified" agricultural program. Once the detailed annotated maps were complete, the extension service explained in 1939, "the material will be made available to the Extension Service, Agricultural Adjustment Administration and other government agencies operating with the county who will shape their programs accordingly. . . . If a cash grain farmer applies for a rehabilitation loan to the [Farm Security Administration] for instance . . . , and it is shown that his farm is located in an area which his community land-use committee has mapped and classified for grazing, a cash grain farming loan will not be made."[133] Tripp County was among the first five counties in the state to be so mapped, with the aim of moving to a unified county agricultural program. An extension specialist from Brookings was assigned to "assist in the detailed mapping and land classification work." A county agricultural policy committee consisting of the "heads of the various agricultural agencies operating in the county" named twelve farmers to serve on a "county land-use committee." The agency heads served as ex officio, nonvoting members of the land-use committee.

The process was completed in 1941, when *Land Use Planning in Tripp County* was published by the Tripp County Land Use Planning Committee. Probably written by the county extension agent (and mimeographed, with a printed map, by the state extension service), the report described itself as representing "the thinking of the farmers of each community relative to the use of their own land and the many problems with which they are confronted in the development of an economically sound agriculture in this region." The members of the committee "combined observations from their own experience and experimentally developed facts" in the report.[134] The central product of the report was the "Land Use Area Classification Map" and the associated recommendations. As can be seen in Figure 3.24, significant areas were classified as "in farms but unsuited to arable farming" (A areas), and "in farms, but questionably suited to arable farming" (C areas) (the categories had been devised for use by county committees by the Department of Agriculture).[135] The committee recommended that the A areas undergo a "transition . . . from a farming area to a ranching area and should be done as soon as possible." To ease the transition, the committee also recommended that taxes be levied "based on productivity."[136] The available records (including the local newspaper) do not indicate how the committee arrived at this conclusion—which would inevitably impact both farm incomes and property values if implemented—and it is not clear that there was even a majority vote, much less a consensus on the recommendations. We simply cannot know how much the extension agent pushed through an interpretation consistent with his training, regardless of local perspective, notwithstanding the insistence that the "thinking of the farmers of each community" is represented in the report. While the official position of the Department of Agriculture on county land-use planning was that the goal was "the carefully formulated opinions of the people themselves," the extension service and other field personnel were expected to provide maps, data, and framing in such ways as to bring about the desired kind of report.[137]

This chapter has argued, after Foucault, that liberalism with its impulse not to govern too much has been historically accompanied by a process of reform guarding against governing too little. This is because liberalism was from its birth in political economy about something larger than the economy. It was in fact about *the welfare of nations,* or the security of national populations, and such collective goods could not be pursued only by letting sleeping dogs lie. Liberal practices justified themselves in terms of a larger rationale. It was this larger rationale of government as the *care of the population* that opened space in government for practices beyond liberalism, practices that even pushed back against liberal practices. New Deal spokespersons often claimed they sought a judicious balance of liberal and reform practices (for example, of private property and the public good). New Deal reform practices—attending to scale, focusing on newly discovered "natural" processes, and systematic, "democratic" planning—had their own genealogies distinct from those of liberal practices, and I have argued that in addition to the supposedly instrumental goals of ending the Depression and the Dust Bowl and returning to prosperity that the most powerful New Dealers had in mind, it is likely that many of the technicians and intellectuals who worked in the trenches of New Deal reform were also engaged by the *elegance* of the new ways of seeing wholes and parts and the relations between them.

For these people, New Deal habits of mind were truly a *movement*. Such ways of seeing problems and taking corrective action could amount to a career, not just (or even mainly) in the sense of an income or financial comfort, but also (and more) in the sense of a path for making a new and improving self (an informed self, a professional self, an inquisitive self, a "thinking" self). But programs that were pleasing, engaging, or compelling to New Deal reformers came to be anathema to many rural South Dakotans who saw, with no exaggeration, the reform practices as the uninformed and self-absorbed games of those who could afford to play at making a living. These people had no intention of becoming New Deal subjects, as we will see in the next chapter.

4

Making New Deal Subjects

The New Deal reformers were convinced that active intervention was necessary in order to correct the breakdown of the economy and the environmental crises of the 1930s. But the most thoughtful among them were also convinced that while some degree of centralized control and specialized expertise were absolutely necessary, no permanent solution to the problems faced by the nation could be found without a new kind of citizen motivated by felt responsibility appropriate to the threshold that had been reached in the nation's—and in world—history. Such new citizens would recognize the inescapability of social governing, would actively participate in it, and would contribute important insights into the process of solving problems collectively in cooperation with government authorities and trained professionals. In other words, as compared to collective or centralized planning in the Soviet Union or in fascist countries, social government in the United States would be "democratic," both because that was the appropriate form given the American character and because the grass roots could, indeed, see local problems and small, but critical details that professionals governing at a distance could not. As we saw in the last chapter, the architects of planning even considered the active stimulation of novel thinking by groups outside of—and potentially opposed to—political authority as a necessary part of planning, simply to increase the likelihood that the diagnosis or treatment of problems would be practically effective. The prospect of mobilizing the grass roots in a *social movement* of reform was clearly as exhilarating to some New Dealers as it was politically naive. This chapter will survey both the plans for making New Deal subjects—or otherwise getting individuals to behave as called for—and the range of responses from the grass roots.

The New Dealers' View

The reformers presumed that the emergency of the Depression and drought necessitated bold action and strong measures—carrots and sticks—to get people to act in the necessary new ways. While the Agricultural Adjustment Act (AAA) was being drafted, Assistant Secretary of Agriculture Tugwell wrote in his diary in January 1933 that it would be possible to control the national supply of agricultural commodities "by devising a mechanism through which farmers can bring the interests of all into concert with the individual interest of each. Under this plan it will pay farmers, for the first time, to be social-minded, to do something for all instead of for himself alone. We thus succeed, we think, in harnessing a selfish motive for the social good."[1] Chester C. Davis, head of the Agricultural Adjustment Administration, was also confident of the inducements incorporated into the AAA: "By making these payments only to those farmers who cooperate in adjusting their production, the adjustment act has provided a skillful method of identifying the interests of the individual with those of the group.... Such is the benefit payment—an equitable compensation for service rendered, and in addition an instrument of hopeful experiment in the direction of economic and social control."[2]

But few if any of the New Deal thinkers would have been comfortable with the idea of simply paying farmers to do what was necessary without any internalized change in how farmers saw their interests. Secretary of Agriculture Henry C. Wallace pointed out that farmers' crop histories and acreages contracted under the AAA were published in local newspapers—to generate transparency in order to weed out cheating. But Wallace made it clear that this was far more than simply a technique of enforcement, and that it had the potential to provide object lessons to farmers. Because local production-control associations were responsible for rectifying discrepancies between the terms of the individual AAA contracts and the actual acreages planted by individual farmers, and because a fraudulent claim could take cash out of the pockets of other members of the association, "these men *learned,* perhaps for the first time, what is involved in making individual interest coincide with the interest of the group." Wallace intended for everyday citizens to "realize how much a part of the Government they are, and how much the Government is a part of them." Of critical importance for Wallace was that "these cooperating growers have demonstrated their willingness to undergo a certain amount of social discipline for the larger purposes of the group."[3]

Ultimately, most of the reformers understood, it would be necessary to educate farmers about what they had to gain, materially, through New Deal programs and through cooperation with their fellow farmers, and what they had to lose by staying out. The soil conservationist in the extension service in Brookings, South Dakota, wrote to the project director of the Winner–Dixon Soil Conservation District, "[i]n all the education meetings that I hold the most common question that I hear is . . . 'How much does it cost?' My reply is that conservation doesn't cost, it pays."[4] The challenge was to get this (supposedly sound) information to farmers, which would require systematically educating them. So, for example, a Soil Conservation Service (SCS) script for a filmstrip lecture said of strip cropping and maintaining a cover crop on the soil that "[t]he profitable results of these simple 'horse sense' farming methods the average farmer can put into practice are indicated strikingly in this picture," corn cane (a soil cover) on a "cooperator's farm that only a few months before was bare, blow dirt, seeming out of control."[5] The *Winner Advocate* quoted a cooperator in the Winner–Dixon Soil Conservation District on the bottom line regarding contour plowing: "Even though I expect it to be a little more inconvenient, I believe contour strip farming will prove more profitable to me than our old system of farming up and down slopes." Contour plowing would help retain moisture from precipitation through the year, and would thus improve chances of better yields in a dry summer. This cooperator, the article explained, was also "contour furrowing his pasture, terracing a small alfalfa field, establishing a farm shelterbelt . . . and retiring a part of his land to grass." "We now plow horizontally," the article concluded, "following the curvature of the hills and hollows on a dead level, however crooked the lines may be. Every furrow thus acts as a reservoir to receive and retain water, all of which goes to the benefit of the growing plant instead of running off into streams."[6] This could not help but appeal to the thinking farmer, the author of the article must have reasoned. The following week, the same author asserted that farmers who adopted these practices were "increasing the value of their own farms and the likelihood of a more uniform income."[7] Ultimately, the New Dealers were convinced, it would be necessary to get famers to rethink "the whole business of farming," including "soil management, crop and livestock production, farm management, tree plantings and wild life under conservation."[8] The aim of the Tripp County extension agent was to get his charges to become "thinking farmers" who were "broad in thought and action."[9]

New Deal technical experts commonly had faith that "scientific" or empirical knowledge stood on its own, was neutral and nonpolitical, and, when effectively disseminated (which sometimes required the public to be taught a little method, some appropriate theory, and a few simple facts), nonexperts would see the light and accept the road to progress as defined by the experts. Even more ambitiously, many New Deal political leaders and visionaries, and technicians in the field, believed that the grass roots and the experts would cooperate on solving problems, with each group providing its contribution to the solution; the unstated premise was that the experts needed to lead or otherwise guide matters that were ultimately dependent on scientific fact. This all came together in the concept of agricultural planning that was described in chapter 3. The Tripp County extension agent wrote in his annual report in 1941:

Theoretically, the prime motive or purpose back of the land use planning program is coordination of the thoughts and efforts of farm people in dealing with their own problems, coordination of local governmental activities to conform with the coordinated thinking of farm people, coordination of state governmental activities to conform with the thoughts and activities of a coordinated farm personnel approach to agriculture's problems, a coordination of the almost innumerable activities of the federal bureaus and departmental heads that are now dealing with agriculture's problems. This coordination aims at a more effective solution of the

problems affecting agriculture and also aims at a democratic approach
to the solution of the problems of agriculture. The coordination of the
thinking and planning of the farmers and the activities of the various governmental agencies should not be attempted and can not be achieved by
the farmers alone or by the representatives of the agencies alone. *The
thinking, planning and action of all groups must be integrated and as it were
assimilated by the body politic, through the assistance and cooperation of all
interested individuals, farmers, research specialists, extension workers, and
the representatives of the various governmental agencies.*[10]

The extension agent did not explain how this "coordination" would be
secured, likely because he was convinced that the experts had the facts of
their side and the rest would naturally follow.

Indeed, the New Dealers never doubted the leadership role of the
paid, professional expert in all this, and clearly recognized the limited
role that dirt farmers could have in making technical "delineations." The
purpose of consultations with farm people seems to have much more
to do with what we might call consumer research or simply marketing
on the part of the reformers than with farmers actually contributing
their experience or practical knowledge to planning in a "democratic"
way. In 1938, the land-planning specialist provided to South Dakota by
the Farm Security Administration described the meetings he had held
with county committees on agricultural planning:

We supplied maps and statistics on type and size of farms, present crop
cover, livestock number, soils, topography, climate, distance to market,
risk, ownership, tax statuses, certain public finance data, problem areas,
etc. In the meetings we interpreted this data in terms of proper land utilization. . . . On the basis of the meetings held so far . . . it seems that the
County Committees will make very few delineations that we could not
make in our office without the meetings. Their delineations will be largely
as our own basic data suggests. This is not criticism whatsoever of the
Committees, this is a problem too technical for an inexperienced group
to handle with a relatively short period, having given it no prior thought
in these exact terms. . . . We have, however, come away from these particular meetings feeling that they were still worthwhile because they seem to

create more local interest in the various adjustment programs. It gave local people an opportunity to express themselves on the various governmental programs, which at times they said functioned at cross purposes. There were some who resented the adjustment programs, and it gave others an opportunity to answer them.[11]

The purpose of meeting farmers was not for them to convey information about farming or erosion based on their practical knowledge, but to facilitate local *dissemination* of the reform models, by getting farmers interested, letting them speak, and allowing their own neighbors already sold on conservation measures to address their complaints in ways that promoted the new reform practices.

A large part of the challenge faced by the reformers in securing uptake of their models among the grass roots is that the payoff of conservation measures turned out to be a bit more complicated than had been hoped. The extension service conservationist who insisted that conservation does not "cost" but "pays" was concerned to come up with material to back up his claims, and he asked the Winner–Dixon Conservation District to provide some figures on "contour farming, strip cropping, tree planning, dam building, terrace construction," and so on. The project director responded with a "guesstimate" of costs, but added that "[f]ollowing your line of thought that these practices pay rather than cost, it would be necessary to determine the value ... derived from these practices in contrast with not using the practices. ... In many cases there may not be an increase in yield but the soil will be conserved so that it will produce crops, 10, 25, or 50 years in the future whereas without the practices it may be non-producing in the same length of time. ... There will be years when certain practices will not give results in increased yields over the use of no practice on similar land. ... Unless we take a long-time view of conservation, it will be very difficult to show where some of the practices justify their cost by immediate increases in crop yields."[12] This was not good news, because as the planning committee of the Winner–Dixon project put it, "[i]n the last analysis each practice must prove its worth by offering more advantages than disadvantages to the land operator in order to be continued and to spread over other areas."[13] Indeed, farmers reported that there were disadvantages to conservation measures. The project manager for the Winner–Dixon Soil Conservation District commented in 1938 on "the objection to strip cropping based on such things as increased grasshopper damage, more hot wind damage along the edges, and substantial losses to cropping operations. These objections were shared by farmers as well as some of the members of both the project and regional staffs. We are meeting that problem by pointing out that we do not have a careful enough check of results over a long period of time to justify a definite conclusion and until such results are obtained we should withhold our judgment."[14] Even when farmers agreed that the measures were worthwhile, they could not afford the time or expense to install the necessary fixtures, or were simply unwilling to unless they were provided free by the SCS.[15]

Indeed, compelling theory existed in agricultural economics that rational farmers would not, in fact, adopt conservation measures of their own accord. As early as 1913, Lewis C. Gray, who would become a major figure in New Deal land-use planning, argued that "it is not necessarily true that . . . conservation is the method which results in maximum profits," and that in fact "methods of conservation are likely to increase the economic burden in the present."[16] Ultimately, Gray recognized that conservation was a *social, not individual utility,* and needed to be understood in terms of intergenerational equity, an *ethical,* not (liberal) economic matter:

> [C]onservation requires that individuals lessen their consumption today in order that other individuals may enjoy the results of the abstinence. Hence, in so far as it involves the saving for the enjoyment of other generations what we might use for ourselves, it constitutes a type of ethical requirement which is upon a higher level than any that has heretofore existed, an ethical requirement entirely novel it its scope. The ethical field is to be widened to include unborn generations; not only those which will appear in the immediate future but also those which are yet enshrouded in a future limited only by the uncertain period of human life upon the earth. Few individuals have achieved an ethical level sufficiently exalted to induce them to curtail present enjoyment for the sake of shadowy generations to come. Let any policy be imposed at the present day the consequences of which are recognized by the general public as resulting in serious curtailment of present enjoyments in the interest of a most distant

future; and one would not have to be a cynic to predict an uprising of the individual against the organs of social control.[17]

Gray wrote this long before the New Deal, but his focus on the ethical goes directly to the challenge faced by New Deal theorists: it would be ultimately necessary to change not just minds, but hearts.

Iowa State University agricultural economist Walter Wilcox came up with a different—but equally disappointing—prediction in 1938, based on interpreting conservation as a form of capital maintenance. When the rate of return on farming—the ratio of income to costs of production—drops below the market rate of return on investment in general in the economy, "capital replacement will not take place." In the Great Plains, Wilcox argued, "[s]oils . . . are not far different from gold-ore deposits"—meaning that cash-crop production leads inevitably to degradation of fertility, and erosion control measures could do no more than slow down the loss. "No educational program," Wilcox concluded, "will be effective in inducing conservation under such conditions. If range- and cropland conservation in the Great Plains is really wanted, society must be prepared to give up a part of its current income from these lands. The ranchers, wheat raisers, and other farmers will not do it voluntarily and without compensation." But whether "society" should do that, Wilcox recognized, and to what extent, is *not an economic question.*[18] We shall return to the question of moral responsibilization momentarily.

There is no reason to assume that farmers were not interested in conserving the fertility of their land, and some agricultural experts in South Dakota, and perhaps in Washington, recognized that farmers were already "thinking" when they chose the options they did in production. The problem lay with the *conditions* they faced, not the "knowledge" or even the lofty "ethics" they supposedly lacked. These advocates rejected all suggestion that farmers were not already acting rationally, even ethically, or that the challenge was simply to "enlighten" farmers as to best practices and moral obligations. While Richard Hofstadter may or may not be correct in asserting that American farmers in general were as committed to speculation as to producing crops, it is important to recognize that at least in the Rosebud country, farmers were petty commodity producers who could not shift their "capital" to alternative "investments" such as conservation measures without profound disruptions to personal, family, and community life, and who were driven by a form of what Marx called the "silent compulsion of economic relations."[19] The South Dakota State Planning Board said as much in its report *Land Use Problems in Central South Dakota, 1937* (Gregory and Tripp counties were included in the study area). The problem was not the lack of awareness of how overgrazing, for example, caused damage, but how silent economic compulsion forced the hand of producers:

> Operators who have too little land supporting too many head of livestock can look at the general situation and agree that when the land is used too intensively, foraging animals are capable of making grassland vulnerable to erosion by tearing the grass out by the roots, disturbing the protective sod, and exposing the soil to the wind. An individual who looks at this situation may agree that his own grazing practices are lacking in foresight; but when his herd is barely paying him a living income, a reduction in numbers is a difficult choice to make, when the alternative is so nebulous a goal as coordinated land planning. This attitude is understandable from the operators' view, though continuation of present practices will necessitate more and more abuse of the grasslands as time goes on, just to preserve present standards of income. The need for a planned approach to this dilemma is obvious.[20]

The SCS district conservationist attached to the Clearfield–Keyapaha Soil Conservation District in Tripp County also recognized the problem. In a 1939 report to his superiors, he wrote: "'In order to make a livelihood now, many people find it necessary to do things to the soil that are not for their own long-time interests or for the interests of posterity. How can these people promote long-time interest without sacrificing their own present necessities? How can the national interest and the individual interest be reconciled?' . . . This question affects people everywhere, but it is most acute where human misery is most acute—where people are trying to scratch a living from submarginal land unfit for farming. . . . Both the soil and the people suffer as a consequence."[21] The New Dealers struggled to find a way around this stubborn disconnect, short of paying farmers to practice conservation (which, of course, the AAA did in part).

Given the doubtful coincidence between existing individual interests and New Deal agricultural programs, even if farmers adopted a "long-time view," it is not surprising that government officials often slipped into metaphors of war—as we saw Roosevelt do in chapter 3 at the beginning of the New Deal—in their attempt to motivate farmers to think about present economic incentives and constraints. A war, after all, requires citizens to be prepared to sacrifice for the greater good of the nation. Secretary of Agriculture Henry A. Wallace described erosion as a "war at our feet," and in 1939 he insisted that conservation of physical and human resources amounted to the "moral equivalent of war."[22] In 1940, Hugh H. Bennett, director of the SCS, told the National Education Association of his concern that "so few people of the United States . . . realize what soil erosion has cost and is costing our nation, or how rapidly the losses are taking place." The danger erosion posed to "national security" necessitated nothing less than "militant support of soil and water conservation."[23] In fact, it was World War II that gave New Deal conservationists the most powerful argument in favor of conservation. As the *Dakota Zephyr*, a newsletter for farmers published by the SCS and the state extension service, urged its readers: "A munition[s] worker's slogan is, 'A man who relaxes helps the Axis.' Prevent erosion and conserve natural resources."[24]

Other New Deal intellectuals appealed to the farmers' moral obligations as citizens with responsibilities to "society" and "future generations." In an article titled "Society and the Farmer Have Mutual Interests in the Land," Undersecretary of Agriculture Milburn. L. Wilson argued that "a new concept of the farmer's and society's interest in the land has appeared and gained acceptance. Put very broadly, this new concept assumes that society has an interest in the privately owned farm which is at least equal to the interest of the owner himself. If this assumption is sound . . . obviously it throws new duties both upon the landowner and society. It becomes the duty of the landowner so to handle his land as to conserve the soil and its fertility in the interest of society, and it becomes the duty of society to assist the landowner to make the best use of his land. Thus the individual landowner and society share the responsibility of preserving our lands for the generations to come."[25] Lewis C. Gray made the argument that there was a legal limit to what the individual could do with his private property, and that compulsory measures to protect the land were perfectly constitutional. Even in our liberal democracy, the right of private property is never absolute but is always "limited by certain governmental rights," such as taxation, eminent domain, and police power ("the right and obligation of government to provide for and safeguard the health, safety, and morals of its citizens"). But there was a new, additional consideration: "a growing opinion that land is vested with a paramount public interest, that private landownership is granted by society rather than being an inherent individual right."[26]

But it was Secretary of Agriculture Wallace who made the most moralizing appeals in the project to responsibilize both farmers and those who depended on farmers. "It was selfishness that has destroyed our natural resources," and Wallace called for "a new working philosophy of American husbandry, both on the farms and in town—one which emphasizes not only the security of the soil itself as our basic resource, but the ultimate security of all who live on this soil, now and for all the generations to come." "Conservation is a way of life; people have to change their minds, their attitudes, their ways" in learning an "ethics of agriculture."[27] In a 1934 article titled "Spiritual Forces and the State," Wallace rejected coercive, disciplinary, and even technical advice to farmers as insufficient to bring about the proper New Deal citizen. "I am deeply concerned," he wrote, "because I know that the social machines set up by this Administration will break down unless they are inspired by men who in their hearts catch a larger vision than the hard-driving profit motives of the past. More than that, the men in the street must change their attitude concerning the nature of man and the nature of human society. They must develop the capacity to envision a co-operative objective and be willing to pay the price to attain it. They must have the intelligence and the will power to turn down simple solutions appealing to the short-time selfish motives of a particular class." What was called for was nothing less than "changed human hearts." There was still great promise of progress based on science and machinery, but "we can not enter into these possibilities until we have acquired a new faith, a faith which is based on a richer concept of the potentialities of human nature than that of the economists, scientists, and business men of the nineteenth century." Wallace anticipated—or hoped for—a return to an older Christianity, before Protestantism became fused with the gospel of laissez-faire. This would happen not by "external compulsion but . . . will spring from the hearts of the people because of an overwhelming realization of a community of purpose." A "spiritual co-operation," ultimately embracing "one world," would need to "grow side by side with a new social discipline."[28]

If, as Karl Polanyi wrote in his 1944 *The Great Transformation*, that— pace John Locke—capitalism is rooted in the "fictitious" commoditization of land, the philosophers of New Deal conservation were asking farmers to decommoditize their land, at least partially. As the *Dakota Zephyr* quoted an agricultural economist in the Bureau of Agricultural Economics: "Land is not a commodity. Land is not the product of man, nor with all the ingenuity of classical economists can he ever mix his labor with anything that is not land and thereby fashion land. Land is the gift of Nature entrusted to man's keeping upon which he may project his energies of mind and muscle and thereby support life and fashion a civilization."[29]

Finally, before turning to examine local resistance to and translations of New Deal programs, we must consider the planning that went into "selling" the Indian Reorganization Act (IRA) and other Indian New Deal programs. I have treated this topic directly and in depth in earlier work, and will only briefly summarize the relevant material here.[30] Personnel in the Bureau of Indian Affairs (BIA) and the solicitors' office of the Department of the Interior spent a great deal of time, intellectual creativity, and bureaucratic energy coming up with plans for Indian people and tribes, as we saw in chapter 3. They spent much less time planning how to get Indian people to cooperate, or otherwise become new Indian subjects. This was primarily a result of the legal supervision that the Interior Department retained over Indians and tribes. Because both individual allotments and tribal land were held in trust for Indians by the United States, the government did not in general need the permission of Indians or tribal governments to do what it saw as its fiduciary best for Indians and tribes. Thus, Indians did not need to be convinced that range units and enforcement of stocking limits were in their "best interests," in the way that non-Indian farmers who owned their land, or rented land, in fee had to be convinced to practice conservation measures and paid cash benefits to limit production.

In the case of new IRA tribal government, the Constitution and By-Laws of the Rosebud Sioux Tribe were said to be drafted by a local (Lakota) committee, but this supposedly grassroots work was heavily shaped by BIA agents using a suggested outline provided by the BIA. Felix Cohen, assistant solicitor in the Interior Department, and Fred Daiker, assistant commissioner of Indian affairs under John Collier, also worked with a Rosebud committee on the document for a week.[31] Because the constitution needed to be ratified by the tribal electorate under the terms of the IRA, the Rosebud superintendent was instructed by the BIA central office to "so organize your personnel and Indian leaders that the constitution will be fully and clearly explained to all of the Indian voters of your reservation."[32] Even though there was strong opposition to the new constitution, including the charges that it was "rammed down our throats" (that is, pushed too aggressively, without sufficient time for consideration) and that many people, particularly the older and more traditional people, did not understand its contents (a Lakota version of the final draft of the constitution had not been provided), it was ratified by a vote of 992 to 643.[33]

The BIA had a role in shaping the actions of the new (1936) IRA tribal council. Because the constitution (1935) and the law-and-order code (1937) were essentially written by the federal government, the tribal council was not clear on its powers or the limits to those powers, and there is evidence that the council—or at least some council members—took the BIA's word for it on at least some occasions when the BIA's opinion was not entirely based on the law but on Collier's and senior BIA officials' concern to protect "native culture," even against native government.[34] More critically, the text of the constitution itself included very serious provisions for legal supervision over tribal council actions by the federal government.[35] Approval or review by the secretary of the interior was required for exercise of the following constitutional powers by the tribal council: to appropriate tribal funds not raised by the council itself; to exclude from the reservation those not legally entitled to reside there; to regulate the membership of the tribe; to promulgate a law-and-order code and establish a reservation court; to regulate the inheritance of property other than allotted land; and to appoint guardians for minors and mental incompetents.[36] The BIA used the provisions for secretarial supervision to head off what it considered to be potential violations of the individual liberties of tribal members. The superintendent disapproved a council ordinance limiting the amount of peyote that could be legally ingested by a member of the Native American Church in 1938.[37] He vetoed a 1937 ordinance prohibiting the meeting of organizations opposed to the tribal council without the council chairperson's approval, advising that it constituted a "violation of the right of free speech as guaranteed by the constitution of the United States." The superintendent's veto was sustained by the BIA in Washington.[38]

There had been ideas when the IRA was being drafted that tribal council actions could be appropriately restrained by a formal system of checks and balances built into the tribal machinery, including a national Court of Indian Affairs to which tribal decisions could be appealed. In the end, however, it was thought that separation of powers and checks and balances were too complicated to deliver as a package to Indian people and that they would be better served by the guiding hand of federal supervision.[39] We will shortly return to examine how Lakota people responded to the Indian New Deal.

Resistance and Translation

The New Deal reformers may have been convinced that, as the Great Plains Drought Area Committee wrote in 1936, "[t]here is no ambiguity as to what is meant by 'the good of all concerned,'" but the matter of the common good (of individual property owners and producers) was precisely what South Dakota farmers worried about when it came to New Deal programs.[40] One of the sources of friction between New Deal agricultural theory and dirt farmers in the Rosebud country was the former's revisionary view of liberalism as a selfishly individualistic way of life and the source of all Depression and Dust Bowl problems, and which needed to be overcome by *collective* entities organized, or at least initiated, by government. Urban liberals—such as those in government in Washington, and in the brains trust—may have understood liberalism in terms of antisocial, or (overly) "possessive" individualism, but South Dakotans didn't see it that way; in fact, they did not even use the term "liberal" to describe their market- and property-based vision of community. Brief mention was made in chapter 1 of historian Jon Lauck's analysis of the role of *republicanism* in South Dakota political culture.[41] Republicanism

(not in the sense of the Republican Party, although many South Dakotans and red state citizens may well say that it *is* in that sense), with its
commitment to community and nation, was and is a check on liberalism
understood as the pursuit of mere self-interest, something they attribute
to "liberals" understood in the current colloquial sense in the United
States. If we put this in Foucauldian terms, we might say that rural South
Dakotans are decidedly *republican-liberal subjects*.

The rural republican tradition of community is well known by scholars, and some have even called it "collectivism." As Currin V. Shields
pointed out—in the midst of 1950s McCarthyism, no less—a "venera-
ble American tradition of collectivism" sat alongside individualism in
American history.[42] Shields had in mind "empirical collectivism," which
does not *presume* action at the collective level as the appropriate scale
(as more left-leaning forms of collectivism did, as in the New Deal),
but that is open to group action when it makes practical, demonstrable
sense: "The empirical collectivist assumes the distinctive position that
collective action should be employed only when necessary to solve practical problems confronting the community. Holding that the community
should undertake collective action when a problem comes within the
purview of public concern, he likewise maintains that the *type* of collective action depends upon the specific character of the problem and
the conditions for its solution—in short, upon the actual situation itself"
(105). Indeed, although Shields does not say so, it is obvious that without
such a readiness for individuals to cooperate in collective action, it would
be impossible to take seriously Locke's or any other classical liberal's contract theory of the state, much less a republican theory of governance.
In fact, it is through empirical collectivism that the general interest is
discovered: the empirical collectivist holds that "public action taken to
dispose of a problem should redound to the benefit of the entire community. . . . [H]is primary concern is with the general interest, rather than
with any special interest within the community" (ibid.). Shields goes on
to say that empirical collectivism in America "developed . . . in direct
response to American frontier experiences" (107):

[F]rontier settlements became veritable laboratories for developing and
testing forms and techniques of collective community effort. The result

was that, during the period prior to industrialization and urbanization of American life, the impetus behind the development of a collectivist tradition in America came from the frontier experiences of small farmers, mechanics, and tradesmen who were colonizing this continent and converting it from a vast wilderness into a prosperous and populous nation. . . . To the frontiersman doctrinaire liberalism was either unknown or regarded, like other quaint European importations, as outlandish nonsense unbefitting a practical people. . . . For the American settler the notion that "natural" economic laws rule mankind in a fearsome grip could not but mark a shocking contradiction of his and his compatriot's experience. For sound reason he knew that "natural" men, by industry and courage, through collective as well as individual effort, could create a kind of world akin to the world they wanted. . . . [T]he empirical collectivist rejects alike the contentions of the laissez-faire liberals and of their socialist critics. (7–8)

Empirical collectivism had many champions in South Dakota and can best be observed in the wake of the election of progressive Republican Peter Norbeck as governor in 1916. When he took office in 1917, Norbeck urged the legislature to give consideration to a rural credit program, a state coal mine and cement plant, state hail insurance for farmers, and state stockyards and state-owned terminal grain elevators. The legislature moved forward on the credit program, the state coal mine and cement plant, and state hail insurance.[43] Regarding the credit program, Norbeck "argued that the State could use its credit to borrow money at cheaper interest rates than could an individual farmer and in turn loan it directly to farmers at an interest rate only enough higher to cover handling charges."[44] By 1922, almost $36 million had been lent to farmers to purchase land, pay down indebtedness on land, make improvements on farms, or purchase livestock or equipment.[45] The program was a bust financially—in part because it did not always collect or foreclose on farmers—but it was a hallmark of the willingness of South Dakota *republicans* (both Democrats and progressive Republicans) to act collectively.[46]

The South Dakota Farmers Union was a particularly strong advocate of cooperation (a much more palatable term to South Dakotans, no doubt, than collectivism) among farmers. Local chapters organized in the Rosebud country as early as 1914, and Edward H. Everson, a son of the Rosebud country who became president of both the state (1928–34) and national (1934–37) Farmers Union, as well as South Dakota secretary of agriculture, was a tireless spokesman for cooperation rather than individualism.[47] Everson was deeply philosophical but also espoused a hard-nosed analysis of the difficulties farmers were facing after World War I. He insisted in a 1931 radio broadcast—at the opening of the Great Depression with its drought and grasshopper infestation—on WNAX in Yankton that Christian love was the only source of "genuine happiness," and that "[w]hile love and co-operation are not synonymous terms, they are very closely allied, for love begets co-operation as hatred begets competition." This is the *moral* version—and vision—of empirical collectivism, which we need to think of as an "indigenous" program of responsibilization already in place when the New Deal reformers arrived not only to teach farmers how to move beyond individualism, but to install a new public, social morality that would fundamentally reform rural citizen subjects. Everson had in mind in his critique a particular kind of competition—between units of very different size, which is to say the domination of the market economy by "trusts and monopolies." The solution was the "combination of a number of the smaller and weaker units [that] may easily compete with the larger units."[48] Here was the rural version of scaling up—yes, rural people had their own version of scaling up—that the New Dealers proposed to implement in a very different form. In his president's column published in the same issue of the union organ, Everson asked, "will we continue as individualists and as competitors both as producers and in developing economic and bargaining power as those who exploit us want us to do? We are asking you members through your county unions to quit being competitive individualists and combine your economic bargaining power for the purpose of unloading the excess baggage placed upon you by other organized classes."[49]

The Farmers Union was not opposed to the free market or private property, which were presumed necessary for producers to exchange the goods they produced for sale, but it was opposed to what Everson called "capitalism" in which the market and the fair distribution of the fruits of labor were distorted by money power and the concentration of enterprise.[50] As the director of education for the South Dakota Farmers Union explained in 1931, "[i]f everyone exchanged with everyone else, there should be enough for all, everybody would have a job and business keep going. The trouble is that some have been taking too much."[51]

In a letter to the editor of the *South Dakota Union Farmer,* the president of the Tripp County Farmers Union laid out a general theory of the agricultural economy, one that was quite consistent with orthodox liberalism in its vision of a free and fair market as the natural state of things.[52] But it included a heavy dose of agrarian and Progressive Era critique of the "unnatural" distortions of the free market brought on by monopoly and trusts. In the beginning—in the United States at least—the farmer was an individualist who produced his own subsistence but traded his surplus goods on the market for currency with which to buy the necessities he could not produce himself. At that time, "the natural laws of supply and demand more or less ruled." Exchanges existed, but "[t]here were no . . . unnatural influences that could break the power of supply and demand":

> But as years rolled on these exchanges became a power within themselves and finally developed into trusts and monopolies in restraint of trade. . . . By and by these financial or money tyrants became better organized, co-operating with each other, thereby eliminating competition and were more able to control and force unnatural conditions for their own individual benefit and to the detriment of the rank and file of the commonality and this power has grown unknowingly to the common people. . . . These unnatural, inhuman elements of power have gradually usurped the people's power and every depression period is more prolonged and more serious than the one prior. . . . [T]hese powers with the aid of the almighty dollar have been able to dictate all laws and all governmental politics.[53]

What allowed this to happen, and what was the way out?

> Now during all these changes in organized efforts the poor ignorant farmers . . . have remained the same. The most independent, single individualist of this animal kingdom, and . . . today the average farmer gives little attention or thought to . . . his brother farmers or the pubic as a whole. . . . In fact, the farmer knows only one task master and that is his own single individual operations, regardless of the welfare of his fellowman. There is

only one element that the average farmer is willing to co-operate with and that is the Divine Power over us all and sometimes we are not in complete harmony with him, our Creator. So the average citizen being an individualist, battling for self and self alone gives all other . . . co-operative organizations of wealth full sway.

As "centralized wealth" has "eaten up (Devoured)" the "small fries," the "farmer has been . . . forced from a business back to just a mode of living . . . down to the standard of the average peasants of the old world under Kings and monarchs." Such is capitalism, as opposed to the free market: "We are not forced by laws of supply and demand; not by the laws of nature, but by the law of the almighty dollar, centralized, concentrated and organized to fleece the public of their just and rightful earnings from the sweat of the brow. . . . [W]e farmers have been deliberately robbed of our just heritage, our profits and prestige—that rightfully belongs to us."[54] The writer notes, ironically, that the sons of farmers were heeding the call to "Go east, my boy, go east," where unions had increased wages through collective action: "[I]f we farmers were as well organized as Union labor, there would never have been this condition. For we could then lock forces and march on to victory side by side with the other laborers of the nation."

Farmer cooperatives were one obvious solution to this dire situation. In 1922, Congress enacted the Capper–Volstead Act, which exempted farmer cooperatives from antitrust liability, and was referred to as "the Magna Carta of Cooperative Marketing." Congress passed the Grain Futures Act in the same year, prohibiting discrimination against co-ops by boards of trade or chambers of commerce (a common occurrence). The Division of Cooperative Marketing was established in the Bureau of Agricultural Economics of the USDA in 1926.[55] The South Dakota Farmers Union took up the cause. In 1924 it acquired a private insurance company in Burke, South Dakota (in the Rosebud country), renaming it the Farmers Union Mutual Insurance Company of South Dakota.[56] More important for farmers in the Rosebud country, the Nebraska Farmers Union established a livestock marketing cooperative at Omaha at the terminus of the Chicago and Northwestern line from the Rosebud country, in 1917.[57] The Nebraska Farmers Union also opened a cooperative at

Sioux City, Iowa, in 1918, which was heavily patronized by South Dakota farmers.[58] The South Dakota Farmers Union opened a livestock marketing cooperative at Sioux Falls in 1929.[59] In 1916, members of the Farmers Union in the Rosebud country purchased the Doane-Sears grain elevator in Winner to "handle all kinds of grain for shipment," and by 1931 it had established a creamery in Burke.[60] Yet the cooperative movement in the Rosebud country—and in South Dakota more generally—never approached the vision of those who advocated cooperative marketing as a solution to the atomism of farmer producers. And for those who were committed "co-operators," such as Edward H. Everson, farmers remained mired in individualism in ways that were harmful.

The legislature, under Norbeck's encouragement, also gave serious consideration to establishing state terminal elevators and stockyards.[61] Norbeck was succeeded by his lieutenant governor, William H. McMaster (also a progressive Republican), who in 1923 ordered the highway department to sell fuel to the public significantly below the price charged by the oil companies. The legislature formalized this authority in 1925.[62] Governor McMaster also allied himself with the Farm Bloc in Congress and supported the McNary–Haugen Bill of 1924, which sought to raise farm prices to parity with industrial prices by government purchase of the domestic surplus whenever it depressed prices below the specified parity price. The government might dispose of the surplus overseas or store it; any loss would be covered with an equalization fee charged to producers. Norbeck also supported this legislation from his position as a U.S. senator.[63]

With perhaps an even wider divergence from orthodox liberal practices, the Farmers Union (both the South Dakota branch and the national union) eventually came to advocate for federal price setting for farm products that would guarantee that farmers receive their "cost of production." President Everson of the South Dakota Farmers Union testified before the Senate Agriculture Committee in 1932 in favor of a cost of production bill.[64] More generally, Everson told his radio audience in 1933, "[w]e must see to it that there is a more equitable distribution of the earnings of society."[65] When the local district of the South Dakota Farmers Union held its meeting in White River in Mellette County in 1932, the members passed the following resolution: "Whereas, the inequitable distribution of new wealth [produced by farmers and workers] together with excessive taxation leads to confiscation and the downfall of nations and whereas, wealthy financial interests have usurped the power of the people through the enactment of legislation and special privileges, discriminating against the masses, therefore we demand repeal of such laws that have proven detrimental to the general welfare either by Congress and Legislature or by referring the same to the electors of our state."[66]

The point to glean from this description of South Dakota republicanism and the Farmers Union is that rural South Dakotans *had their own version of "the thinking farmer" and of moral and political responsibilization*. Given this, it comes as little surprise that farmers, ranchers, and businesspeople in western South Dakota tended to doubt the validity of the New Deal collectivist solutions (which must have seemed starkly *nonempirical* from their point of view) to their difficulties. Indeed, many of them were scandalized, as historian Paula Nelson describes:

> To the west river residents—most of whom were first or second generation settlers—the mark of success and development was increasing population; decreasing population signified regression into an earlier historical epoch, when vast stretches supported tiny numbers of Indians and ranchers. In contrast, many of the federal policies for the region contemplated the partial depopulation of the region, either directly (for example, the resettlement and grasslands programs) or indirectly (by conversion from tillage to ranching); for the federal policymakers and bureaucrats, population loss represented progress in adapting to the uses of the land and moving people into more productive areas. Thus, what the residents viewed as progress was considered irrational nostalgia by the planners, while the planners' vision was seen by the residents as a giant leap backward into the region's past.

No one doubts that some New Deal "benefits" were critical for families to survive the 1930s, but, as Nelson observes, they had "a deep-seated ambivalence about the benefits of federal assistance."[67]

Relief and AAA payments clearly saved the day for farm families that did not leave—along with their hard work and sacrifice, of course. As a farmer from Murdo, South Dakota, just north of Mellette County, wrote to Senator Norbeck in 1934, farmers had not been "enthusiastic over the

Triple A," but "[t]heir needs were so terrible that they grasped at a possible cash payment . . . as a drowning man would grasp at a rope."[68] The *Gregory Times-Advocate* editorialized in the summer of 1933: "[W]hile this paper has not been a very strong advocate of the present crop reduction law, it will have to be admitted that the seventy thousand dollars to be prorated among the wheat growers of this county will be more than helpful at this time."[69] But New Deal programs—especially the attempts to replace crop farming with ranching and return cropped land to grass, as well as the crop reduction program—were part of a fundamental attempt to *manage devaluation,* not to valorize farms or ranches for "the good of all concerned," which must have clearly seemed to leave out those who actually lived and produced in the Rosebud country. To their credit, the New Dealers were committed to intervening humanely in an otherwise catastrophic process of devaluation, which they recognized would entail loss of assets being passed on by corporations (banks and other corporate creditors, and agricultural processors) to farmers if nothing was done to prevent it. But from the standpoint of many South Dakotans, the danger was that the New Deal programs could, by so explicitly and pejoratively (it was felt) identifying agricultural "problem areas" or seeking to ban farming in certain zones and limiting the production on working farms, actually *hasten and exacerbate the devaluation of farms.* Even if bad (for South Dakota) publicity disseminated by the federal government had no role in the actual process of devaluation, it is important to bear in mind how desperate South Dakota farmers were. Figure 4.1 graphs the depreciation of the value of farms and buildings in the Rosebud country as a result of the drought and depression. Some of this devaluation was absorbed by insurance companies, banks, and land companies, and some by the South Dakota Rural Credit program, but most of it was absorbed by the farmers themselves. The crash is also reflected in the percentage of taxable farm land in tax delinquency in 1938. This both resulted in tax-delinquent land being seized and sold by counties for back taxes (which further devalued land), as well as extreme fiscal pressures on local governments, increasing their difficulties paying their obligations on the declining tax revenues they could raise. As a former National Resources Board consultant provided to the South Dakota State Planning Board wrote in 1936, the situation amounted to "overinstitutionalized"

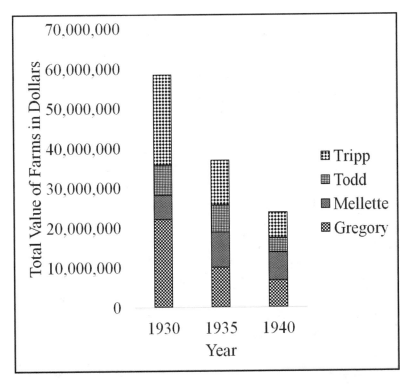

FIGURE 4.1. Loss of farm values (land and buildings). For Gregory County, 26.7 percent; Mellette County, 45.2 percent; Todd County, 33.6 percent; Tripp County, 33.6 percent. Data from U.S. Census, Agriculture.[72]

local government (too many county and township governments, too many school districts) having been established in "sub-marginal land areas."[70] Of course, from the point of view of most rural South Dakotans, this was all a crisis and a tragedy, but not something that would be helped by "going backwards." As historian John E. Miller succinctly describes it, rural South Dakotans saw the picture of overinstitutionalization painted by the New Dealers as "false, and . . . dangerous." The "fear [was] that such a negative portrayal would harm the state's image, discourage tourists and investors, and stimulate residents to flee."[71] All this threatened a vicious downward spiral.

T. E. Hayes of Perkins County (in the northwestern part of the state), a regular columnist for the *Dakota Farmer*, wrote in 1935 that he saw "things going in reverse" and blamed the agricultural experts. "Only a few years ago" (during the period of sod-busting liberalism), extension service agents in western South Dakota had insisted that the way forward

> was to break up most of the original prairie sod and make the land produce two or three times as much as it was doing in its natural state. The agent held and talked at many meetings, visited many farms—always telling how this land that was so rich could produce such a lot more if certain methods were followed. Farmers took the advice given. It often meant borrowing money to build fences, to buy machinery, to remodel buildings, to buy and seed certified seed, establish fields of alfalfa, and so on. Then, by following the advice given . . . farmers built for themselves homes, expecting to spend the rest of their lives on them, and leave them for their children. . . . Now, after doing all this, they tell us it is all wrong. This land is not capable of producing enough to pay expenses entailed; we cannot not raise enough on this sub-marginal land to pay for roads and schools necessary. Further, we are pursuing a type of agriculture for which this area is not adapted. . . . Right here is where the extension service and I part company. After that service, more than any other thing, has led us along this way of producing two blades of grass where one grew before, and through taking their advice, we have gone so far into this program that all our years of hard work, all our hard-earned resources, have been put into it, all our small towns established, our township roads built with our . . . money. They have the nerve to tell us it is all wrong; that this land should be let go back to prairie; that farmers should be removed from this western part of the state; and it should be parceled out in big ranches.

Hayes scoffed at the idea that the government would be able to remove people from the land just so "these wise birds can have their way." "America, or western South Dakota, is not Russia, or any of those countries under the feel of a dictator," and "if it rains this year they will need the army to move the bulk of the people out of this west river country—and then some. These people have not fought with blizzards, drouth and grasshoppers for more than a quarter of a century, and then be willing to get out because some fellows back east had a sort of fool brain wave."[73]

The resentment of the idea of "retiring" land from farming in South Dakota west of the Missouri River was made clear by an editorial from the *Arizona Daily Star* reprinted in the *Gregory Times-Advocate*:

> The refusal of the farmers of the drouth stricken region of western South Dakota to obey the federal . . . proposal for whole sale evacuation of this region is an encouraging sign of the times. In effect it is a reassertion of that spirit of independence and self-reliance which, during the past century, developed the United States of America. It is also a warning to those New York college professors led by Prof. Moley and Prof. Tugwell that the American people cannot be regimented into a planned economy and life of professional experimentation. Rather than give up their homes on the soil they have learned to love and submit to minute direction of their lives by the federal government these hardy farmers of western South Dakota would rather endure all the hardships to unprecedented drouth and by their own self-reliance eke out their living in hopes of better times ahead.[74]

The issue heated up after the National Resources Board released its first report in December 1934. The report included a national map depicting most of South Dakota as consisting of "areas in which it appears desirable to encourage permanent retirement of a substantial part of the arable farming and develop constructive use of the land not to be in farms"[75] (see Figure 4.2). The intent of the classification, according to a representative of the National Resources Board, was not to argue for "taking South Dakota out of production, but changing production to more gainful uses" (such as grazing and hay production, rather than cash-crop production), but it was admitted that "some people should be removed from that territory" to make agriculture more productive for those who remained.[76] Commentary in the Pierre *Capital Journal* was reprinted in the *Gregory Times-Advocate*:

> The government planning boards are certainly suggesting a wrecking of this state, so far as its prospective development is concerned from an area standpoint. . . . [The National Resources Board] suggests a consolidation of our state education institutions, abandonment of highways except a few

cross country roads for the benefit of tourists from the Great Lakes to the Rockies and as a natural sequence undoubtedly discontinue some of the existing railroad lines. This is simply ridiculous. . . . If this program is carried out, it will undoubtedly be necessary to consolidate a whole lot of counties into [very large counties]. It will probably be necessary to consolidate some of the county officers. It would reasonably reduce our legislature to a one body organization. It would cut out at least two thirds of the newspapers of the state, and when the program is finally finished farms that have produced as much as 16,000 bushels of wheat by a single family endeavor, would become prehistoric dots on the map of the nation that might properly be referred to as the inland island of adventure of a lot of hopeful and aspiring people, who a generation ago secured for the state the reputation of being the wealthiest per capita in the nation.[77]

In other words, the federal "adjustment" programs—adjusting "down" or "back"—were far from simply insulting, but threatened to undo the growth and undermine the regional growth coalitions we examined in chapter 1—at least from the point of view of those who had built the farms and towns, had helped to feed the country, and had added value to the state and to their own farms, businesses, and towns.

In 1936, the Resettlement Administration, headed by Rexford Tugwell, released a documentary written and directed by filmmaker Pare Lorentz, *The Plow That Broke the Plains.*[78] A lyrical script with a clear moral is read by the narrator: a land "without rivers, without streams . . . A country of high winds, and sun . . . and of little rain":

By 1880 we had cleared the Indian, and with him the buffalo, from the Great Plains, and established the last frontier . . . Half a million square miles of natural range . . .

First came the cattle. . . . For a decade the world discovered the grass lands and poured cattle into the plains.

[Then,] the railroad brought the world into the plains . . . new populations, new needs crowded the last frontier. Once again the plowman followed the herder and the pioneer came to the plains.

"Wheat will win the war!" . . . "Plant the cattle ranges." . . . Then we reaped the golden harvest . . . we really plowed the plains.

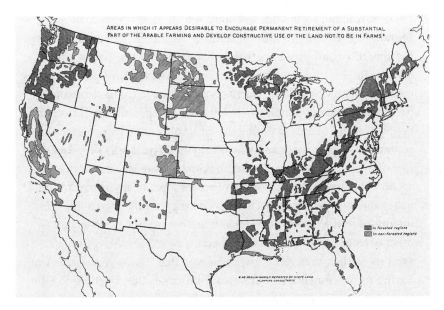

FIGURE 4.2. Farming areas prescribed for retirement, 1934. National Resources Board, *A Report on National Planning and Public Works in Relations to Native Resources* (Washington, D.C.: U.S. Government Printing Office, 1934), 16.

By 1933 the old grass lands had become the new wheat lands . . . a hundred million acres . . . two hundred million acres. More wheat! . . . A country without rivers . . . without streams . . . with little rain. Once again the rains held off and the sun baked the earth. This time no grass held moisture against the winds and sun . . . this time millions of acres of plowed land lay open to the sun. . . . Baked out—blown out—and broke. Year in, year out, uncomplaining they fought the worst drought in history. . . . Last year in every summer month 50,000 people left the Great Plains and hit the highways for the Pacific Coast, the last border. Blown out—baked out—broke . . . nothing to stay for . . . nothing to hope for . . . homeless, penniless and bewildered they joined the great army of the highways.[79]

The Plow That Broke the Plains was screened at a meeting of the Winner Rotary Club in 1940, and was probably also shown in other venues in the Rosebud country.[80]

Local reaction to the documentary was clear. Congressman Karl E. Mundt, Republican of Madison, read a speech in Congress excoriating the film. He began by insisting that the issue was one of "self-preservation," because the effect of the film was "to bring distress to my section of the country." "By trying to keep tourists from visiting it, trying to discourage people from the surrounding country buying [especially land] from the people within this area, pointing the finger of condemnation, scorn and contempt at a group of people whose activities have largely kept America from complete economic collapse, the Government is handicapping this section."[81] Although Mundt was to become a politically successful red-baiter and must have known that he was exaggerating by attributing evil intentions to the federal government, there was unquestionably an element of truth here—that federal programs risked devaluing local assets even more than they already were depreciated.[82] Mundt succeeded in having the documentary withdrawn from circulation by the U.S. Film Service.[83] The *Gregory Times-Advocate,* among other papers (especially Republican ones), "greatly appreciate[d] . . . Congressman Mundt . . . for the work he has done to stop the showing of the picture. . . . The picture was . . . for the purpose of making it appear that South Dakota and a large part of the entire Northwest was but a dust driven desolate place, in order to bolster up the [submarginal] land buying program and other new deal theories made up by a few chair warmers in Washington."[84]

South Dakota even tried to reinvigorate the old standby of the regional growth coalition—boosterism—in the face of the politics of devaluation launched by the New Dealers. In 1936, the state Rural Credit Board, holding properties defaulted on by farmers who could not make the loan payments or who had abandoned their farms, released a piece of promotional literature titled *The True Story of "The Plow That Broke the Plains" in South Dakota.* "We readily admit," the brochure began, "that we have suffered great hardships, not only from weather conditions and grass-hopper infestations, but from war boom indebtedness, depressed grain and livestock prices and reciprocal trade treaties that do not reciprocate for agriculture." But "these conditions are not normal and . . . they are not the true pictures of the South Dakota we know and love." Federal and state statistics actually "belie the reports that have blackened the name of Western agriculture." In fact, "South Dakota's farmers' average income far exceeds that of the average American farmers." "Corn is king," the brochure boasted, recuperating the familiar boosterism from the early twentieth century, and "[t]here is no county in the state where corn will not grow." It included a photograph of wheat in Tripp County, where "[i]t is not uncommon to raise twenty bushels of wheat to the acre," and "in many cases, the net profit from one crop will pay for the land at current values."[85]

It is true that there was *some* overlap between the perspectives of some of the New Deal reformers and some South Dakotans about the causes of the Depression, and the problems faced by farmers specifically. There was agreement, for example that the tariff had harmed farmers. Manufacturers, because of their political influence, had secured protections against cheaper foreign manufactures and were able to maintain artificially elevated prices that farmers had to pay if they wanted tractors, plows, and household goods. On the other hand, because there was a surplus of farm products relative to domestic demand, the agricultural tariffs in place did not help American farmers. This position of the farmer between a rock and a hard place was well known by agricultural experts, agrarian editors, and farm leaders since the postwar agricultural depression of 1921. It was also a central concern of the New Deal, which the Agricultural Adjustment Act was meant to correct by reducing production to the level of effective domestic demand, thereby raising agricultural prices on the market and paying farmers cash benefits that would raise their income to a level closer to what they had received prior to the postwar deflation. There were also those in the government who agreed with rural South Dakotans that the commodities markets, particularly in grains, could be and had been manipulated by traders to corner the market, and many also agreed that "middlemen"—the grain mills and bread distributors, for example—were reaping the lion's share of the prices paid for food by consumers, squeezing out the farmer's chance to receive higher prices.

Beyond that, however, most editors, farm leaders, and farmers in South Dakota parted company with the New Deal programs. The New Dealers' emphasis on the problem of "the farm surplus" and production control as the solution was deeply counterintuitive for most South Dakotans. John Simpson (Iowa), president of the National Farmers Union, surely spoke for most South Dakotans when he said in 1934 that "what we have overproduction of is empty stomachs and bare backs."[86] If people were hungry and in poverty in the cities, could anyone in their right mind speak of "overproduction" of staples? Edward H. Everson said in a radio address in 1931 (before the New Deal, but when the Hoover administration was already trying to dispose of the domestic surplus) that the farm problem is "a problem of loss of buying power and underconsumption more than of surplus."[87] It was the unemployment of workers in cities, not overproduction, that explained why farmers could not sell enough even to meet their expenses. The president of the Tripp County Farmers Union was more explicit and more blunt about the glaring contradiction of the Depression: "the United States soon after the greatest era of prosperity known in history, today has six million of unemployed workers, men that want work, men that will work if opportunity presents itself. There is today hunger and malnutrition threatening and in the face of the greatest era of [potential] production known to mankind, surpluses galore and money that is [available] for investments and no takers that can offer assurance of security. Will Rogers was right when he said that he had never before heard of the monkeys starving, when the ground was literally covered with cocoanuts."[88] The Farmers Union was opposed to the production-control logic of the AAA and called for price guarantees that would secure repayment "cost of production" for farmers.

Not surprisingly, the AAA came in for creative derision. In January 1934 the *South Dakota Union Farmer* reprinted a letter to the *Chicago Tribune* from an Illinois farmer mocking production control: "I am a farmer living near Naperville, Ill., and I am writing for information. I have two old cats which I think will soon have kittens, and I would like to know what to do. I don't know just what code cats fall under. Should I write to Mr. Wallace, Gen. Johnson [in charge of the National Recovery Administration], or to Prof. Tugwell himself? No doubt there are too many cats now. Can I get some government benefit by eliminating them, or should cats be stimulated? Please let me know as soon as possible as the kittens may appear any day."[89] But, of course, it was ultimately no laughing matter, and the depth of the resentment is obvious in the appeal to the divine by some. Commentator T. E. Hayes (from Perkins County in the northwestern part of the state) was clearly scandalized by the idea of production control, land retirement, and returning cropland to grassland. He wrote in the *Dakota Farmer* in 1934 that

> [t]he majority of our farmers have the idea firmly fixed in their minds that the [drought] is retribution. It is generally conceded that the Creator sent us a good supply of food and the material for making clothes to wear; that we, as a nation, were especially favored in this respect. Then, to put the thing in bald language, the people elected or appointed to power decided to control the bounties of Nature and God—to which the Creator replied, "If you don't want these things and are destroying, and trying to control the output, put a limit on God and Nature, saying you must only give us so much then, the earth shall not yield her increase, you must be shown how puny and small man is when he tries to gamble with nature and God."[90]

Most South Dakota commentators on the New Deal were more secular and more political, if no less ideological. A December 1934 Sioux Falls *Argus Leader* editorial argued that the New Dealers were going overboard in suggesting that erosion be tackled with "planning boards and appropriations to take action. The idea that such erosion might be an individual problem to be handled by each land owner in accordance with his desires seems to be out of the picture." "If he feels that the erosion is sufficient to warrant correction," the paper reasoned, the owner "can take steps to do so, improving his own property at his own expense. This would be in accordance with the American system." "The government," the paper worried, "is trying at every turn to do things for the people that they should do if they so desire for themselves."[91]

It is noteworthy that a full decade before F. A. Hayek was to argue that planning and social government were, in fact, "socialism," not to mention "the road to serfdom," many of South Dakota's agrarian intellectuals were explicitly identifying the New Deal as a move toward totalitarianism, if not totalitarianism itself.[92] For many, there was little difference between left and right forms of tyranny. In the same editorial in which he invoked God and Nature, T. E. Hayes asserted that, "In our own America, we have the 'Brain Trust,' who now control our finance, our industry through the NRA [National Recovery Act], our agriculture through the AAA, with Secretary Wallace asking for power to absolutely control the farmer and all his doings. We are supposed to be a free and independent people. Do we really want Fascism, Nazism, Soviet, or the Brain Trust?"[93] The editor of the *Gregory Times-Advocate* pointed out in a 1934 opinion piece "[t]hat a person may conduct his private or business affairs as he chooses is one of the underlying principles of the federal constitution," and he cited the "'rugged individualism' that developed the natural resources of the nation and made these United States the most progressive nation of the world." Yet Roosevelt, he complained, had chosen "as his advisors a group of college professors, who for the most part are socialistic in behavior or what has been termed 'parlor reds.' . . . Individualism seems to have been discarded and in its stead has come group action under government supervision."[94] By July 1934, the editor insisted that "Tugwell has been classed by any truly patriotic American as being Public Enemy No. 1 as concerning American institutions which guarantee to us liberties we now enjoy. . . . Tugwell is hungry for power to carry out his socialist and communist schemes."[95] The paper called the Grass Mountain Colony (discussed in chapter 3) a "socialistic community planned for Indians."[96]

It seems reasonable to assume that painting the New Deal as socialist, communist, fascist, or Nazi probably went beyond the terms that most South Dakotans would have used. Most probably assumed that the government, and even the brains trust, were trying to help farmers and not simply build their own despotic regimes, however misguided the attempt. At the same time, most South Dakotans seem to have been uneasy with the degree of collective or centralized planning, or planning by paid experts, that went into the New Deal programs, and no doubt saw this as an assault on their property rights and individual freedom that might or might not be justified by the material benefits they received. On the other hand, it is worth recognizing that the outraged vilification of the New Deal—especially, for example, Tugwell and the brains trust—may have pointed to something deeper. As I suggested in chapters 2 and 3, the rationalities or "content" of specific regimes of governmentality—civilizing Indians, modernizing farmers, managing the supply of agricultural products, minimizing soil erosion—have *some* arguable relation to real processes and real problems confronted by people intent on improving things. But they are not only to be understood, or not best understood, as ultimately "rational" systems that exist because they were empirically effective or somehow empirically suited to the problems at hand. This is a major Foucauldian intervention into studying the history of governing. We need to approach regimes of governmentality without presuming that they *ever* represent progress, no matter how good they are at selling themselves in terms of progress. To study a *regime of governmentality* is different than to study the outcome or validity of a "policy." Policy study generally entails analysis of the effectiveness and validity of the policy (in its *own* terms). A regime of governmentality—as a critical concept, and as used in this book—can only be described in terms of its emergence ("birth") and functioning, both of which are saturated with intellectual arbitrariness (in the anthropological sense of "the arbitrary"), historical accident, and micro-, even petty, power. The point is not to examine the regime in its own terms, but to ask how those terms appeared, and how they shape what appears valid and not within a self-referential field of discourse and practice. The New Dealers, especially the brains trust and more local reform intellectuals in the Agricultural Adjustment Administration, the SCS, the extension service, and planning boards, surely meant to do "good" and to be effective. But they also, in the process, expanded their fields of professional vision and power (the vision of "problems" to be corrected, and the power to define both problems and solutions and to call upon others to follow their official lead) along lines that became open to them essentially by historical accident. As I argued earlier, governing needs to be seen not as a form of human mastery (especially not as a progressive, improving human mastery), but as the outcome of practices of governing flowing, morphing, seeping into new niches that governing itself creates. As we saw Paul Rabinow observe in chapter 2, "[t]he end of good government is the correct disposition of things—even when these things have to be *invented* so as to be well governed."[97]

In this light, the scandalized views of some of the South Dakota commentators on the New Deal might easily take on a significance beyond what might sound to modern ears like a straightforward, well-worn, well-known, red-baiting, "red state" ideology. As I write this in the summer of 2016 during the campaigns for presidential nominations, it is indeed tempting to see the outraged South Dakota writers who excoriated the New Deal and its intellectuals in the 1930s as merely the origin of the present—red state/blue state, or Christian right/left-liberal—political topography. But that would be a serious historical error. Rather than seeing the critics' comments as "merely ideological," we need to take seriously the advice of anthropologist Lila Abu-Lughod, who urges us to see resistance as a "*diagnostic* of power." "[W]here there is resistance, there is power," and we should follow the lines of resistance carefully to uncover forms of power that are not easily recognized for what they are, and that even the resisters may be unable to explicitly articulate.[98] Abu-Lughod has in mind, specifically, forms of power Foucault called *subjection,* and that is the apt concept to apply here. In "The Subject and Power," Foucault identifies three forms of struggle: "against forms of *domination* (ethnic, social, and religious); against forms of *exploitation* which separate individuals from what they produce [class struggle]; [and] against that which ties the individual to himself and submits him to others in this way (struggles against *subjection,* against forms of subjectivity and submission)."[99] Subjection is a

> form of power [that] applies itself to immediate everyday life which categorizes the individual, marks him by his own individuality, attaches him to his own identity, imposes a law of trust on him which he must recognize and which others have to recognize in him. It is a form of power which makes individuals subjects. There are two meanings of the word *subject.* Subject to someone else by control and dependence, and tied to his own identity by a conscience or self-knowledge. Both meanings suggest a form of power which subjugates and makes subject to.[100]

Following the approach of Abu-Lughod and Foucault, what was the target of those South Dakotans—and many others across the United States in the 1930s—who spoke of the New Dealers as communists, fascists, or Nazis, or even just arrogant professors who wanted to experiment on people? I would suggest that it was not only the threat of loss of what they saw as their property rights and the rights to what they produced, or the loss of the value of their farms (although all this was real enough). It was also the threat of a revolutionized map of the world—how the world is put together at an ontological level in terms of everyday knowledge and expectations about property, labor, value, and community, and, of course, the place of the self in that world. To insist on collective action as a necessary *replacement* for supposedly outmoded individual action, for example, was a profound reconfiguration, or an attempt to reconfigure, the elementary touchstones of rural life from the standpoint of the individual. While farm families in South Dakota were familiar enough with "cooperation" and even government intervention into the economy, the idea that collectivism should *supplant* what locals saw as republican individuality or private property, or that individualism and private property were the *source* of all their problems, was an attempt to force, in ways that must have seemed arbitrary and authoritarian, a radical revision at the level of thought and feeling. The level at issue is what the cultural studies thinker Raymond Williams called "practical consciousness," or what anthropologist Anthony F. C. Wallace called the "mazeway."[101] This is the level at which *subjection* operates, here through a power-laden, if well-meaning, process to create *New Deal subjects,* who would change, in conformity with the party line, how they would fit into the world, know themselves, and be known by others (including, but not limited to, the government) as responsible and moral individuals. The New Deal was meant by its most articulate and thoughtful advocates to be not just a correction of the disposition of *things,* but a reordering of the individual into a new kind of actor with a fundamentally different ethical and political orientation, and a radically new understanding of problems, where they came from, and how to solve them. Is it any wonder that rural people might see the family resemblance between the "New Deal farmer," on the one hand, and the "New Soviet Man" (and Woman) or "Good Nazi"?

What's the matter with South Dakota?[102] Why did South Dakotans resist federal programs that were meant to help them and other people like them? The answer is not to be found in generalizations about "conservatism" or "red states," and my argument here has assumed that rural South Dakotans were no less rational than the New Deal reformers who sincerely meant to help them. The fact that so many South Dakotans deeply resented anything that they perceived as derisive of the state is easily understandable, and was—yes—quite rational, as we have seen. There were other explanations for, and solutions to, their agricultural problems that even many of the reformers agreed with but were not in a position to act on, or chose for reasons of political expediency not to. The fact that South Dakotans saw the ultimate obfuscation in the dominant New Deal presumption of an agricultural "surplus"—while Americans were literally going hungry—suggests that they perceived things in some ways *more clearly* (one is tempted to say more radically) than the New Deal reformers did. Rural South Dakota people would no doubt have called this clarity *more Christian*. Federally guaranteed cost-of-production prices for farmers was not an outlandish idea—at least no more so than production control—and could have been paired with expanded food subsidies, or expanded employment, for the hungry.

South Dakotans' inherent resentment of the gaze of devaluation emanating from Washington and other powerful places and actors turns out to have been not only rational but prescient regarding other risks to the state. For it was the devaluation of South Dakota and its population that allowed the Cold War national security complex to contemplate making the state a sacrifice zone, as we will see in the next chapter.

5

Planning Who Shall Die
So Others May Live

Biopower and Cold War National Security

In 1990 I attended a tribal council meeting on Rosebud Reservation at which an elected representative from the Antelope Community rose to complain about media reports on "the buffalo commons." This controversial (in the rural West) idea had made it into the national news because of an article published by Rutgers University planning scholars Frank J. Popper and Deborah Epstein Popper in the *Washington Post*. They argued that, "During the next generation, as a result of the largest, longest-running agricultural and environmental miscalculation in the nation's history, much of the Plains will become almost totally depopulated. The federal government should begin planning to convert vast stretches of the region to a use so old it predates the American presence—a 'Buffalo Commons' of native grass and livestock. . . . It is not uncommon to drive 40 miles to a school or movie, a hundred to a clothing store or dentist." "[D]esertion of huge areas of the Plains is inevitable," and the proper role for government would be to buy out the those still there and "tear down the fences, replant the shortgrass and restock the animals, including many bison—creating what we would call the Buffalo Commons."[1] Like many other people living in the shortgrass Plains, the tribal council representative from Antelope was scandalized that his community was so defamed in this scheme—its history described as a great miscalculation, its way of life described as a failure, and its coming disappearance inevitable. Even though the Poppers surely assumed the miscalculation at issue was that of the white settlers, not that of Lakota people on the reservation, this Lakota man sensed the parallel between the "buffalo common's" denial of civilization on the Plains and the long history of describing Indians and Indian country as uncivilized.[2]

The Poppers' buffalo-commons idea was hardly the first time attempts were made at the rhetorical or economic devaluation of rural South Dakota, especially West River (west of the Missouri River). A major part of the New Deal practice in the state was finding ways to get local farmers to cut their losses (with federal assistance, in theory) on "uneconomic units" in supposedly "overdeveloped" areas. Beginning in 1934, the Department of Agriculture began acquisition of uneconomic farms or ranches in Pennington, Jackson, Custer, and Fall River counties in order to assemble land in federal ownership in the Badlands–Fall River Land Utilization Project (see Figure 5.1), which eventually became the present Buffalo Gap National Grassland. The idea was to buy out crop farmers and small ranchers, raze the surplus homes and refence for properly sized range units, install rationally distributed water facilities for cattle, and replace the surplus population with a much-reduced number of viable ranchers. More than one thousand families were targeted to be moved out of the project area, and the "adjustment" also entailed the elimination of roads, the closing of twenty-five schools, and the disbandment of organized townships.[3] While some farmers and ranchers who were barely making ends meet or were "underwater" (as we have come to call the condition in the wake of the Great Recession of 2008) may have welcomed the opportunity to sell out (even if they were not all pleased with the price offered by the government), many South Dakotans in and out of the area deeply resented the whole idea of "retiring" land from farming, as well as the idea that homesteading had made the area "greatly overdeveloped."[4] The New Dealers spoke in such terms as the "promiscuous organization" of school districts and township government (not to mention county government) in territory that could not support the population. Not surprisingly, "the attitude of residents of the area toward their township and their local school district . . . makes them reluctant to give up the local units with which they are familiar."[5]

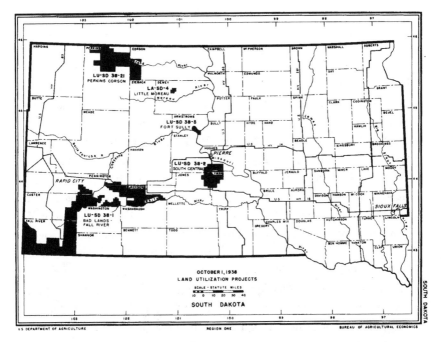

FIGURE 5.1. South Dakota land utilization projects, 1938. The sprawling Bad Lands–Fall River project (including lands in four counties) is in the southwest corner of the state. *The Land Utilization Program, 1934 to 1974: Origin, Development, and Present Status,* Agricultural Economic Report no. 85, Economic Research Service, U.S. Department of Agriculture.

While the New Dealers insisted that these adjustments would actually raise the standard of living for those who remained, locals saw clearly that the entire project was one of systematic devaluation, both in terms of the going price of farmers' and ranchers' assets and in terms of the "rationality" of the development they had brought to the short-grass Plains.

During the Cold War, however, a use other than just ranching—or a buffalo commons—was found for the area. While intercontinental ballistic missiles (ICBMs) were being developed in the 1950s,[6] the Joint Chiefs of Staff (JCS) in the Defense Department took up the question of the siting of ICBM emplacements, and asked the Weapons Systems Evaluation Group (WSEG) to work on the problem: "These weapons must be sited to give them maximum security and effectiveness. On the other hand, since these bases may be prime targets for enemy strikes, it becomes important to consider whether moving such bases to *areas of scarce population* in or outside the Continental United States would *reduce the hazard to our population and institutions.*[7] The WSEG determined that "all ICBM locations considered outside the Continental United States are excessively vulnerable to prelaunch attacks by aircraft and sea-launched missiles," and that "[w]ithin the United States, the north-central region, in and around North Dakota, is nearly optimal, and adjacent areas are not far from optimal."[8] By 1958, it was decided that the Minuteman missile would be sited in "dispersed and hardened launch facilities" so as to "insure that not more than one launcher/missile will be disabled by a 5 MT [megaton] detonation."[9] By 1959, it was decided that "proposed ICBM sites will be critically reviewed to determine that potential danger to civilian population has been minimized as far as practicable without unacceptable operational penalties." Missiles would not be sited closer than fifteen miles to cities of twenty-five thousand or more. In practice, this meant placing missiles west of a line running along the border between the Dakotas and Minnesota, south to the Gulf of Mexico. Malmstrom Air Force Base in Montana was the first base selected to receive the Minuteman, in 1959, and Ellsworth Air Force Base near Rapid City, South Dakota, was selected in 1960.[10] Figure 5.2 shows the Minuteman silos and launch control facilities installed in South Dakota.

At the same time that the Minuteman missiles were going into the silos in South Dakota, President Kennedy and Secretary of Defense Robert McNamara were working on plans for the possibility of fighting a *limited* nuclear war, whereby "population centers" would be avoided as targets by both the United States and the USSR, and it would be "counterforce" targets (such as missile silos) that would be prioritized by both countries in an initial nuclear exchange. The strategy was simple, almost commonsensical. As described to a House subcommittee in 1960 by Air Force Vice Chief of Staff General Curtis LeMay, the idea was that the missile sites in "the less densely populated part of the United States" would "draw some of the enemy ICBMs or submarine-launched missiles away from our population centers which would otherwise be their targets. They will also divert a portion of the total attack away from the more densely populated area of the United States."[11] As Gretchen Heefner puts

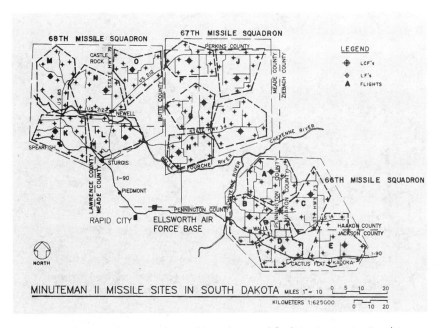

FIGURE 5.2. Minuteman silos and launch control facilities in western South Dakota. Library of Congress, Prints and Photographs, HAER SD-50.

it in her careful and insightful history of the Minuteman missile on the Great Plains, *The Missile Next Door,* from the standpoint of people living in the less densely populated places "the missiles would actually mark rural communities with giant red bull's-eyes as the enemy's prime target."[12] Indeed, late in the game of nuclear war planning, a 1990 map produced by the Federal Emergency Management Agency (FEMA) clearly depicts what would happen to the less densely populated part of South Dakota (Figure 5.3). General LeMay had estimated in 1960 that a Soviet attack on American ICBMs would require ten to thirty warheads to stand any chance of destroying any single silo, because they were optimally spaced so that a single warhead could not significantly damage more than one silo, and the silos themselves would eventually be hardened (with steel-reinforced concrete, including blast doors over the silos to be opened just before launch with explosive charges). The deterrence theory was to make a successful Soviet attack on American missiles so "costly" (in terms of Soviet missiles and warheads) that they would not

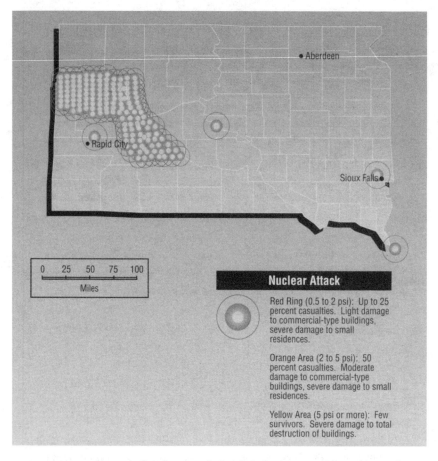

FIGURE 5.3. Hazard of nuclear attack, South Dakota, 1990. *Risks and Hazards: A State-by-State Guide*, FEMA-196 (Washington, D.C.: Federal Emergency Management Agency, 1990).

attempt such an attack. Of course, LeMay admitted, deterrence could fail, and then all bets would be off. But the odds were that it would be the American silos (and the surrounding countryside), not American cities, that would absorb the first enemy blow.[13]

How did South Dakotans in the area respond to all this? Perhaps surprisingly, without apparent fear of being a primary Soviet target or of enemy attack, and with concern only for the price to be paid for the land to be taken for the silos and the inconveniences anticipated. An illustrative example will help make the point. In 1961, a farmer from Viewfield, South Dakota, northeast of Ellsworth Air Force Base, wrote to Senator Francis Case (Republican of South Dakota) about the government's "plan for a Minuteman Missile Site in the center of my farm land." The silo itself would amount to only two to five acres, but his concern was the right of entry that "takes in most of my farm land . . . and takes half of my only pasture. The half of the pasture they want is in the very middle of [my existing pasture]." "They want me to give them the right of entry but we don't feel that this is fair, considering the way it cuts my farm up." He suggested that the purchase could be replaced with a land lease, which would not prevent him from using the land, but more generally, he raised the matter of the placement of the silo on his land, and the whole government process of acquiring silos sites: "There are some places that the site isn't going to do any or very little damage to, others will be improved because of it [by, for example, the construction or improvement of rural roads] and others will be almost completely ruined by it. We have a large family and need all of our farm land badly or a good compensation in place of it." He enclosed a map of his farm and the planned silo (see Figure 5.4). This man did not appear to be concerned at all about any *danger* associated with the missile in the middle of his land.[14]

This chapter will examine the biopolitical rationality by which the president, secretary of defense and other administration personnel, the Joint Chiefs of Staff, the air force, the Strategic Air Command (SAC), and defense intellectuals at the RAND Corporation and elsewhere developed plans to sacrifice western South Dakota (and other rural places) in order to protect U.S. cities in the event of a nuclear war.[15] How did this thinking acquire its "rationality," its quality of seeming to be the only course of action open to those who were responsible for national security? And how was it that in the politics that accompanied the emplacement of Minuteman missiles in South Dakota, the matter of the planned thermonuclear vaporization of a large part of the state remained unstated and perhaps not fully comprehended or faced?

The Birth of the Cold War Regime of Nuclear Strategy

How did the political and strategic touchstones of Cold War thinking about, and plans for, nuclear weapons become not just thinkable but

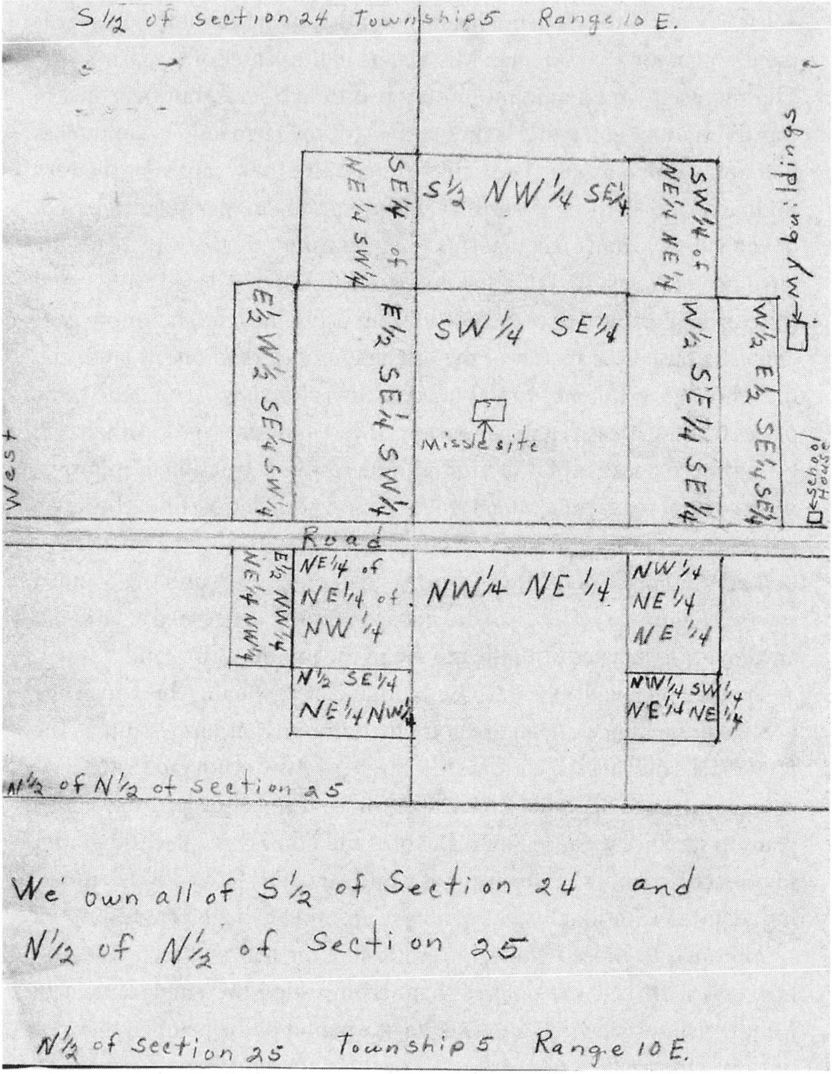

S ½ of section 24 Township 5 Range 10 E.

SE¼ NE¼ SW¼

S½ NW¼ SE¼

SW¼ of NE¼ NE¼

/w/ buildings

E½ W½ SE¼ SW¼

E½ SE¼ SW¼

SW¼ SE¼

Missile site

W½ SE¼ SE¼

w½ E½ SE¼ SE¼

West

Road

E½ NE¼ NW¼

NE¼ of NE¼ of NW¼

NW¼ NE¼

NW¼ NE¼

school House

N½ SE¼
NE¼ NW¼

NW¼ SW¼
NE¼ NE¼

N½ of N½ of section 25

We own all of S½ of Section 24 and
N½ of N½ of Section 25

N½ of section 25 Township 5 Range 10 E.

FIGURE 5.4. Farmer's map of silo in his pasture, 1961. Minuteman Unit, Ellsworth Air Force Base File, Case File 34, Drawer 136 (Old Drawer 140), Box 1, Senator Francis H. Case Collection, Archives, McGovern Library. Mitchell, South Dakota: Dakota Wesleyan University.

seemingly necessary? Assuming, in conformity with the methodological presumptions of this book, that Cold War thinking was not "inevitable," what historical conditions—or historical contingencies—gave birth to the Cold War and the technical strategies for using nuclear weapons? Two historical conditions of possibility made the early Cold War (generally, during the 1950s) nuclear weapons doctrine both thinkable and compelling. One was the emergence of a widely disseminated Manichaean worldview of "democracy" or "the free world" versus communism, in which the Soviet Union was the essential "antithesis" of Western democracy and its inescapable mortal enemy. The other was the related assumption that the Soviets would target American cities with their nuclear weapons. Together, these premises set the stage for the (nuclear) militarization of "society" in which it was understood that civilians were on the front line of an impending war of annihilation with communism. We turn first to the Manichaean worldview of democracy and communism.

While American anticommunism appeared before that the Cold War— from the first "red scare" after the Bolshevik Revolution in 1917—the Cold War witnessed the dissemination within and beyond national security circles of a compelling narrative of the dangers of communism.[16] The immediate origins of Cold War alarm over communism—quite distinct from that over communist possession of the bomb—are often traced to George Kennan's 1947 article in *Foreign Affairs*, written under the pseudonym Mr. X. The article was a revision of the "long telegram" Kennan had sent to Truman's secretary of state, James Byrnes, in 1946, while Kennan was stationed at the U.S. embassy in Moscow.[17] Kennan was concerned about the "absolutism" both within Soviet society and in its international relations, a position based on its deep "skepticism as to the possibilities of permanent and peaceful coexistence of rival forces."[18] Capitalism represented "hostile and incorrigible forces," a "menace confronting Soviet society from the world outside," both in Marxist-Leninist theory and in the self-interested ideological justifications of Soviet despots in "explaining away the maintenance of dictatorial authority at home."[19] There was no getting beyond the Soviet conviction of "the innate antagonism between capitalism and Socialism."[20] Kennan concluded, famously, that the only course of action for the United States was "a policy of containment, designed to confront the Russians with unalterable counter-force at every point where they show signs of encroaching upon the interests of a peaceful and stable world."[21]

By 1950—and in the wake of the Berlin blockade (June 1948–May 1949), the first successful Soviet nuclear test (August 1949), and increasing tensions in Korea—a fundamentally new synthesis on the communist threat crystallized (in secret, at least) in the National Security Council's "NSC-68," a document that historian Walter LaFeber has called "the American blueprint for waging the Cold War."[22] Although the document itself did not see the light of day at the time, except among those charged with managing national security, it is significant both because it represents the thinking of at least some influential thinkers in the defense establishment and because many of its presumptions and ideas did become widely disseminated in American society. Written primarily by Paul Nitze (who had served on the U.S. Strategic Bombing Survey during the war), NSC-68 was a coherent policy statement on the Soviet threat and how to meet it.[23] NSC-68 sounded the alarm for recognizing the emergency of the communist threat to free societies: "[T]he Soviet Union, unlike previous aspirants to hegemony, is animated by a new fanatic faith, antithetical to our own, and seeks to impose its absolute authority over the rest of the world," creating a profound danger in which "this Republic and its citizens . . . stand in their deepest peril." At stake was "the fulfillment or destruction not only of this Republic but of civilization itself. . . . With conscience and resolution this government and the people it represents must now take new and fateful decisions."[24]

Quoting from the Constitution and the Declaration of Independence, NSC-68 laid out the core ideological binary of the Cold War. The "fundamental purpose" of the United States was "to assure the integrity and vitality of our free society, which is founded upon the dignity and worth of the individual." Against this,

the fundamental design of those who control the Soviet Union and the international communist movement is to retain and solidify their absolute power, first in the Soviet Union and second in the areas now under their control. . . . The design . . . calls for the complete subversion or forcible destruction of the machinery of government and structure of society in the countries of the non-Soviet world. . . . The United States, as the principal center of power in the non-Soviet world and the bulwark of opposition to Soviet expansion, is the principal enemy whose integrity and vitality must be subverted or destroyed by one means or another if the Kremlin is to achieve its fundamental design. . . . Thus, unwillingly our free society finds itself mortally challenged by the Soviet system. No other value system is so wholly irreconcilable with ours, so implacable in its purpose to destroy ours, . . . no other so skillfully and powerfully evokes the elements of irrationality in human nature everywhere, and no other has the support of a great and growing center of military power.

Communism simply "cannot . . . tolerate the existence of free societies," and "there is no justification in Soviet theory or practice for predicting that, should the Kremlin become convinced that it could cause our downfall by one conclusive blow, it would not seek that solution."

And there was evidence that the USSR was "developing the military capacity to support its design for world domination" and "possesse[d] armed forces far in excess of those necessary to defend its national territory." Soviet "production capability," in the estimation of the Central Intelligence Agency (CIA), the armed services, and the Atomic Energy Commission, could yield a "fission bomb stockpile" with dramatic rates of increase. Beyond fission bombs, "[t]here is some evidence that the Soviet Union is acquiring certain materials essential to research on and development of thermonuclear weapons." The Soviet Union also had "an atomic bomber capability already in excess of that needed to deliver available bombs." Factoring in an "accuracy rate" of bomb placement similar to that of the United States (40–60 percent), the year 1954 "would be a critical date for the United States" because the Soviet Union might then be able to deliver "100 atomic bombs on targets in the United States," resulting in "devastating attacks on certain vital centers of the United States and Canada." The clear and present danger for the survival of the United States was inescapable: "The possession of atomic weapons at each of the opposite poles of power, and the inability (for different reasons) of either side to place any trust in the other, puts a premium on a surprise attack against us." Indeed, once the Soviet Union "calculates that it has a sufficient atomic capability to make a surprise attack on us, nulli-fying our atomic superiority and creating a military situation decisively in its favor, the Kremlin might be tempted to strike swiftly and with stealth." NSC-68's narrative transformed the quantitative assessment of risk into a qualitative state of emergency.

What is important to draw from NSC-68 is the emerging discourse of alarm—the conviction that the Soviet Union and communism were threats to the democratic way of life, to national existence, and to the very physical survival of many millions of Americans. While NSC-68 itself was secret, it articulated assumptions and convictions that were either emerging publicly or soon to emerge in the United States. For our pur-poses, it is useful to read NSC-68 in conjunction with historian Richard Hofstadter's 1952 *The Paranoid Style in American Politics*. Hofstadter—courageously, given the times—used McCarthyism and the John Birch Society as two of his main exemplars of the paranoid style, which he saw as an *institutional* framing of danger and defense, not a personality trait; but his ideas clearly apply to the Cold War vision, by no means idiosyn-cratic, articulated in NSC-68. Indeed, it is obvious that Hofstadter had the larger Cold War vision in mind in writing his book. "The central image" in the paranoid style, he writes, "is that of a vast and sinister con-spiracy, a gigantic and yet subtle machinery of influence set in motion to undermine and destroy a way of life." In terms closer to the Foucauldian ideas used in this book, one could say that we are describing the dis-cursive eruption of an emergency and general form of problematization associated with that emergency. Hofstadter goes on:

> The distinguishing thing about the paranoid style is not that its expo-nents see conspiracies or plots here and there in history, but that they regard a "vast" or "gigantic" conspiracy as the *motive force* in historical events. History *is* a conspiracy, set in motion by demonic forces of almost transcendent power, and what is felt to be needed to defeat it is not the usual methods of political give-and-take, but an all-out crusade. The par-anoid spokesman sees the fate of this conspiracy in apocalyptic terms—he traffics in the birth and death of whole worlds, whole political orders, whole systems of human values. He is always manning the barricades of civilization. He constantly lives at a turning point: it is now or never in

organizing resistance to conspiracy. Time is forever running out. Like religious millenarians, he expresses the anxiety of those who are living through the last days and he is sometimes disposed to set a date for the apocalypse.[25]

All of this is obvious in NSC-68, including the dating of the apocalypse (1954, when the Soviets would be sufficiently advanced in weaponry and delivery to wage a successful attack on the United States), or at least its impending points of highest danger (which, of course, continued to be reinvented in the form of "gaps" over the course of the Cold War).

How much things had changed on the *public* stage—not just in secret memos such as NSC-68—is indicated by the Republican platform of 1952. While the main point of the document was, of course, less to sound the alarm than to vilify the Democrats, who had worked "unceasingly [since 1933] to achieve their goal of national socialism," the tactic was to articulate concisely the communist threat that came to be taken more and more seriously by more and more people of all classes and both parties. "[M]ore than 500 million people of fifteen different countries have been absorbed into the power sphere of Communist Russia, which proceeds confidently with its plan for world conquest." The Democrats had "betrayed" the "moral incentives and hopes for a better world which sustained us through World War II . . . and this has given Communist Russia a military and propaganda initiative which, if unstayed, will *destroy us*." Communists are "despots, who . . . consider that murder, terror, slavery, concentration camps and ruthless and brutal denial of human rights are legitimate means to their desired ends." In order to build a national defense prepared for a potential Soviet threat, the United States should develop sufficient forces—"including atomic energy weapons in abundance"—to "deter sudden attack or promptly or decisively defeat it."[26]

It is important not to underestimate the Cold War as a *cultural context* that made some ideas sound more reasonable, sensible, or prudent than others, and that would render certain kinds of regulatory or governing regimes more compelling or seemingly better choices. The Cold War entailed a cultural formation, complete with metaphors and symbolic resonances that fed off one another. Among the key energizing metaphors was the idea that communism had the properties of an invasive bacterium or virus. This had particular relevance in the realm of ideas about communist subversion at home (spies and disloyal Americans) and abroad, but ideas about hostile foreign matter must have also added to the general sense of the inescapable *hostility* and *mortal danger* of communism for the free world generally.[27] We should also note that the military danger to the United States was not just written, heard, and talked about, but *performed* into common sense through civil-defense drills that Tracy Davis describes as "rehearsals for nuclear war."[28] Readers of my generation will recall the "atom drills" in elementary school, not to mention the fear of communists.

The power of the discourse of a deadly emergency to awaken concern should not be underestimated, and to suggest that it amounted to a paranoid institution is not to imply that it was easy to ignore by sensible people, or that we know better in the present. That is not at all the theme of this book; the idea, on the contrary, is to understand "the natives' point of view," to see how perfectly mainstream, moral, and thoughtful people could come to think—and, as leaders or officials, plan, often in secret—in the terms described. Even those who thought the Cold War call to arms was overblown (except perhaps for members of the Communist Party) found themselves admitting that there was a real danger from communism to the United States and to Western Europe—the challenge was, as in the New Deal, not to govern (in this case, national security) *too little.* Those who were legally and morally accountable for the security of the nation found that they *could not responsibly ignore the possibility that some, if not most, of the emergency was real. Reasonable prudence demanded as much.* While petty political and careerist opportunism, political and bureaucratic "self-interest" and even "empire building," and crackpot paranoia outside the realm of mainstream thinking were all clearly part of Cold War history in the United States—indeed, they are part of every system of rationality explored in this book—there was also a compelling impulse at the core of the heightened security awareness that led even "impartial" parties to see the good sense in being prepared. How could it not be a monumental blunder not to be prepared, given the stakes for national survival, once *the possibility* was raised, even if it was raised by obviously partisan actors? Even paranoids have enemies.

The conviction that the Soviet Union was the mortal enemy of the West and was intent on destroying the United States, or conquering it, became a key premise in the production of the Cold War subject. The commonsense notion of the communist threat underwrote what Joseph Masco calls the "militarizing of everyday life." This, of course, included the tenet that "citizens should be prepared every second of every day to deal with a potential nuclear attack."[29] The militarization of everyday life also entailed an underlying premise that we have seen clearly articulated in Kennan's long telegram, NSC-68, and the 1952 GOP platform: the assumption that one was literally better off dead than red, and that taking calculated—if potentially catastrophic—risk (perhaps for some Americans more than others, as I am suggesting here) was necessary for the nation and its citizens. As we will see, without this particular form of militarization, the Minuteman silos in South Dakota would not have been so easy to contemplate.

The second historical precondition for Cold War security thinking was the history of American airpower. The dream, and promise, of strategic airpower, from at least the 1930s, was that bombing specific targets that enabled the enemy to fight a war could in itself either win a war or make it substantially easier to win; the idea was that ground invasion might be limited or even made unnecessary by strategic bombing (or even the mere threat of it). Thus, industrial bottlenecks in critical war-related production were apt targets for precision bombing: "Transportation, steel plants, ball-bearing manufacture, food delivery systems, energy supplies, and above all electrical power contained a few vital gears whose destruction would harm vast economic systems. Selective attack would bring systematic disorganization."[30] But there was nothing militarily inherent in the concept of strategic bombing that precluded the bombing of civilians—or area bombing, as it was sometimes called (later, carpet bombing)—and inflicting "pain" on enemy civilians could bring about "demoralization" and undermine national "commitment to the war," as the Germans were convinced in World War I.[31] The United States resisted the concept of area bombing or deliberately attacking enemy civilians or civilization throughout World War II in Germany. Even in the notorious Allied bombing of Dresden in February 1945, the U.S. Army Air Force described its role as "precision" bombing to distinguish its role from that of the Royal Air Force that pursued area bombing.[32]

But a Rubicon in U.S. strategy was crossed, even if pinpointing the time and place is difficult. Initial U.S. B-29 attacks on Japan in 1944 were daylight precision raids, but General Curtis LeMay's XXI Bomber Command in the Marianas Islands "began to speculate about a reversion to an area attack similar to that of the [Royal Air Force] Bomber Command in Europe."[33] Historian Michael S. Sherry argues that the transition was partly the result of the Army Air Force's difficulty in getting measurable results for successful precision bombing, and the relative ease of measuring and documenting the success of area and incendiary bombing (for example, tons of ordnance placed on "target," or square miles of urban area destroyed). This also facilitated quantifying the cost-benefit ratio of man months in bombing to "man months of [Japanese] manufacturing labor" reduced. Such thinking was facilitated by operations research that had increasingly become part of planning and evaluation of strategic bombing, as well as by "the lower value Americans put on Asian lives."[34] Japanese industry was also based on "a vast feeder system of home shops and cottage industries that saturated workers' residential areas and kept the main war industries supplied with parts," and the tight packing of wooden houses in Japanese cities seemed to call for firebombing.[35] Incendiary devices meant to set Japanese cities on fire became the predominant ordnance delivered by the B-29s. The Army Air Force publicly denied that it was targeting civilians rather than "workers," or described its work as "dehousing" workers.[36] At least eighty-four thousand died in the firebombing of Tokyo on March 9–10, 1945, and Sherry estimates that U.S. conventional (nonatomic) bombing killed 550,000 Japanese in total.[37] George Quester argues that "LeMay's headquarters had almost independently reversed bombing policy over Japan, precisely while the United States air planners in Europe were still criticizing the British area bombing offensive, and upholding the American reliance on precision attacks as more militarily efficacious and more civilized."[38]

Area bombing and firebombing, and their effects on Japanese civilians and civilization, inevitably lowered the threshold for the use of atomic bombs because "the distinction between 'military target' and 'city' had [already] totally collapsed" before Hiroshima, as Sherry puts it.[39] When Secretary of War Henry L. Stinson convened his Interim Committee to plan the atomic bombing of Japan in May 1945, the same euphemisms used in firebombing were reiterated:

After much discussion concerning various types of targets and the effects to be produced, *the Secretary expressed the conclusion, on which there was general agreement, that we could . . . not concentrate on a civilian area; but that we should seek to make a profound psychological impression on as many of the inhabitants as possible. . . . [T]he secretary agreed that the most desirable target would be a vital war plant employing a large number of workers and closely surrounded by workers' houses.*[40]

Estimates by the Manhattan Project Atomic Bomb Investigating Group put the immediate death toll in Hiroshima at 66,000 and the casualty toll at 69,000; the figures for Nagasaki were 39,000 and 25,000, respectively.[41] These figures, of course, did not include mortality or morbidity resulting from the long-term effects of radiation.

The Evolution of Massive Retaliation

As historian Edward Kaplan writes, "[i]mmediately after the Second World War, the [air force] saw the A-bomb not as the apocalyptic weapon it later became but as a better means to execute a proved body of strategic thought"—the destruction of industry.[42] The air force and SAC developed plans for attacking the Soviet Union: "The target list which became part of war plan BROILER [1947] called for 34 bombs on 24 cities. The air force HARROW war plan . . . contemplated dropping 50 bombs on 20 Soviet cities. Joint war plan TROJAN, approved in December 1948, called for attacks on 70 cities with 133 atomic bombs. . . . The October 1949 target annex for Joint Outline Emergency War Plan OFFTACKLE called for attacks on 104 urban targets with 220 atomic bombs. . . . The prime objective was . . . to disrupt the Soviet will to wage war."[43] General LeMay, who had directed the assault on Japan, became commander of SAC in 1948 and understood "strategic" bombing as city busting aimed at "industry itself," rather than specific, isolated targets.[44] Of course, the distinction between killing industry and killing civilians had already been blurred, and killing civilians was not only an inevitable collateral effect of destroying industry but also had some credence in airpower theory as a way to break the enemy's will. Thus, it is not surprising that an air force historian would write in 1959 that SAC operational details for

Plan HARROW in 1948 included "aiming points ... selected with the primary objective of the annihilation of the population, with industrial targets incidental."[45]

By 1950, the JCS rationalized plans—without mentioning the annihilation of populations—to include three missions in a nuclear war with a priority order:

BRAVO: the *blunting* of Soviet capability to deliver an atomic offensive against the United States and its allies;

DELTA: the *disruption* of the vital elements of the Soviet war-making capacity;

ROMEO: the *retardation* of Soviet advances into Western Eurasia.[46]

The DELTA mission was described by the JCS in another document as having the goal of "progressively and systematically destroying the industrial base of the Soviet Bloc to the extent necessary that it no longer contributes significantly to the military capabilities of their fighting forces by the end of the emergency phase."[47] This had obvious implications for the survival of both cities and their populations, notwithstanding the euphemistic language.

In an actual attack, SAC considered its "optimum plan" to be a "bomb-as-you-go system in which both BRAVO [blunting of strategic forces by bombing air fields, etc.] and DELTA [disrupting war-making capacity by bombing urban-industrial sites] targets would be hit as [U.S. aircraft] reached them." A Navy officer who attended a 1954 SAC briefing described the explanation of BRAVO and DELTA missions as "skillfully done by showing successive charts of Europe based on one-half-hour time intervals after SAC bombs first hit the Russian early warning screen. Many heavy lines, one representing each wing, were shown progressively converging on the heart of Russia with pretty stars to indicate the many bombs dropped on DGZs [designated ground zeros]. The final impression was that virtually all of Russia would be nothing but a smoking, radiating ruin at the end of two hours."[48]

A 1955 briefing of the JCS by the WSEG estimated the outcome for the enemy of such a planned atomic (including fifteen thermonuclear bombs) attack: "a total of seventy-seven million casualties within the Soviet Bloc of which sixty million will be fatalities," which, "coupled with the other effects of the atomic offensives, may have an important bearing on the will of the Soviets to continue to wage war." The attack entailed "the total loss of 118 out of the 134 major Soviet cities."[49] The Soviet Bloc strategic air forces were estimated to total 1,530 medium bombers, 3,579 light bombers, and 284 atomic bombs. Although 645 Soviet Bloc airfields would be attacked, some airfields would survive even a best-case scenario, and it was estimated that even after the U.S. attack "seventy-five weapons could be lifted against the U.S." Because these were "assumed to be of 60 KT [kiloton] to 1 MT [megaton]weapons," dire consequences would ensue for the United States. This outcome could be mitigated only if "more weapons [were] allocated to . . . insure coverage of potential dispersal airfields, and to insure that all the important Soviet operational and staging bases were destroyed in the first strike."[50]

A key part of U.S. defense strategy was that "[i]n the event of hostilities, the United States will consider nuclear weapons to be as available for use as other munitions." This policy would be made known to aggressors when "a warning appears desirable and feasible as an added deterrent." Thus, the United States was prepared to use nuclear weapons in a first strike (as it continues to be), and as an alternative to stationing military personnel or other assets overseas for conventional warfare against localized Soviet aggression.[51] The strategic stance of retaining a preparedness to strike first with nuclear weapons, and to wreak great damage on an enemy as a deterrent to provocation, nuclear or conventional, was made public by President Eisenhower's secretary of state, John Foster Dulles, in a speech before the Council of Foreign Relations in January 1954. Dulles insisted that aggression could not be contained only with "local defense," which is to say conventional war (with the possible addition of smaller tactical nuclear weapons) in a single theater of operations. Rather, "[l]ocal defense must be reinforced by the further deterrent of massive retaliatory power." A "potential aggressor who is glutted with manpower might be tempted to attack in confidence that resistance would be confined to manpower"—and thus on the enemy's terms—requiring that the United States be "ready to fight in the Arctic, and in the tropics, in Asia, in the Near East and in Europe; by sea, by land and by air; by old weapons and by new weapons." In budgetary

terms, this was not feasible. The better option was to "to depend primarily upon a great capacity to retaliate instantly by means and at places
of our choosing." This, of course, was the threat of massive, first-strike
nuclear attack. Dulles said that an "honorable" peace had been won in
Korea because "the aggressor . . . was faced with the possibility that the
fighting might, to his own great peril, soon spread beyond the limits and
methods which he had selected," alluding to Eisenhower's veiled nuclear
threat over Korea.[52]

Plans for massive retaliation reached their most refined form in
1960 with the first Single Integrated Operational Plan (SIOP). The idea
behind developing the plan had been for SAC, the Navy (which would
soon deploy the Polaris Missile in submarines), and the U.S. Air Force
in Europe to coordinate nuclear war plans in order to avoid duplication
or "fratricide."[53] Eisenhower's defense secretary, Thomas S. Gates, established the Joint Strategic Target Planning Staff, headed by SAC Commander Thomas S. Power, to draft the SIOP. The main significance of
SIOP-62 (which became operational in fiscal year 1962, April 1961) for
present purposes was the massive destruction planned. An "Optimum
Mix of combined Military and Urban-Industrial Target Systems" would
be destroyed or neutralized "in order to achieve the objective of prevailing in general war."[54] But, "the priority" in terms of "*confidence* in being
able to destroy targets" was given to "the urban-industrial targets, and
then to nuclear threat and other forces."[55] Under the category of urban-
industrial targets, 130 cities (of 151 on the target list) were programmed
for attack by SAC alert forces (the first forces to be sent). Four weapons
were to be placed on each target to reach a high level of assurance of
destruction.[56]

How Not to Govern National Security Too Little

The U.S. threat of massive retaliation seemed to many Americans to be
a rational form of containment of Soviet aggression and a deterrent to
Soviet nuclear attack on the United States. This was the case while the
United States had superiority in terms of weapons and delivery systems.
As Soviet nuclear forces caught up with those of the United States in the
second half of the 1950s, massive retaliation fit into a new concept that
some called "the balance of terror." RAND scientist Albert Wohlstetter

reported in 1959 on the "prevalent" conviction that "the atomic stalemate" had rendered deterrence "automatic" and resulted in "the receding probability of war"; he detected a "nearly universal optimism about the stability of deterrence."[57] The idea was that initiating an atomic war was mutually deterred because such an action would result in the national destruction of the party initiating such war. This position eventually became known as "mutually assured destruction" (MAD).

But defense intellectuals (including Wohlstetter), both at RAND and in universities, came to question this policy. Sophisticated arguments began to be made that massive retaliation/MAD risked, in the terms I have been using, *governing national security too little*. The critics agreed that deterrence was *not* automatic or guaranteed, and that a general nuclear war with the Soviet Union was possible, if not probable, in the long run—through accident, miscalculation, changes in relative force capabilities, or some other failure of deterrence. If nuclear war could happen, it needed to be faced squarely by responsible policy makers. RAND scientist E. J. Barlow wrote in 1959, "[t]o many people the consequences of . . . [deterrence] failure seems so horrible, so total, that it is felt such a war could never happen and the subject should be dismissed out of hand. The policymaker cannot allow himself the luxury of this dismissal."[58] These strategists insisted that how a nuclear war could be fought, survived, and even won were precisely the questions that needed concrete and objective answers. Paul Nitze argued in 1956 that "the word 'win' is used to suggest a comparison of the postwar position of one of the adversaries with the postwar position of the other adversary. In this sense it is quite possible that in a general nuclear war one side or the other could 'win' decisively." "[I]n a nuclear war fought with some degree of reason one side may very well 'win' in this . . . comparative sense and the other side lose. The victor will be in a position to issue orders to the loser and the loser will have to obey them or face complete chaos or extinction. The victor will then go on to organize what remains of the world as best he can."[59]

Nitze and others who wanted to plan for fighting a nuclear war with reason had some good news, at least theoretically speaking. A *rational* nuclear war fighter—East or West—would not launch a first strike aimed at annihilating the opponent's cities or even industry (even though that was in fact what the U.S. war plan called for at the time). Rather, "the attacking side . . . would logically concentrate the full power of its initial atomic attack on the military . . . capabilities of the other side. The attacker's object would be to destroy, in the initial blow, a large portion of the base structure from which the defender must launch his retaliatory action." "He will . . . want to destroy only as much of the enemy territory as is necessary for him to impose his will and get on with the job of making the world what he wants and can make of it."[60] This inherent logic of the strategic nuclear game itself could be enhanced by additional measures. The United States should develop a "widely dispersed base system" and enhance its retaliatory capabilities to the point of "superiority." This would not only make it more difficult for an opponent to disarm the United States in a first strike but would provide insurance against attack on U.S. cities by making it "irrational:" "Every weapon he wasted on a city would be a weapon he could not use against our dispersed retaliatory base structure and a further contribution to the overwhelming destruction of his own cities which his attack would have initiated." *Here was the entry of biopolitics into U.S. nuclear strategy.* The United States (and its enemies) could "locate military air bases more than a given distance, say 20 miles, from major population centers," and bombing against military targets did not need to use (there was no rational reason for them to use) "high-yield thermonuclear weapons." "Certainly, smaller population centers might be destroyed by near misses or other accidents, but is this not wholly different from the purposeful mass destruction of the urban populations of the world?"[61] Henry Kissinger was also optimistic that city-busting atomic warfare might be avoidable, because rationally, a nuclear strategy of attrition against industry and population would be "the most wasteful strategy," and "nuclear weapons may be . . . more decisively employed on the battlefield or against military installations such as airfields than against production centers."[62]

Herman Kahn's *On Thermonuclear War,* published in 1960, was meant to survey the full range of what the United States might do to decrease the risk of war and to help ensure national survival in the event that deterrence failed. Kahn had been an old RAND hand, and he agreed with the kind of thinking that Nitze and Barlow were advocating: a lot could be done by responsible leaders to make things better in the realm of national security. Kahn insisted that nuclear war was fightable, survivable, and winnable, and he itemized the alternatives to massive retaliation, alternatives that could have an important effect on how many Americans were killed and how quickly the United States could recover from a nuclear war. Kahn's book is best known for his optimistic assurances about human survival in the face of thermonuclear radiation and national political and economic survival in the face of destruction. He had a lot to say about civil defense, and about preparations for postwar recovery. But he also insisted on the importance of methodically planning out the potential options for fighting a nuclear war rationally and successfully. For example, "[t]he more SAC is protected by hardening and dispersal, the more it acts as a 'Counterforce' by drawing the enemy's attack away from cities." And rational nuclear war fighters (on both sides) might even opt for "completely or almost completely avoiding cities" because this would "maximize their post attack blackmail possibilities" (in other words, holding the civilian population hostage has a tactical pay-off greater than initial obliteration of dense, urban populations).[63]

These were some of the critical ideas about what we might in current terms call a "smart" nuclear war that were floating around among defense intellectuals when the Kennedy administration took office in 1961. In February, Kennedy's new defense secretary, Robert S. McNamara, was briefed on SIOP-62 (which would go into effect in April). McNamara was one of the "whiz-kids" who had worked in the Office of Statistical Control in the Army Air Force in World War II, and he went on to run the Ford Motor Company. At the 1961 briefing, McNamara "asked questions on ratios of force structure versus damage, pursuing it from a statistical approach." But he was also concerned about radiation effects. While he understood the value of assigning four weapons per target "to ensure a high probability of getting one on a DGXB [designated ground burst] . . . he worried that the fallout would be 'fantastic,'" and he "[e]xpressed concern over the amount of damage that was being obtained by SIOP-62." He "felt that the casualty figures for Russia and China were probably conservative."[64] The effects of delivering SIOP-62 upon the enemy, of course, had direct consequences for the U.S. homeland in how its adversaries would respond. McNamara sent Kennedy an analysis that rejected a single U.S. strategy of massive retaliation (even though it was not always called that, but nevertheless amounted to it) as both too blunt and too reactive. Clearly influenced by the critical ideas raised by defense intellectuals, McNamara insisted that "[t]he conduct and outcome of a big nuclear war is worth caring about, more than any war in history. The success of deterrence cannot be guaranteed. If nuclear war comes and is unlimited and uncontrolled, it would be suicidal. We must do what we can to prevent this disaster, to improve the war's outcome, to terminate it under favorable military conditions, and to limit the damage to our allies and ourselves." For McNamara, a system of graduated deterrence, credibility of deterrence against all levels of Soviet aggression, and maximum protection of Western civilization and population through limited (targeted) warfare were all benefits of a single system that needed to be installed. The United States must plan for the use of its nuclear weapons "in a careful and discriminating way" so as to convince "the enemy not to attack our civil society in wholesale fashion." Civil defense would also, of course, be part of the package to limit damage to the United States, and an enhanced ability to fight with conventional, nonnuclear forces in local wars was also required. "Perhaps our most fundamental weakness in the strategic area," McNamara said, "is the lack of flexibility in our ability to respond. With a vulnerable strategic force [at the time both missile sites and strategic air bases were assumed to be at risk from Soviet bombers], with the expectation that the tempo of action in nuclear war would be incredibly fast, we have been forced into a single strategy for retaliation. . . . We must move as rapidly as possible not only to create the survivable forces and control systems necessary to give us a range of choices, but also to develop strategies at the highest level for a wide range of general war contingencies."[65]

By October 1961, the JCS had drafted a new policy, reflecting the Kennedy administration's desires, which spelled out U.S. objectives "in the event of general war":

(1) To destroy or neutralize the military capabilities of the enemy, while retaining ready, effective and controlled US strategic capabilities adequate to assure, to the maximum extent possible, retention of US military superiority to the enemy, or any potential enemies, at any point during or after the war.

(2) To minimize the damage to the US and its Allies, and in all events to limit damage to a level consistent with national survival and independence.

(3) To bring the war to an end on the most advantageous possible terms for the United States and its allies.[66]

These objectives, as well as flexibility in strategic response to a Soviet attack, were incorporated into the Single Integrated Operational Plan 63 (SIOP-63), which became effective on August 1, 1963.[67]

In June 1962, McNamara made an important speech at the University of Michigan that highlighted the emerging biopolitical rationale for nuclear war planning. McNamara told his audience that the retaliatory capability of the United States was a strong deterrent that made a Soviet attack "highly unlikely," but that it also could not prudently be ruled out. Accident, a failure of its leaders to act rationally, or a miscalculation or misunderstanding were possibilities that could make deterrence fail, so the United States and its allies must "frame our strategy with this terrible contingency" in mind. The United States had concluded that its "principal military objectives, in the event of a nuclear war stemming from a major attack on the Alliance, should be the *destruction of the enemy's forces, not his civilian population.*" The biopolitical goal—concerning the enemy's population, but ultimately the U.S. population—was to give "a possible opponent the strongest imaginable incentive to refrain from striking our own cities." Avoiding enemy cities could induce a similarly limited Soviet response because the United States would still have "sufficient reserve striking power to destroy an enemy society if driven to it." The Soviet Union would thus be encouraged to limit its own response to a U.S. strike in order to avoid a full-blown follow-on U.S. response to its attack. "[W]e believe that the combination of our nuclear strength and a strategy of controlled response gives us some hope of minimizing damage in the event that we have to fulfill our pledge" to retaliate. The message clearly received in the United States and abroad was a policy of "no cities"—at least in the initial phase of war.[68] McNamara included in a report to Kennedy in the fall of 1962 statistics showing that a Soviet attack on both military and urban-industrial targets could produce 95 million U.S. deaths, while an attack limited to military targets would risk only 30 million U.S. deaths.[69] The numbers must have been startling, both to McNamara and to Kennedy, and a strong incentive to plan for limited nuclear options. One cannot help but wonder if they had read and been thinking about Herman Kahn's *On Thermonuclear War*: "If we have a posture which might result in 40 million dead in a general war, and as a result of poor planning, apathy, or other causes, our posture deteriorates to 80 million dead, we have suffered an additional disaster, an *unnecessary* additional disaster that is almost as bad as the original disaster."[70]

The no-cities message was also meant for the Soviets, of course. It seems very likely that McNamara and other defense specialists in the administration were familiar with Thomas Schelling's work on game theory and limited war. A Harvard economist, Schelling's 1960 *The Strategy of Conflict* raised the possibility that belligerents could bargain "tacitly" in the midst of war in order to coordinate their actions within limits. One way this could happen was through "unilateral negotiation" in which one party either declares or tacitly signals an intention to limit his actions.[71] Schelling was not optimistic that nuclear war could be limited once it had started because he was not convinced there were any natural or obvious thresholds in nuclear escalation, but McNamara's no-cities announcement was a textbook case of attempting such a (qualitative) threshold via "unilateral negotiation." In the face of the no-cities statement, it was possible to imagine that rational planners and managers of nuclear war on the opposing side might respond by staying their own hand. In other words, it was not just the backup "blackmail" of targeting Soviet cities, or of holding the Soviet population "hostage," that would motivate Soviet forces not to attack U.S. cities, it was also the potential mutual understanding of the mutual benefit of playing the game of limited nuclear war—limited to counterforce targets, without escalation to countervalue targets unless made necessary by the opponent breaking the rules of the game.

But no cities as a U.S. strategy that would rationally entice or compel the Soviets into a parallel, limited counterforce strategy had its doubters among security officials. The CIA's National Intelligence Estimate of July 1962 reported that "The current Soviet targeting concept reflects the view that . . . victory requires the reduction of all elements of the Western warmaking potential. These elements include: the bases of strategic delivery systems; nuclear weapons facilities; communication and government centers; military and war supporting industry. We have no evidence that avoidance of heavy civilian casualties is among the objectives underlying Soviet targeting."[72] When the Net Evaluation Subcommittee reported to Kennedy and the National Security Council (NSC) in September 1963 on its war gaming for the projected situation from 1964 through 1968, it laid out among its assumptions the presumed Soviet objective—in both a first strike and a retaliatory strike—to attack both strategic forces and the "US urban-industrial complex:" "It should be emphasized that in our judgment the Soviet force structure throughout the period made it illogical for them to execute a controlled response attack—either in retaliation or pre-emption. Hence, in all [war-gamed] attacks the USSR fired at all targets from the outset."[73] It is also the case that the JCS and the air force commanders had doubts about the technical and tactical possibilities of separating out limited responses from more destructive ones, and about the likelihood of limiting damage to the United States.

McNamara attempted to deflect such criticisms of no-cities/limited, counterforce nuclear war by reasoning that, "[i]n talking about global nuclear war, the Soviet leaders always say that they would strike at the entire complex of our military power including government and production centers, meaning our cities," and that the United States in that case "would have no alternative but to retaliate in kind." Nevertheless, it was not possible to "forecast the nature of a nuclear attack" by the Soviets, and

> [i]t would certainly be in their interest as well as ours to try to limit the terrible consequences of a nuclear exchange.... By building into our forces a flexible capability, we at least eliminate the prospect that we could strike back in only one way; namely, against the entire Soviet target system including their cities. Such a prospect would give the Soviet Union no incentive to withhold attack against our cities in a first strike. We want to give them a better alternative. Whether they would accept it in the crisis of a global nuclear war, no one can say. Considering what is at stake, we believe it is worth the additional effort on our part to have this option.[74]

Nevertheless, by late 1963, McNamara backed off advocating a flexible response as a means of limiting damage to the United States in the event of a nuclear war, although he never gave up on the idea entirely. In a December memo to President Lyndon Johnson, he quoted the chair of the JCS in supporting his recommendation: "Recognizing that . . . it is not possible to assure the limiting of damage, in loss of life, to the United States to a level . . . suggested by the Secretary of Defense, we consider that . . . [a] vital first objective to be met . . . by our strategic nuclear forces should be the assured capability of destroying singly, or in combination, the Soviet Union and the Communist satellites in Europe as national societies." McNamara explained to President Johnson that the United States then had three "general nuclear war objectives." "'Assured destruction' of the Soviet Union" meant a U.S.

> ability to destroy . . . the Soviet government and military controls, plus a large percentage of their population and economy (e.g. 30% of their population, 50% of their industrial capacity, and 150 of their cities). The purpose of such a capability is to give us a high degree of confidence that . . . we can deter a calculated deliberate Soviet nuclear attack. . . . The calculations made to test this ability are our best estimates of the results of possible Soviet calculations of what we could do to them in retaliation if they were to attack us. This calculation of the effectiveness of U.S. forces is not a reflection of our actual targeting doctrine in the event deterrence fails.[75]

This appeared to leave open the option of a more "damage limiting" (including no-cities) response to a Soviet first strike, and he was still making public statements in favor of pursuing a flexible capability (which would require systemic technical, operational, and tactical changes in SAC) as late as 1966.[76] But McNamara admitted that "counterforce attacks may not hold great promise in the later part of the 1960s if the Soviets hardened and dispersed their ICBM force and build up their missile submarine force as we now expect them to do." Furthermore, U.S. fatalities would be "great even if urban-industrial areas are not directly involved." For example, McNamara projected that while a U.S. response to a Soviet strike in which only Soviet urban-industrial targets were destroyed would result in 195 million American fatalities, counterforce targeting (which would in theory both reduce remaining Soviet strategic forces and persuade the Soviets to avoid attacking U.S. cities) would limit damage only minimally, resulting in 183 million American fatalities.[77]

McNamara oversaw the development SIOP-64 (later shortened to SIOP-4), which became operational in 1966. A declassified document drafted in 1972 by a committee chaired by President Nixon's national security adviser, Henry Kissinger, gives us a glimpse into the plan. SIOP-4 laid out three objectives:

—Destruction of nuclear offensive threats to the United States and its allies in order to limit damage.

—Destruction of a comprehensive military target system, in order to assist in destroying overall Soviet and other Warsaw Pact military capability.

—Destruction of war-supporting urban and industrial resources. (The . . . goals are to inflict moderate damage in 70% of the war supporting industry and to destroy 30% of the people.)

Three tasks were delineated to achieve these objectives:

—Task ALFA includes strikes on ICBM and IR/MRBM [intermediate range/medium range ballistic missile] sites, bomber bases, ballistic missile submarine bases, local military command and control sites, nuclear weapon storage sites, and defense suppression targets.

—Task BRAVO includes strikes on tactical airfields and other military targets critical to the overall conduct and direction of military operations.

—Task CHARLIE includes strikes on urban/industrial targets and military targets colocated with cities.

SIOP-4 also provided for five attack options, three preemptive and two retaliatory. Urban-industrial targets were not listed in three of these options. Critically, however, "the smallest preplanned SIOP option which can be ordered against the Soviet Union involves about 2,500 weapons." At bottom, plans under SIOP-4 could not "significantly limit damage to the United States and its allies," and could not "insure termination of hostilities under conditions advantageous to the United States as measured in terms of residual military resources and limitation of damage to the U.S. urban/industrial base."[78] McNamara had wanted "options to permit withholding of reserve forces from initial attack; to avoid attacks on urban-industrial populations, and government control centers," but the JCS explained that "[t]he capability simply did not yet exist to permit avoidance of enemy non-military centers and population in an attack."[79] Operational and tactical capabilities for delivering a wartime nuclear strike against the Soviets may well not have been much advanced from where they were in 1960—at the height of massive retaliation—in terms of limiting damage or fighting a nuclear war rationally with the aim of surviving and winning.

The Dream of Saving the Cities Returns

The imperative raised by Herman Kahn and other RAND defense intellectuals—the idea that it would be *irresponsible* for those charged with national security not to think about managing nuclear war for the best possible outcome—was compelling enough that the goal of minimizing American deaths and the destruction of American civilization could not be ignored for long, whatever the operational, logistical, or tactical challenges. Even those who might have worried that planning for "limiting" atomic war might actually hasten it, and who thought that we were all best served by mutually assured destruction, must have found the RAND warning difficult to ignore or suppress. How would they answer to a "second disaster" or more Americans killed than was necessary, if they had done nothing to avoid it? So, in his first annual report to Congress on foreign policy in 1970, President Nixon asked rhetorically, "Should a President, in the event of a nuclear attack, be left with the single option of ordering the mass destruction of enemy civilians, in the face of the certainty that it would be followed by the mass slaughter of Americans? Should the concept of assured destruction be narrowly defined and should it be the only measure of our ability to deter the variety of threats we may face?"[80] At the time, an NSC report had estimated that an all-out U.S. strike on the Soviet Union could kill 40 percent of its population, 90 million. The consequences for the U.S. population of

Soviet retaliation (because some Soviet nuclear assets would always survive an American attack) were obvious.[81]

In January 1974, Secretary of State Henry Kissinger provided Nixon with a new proposal for the JCS to develop plans for more flexible options for limited war fighting, and Nixon signed National Security Decision Memorandum (NSDM) 242.[82] Escalation control would be pursued by developing "options [to] (a) hold some vital enemy targets hostage to subsequent destruction by survivable nuclear forces, and (b) permit control over the timing and pace of attack execution, in order to provide the enemy opportunities to reconsider his actions."[83] The Defense Department provided the JCS with additional guidance for the development of operational plans:

> Control of escalation requires both sides to show restraint. Such restraint could stem from a combination of self-interest and coercion. In an effort to deter the enemy from escalation and to coerce him into negotiating a termination of the war acceptable to the United States, the U.S. should maintain the capability to effectively withhold attacks from additional targets highly valued by the enemy leadership. . . .
>
> U.S. nuclear weapon employment plans should provide the National Command Authorities with the ability to conduct nuclear war at various levels of intensity within clearly defined boundaries. These boundaries are intended to signal to the enemy our desire to keep the war limited.[84]

Even before Nixon signed NSDM 242, his defense secretary, James R. Schlesinger, announced publicly that some U.S. ICBMs were being reprogrammed to target Soviet military sites, such as missile silos, in addition to cities.[85] As the *New York Times* described the supposed rationale for the new policy, "[i]nstead of hitting cities and killing millions of civilians, the enemy's military forces would be attacked, as in old-fashioned wars. Military men, trained for war fighting, find this approach particularly attractive. Instead of responding to a Soviet nuclear attack against American missiles with a blow against Soviet cities, which would bring down Russia's remaining nuclear warheads on American cities, President Nixon has asked for the option of making a limited counterforce response against the remaining Soviet missiles first."[86] In September 1974,

Schlesinger briefed the Subcommittee on Arms Control of the Senate Committee on Foreign Relations on the new policy and showed a slide of U.S. strategic nuclear force locations that were then targeted by the Soviet Union. "The main point that one gets from the ... slide," Schlesinger assured his audience, "is the nonlocation, by and large, of the strategic nuclear forces targets located in the United States and the urban populations of the United States."[87] Limited, counterforce war made biopolitical sense because strategic nuclear assets in the United States were located outside major population areas.

Whatever real progress the Nixon and Ford administrations were able to make in getting operational plans for limited nuclear war adopted by the military, the Carter administration felt compelled to renew the pursuit for nuclear options, and Carter issued Presidential Directive 59 (PD-59), "Nuclear Weapons Employment Policy," in July 1980.[88] PD-59 was based on the goal of providing *measured* credible deterrence against a full range of possible enemy attacks, abroad and at home, nuclear as well as conventional, which was now referred to as a "countervailing" strategy but was essentially an iteration of McNamara's graduated deterrence. The SIOP was to be revised to provide for preplanned "flexible sub-options that will permit ... sequential selection of attacks from among a full range of military targets, industrial targets providing immediate military support, and political control targets, while retaining a survivable and enduring capability that is sufficient to attack a broader set of urban and industrial targets." PD-59 recognized the particular reality of U.S. ICBM silos being "vulnerable to preemptive attack" (the understanding was that targets such as the Minuteman silos and launch control sites and Ellsworth Air Force Base would be attacked first, before the cities), and the SIOP revision was to allow for "launching nuclear weapons on warning that an [enemy] attack has begun." Flexibility would also be introduced into the SIOP through the "ability to design nuclear employment plans on short notice in response to the latest changing circumstances." Countervailing strategy would allow the president "to choose to put the major weight of the initial response on military and control targets," and to "limit collateral damage [of] urban areas, general industry, and population targets outside these categories." The latter were, of course, still potential targets, but classified as "withholds" in early stages of strategic escalation, to give the enemy incentive to forgo attacks on the U.S. population or attacks with high "collateral damage" (civilian deaths), and to provide leverage—through the threat of attacking his cities—to bring the enemy to the negotiating table in order to end the exchange. All of this would require enhancements of intelligence, command and control, and communications.[89]

In August 1980, Carter's secretary of defense, Harold Brown, delivered a speech at the Naval War College on the new policy. The countervailing strategy had as its aim "that no potential adversary of the United States or its Allies could ever conclude that aggression would be worth the costs that would be incurred. This is true whatever the level of conflict is contemplated." Deterrence, in other words, "must restrain a far wider range of threats than just massive attacks on U.S. cities," including "deterrence of conventional aggression." The credibility of U.S. deterrence inevitably required "giving greater attention to how a nuclear war would actually be fought by both sides if deterrence fails." Soviet "political and military control, military force both nuclear and conventional, and the industrial capability to sustain a war" would be targeted first, but, "of course, we have, and we will keep, a survivable and enduring capability to attack the full range of targets, including the Soviet economic base."[90] The clear assumption was that through escalation control, strategic military assets in the United States (such as the Minuteman sites and Ellsworth Air Force Base) would be reduced prior to attacks on U.S. population centers, and the exchange could be dampened to prevent the latter attacks.

In 1981, President Ronald Reagan signed National Security Directive 13 on "Nuclear Weapons Employment Policy." The directive accepted the underlaying theory of earlier designs to prepare to fight a nuclear war rationally so as to minimize damage to the United States. Reagan's directive was perhaps more blunt, stating that the United States "must prevail" in a nuclear war, and that it must be "prepared to wage war successfully." But this was not qualitatively different from the two-decades-long pursuit of what had previously been called "graduated deterrence," "countervailing strategy," and the like. Reagan is remembered, of course, for "Star Wars" (his Strategic Defense Initiative), but the policy in place during his presidency was the long-standing one of giving the president the capability in a nuclear war to "pursue specific objectives . . . at any given time, from general guidelines established in advance." The United States "must have the capability to attack the widest range of targets in a way that serves our national interests."[91] How actionable such a capability was remains an open question both in terms of operational, logistical, and tactical capacities and in terms of outcomes in an actual nuclear war.

The Biopolitics of Nuclear War Plans

Foucault defined biopower as "the entry of life into history."[92] I am arguing here that the entry of life into national security is also usefully understood as biopower—and as an important threshold in thinking about how the nation and its people can be protected and their welfare secured. We will now briefly survey Foucault's ideas on biopower before returning to the dream of protecting Americans in nuclear war, to the extent rationally possible.

Like most of his concepts, Foucault was not consistent in what he chose to emphasize with his concept of biopower or biopolitics (the terms are often used interchangeably, although the latter places emphasis on the *political struggles* over the former). He introduced the concept in 1976 when he contrasted it against the premodern form of power that resided in the sovereign. The sovereign exercised "the right to *take* life or *let* live," but this was a distinctly limited form of power. Modern power (developed since the seventeenth century), by contrast, is a capacity "to incite, reinforce, control, monitor, optimize, and organize the forces under it: a power bent on generating forces, making them grow." Biopower is a "life administering power" that goes beyond merely taking life or letting live to "*foster* life or *disallow* it to the point of death."[93] As Foucault put it in a lecture, biopower is the capacity "*to make live or to let die,*" as would a breeder of plants or animals, or a gardener.[94] "A power whose task is to take charge of life," biopower "needs continuous regulatory and corrective mechanisms. . . . Such a power needs to qualify, measure, appraise, and hierarchize, rather than display itself in its murderous splendor," as does sovereign state power.[95] Critically, biopower has two axes: the discipline of bodies and the regulation of populations.[96] Clearly, the concept of biopower encompasses all the practices of governing that we have so far examined in this book. But Foucault used the concept of biopower to place emphasis more specifically on the *bio* in governing, and pursuing this emphasis will allow us to examine how the planning of nuclear war entailed a new way of governing the countryside.

Foucault did not argue that sovereign power—the power to take life and let live—had disappeared from history with the appearance of biopower. After all, prisons, capital punishment, and the use of atomic weapons are paradigmatic examples of taking life that have lived on in modernity. Rather, he spoke in terms of "the 'governmentalization' of the state," and the implantation of biopolitical reasoning into state-rationality.[97] Foucault seems at times to suggest that state-rationality or reason-of-state (what he calls "sovereignty," the "juridical," or simply the "law") is inherently homicidal in its internal logic, and that if it is to survive in the present, it can act out its internal logic only by cloaking itself with biopolitical (and pastoral) justifications for purposes of political legitimation.[98] This is unfortunate wording on Foucault's part, because he almost surely did not mean to suggest that the state was driving history, but that biopower itself was in the driver's seat. More in keeping with the thrust of his narrative is to recognize that state-rationality itself was transformed by the appearance of biopower; state apparatuses took up the biopolitical game of pastoral care not as a cloak, but as their reason for being, as their internal logic.[99]

But if state apparatuses became governmentalized or pastoralized through the incorporation of biopower—focused on the welfare and best interests of individuals and populations ("power that exerts a *positive* influence on life")—how can we explain the ongoing murderous splendor of modern states?[100] As Foucault points out, "wars were never as bloody as they have been since the nineteenth century, and . . . never before did regimes visit such holocausts on their own populations."[101] The explanation is to be found in the logic of biopower itself: "If genocide is indeed the dream of modern powers, this is not because of a recent return of the ancient [sovereign] right to kill; it is because power is situated and exercised at the level of life, the species, the race, and the large-scale phenomena of population."[102] Biopower has the inherent potential, perhaps the predisposition, to *fold back upon itself.* Foucault illustrates this with the appearance of modern racism.

Modern racism is a (systemic, or path-dependent) transformation or mutation of biopower understood as the pastoral care of individuals and the population; it operates by "introducing a break into the domain of life that is under power's control: the break between what must live and what must die," in the service of the welfare of "all." Racism acts "to fragment, to create caesuras within the biological continuum addressed by bio-power."[103] Modern racism originates historically in Western colonialism, "or in other words, with colonizing genocide," and is based on the logic of "evolutionism," or, in the American case, social Darwinism.[104] But Foucault's paradigmatic case of modern, biopolitical racism is the Nazis. The role of racist evolutionism in Nazism needs no further explanation here. But it is important to recognize that Foucault understood racism in terms broader than "ethnic racism."[105] It includes, for example, the biologization of the criminal. The death penalty, for example, is biopolitically thinkable because of "the monstrosity of the criminal, his incorrigibility, and the safeguard of society."[106] Foucault also saw Stalinism as a form of "racism of the evolutionist kind, biological racism" in the way it "deal[t] with the mentally ill, criminals, political adversaries, and so on."[107]

Given Foucault's much broader understanding of racism in comparison to our common usage of the term in the United States, it might be better to think of his argument about the biopolitical fold as including what we know as modern racism, but also including other forms of administrative and political essentialization or labeling-with-a-vengeance that go beyond the strictly racial. What the strictly racial and the other forms of essentialization have in common, and that Foucault meant to emphasize in categorizing them all as "racism," is two core, inescapable concerns of biopower: evolutionary competition, and "the naked question of survival," of the larger population (or "the people").[108] If we can understand naked questions of survival as the root of biopower—and modern racism as one of its historical expressions—it is not distorting Foucault's insights to add to his analysis of the *racial* fold in biopower an analysis of the *spatial and the demographic factor* in biopower. By "spatial and the demographic" I mean the division of national space into zones of differential value in terms of life—this is still biopolitics, but not racial as we usually understand it (for present purposes, the term "racial" is better reserved for the more directly racial matters described throughout this book). States certainly claim sovereignty that is "fully, flatly, and evenly operative over each square centimeter of a legally demarcated territory," suggesting an "equality" of the relationship between the state and all localities and their subpopulations within its borders.[109] This was one of the key rationalities of the formation of national space described in chapter 1. And the modern nation-state *may* well have an internal logic that favors "civil equality," making differentiations among citizens somehow more difficult than they might otherwise be (although this must remain an open question).[110] But just as the emergence of racism complicates the picture in significant ways, other biopolitical challenges—real or imagined—also make the "universality" of space, place, and person within the nation-state *improbable*. Indeed, the biopolitical problem of nuclear war made the very notion of treating national space and population as "equal" or interchangeable a distinctly *bad policy*, even *irresponsible* on the part of any leader who thought in such terms.

Spatial and demographic discriminations were not invented by defense intellectuals or strategic nuclear managers. As mentioned, there has been a historically recurrent tendency to differentiate regions in a specific way—in terms of a supposedly objective measure of development (or "evolution"). We saw this in Turner's model of different zones of "social evolution" of the nation (chapter 1). As historian William Cronon has persuasively demonstrated, it is very instructive to read Turner *structurally*—the different zones are not necessarily, or primarily, stages of ongoing evolutionary change, but stable zones of development determined by distance from metropolitan markets. Based on his reading of Johann Heinrich von Thünen's *The Isolated State* (1826), Cronon lays out the economic zones (based on distance from market) that outlie the metropolis in the case of U.S. history, and Chicago in particular (Figure 5.5). This zonation accounted for the differential population densities and quantity of built environment—the differentiation of the value of place— across national space. This kind of analysis served as the basis for central place theory in geography.[111] The point to emphasize for present purposes is that under the right conditions—the threat of total war and national annihilation—the differentiation of national zones on the basis of the density of population and built environment (distance from metropolises, in von Thünen's model) becomes the inevitable basis for strategizing about who should die that others might live.

As mentioned at the start of this chapter, the biopolitics of counterforce thinking was rooted in the differentiation of "populated" from

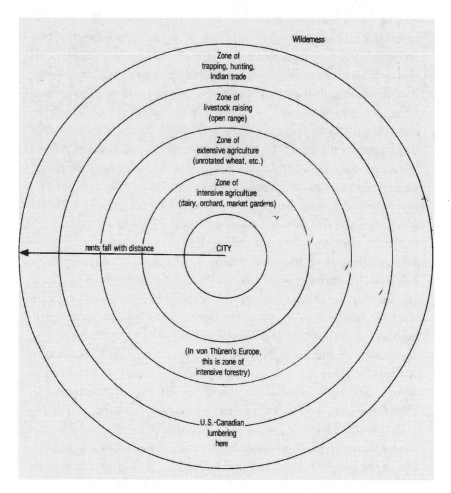

FIGURE 5.5. Zones of valuation and distance from metropolis. William Cronon, *Nature's Metropolis: Chicago and the Great West* (New York: W. W. Norton, 1991), 49.

"unpopulated" areas, or areas of "low population." As geographer Matthew Farish puts it, national security in the atomic age has always been "profoundly geographical." The specific dangers—both blast and radiation—of the bomb forced upon defense intellectuals the recognition that "American society might be geographically recalibrated to reduce this risk."[112] Early thinking on these matters entailed designing cities, as the American

Institute of Planners put it, to be less "profitable targets to an attacker and so [to] discourage attack." Of key concern was that "[n]early one-fifth of the nation's population and 27.6 per cent of its manufacturing employment is concentrated in its top five metropolitan areas. The top fifteen contain 30 per cent of the total population and 40 per cent of the manufacturing employment. The top forty contain 40 per cent of the total population and more than half of the manufacturing employment."[113] Tracy Augur (an old New Deal hand who had worked as a planner for the Tennessee Valley Authority) warned in 1948 (in anticipation of the Soviet bomb) that the concentration of American industry and specialized expertise in cities was "of a kind with our 1941 concentration of naval strength at Pearl Harbor. Because concentrated, they are easier to hit" and actually created an incentive for enemies to develop the atomic bomb.[114] Augur proposed an elegant solution. Anticipating the logic of Minuteman missile siting in South Dakota, he explained that a city of 1 million people might be dispersed in "a cluster or some twenty units averaging about 50,000 each and separated from one another by four to five miles of open country":

> From the standpoint of airborne attack the concentrated city undoubtedly offers the better target area. Its 63 square miles is solid urban territory. An A-bomb placed anywhere within it would do tremendous direct damage and large secondary damage through the spread of conflagration and panic in the crippling of city functions. If an area of like diameter is superimposed on any part of the cluster formation, not more than three or four of its twenty units will lie within it. At least four-fifths of the enclosed area will be open country. A bomb placed within the nine mile [cluster] would have only a one in five chance of a direct hit on urban territory. . . . A one in five chance of losing a city of 50,000 is . . . better than a one in one chance of losing a larger portion of a bigger city.[115]

What is more, the clustered metropolis would lose none of the economic, social, or cultural benefits of the nucleated metropolis because commuting between clusters would be easy. And residents would have the added benefits of the absence of congestion and access to green space. Finally, this design could be achieved without additional cost, because the United

States was then engaged in a great building boom. Because homes, roads, and infrastructure would be built anyway, it would take only the espousal of a plan to see that the new building conformed to the cluster design rather than adding to the existing urban agglomerations.

Yale professor Bernard Brodie, who would work for RAND and become a well-known defense intellectual, was skeptical of the planners' cellular (or, alternatively, linear) cities and believed that potential adversaries would simply build more bombs to achieve coverage. He assumed that cities could not survive a nuclear attack, and that suburbanization of the population was the best option, as well as moving vital industries out of cities—what he called "compartmentalization."[116] Critical here was military assets "independent of the urban communities," which were expected to be goners. De-urbanization of essential industries and services would also enable the predicted "exodus from the cities by which alone their lives can be safeguarded" in case of attack.[117]

Thus, before the perfection of the theory of counterforce—and the development of weapons capable of such tactical use—cities were presumed to be the primary targets (along with Air Force and other large military installations), and the countryside was seen as a survival zone (excluding, of course, the fact of fallout, which was not on the radar screen of defense thinkers until the second half of the 1950s, after the hydrogen bomb tests). Evacuation of urban populations in the event of a crisis or warning of attack was the first form of "civil defense."[118] As Matthew Farish paraphrases a 1955 Federal Civil Defense Administration pamphlet, *4 Wheels to Survival,* "Automobiles effectively became a 'small movable house' for the maintenance of the nuclear family in times of emergency, and a link to the authoritative civil defense radio broadcasts . . . that would direct traffic out of cities in orderly fashion."[119] In fact, the idea of surviving a nuclear war (or prevailing over the Soviets) found its entry point into the national security discourse through the idea of the salvation offered by the countryside. In RAND's 1959 *Is Deterrence Enough or Should We Be Prepared to Fight a General War in the 1960's?* E. J. Barlow informed his readers that "it is *not* necessarily true that a general war would destroy our population; there is some hope our nation could survive these radioactivity effects."[120] The key to this would be the less-urbanized zones ("B country") that are likely to survive the blast and

fire of city-busting enemy attacks: "'B' country [is] the more likely sur-
vivor of at least the physical damage of a war, and therefore a more likely
repository of our hopes for rebuilding the nation," and most likely to
benefit from fallout shelters (because the danger to this area will be radiation, not blast and fire that may well destroy urban populations).[121] Yet,
looking ahead to counterforce, Barlow pointed out that the wise policy
planner will nevertheless consider a strategy of dispersed and otherwise
protected nuclear retaliatory forces so that enemy nuclear fire would be
"soaked up" and "pulled away from a direct attack upon our cities and
our people."[122]

Cold War Subjects in Western South Dakota and Beyond

While nine Titan missile sites were still being constructed near Rapid
City, South Dakotans learned in January 1961 that Ellsworth Air Force
Base would be the center of a complex of 150 Minuteman missiles, in
addition to its fifteen B-52 bombers and twenty KC-135 tankers.[123] The
Rapid City Journal was quick to report that the Minuteman program "will
herald vast economic benefits for the entire West River region, as well as
Rapid City." The paper cited the optimism of the president of the Black
Hills Board of Realtors about the effects of the "$60 million construc-
tion project" on the real-estate market. The president of the Rapid City
Chamber of Commerce was paraphrased on the program as "encouraging steady economic growth." Workers would move in for construction
of the missile complex, to be followed by the military personnel to operate the complex. The secretary of the local building and trades council
said that "over 500 plumbers and about the same number of electricians
will have come into the area when skilled labor needs reach a peak on the
Titan projects. They will stay if Minuteman work is available."[124] By June
1962, the South Dakota Highway Department had spent "$2.5 million in
defense department funds for special improvements to about 500 miles
of roads and bridges leading to the sites" in order to support the construction and missile transport and maintenance loads.[125] Even rural electric
cooperatives would benefit by providing power to the complex, and were
investing $2.5 million in upgrades by August 1962.[126] Indeed, the classic
South Dakota boosterism examined in chapter 1 was renewed in the case
of the Minuteman. Three months before Ellsworth had been officially

chosen by the Air Force for the complex, a cashier at the Blackpipe State
Bank in Martin (in Bennett County, originally part of Pine Ridge Reservation, and still containing reservation trust land) wrote to South Dakota
Republican congressman Francis Case, "I hear on TV where it might be
possible that they will construct some more missile bases in this area. . . .
To sort of put our bid in early . . . [d]o you think that our area might
be considered? We surely would like to get some such here. . . . Actually
Martin . . . has never had any government construction." Case requested
that the Air Force "take a look at some of the buttes in the Bennett County
area and see if they would lend themselves to use for the proposed Minuteman unit." Responding to Case, the Air Force instructed SAC "to
include consideration of possible use of the buttes in Bennett County for
the Minuteman missile," although sites were never located there.[127]

The management of construction of the Minuteman complex, including the acquisition of land, was assigned to the Army Corps of Engineers.
To orient landowners for the process, the Corps issued a pamphlet, *Facts
about Minuteman Land Acquisition*, which explained that the final sites
had been selected "to fit required geographic locations . . . and to have
the least adverse effect on local community and private property interests." "No substantial amount of land at any one site will be retired from
productive use," and "[e]very effort has been made to plan so that it will
create the least possible disturbance to the normal ranching, agricultural
and other usual activities in the area."[128] About four acres would be required during the construction phase for each site (both silos and launch
control facilities), for which the landowner would sign a right of entry.
About two acres were to be ultimately purchased by the government
at each site after construction, and easements would be negotiated for
access roads, underground cables, lines of sight from the silos to azimuth
markers (for aiming the missiles), and restrictive use areas (for "safety").
In consideration of relinquishing such property rights, landowners would
receive fair market value, defined by the federal courts as "the amount
which would be agreed upon between a willing seller and willing buyer,
neither of them being obligated to sell or buy. It is the Corps of Engineers' desire and duty to pay the property owner 'just compensation,'"
in conformity with the Constitution's Fifth Amendment.[129] Previously
the Corps had offered a nonnegotiable price in land acquisitions, but a

new policy was now in place: "The representatives of the Corps will contact the owner and negotiations will proceed on the same basis as would be involved in the barter and sale of real estate generally."[130] Local real-estate appraisers would be contracted to help assess market value. If agreement could not be reached, or if the landowner refused to sign the right of entry, condemnation proceedings would be instituted in federal court.

By March 1961, landowners were already dissatisfied with the process and had organized the Missile Area Land Owners Association (MALOA) "for the securing of information affecting our property and the value thereof and the use to be made of same, and in order to obtain appropriate and proper legal advice and representation in all negotiations, agreements, and proceedings."[131] The president of the MALOA explained that the right-of-entry instrument ranchers were being asked to sign bound them to allow construction for two years, but without any payment or even an agreed price to be paid at completion of construction. This was particularly unacceptable to ranchers because, by comparison, "contractors and suppliers are not asked to sign contracts without provisions for time and amount of payment."[132] Another key concern of landowners was the general devaluation of land not directly purchased by the government because of the presence of a silo on a ranch, in part because of "how it may interfere with the normal operation of the [ranch] unit." The vice president of the MALOA must have spoken for many when he wrote to Congressman Case:

> [W]e all realize the need for a deterrent force, and missiles seem to be the force indicated at this time. We realize the need for a place to put them, and as our area has been chosen for them, we will somehow have to make the best of it. But it would make it so much easier to cooperate if we could be met at least half way, with businesslike terms for an agreement for final settlement. We do have certain rights and it would seem that these rights should be respected even in the face of this emergency. Some of the landowners affected (and really a good many of them) have worn the same uniforms that some of the people we are dealing with now are wearing; and some including my self have a son or sons in the armed services, and are in various places all over the free world.[133]

The vice president of the MALOA reported that the government negotiators had gone so far in their dealings with landowners as to "hint that
we might be subversive in our attitude and thinking."[134] There was some
resentment among other South Dakotans about the apparent fuss being
made by the MALOA. A (non-Indian) rancher on the Cheyenne River
Reservation called the resistance of the landowners a "sad affair" and
informed Case that "my family and I wish to offer to give the government for free enough land for a site here."[135] The Sioux Falls *Argus Leader*
accused the MALOA members of

> trying to get every nickel out of Uncle Sam that the traffic will bear. . . .
> They're demanding not only payment for the land, but . . . severance
> damages for the inconvenience which Air Force men will put them to by
> jeeping to missile sites in the middle of a pasture. . . . There are a lot
> of inconveniences in this world of 1961. The hot breath of the Russians
> in the race for space and for supremacy on this globe is one of them. . . .
> Can the government demand much of some citizens . . . and let [other]
> citizens demand extra payment for minor inconveniences caused by a
> missile site?[136]

But was the MALOA really trying to price-gouge the government?
First, we need to recall that this part of South Dakota, not even in the
aridity "transition" zone of the Rosebud country, but further west and
drier, was a very difficult place to make a living in agriculture and had
been one of the federal target zones for removing population during
the New Deal. Margins were extremely tight for ranch families. The vice
president of the MALOA put it aptly to Case: "In an area where the major
battle is with the elements, and for some there has been some measure
of success, this could well be the 'straw that broke the camel's back.'"[137]
Ranchers could not afford not to worry about silos and associated emplacements and activities potentially interfering with their future ability
to harvest enough hay or feed (some missile sites were in hay or crop
fields), to rely on water-spreading systems and wells, to move cattle from
summer to winter pastures, to plow for crops (which might be impossible because of buried cables), to keep their livestock calm, and so
on.[138] The Corps negotiators "hinted that our land values would go up,"

the vice president reported, and "I realize that this is true of most projects, especially in metropolitan areas." But for ranchers in the missile area, "with . . . [government] taking of land . . . [the rancher's] economic situation will become more critical, and it will become more difficult for him to carry on normal operations."[139] Hardly "minor inconveniences," as the *Argus Leader* had put it. If MALOA members seemed "calculating," it was because they could not afford not to be. Hay land, after all, "is the heart of the ranching operation which is just as important as the rocket engine is to a missile and without either one the end product would not come into operation," a local lawyer made clear to the Corps.[140] When some landowners refused to sign the right-of-entry instrument, condemnation proceedings were initiated in federal court.

There was, inevitably, also moral outrage over the way that the ranchers felt the Corps was trampling on ranchers' property rights (see chapter 4 for the larger picture from the standpoint of the grass roots). They were, of course, more than a little aware of the Constitution's Fifth Amendment "taking clause" (the parallel to Lakota knowledge and invocation of treaty rights is noteworthy, although Lakota people did not raise such rights regarding Minuteman, even though their downwind proximity put them at extreme risk). And they were aware that other parties who contracted with the government on the Minuteman project were treated— and compensated—much differently. The vice president of the MALOA pointed out that the landowners received an average of $659 per site— mere "pin money"—out of a total cost of $3 million per sited missile. The landowner "should be paid the same as anyone else connected with the Defense program," but instead we "are now going through the biggest land grab in the history of our Government."[141] Obvious here is the parallel to agrarian arguments during the Depression that the "middleman" (buyer, processor, futures investor) was taking the profit from the farmer's work.

Thus, the Cold War subject in South Dakota was complicated—on board about the dangers of communism and the necessity for a strong nuclear defense, and even the necessity for individual sacrifice, but also attuned to questions of equity, fairness, and the close margins families faced in ranching. But we need to attend to additional complexities in the Cold War subject. We need to pay attention to what was *not* said, what South Dakotans (both non-Indian and Indian) may not have been aware of, what they may have chosen not to think or talk about, and what could not be articulated because it was tacit or even unthinkable. All of this is also part of producing Cold War subjects in South Dakota.

Some South Dakotans worried about the silos being sited "too close" to people's homes—they did not "want them on their doorsteps"—but this had either to do with their unsightliness or the potential danger from accidental explosion of the Minuteman's solid fuel.[142] South Dakotans apparently accepted the deterrent theory for Minuteman. When the Minuteman project was announced, the *Rapid City Journal* explained the "underground silo theory" in terms of "forc[ing] an aggressor to expend more missiles than he could afford just to have a reasonable chance of hitting the stationary sites," which were "built to withstand a near miss by a nuclear bomb."[143] The *Argus Leader* opined that "the West River country is sprouting missiles all over the place" precisely to *prevent* "a Russian missile dropping on South Dakota."[144] South Dakotans also likely understood that this deterrent effect protected all of the United States, including western South Dakota (and it certainly did not seem to be realized that the Minuteman might protect the rest of the country *at the expense* of risking enemy attack on South Dakota missile sites). South Dakotans were aided and abetted in this confidently evasive thinking by the framing of the issues offered by the air force and the Corps of Engineers. "The Minuteman will create no hazards for its neighbors," the pamphlet *Facts about Minuteman and Land Acquisition* assured it readers.[145]

There was a debate within the Defense Department about how close to homes, or other places where civilians might be found, Minuteman silos might safely be located, and this was reported in the *Washington Star* in May 1962. While the Armed Services Explosives Safety Board issued a minimum distance requirement of 1,300 feet to protect against the potential effects of an accidental fuel explosion "equivalent [to] 40,000 or 50,000 pounds of TNT," the air force insisted that "such an explosion would equal only about 20,000 pounds" (a higher yield than the sixteen kiloton Hiroshima bomb) and that the "minimum distance of a little more than 600 feet would be sufficient." Reassuringly, "[a]ll parties to the dispute emphasize that the problem does not involve the nuclear warhead of the Minuteman missiles. The danger is from possible explosion of the fuel that propels the rockets, not from accidental explosion of the warhead *or from possible wartime enemy attacks,*" according to the *Star*. *As to the latter,* "All sites are more than 20 miles from any town of more than 25,000 population. This is the distance considered necessary by the Air Force to minimize civilian casualties during an actual enemy attack on American missile sites."[146] The *Star*—and the air force—were silent about what would happen to towns of fewer than twenty-five thousand souls.

There were those who thought outside of the box proffered by the air force and the Corps. If no South Dakotans in the missile area, least of all ranch owners, read the article in the *Washington Star* (it seems unlikely that any would have had access to a Washington newspaper), Congressman Case, or his staff, certainly did, and it is a testament to his vigilance over the interests of his constituents back home that he made inquiries about the dispute with the secretary of the Air Force, who explained the rationale for the Air Force's small safety zone around each Minuteman silo.[147] Case had long-standing concerns about the dangers that the missiles presented on South Dakota soil. In August 1961, a brief article—remarkably so in comparison to the hype about the boom to be expected from the Minuteman—in the *Rapid City Journal* reported that "South Dakota has several prime targets in case of nuclear war, Sen. Francis Case . . . said today." These included, in addition to the missile sites, Ellsworth Air Force Base, an airport at Sioux Falls, and dams on the Missouri River. "Plain prudence suggests that the cities of Pierre and Yankton, Sioux Falls and Rapid City organize for possible attack and that they as well as towns and farm homes downwind from target areas prepare to survive trouble," Case was quoted as saying.[148] In fact, the state civil defense agency had drawn up a list of ten target counties as part of the national Operation Alert (1961), counties that were most likely to "suffer the immediate and direct effects of a nuclear attack (blast, heat, and initial radiation)."[149] Most citizens may not have known the details of this, but local civil defense officials certainly did. Yet, there is no indication in the archives or the newspapers that South Dakotans paid any attention to what would happen to the ranches and small towns in and near the missile area—including the Rosebud country. How much that failure to grasp the danger was an effect of ignorance of the facts, and how much it was a product of willful—if understandable—evasive thinking, is more difficult to unravel. It was not until the late 1970s and the 1980s that at least some South Dakotans came to a dawning realization of the potential danger they were in as a result of counterforce, no-cities nuclear strategies, and their proximity to strategic weapons. Gretchen Heefner describes the *epiphany* of rancher Marvin Kammerer near Ellsworth Air Force Base in 1979, when he witnessed the emergency takeoff of the base's B-52s— either a drill or a false alarm (Kammerer later believed it to have been the latter): "To Kammerer it looked like every single bomber had taken off and was soaring up and out toward the North Pole, presumably the shortest distance to their Soviet targets. It would take about 30 minutes for the Soviet ICBMs to arrive, Kammerer knew; he did not have enough to time to find his family. All he could think of was that on that morning he had not hugged anyone goodbye."[150]

This disquieting awareness might have appeared earlier and among more than some South Dakotans. If anyone had been listening in South Dakota—and we can assume that Congressman Case *was* listening, or at least skimming the transcripts—the Holifield Subcommittee on Military Operations held hearings on civil defense and missile sites in March 1960 while Minuteman was still in the planning stage. Congressman Chet Holifield (Democrat of California) opened the March 30 session by explaining: "We are concerned over the civil defense implications of hardened missile sites within the continental United States. According to information already made public, the planned locations of some of these missile sites will jeopardize various populated centers in the event of a concentrated enemy assault against these missile bases. Because of the widespread fallout of deadly radioactive particles in the event of an enemy attack, *the location of these sites may also endanger the great agricultural heartland of the Nation.*"[151]

The subcommittee then heard from General Curtis LeMay, air force vice chief of staff. LeMay's testimony must have further disturbed Holifield, and it would certainly have disturbed Case had he been present. LeMay explained that silo hardening made it necessary for the Soviets to assign ten to thirty ICBMs "to knock out one of our missile sites," and that with additional hardening in the future, the range would increase to twenty to forty weapons. The point was to make destruction of the U.S.

retaliatory missile force so costly and so difficult that no rational Soviet leader would attack any target in the United States for fear of the massive retaliation to follow through U.S. ICBMs, thus "dramatically increas[ing] the effectiveness of our deterrent posture." The enhanced danger that, should the Soviets try, they would do so with increasingly multiple warheads (or larger ones) "placed" on multiple targets, seems to have escaped the general. Then LeMay explained (as quoted near the beginning of this chapter) that if deterrence failed, the existence of the Minuteman missiles would force the Soviets to attack them first (to ensure their own national survival), thus drawing attacks away from "the more densely populated area of the United States."[152]

General LeMay articulated a rationale that was to become standard fare in subsequent years: "In the selection of specific locations for ICBM sites within the United States, the Air Force has given due regard to the potential danger to the civilian population from such sites. Missile bases are so located that the direct effects of a nuclear attack—blast, heat, and prompt radiation—are minimized as far as practicable. The general area selected for ICMB units encompasses the less densely populated part of the United States."[153] Those who would absorb the immediate effects of Soviet attack were not even worth naming—or best not named. In order for their annihilation to be *tacitly accepted* as a necessary cost (literally, in the world of cost-benefit analysis), their annihilation was best not even raised as a pertinent fact. It is important to understand that this was not an argument about national "sacrifice." Sacrifice is an old (indeed, Old Testament, but also indigenous) and premodern metaphor that en-\tails the full recognition of the value of what is offered up, what is to be lost by the person who sacrifices. As in the story of Abraham and his son Isaac, sacrifice assigns moral weight to the suffering of the one who forfeits something of her or his own. It has obvious relations with—binary differentiation from—the equally moral metaphor of punishment. There is no doubt that the metaphor of sacrifice has been invoked many times in the realm of war—involving both "combatants" and "noncombatants"— over the last few thousand years, both as a battlefield tactic and as an explanation for what we now call "strategic decisions." But the thinking under examination here—the choice of western South Dakota and other ICBM sites in the United States as planned enticements for Soviet nuclear targeting—is better understood as biopower. The decision was arrived at not by asking people to make sacrifices but by coolly and logically calculating how to fight a nuclear war rationally. In such a biopolitical machine, moral value is assigned to those who accept the responsibility to make the "hard" decisions for the nation, even if they have to be kept secret or distorted for public disclosure. As Foucault would no doubt tell us, this was something new in the twentieth century, but not at all limited to the world of nuclear security.[154]

It is telling that *the critics of limited-war theory never raised the question of the immediate effects of enemy weapons on those living in the less densely populated parts of the country.* They were left out of frame—a necessary cost, if they were recognized at all—either because they had "agreed" (in a "market" transaction) to the location of the silos in their pastures and hay fields, or because such siting of the silos was "necessary for national defense," that is, it was "the only way" to limit the overall destruction of the nation and to minimize the national casualty rate. Because national security by its very definition required that one scale up one's balancing of costs and benefits, what alternative was there to losing the less developed parts of the country for the more developed, letting "country B" die so that "country A" might live? Congressman R. Walter Riehlman (Republican of New York), whose district included the county in which Syracuse is located, commended the decision to locate the silos in "areas where the least amount of population [would be] affected by attack," but he pointed out that the Holifield Committee was concerned about radiation effects beyond the missile areas: "The prevailing winds . . . would naturally tie in with an attack and its effect upon our population."[155] The key question was what would happen to cities "downwind," as Holifield put it, from the missile silos.[156] Ralph E. Lapp, a nuclear physicist who had worked on the Manhattan Project, also testified for the Holifield Committee and argued that the effect of "some 30 megatons land[ing] on each ICBM target" would be the same as a general atomic attack on the homeland.[157] In other words, the problem with drawing enemy fire away from cities with missile silos as targets is not the destruction of the population in the immediate area but the fact that the bulk of the nation's population would also suffer the consequences through delayed fallout.

This was the central theme of public criticism of "limited war" for the rest of the Cold War.[158] Never was the prompt destruction of people in western South Dakota—or the other missile areas—even recognized, much less questioned in the available record. It must have seemed to be such a small but inevitable price to pay that it was not even worth discussing (and South Dakotans seemed to accept the deal on some level by their silence). No "defense intellectual" at RAND or SAC planner ever calculated how many people living in specific places such as the western South Dakota countryside would be sure to die from blast, heat, and prompt radiation in order that millions of unspecified (beyond the fact that they lived in "populated" areas) individuals might probabilistically survive who might otherwise have died in a general Soviet attack focused on metropolitan areas and cities. This was a critical, if always unstated, component of "the banalization of the U.S. nuclear weapons in everyday American life" described by Joseph Masco.[159]

In the wake of his announcement of what became known as the "Schlesinger Doctrine," Gerald Ford's secretary of defense, James Schlesinger, briefed the Senate Foreign Relations Committee's Subcommittee on Arms Control on the "effects of limited nuclear warfare" in September 1974. He drew out the differential effects of an enemy counterforce attack, versus a "full-scale attack" (Figure 5.6). While a full-scale attack "would give us prompt fallout plus fatalities on the order of 95–100 million," a Soviet attack limited to ICBM silos might produce collateral damage of (only) 300,000 fatalities, or (again, only) 800,000 if Whiteman Air Force Base in Missouri was included (it had been excluded because of its unusual location upwind from St. Louis).[160] Critics were, not surprisingly, suspicious of these fatality estimates, and the Defense Department followed up the briefing with a detailed analysis in 1975 of the variables involved in estimating collateral civilian fatalities in Soviet counterforce strikes, including the number, size, and detonation altitude of warheads placed on silos; weather; and civil defense.[161] Although this report significantly raised the number of civilian fatalities from limited war—as high as 18,300,000 in an attack on ICBM silos—this still paled in comparison to the 95–100 million for a full-scale attack.[162]

The subcommittee's 1975 report, *Analyses of Effects of Limited Nuclear Warfare,* also included an analysis by physicist Richard Garwin, who

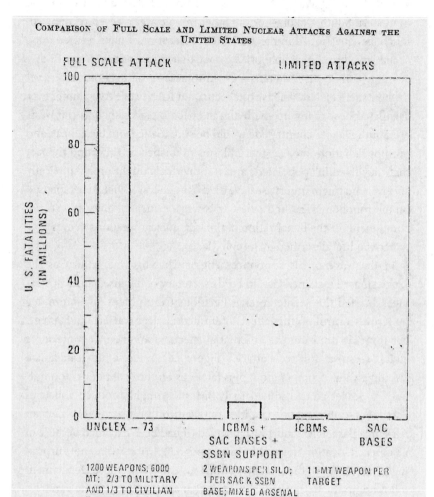

COMPARISON OF FULL SCALE AND LIMITED NUCLEAR ATTACKS AGAINST THE UNITED STATES

FULL SCALE ATTACK   LIMITED ATTACKS

U. S. FATALITIES (IN MILLIONS)

UNCLEX — 73

1200 WEAPONS; 6000 MT; 2/3 TO MILITARY AND 1/3 TO CIVILIAN TARGETS

ICBMs + SAC BASES + SSBN SUPPORT

2 WEAPONS PER SILO; 1 PER SAC & SSBN BASE; MIXED ARSENAL

ICBMs

1 1-MT WEAPON PER TARGET

SAC BASES

FIGURE 5.6. Massive attack versus limited attacks on military targets. Briefing on Counterforce Attacks (Appendix), *Analyses of Effects of Limited Nuclear Warfare*, Subcommittee on Arms Control of the Committee on Foreign Relations, U.S. Senate. 94th Congress, First Session (Washington, D.C.: U.S. Government Printing Office, 1975), 111.

had worked on design of the hydrogen bomb. The document included a national map of fallout patterns from Soviet attacks on missile sites and SAC bases on a "'typical' winter day" (Figure 5.7), clearly showing how a Soviet counterforce attack would entail much more than the destruction of purely military assets (note that the Rosebud country would receive high levels of radiation). Garwin's analysis was also accompanied by state maps annotated with hand-drawn designations of blast zones at SAC bases and ICBM sites and fallout tracks. Garwin's map of South Dakota

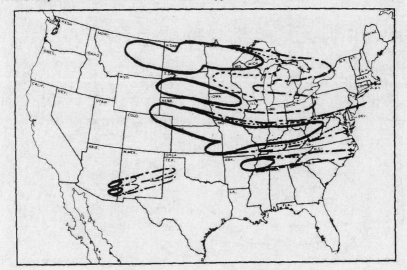

FALLOUT PATTERNS FOR A "TYPICAL" WINTER DAY

This map illustrates the sensitivity of the fallout pattern to the characteristics of the winds blowing at the time of the attack. The patterns shown were calculated using the same assumptions as those used to produce the previous map but winds for a "typical" winter day were used instead of winds for a "typical" March day.

450 REM to persons with a protection factor of 3
200 REM to persons with a protection factor of 3
2 microcuries per square meter of Sr-90

FIGURE 5.7. National fallout pattern for attack on strategic military targets in the United States. Statement by Richard Garwin, in *Analyses of Effects of Limited Nuclear Warfare*, Subcommittee on Arms Control of the Committee on Foreign Relations, U.S. Senate. 94th Congress, First Session (Washington, D.C.: U.S. Government Printing Office, 1975), 52.

is reproduced in Figure 5.8. The blast area at the left of the map (designated as the area enclosed by two meandering parallel lines, and marked with perpendicular crosshatching) "would experience at least 4–5 pounds per square inch of blast pressure and wind speeds in excess of 120 mph. Most ordinary houses would be destroyed." This area, as well as the eastward fallout track (designated by parallel, up–down lines), would receive 450 REM, a level sufficient to "result in at least 50 percent of the people in the area being killed by radiation sickness." The track continued east-northeast, with lower lethality, through Minnesota (north of Minneapolis) and Wisconsin and into Canada. Again, the clear message was not about the small towns and ranchers surrounding Ellsworth Air Force Base and the silos, but about the threat to population beyond the Soviet

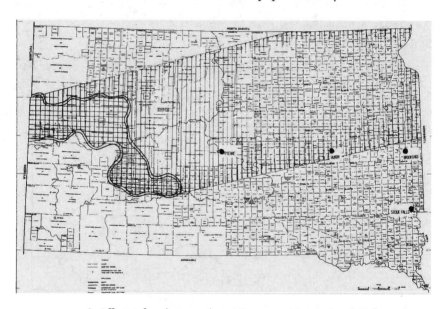

FIGURE 5.8. Effects of nuclear attack on Minuteman sites in South Dakota. Statement by Richard Garwin, in *Analyses of Effects of Limited Nuclear Warfare*, Subcommittee on Arms Control of the Committee on Foreign Relations, U.S. Senate. 94th Congress, First Session (Washington, D.C.: U.S. Government Printing Office, 1975), 91. Two parallel, meandering lines surrounding perpendicular crosshatching mark the blast zone with overpressure of 4–5 pounds per square inch and winds in excess of 120 miles per hour; radiation of 450 REM, killing one-half of people exposed. Parallel vertical lines indicate radiation of 450 REM, killing one-half of people exposed.

target zone.[163] It is very unlikely that anyone in South Dakota even saw these maps, much less discussed them at the time.

Herman Kahn readily admitted in *On Thermonuclear War* that in the wake of a nuclear war fought rationally against the Soviets, not "every part of the country would be habitable." If "the Strategic Air Command [were] moved away from cities and into the Rocky Mountains or the Great American Desert [the Great Plains] . . . then some wars might easily result in the creation of large areas that one would not wish to live in" because of radioactive contamination; it was unlikely that such areas "would ever be decontaminated." But he was quick to point out the good news: "Some people might be willing to visit and perhaps hunt or fish for a few weeks (the game would be edible)." Here we have a post–nuclear-war buffalo commons (except that there would be no humans left in it at all). But more important, other parts of the country would be completely habitable, if with somewhat more radiation than the population had been exposed to prior to the nuclear war.[164]

Of course, the almost completely unthinking write-off of places like western South Dakota could not always be sustained simply by cost-benefit thinking about "national survival." Sometimes nervous laughter was necessary to *euphemize* what the planners themselves *recognized* (on some level) they were doing. In September 1975, the National Security Council discussed plans for a mobile ICBM system (that would eventually become the stationary MX missile). President Ford pointed out that "[t]he biggest problem is selling Congress on the location. Everybody wants it in somebody else's backyard." At that point, the plan was for a mobile ICBM field "in the West, [where] we have significant amounts of federal land that are unoccupied. West of Salt Lake and some in Idaho." Ford quipped, "You would be surprised how many coyotes have to be preserved! (Laughter) It's a totally different world."[165] Thus, long before the phrase "coyote nowhere" became common parlance in the urban lexicon to invidiously designate "uncivilized" places, the idea that ICBMs could be placed where (putatively) only coyotes roamed was a concrete euphemism in national-security thinking.[166] Indeed, the humor in Ford's quip hinges on the idea of only nonhuman animals being put at risk, while the larger reality is comically disposed of in a stunningly Orwellian (via Marcuse) way. This was not black humor, but humor meant to emphasize the absence of humans (or at least humans worth thinking about) from the landscape. This is part of the discursive marginalization of the "price" that real, historical people in rural and small-town South Dakota (and "country B" generally) would pay in the scheme to save "country A." In this carefully protected, self-referential, and self-contained discourse, the missile silo in the rancher's pasture, or the missile silo *two and one-half miles* west of Main Street, Kadoka (population 815 in 1970), South Dakota, are evasively excluded from attention. So is Rosebud Reservation and the larger Rosebud country.[167]

Thus, governing the countryside entailed optics—or, we might be apt to put it, optical illusions—that both occluded what could happen in rural South Dakota (as we have seen here) and focused sustained gaze on what should happen to improve South Dakota and its people. In the next, and final chapter, we will turn once again to a case in which would-be governors intervened to fix what was perceived as wrong with South Dakota—in this case, wrongs pertaining to race and rights.

6

Voting Rights, or How a Regulatory Assemblage Governs

Todd County on Rosebud Reservation was formally organized in 1982 as a result of an out-of-court settlement reached in a Voting Rights Act case between the state of South Dakota and the U.S. Justice Department. The organization of the county followed eight years of litigation and political struggle, and the outcome advanced the voting of Indian people in the view of the Justice Department because it gave them the right to vote for the county officials who govern them. But many, if not most, people of Todd County, both Indian and white, saw the outcome as a *diminishment* of their fundamental rights. Oglala Lakota tribal member Tim Giago, who edited and published the *Lakota Times,* gave clear expression to the viewpoint of many Rosebud Sioux tribal members in Todd County when he wrote, "Indian tribes do not want to become counties or colonies subject to state jurisdiction. The Indian reservations are the last foothold left to the Indian people on a continent they once owned and encroachment upon those lands is verboden [sic] no matter the circumstances."[1] In other words, even gaining Indian voting rights does not justify organizing a county on Rosebud Reservation. The U.S. Supreme Court had determined in 1977 that the counties of Gregory, Tripp, and Mellette that had been opened to non-Indian homesteading (see chapter 1) were no longer part of Rosebud Reservation.[2] Only Todd County remained of the original reservation (see Map 1.3), and now the tribe found itself confronted by the sudden presence of a state subdivision with a jurisdiction spatially overlapping its own on the last intact remnant of the reservation. Rosebud tribal officials and local Indian opinion leaders had deep suspicions of county and state government, which they saw, not at all unreasonably, as hostile to tribal sovereignty.[3]

At least some non-Indians in Todd County were also unhappy with the outcome of an organized county government. To begin with, there was the question of how the (mostly white) owners of taxable land in the county (the white population was only 22 percent of the county total in 1980) would be able to cover the costs of a county government without excessive property-tax rates, and this heightened the resentment many felt over the tax exemption for Indian trust land; it seemed an unfair burden placed on whites, because Indians too would benefit from the county government (which would provide a range of services to all residents, from drivers' licenses to food stamps). And then there was the fact that an organized county government had been *mandated* by a court far off in Washington (the U.S. District Court for the District of Columbia), without a vote by local people. Reiterating the Jeffersonian model of scaled and pointedly "bottom-up" democratic space and government examined in chapter 1, the *Todd County Tribune* complained, "Normally, governments are formed by the people who will live with it via a referendum vote, not by a higher power that says, with dictatorial overtone, 'You shall . . . like it or not.'"[4]

This chapter will examine the history of the legal and political conflict that led to the organization of Todd County on Rosebud Reservation. Part of the story concerns two legal-political apparatuses in the contemporary United States: protecting the voting rights of racial minorities (the voting-rights apparatus), and the recognition of treaty rights and protecting tribal sovereignty (the treaty-rights apparatus).[5] I use the term "apparatus" (French *dispositif*) in the Foucauldian sense: "a thoroughly heterogeneous ensemble consisting of discourses, institutions, architectural forms, regulatory decisions, laws, administrative measures" that "at a given historical moment [responds] . . . to an *urgent need*."[6] Both the treaty rights and voting rights apparatuses include relations between official institutions (courts, tribes, states, legislatures), and official decision making and official legal pronouncements, but they also include "lay" or "folk" discourses, decisions, and other practices and actions.

This will become abundantly clear as we follow the conflicts described in this chapter.

Although there is no inherent reason that these two apparatuses should come into conflict—tribes, tribal members, and their advocates regularly speak, for example, of Indian people having "dual citizenship" in both their tribes and in the United States and the states—in this case they did come into conflict because of the (contingent, historically accidental) way that the pursuit of Indian (and non-Indian) voting rights unfolded in the context of treaty rights as a central concern for people on and near Rosebud Reservation. The voting-rights apparatus was deployed on the ground or "in the trenches" (an apt metaphor because of the adversarial context of its deployment) in a way that ended up eclipsing and dislodging what Lakota people saw as their treaty rights. In the end, Indian people gained voting rights for their county officials but at the cost of a significant challenge to tribal sovereignty and tribal territorial jurisdiction—the presence of a county government organized under state, not tribal, law.

Previous chapters have described regimes of governance as primarily coherent programs consisting of problematizations, optics, policies, and practices that have been given common names by the actors in ways suggesting internal consistency in the regimes—"civilizing Indians," "modernizing farmers," "production control," "Indian self-government," "soil and water conservation," "democratic planning," "graduated deterrence," "no cities," and so on. It has also been clear in the cases we have examined who the programmers were and who the targets of the programs were. We have noted that these programs may or may not have been successful in achieving the goals of the programmers—my assumption has been that effectiveness had little to do with the persistence of any particular program—and that they entailed some friction, translation, and resistance at the point of contact with their human targets. This chapter examines another manifestation of government, much more complex because two distinct strategies of governing were brought into competition with each other.

In order to bring this complexity into focus, I use the term "assemblage" in this chapter to describe the evolving legal and political conflict generated by the active use of the two strategies by situated actors. While the concept of assemblage has been used by scholars to emphasize many different dimensions of complex and hybrid subject matter under analysis, I use it to focus attention on a particular kind of complexity at work in the fraught history of the treaty-rights apparatus and the voting-rights apparatus as they worked themselves out in the Rosebud country.[7] An assemblage is not an institution (such as "the law," the state, the county, the tribe, the Bureau of Indian Affairs, the Justice Department, Congress, South Dakota, a legislature, or a court) although it includes processes and elements and personnel of such institutions. An assemblage includes apparatuses (in this case, treaty rights and voting rights), but it does not have any "dominant strategic function" that Foucault attributed to apparatuses, nor is anyone or any one group "in control."[8] The assemblage described here includes actors who are *political and legal opponents,* yet are nevertheless caught up in the same ensemble of political and legal rights struggle that enmeshes them both. An assemblage, here, is the collection of variously interested parties (along with their idiosyncratic "personalities"), legal-political expertise and discourses (some professional, some lay), and legal and political tactics (some rational and effective, some not) that contingently unfold in a specific conflict in ad hoc and contingent ways. This assemblage is a "formation" in only the most fleeting sense—it existed for the length of the conflict. Once the conflict was "resolved" (admittedly in ways that left an extremely bad taste in the mouths of many, if not most, of the actors), the assemblage withered away—but not, of course, without lasting effects. Another way of putting this is that an assemblage is the entangled political-legal *games* in a general area of conflict as that conflict is played out in its full complexity. *Assemblage* thus refers to an "uncertain and unfolding process . . . that is at most only very partially under any form of deliberate control," although the differentials in power among the actors will be plain enough in the description that follows.[9]

Despite this complexity, the assemblage examined in this chapter had the effect of *governing* lives in two senses. First, the conflictual assemblage included an ongoing (but path-dependent) process of decision making through legislatures, courts, and state and federal agencies. These decisions officially guided, or at least were officially said to be guided, by the treaty-rights and especially the voting-rights apparatuses—as we will see, even judges deploy apparatuses tactically (and thus reproduce them) in order to render "clean" decisions. These decisions had concrete regulatory (and political) effects in defining the precise rights and obligations of citizens and units of formal government under the law. What Indian tribes and Indian people can and cannot do (without risking legal repercussions) in and out of Indian country is more or less clearly defined in the corpus we call federal Indian law, which was activated, and modified, in the assemblage examined here (in other words, the assemblage altered the treaty-rights apparatus). What non-Indians, state and local subdivisions, and even the federal government can do in and out of Indian country concerning Indians and tribes (again, without legal repercussions) is also defined in Indian law as made by Congress and the courts. The same is true for the voting-rights apparatus. What rights people can exercise as voters and what is required and prohibited on the part of local, county, and state government regarding voting is fairly strictly determined by law (even while under continuous change via litigation and legislation). The outcome of legal or related regulatory disputes is, again, never predictable or even reliable or stable over time, as will be clear in the case examined here. This may well be the most important, or at least the most intellectually and critically noteworthy, fact about how government most commonly works in our daily lives.

We turn first to the initial appearance of the voting-rights apparatus in the Rosebud country, what we might think of as the first volley in the opening of the adversarial assemblage that locked self-mobilizing actors into conflict. Because of the complexity of the unfolding conflict, and because *that complexity is a core lesson* about the way that a legal assemblage "governs" in unexpected and unpredictable ways far beyond the goals or view of "regulators," the legal and political history is narrated in detail (although still highly condensed and without bringing in all historical details of the litigation). The reader is encouraged to refer to Figure 6.1 as necessary to follow the trajectory described in the chapter.

Voting-Rights and Treaty-Rights Apparatuses

Todd County was established by an act of the state legislature in 1909. By that time, there were already hundreds of non-Indians living in the county (see Figure 6.2). Although lands in Todd County were never declared surplus and opened to homesteading as had been the case for

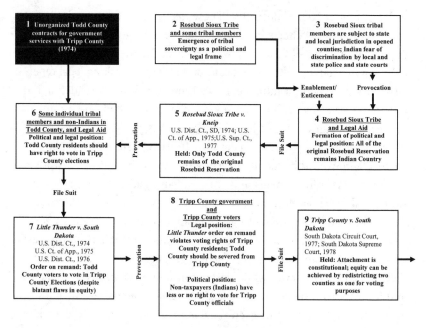

FIGURE 6.1. The complex assemblage of conflict over voting rights and treaty rights.

Gregory, Tripp, and Mellette counties, an Indian allotment could be fee-patented (its trust status removed) if the allottee was administratively declared competent to manage her or his affairs and lands in hopeless heirship fractionation or that were deemed not needed by the allottee could be sold as fee land through the BIA. Such lands were quickly bought up by non-Indians, and the non-Indian (almost always white) population of Todd County rose from 231 in 1910 to 1,588 in 1980. The non-Indian population on deeded land was in general not subject to federal jurisdiction, nor did it receive federal services meant for Indians.[10] Whites thus depended, at least officially, on state civil and criminal jurisdiction for protection on the reservation.[11] The challenge for non-Indians in Todd County, however, was that because there was relatively little taxable (fee-patented or deeded) land in the county, they could not afford to organize with a board of commissioners, a staff, and a county courthouse. Thus Todd County was initially attached to Lyman County "for judicial purposes."[12] In 1923, Todd County was attached to neighboring

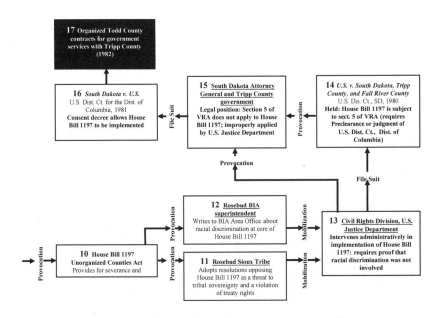

Tripp County (which had been opened for homesteading and organized with a board of county commissioners in 1909) not only for judicial purposes, but also for recording of deeds, mortgages, and foreclosures.[13] The assumption in this practical arrangement was that "attachment" would no longer be necessary as the trust status was eventually removed from Indian lands as Indians became "competent to manage their own affairs," the reservation and "Indians" would disappear as legal things, and Todd County would graduate to full county organization paid for by its Indian and non-Indian property taxpayers (because the Indian Reorganization Act halted allotment and its process of removing the trust status from Indian lands, this resolution was never to happen). In the meantime, Tripp County received as revenue the property taxes raised in Todd County in return for the services it rendered Todd County. By 1967, the responsibilities of Tripp County for Todd County were listed as "administration of governmental and fiscal affairs including all state, county, judicial, taxation, election, recording, canvassing, and foreclosure

Year	White	Indian	Total
1910	231	1,933	2,164
1920	871	1,912	2,783
1930	3,121	2,776	5,897
1940	2,653	3,058	5,711
1950	2,090	2,646	4,736
1960	1,936	2,725	4,661
1970	1,995	4,600	6,595
1980	1,588	5,688	7,276
1990	1,431	6,883	8,314
2000	1,138	7,747	9,050
2010	921	8,468	9,612

FIGURE 6.2. Todd County population by race. Source: U.S. Census, Population.

purposes."[14] This was one of only three county "attachment" arrangements in the United States; the other two were unorganized Shannon County on Pine Ridge Reservation, which was attached to Fall River County, and unorganized Washabaugh County, also on Pine Ridge, and attached to Jones County.[15]

This was a commonsensical arrangement for a reservation county with a relative handful of non-Indian residents on deeded land. Indians would be governed by the federal government, and from 1936 by the tribal government (based on a constitution ratified in 1935), from both of which they would also receive government services. Non-Indians would be governed by, and would receive their government services from, neighboring Tripp County, which would also collect property taxes from owners of deeded land in Todd County in order to cover (in theory) the expenses entailed. This must have seemed to all—including Indian people who gave it any thought at all—like a simple version of what is today called an intergovernmental contract (see Figure 6.1, box 1).

Enter South Dakota Legal Services ("legal aid"), whose office was in Mission in Todd County. Remarkably smart and creative, young staff attorneys had become both experienced and activist in using federal Indian law in the interests of Indian people and the tribe. In this regard, their legal work both invoked and added to what I am calling the treaty-rights apparatus—the set of legal principles and actionable interests that both the Rosebud Sioux Tribe and individual tribal members depended upon. But as good advocates for their clients, the attorneys were prepared to use whatever body of law might yield progress in social justice. By the 1970s, many Indian people, as well as non-Indians, in Todd County came to have dealings with the Tripp County government: property taxes when they owned deeded land; recording of deeds and foreclosure proceedings on Indian-owned fee land; automobile registration and drivers' licenses; food stamps; and voter registration and elections. In 1974, the legal aid attorneys developed a powerful argument that challenged the arrangement by which Tripp County officials governed Todd County citizens; Todd County citizens were not allowed to vote for the Tripp County officers who governed them. A suit was brought on behalf of six plaintiffs living in the unorganized counties on Rosebud and Pine Ridge reservations.[16] One of the legal aid attorneys who was privy to the thinking told me recently that "really, it was a no brainer, along the lines of taxation without representation," but in fact it was a creative piece of lawyering that threatened to upset local arrangements in very significant ways, positively or negatively, depending on one's situation.[17] The discussion here will focus primarily on the plaintiffs from Todd County and the defendants, Tripp County and the state of South Dakota. One of the Todd County plaintiffs was an Indian from Mission, and one was a non-Indian from Parmelee.

The complaint in *Little Thunder v. South Dakota* succinctly articulated the civil-rights—not treaty-rights—issue the attorneys had come up with regarding the attachment scheme. Tripp County "has the power and the duty to govern the affairs of . . . attached [Todd County], and [Todd County] is taxed for the cost of its administration. Moreover, elected county officers of [Tripp County] automatically hold their respective offices in governing [Todd County], and part of their salaries is paid from taxes levied upon persons residing in [Todd County]. Persons living in [Todd County], however, are unable to vote for these officials." The plaintiffs were thus denied "any direct voice in the selection of those who will administer their local [government], which . . . [has] a direct, immediate, and substantial effect on their daily lives." Their "interest . . . in good local government is as direct and substantial as that of the voters in" Tripp County. At issue was "an invidious and irrational classification between two classes of people," which served no "compelling state interest." In short, the arrangement was "violative of the Equal Protection and Due Process Clauses of the Fourteenth Amendment to the United States Constitution."[18]

The complaint described the issue as one of "geographical discrimination," not racial discrimination, no doubt because the plaintiffs' attorneys did not want to flag the special legal status of Indians in Todd County (which the attorneys tactically omitted from the filing) by mentioning the word *race*. The geographic denial of equal protections was laid out in the brief:

> an unorganized county and the organized county to which it is attached . . . form a single governmental unit. Both are governed in the same manner by exactly the same personnel. Both pay taxes to support the county services which are provided to both through exactly the same agencies. And yet . . . [the arrangement] divides the qualified voters of this single governmental unit into two classes of otherwise qualified voters, the one class being allowed to have a voice in the local public affairs of the unit of local government, and the other being entirely denied such a voice.

But the assertion that both Tripp and Todd counties were "governed in the same manner" omitted the extremely weighty—and glaring—fact that Tripp County officials did not have civil or criminal jurisdiction over Indians in Todd County, except for taxation of fee land (see Figure 6.1, box 4).[19]

While the legal aid attorneys' legal argument may have seemed technical or abstract, local people understood the underlying issue in very concrete terms. It was potentially, from the standpoint of white people living in Todd County, about taxation without representation. To white people living in Tripp County, the suit was an outrageous attempt by (mostly Indian) people in Todd County, or those representing them, to exert control over Tripp County government. The lawsuit caused an immediate lining up of the "sides" among not only local officials but the general population.

In order to understand how Indian people in Todd County favored, or came to favor, this suit, we need to examine the wider context of political activism and litigation at the time, and in particular the treaty-rights apparatus that was undergoing a transformation at the same time that voting rights became a question in the Rosebud country. American Indians received the right to vote in 1924, when they were declared citizens, and voters on Rosebud Reservation have been frequently visited by candidates for elective office—especially Congress—ever since. There is no historical evidence of attempts to prevent Indians from voting since 1924, and "voting rights" were never a political issue prior to 1974.[20] In addition to federal elections, Indian people on Rosebud voted in state and local elections. Indians living in Mission and St. Francis in Todd County (both incorporated under state law) voted for municipal officials, and Indians living in Tripp County voted for county officials, and, when they lived in Winner, for municipal officials.

This is not at all to say that Indian people had not long been concerned with forms of racial discrimination other than those pertaining to voting rights. The most well-known activist from Rosebud Reservation attended the March on Washington in 1963 and was an important spokesperson in South Dakota regarding the civil rights of Indians.[21] But while Lakota activists and many "grassroots" people never disengaged from the struggle against racial discrimination, by 1974 they were at least as concerned, if not more so, with treaty rights, understood in a new, *indigenous nationalist* way. Vine Deloria Jr. dates the political birth of the tribal sovereignty movement to the Trail of Broken Treaties caravan that descended on BIA headquarters in Washington in 1972, and the occupation of Wounded Knee on Pine Ridge Reservation in 1973 by the American Indian Movement and Oglala Lakota people who identified themselves as traditional Lakota. Deloria's book, *Behind the Trail of Broke Treaties: An Indian Declaration of Independence,* published in 1974, was a key manifesto in the emerging movement and had an important role in the wide dissemination of the treaty-rights apparatus and the nationalist ideology of tribal sovereignty.[22] Although treaty rights had been invoked for a long time by Lakota people—from at least as early as the 1868 treaty (discussed in chapter 1)—it was transformed in the 1970s with Deloria's (and others') insistence on reading treaties as *international agreements between sovereigns.*

A key lawsuit at the core of the treaty-rights apparatus was *Rosebud Sioux Tribe v. Kneip,* filed by legal aid attorneys in Mission in 1972. The suit—which had been approved by the Rosebud Sioux Tribal Council—sought a declaratory judgment that Rosebud Reservation included all of the original territory as laid out in 1889—including all of Tripp County. Such a judgment would mean that the counties opened to homesteading and now with majority white populations—Gregory, Mellette, and Tripp—would still be Indian country and Indians would *not* be subject to the jurisdiction of the state or its subdivisions, as was the existing state of affairs in 1972. Even more ominous for non-Indians in the opened counties, the Rosebud Sioux Tribe was beginning to flex its sovereign muscles in the terms made newly thinkable by the emerging treaty-rights apparatus. The activist mentioned earlier who had spent many years fighting for Indian civil rights was now the tribal chair and was committed to extending tribal jurisdiction—civil and criminal—over non-Indians on the reservation (which, if the tribe prevailed in *Kneip,* would be all of the original reservation). In April 1974, the tribal council adopted an ordinance assigning the tribal court jurisdiction over "any person" within the original 1889 boundaries of the reservation.[23] Prior to the Supreme Court's 1978 *Oliphant v. Suquamish* holding that tribes may not exercise criminal jurisdiction over non-Indians in Indian country, and its 1981 *Montana v. U.S.* holding severely limiting tribal civil jurisdiction over non-Indians on deeded land in Indian country, there was nothing legally to stop the Rosebud Sioux Tribe from exercising such jurisdiction over non-Indians in Tripp County if it was still part of the reservation, and the latter were alarmed, to say the least.[24] By October 1974, however, the U.S. district court had dismissed the tribe's suit in the *Kneip* case, and the *Little Thunder* suit took on new significance for Indian people.

This was the context (as created by the treaty-rights apparatus that had motivated the tribe to agree to filing the *Kneip* suit) in which the *Little Thunder* case was contemplated by Indian people in Todd County in 1974. Terry Pechota, lead attorney on the *Little Thunder* case, recalls that "Indian clients complained to Legal Services that Todd County was attached [to] Tripp County . . . without any right to vote for the county officers who governed them such as sheriff, clerk of courts, register of deeds, county auditor, and county commissioners."[25] It is very likely that it was the tribe's loss of *Kneip* in the district court that was the source of Indian complaints about their lack of the right to vote for Tripp County officials. Even if neither they nor the Rosebud Sioux Tribal Council had politicked or lobbied for voting rights in Tripp County elections historically, the prospect had become *engaging* because of the loss in the *Kneip* case. There was also the widespread feeling among Indian people that Winner was an anti-Indian town. I was told this numerous times early in my fieldwork in Todd County (beginning in 1985), and it is not difficult to imagine Indian citizens feeling slighted by the "attitudes" of county frontline staff at the Tripp County Courthouse in Winner.[26] If non-Indians in the opened counties could not be brought under tribal jurisdiction, Tripp County government at least could be subjected to the formidable voting power of Indians in Todd County. In other words, Indian support for the *Little Thunder* case most likely originated not primarily from an indigenous standpoint on voting rights in the struggle for justice—they probably had not questioned their lack of the right to vote for Tripp County officials prior to 1974—but from the larger political contest involving reservation boundaries and tribal sovereignty within the treaty-rights apparatus. As the defendant counties and state argued in their brief in *Little Thunder*—with no small insight—the "lawsuit is nothing other than a means of . . . allowing the citizens of the unorganized county to control the governmental affairs of the organized county."[27] Indeed, this must have been precisely the way the stakes in the suit were understood by Indian people in Todd County and non-Indian people in Tripp County.

Returning to examination of the suit, the defendant counties and state responded by invoking the Indian country status of Todd County as a defense. While the plaintiffs had remained silent about the significance of Todd County's being a *reservation* county, about Indian and tribal exemption from state jurisdiction in Indian country, and about the exemption of Indian trust land from property taxes, these facts were critical. "[I]f they are Indians," the defendants argued at trial, no unit of state government "can govern them civilly [or] criminally."[28] As the brief explained:

> The majority of the Plaintiffs . . . are . . . members of either the Rosebud or
> Oglala Sioux Tribe and, as a result thereof, are not taxpayers to either the
> unorganized counties or the organized counties but owe their allegiance
> to the Oglala Sioux Tribe and the Rosebud Sioux Tribe. . . . The unorga-
> nized counties are wholly within the closed portions of either Rosebud or

Pine Ridge Indian Reservations. The majority of the real estate in the unorganized counties is of trust status and not subject to taxation by the unorganized counties, and the majority of the residents of the unorganized counties are enrolled members of the applicable reservations and have no tax responsibilities to the State or unorganized counties.[29]

As everyone was well aware, it was the trust status of Indian land in the unorganized counties that had made the attachment arrangement compelling in the first place.

The lawsuit thus involved attorneys for Indian clients citing civil rights and "geographical discrimination," avoiding mention of either race or Indian country, and attorneys representing state and county governments citing basic Indian law. This is how lawyers usually work—they use the law that will allow them best to advocate for their clients; they frame an argument by foregrounding and backgrounding facts, laws, and precedents in conformity with a legal strategy. The plaintiffs in *Little Thunder* would have had a less credible argument had they described, or even admitted to, Indian people in Todd County having a (very) distinct legal status (it would have undermined the geographical-discrimination argument), or acknowledged the special status of the reservation and the tribal government at the core of the treaty-rights apparatus. Arguing that Indians in Todd County had the same interests in voting for Tripp County officials as did whites in Tripp County required that any legal differences affecting the situation of Indians in Todd and non-Indians in Tripp be elided. In David Delaney's evocative terms, we might aptly describe the plaintiffs' rhetorical strategy as one of narrating a "geography of connections." Indeed, recognizing any significant differences between people in the two counties would have given credence to the original and quite rational, perhaps even compelling, plan to attach reservation counties to neighboring organized counties (but without merging them into a single county). As we have seen, this was precisely the "fact situation" that was emphasized by the defendants, who insisted that the two groups of citizens were anything but similarly situated. In Delaney's terms again, we can usefully name this a "geographical narrative of severance."[30] Another way of saying this is that any body of law can cut both ways in a particular suit, and federal Indian law and treaty rights can be useful for non-Indians, even if they may disapprove of those laws in principle (for example, the common argument that Indian people and tribes are unfairly allowed rights beyond those possessed by other citizens). Thus, the plaintiffs on the reservation limited their narrative to civil rights, and it was the defendants—commonly thought of as hostile to treaty rights—who highlighted the well-settled expectation under Indian law of Indian and tribal exemption from state jurisdiction. Everyone involved—both lawyers and laypeople—knew in effect what the Supreme Court had made clear as early as 1832: an Indian tribe in Indian country is "a distinct community in which the laws of [a state] can have no force."[31] The attorneys for Tripp County wanted to highlight this, even though they almost certainly—as did their clients—resented this particular legal reality, which was commonly seen among non-Indians in the Rosebud country as "racial inequality" and even "un-American."

The federal judge in *Little Thunder* issued his opinion on the same day as the trial, and held that the existing arrangement of attaching unorganized counties to organized counties for practical administrative purposes, without giving voters in the unorganized counties the right to vote for officials in the organized counties, "is not unconstitutional," and that "the legislature has drawn a reasonable line" on voting rights based simply on county of residence. The unorganized counties' claim was simply "without merit."[32] The district court implicitly adopted the geographic narrative of severance, which would recognize the distinctly different political-legal situations of Indians in Todd County and residents in Tripp County—in other words, recognizing that the treaty rights of tribal members made a mockery of the claim that the two counties could be reasonably seen as a single unit.

The plaintiffs in the unorganized counties appealed to the U.S. Court of Appeals for the Eighth Circuit, which reversed the district court holding in June 1975. While the state and organized counties had insisted that "nothing more than a geographic residency requirement is imposed" (indeed, as we have seen, Indians who resided in Tripp County could vote for Tripp County officials, apparently without challenge), the appellate court reasoned that "[t]his view is too simplistic."[33] The court adopted the geographic narrative of connections urged by legal aid in the district court case, declaring that "each of the unorganized counties and the organized county to which it is attached form a single unit of local government," because the officials in the organized counties "exercise the same authority and are impressed with the same obligations towards the unorganized counties as towards their own organized county."[34] The case was remanded to the district court for appropriate resolution (Figure 6.1, box 5).

In conformity with the geographic narrative of connections advanced by the legal aid lawyers, the appeals court made its decision without recognizing the established fact that federal Indian law prohibited state jurisdiction over Indians in Indian country and that almost all land owned by Indians in Todd County was untaxable trust land. Thus, the court's statement that the organized counties "exercise the same authority and are impressed with the same obligations towards the unorganized counties as towards their own organized county" either purposely excluded the concrete effect of federal Indian law in this case (most likely) or at best was based on extremely short judicial memory (not likely). In 1973, a three-judge appeals panel (including one judge who would later sit on the 1975 *Little Thunder* panel) revisited criminal jurisdiction in Indian country in a reservation boundary case concerning the Cheyenne River Reservation in South Dakota. The judges proceeded from the crystal-clear presumption that if a crime had taken place on the reservation, "then South Dakota had no jurisdiction to charge and convict . . . an enrolled member of the Cheyenne [River Sioux] Tribe, for the rape of a . . . librarian at Eagle Butte." This necessarily followed, the court explained, from federal law that gives *exclusive jurisdiction* over rape by an Indian in Indian country to the United States. This was well-established, fundamental Indian law at the core of the treaty-rights apparatus. The court found that, indeed, Eagle Butte was in Indian country (despite the opening of the area to homesteading) and that the state had illegally convicted and imprisoned the tribal member.[35] Some eight months later, an Eighth Circuit panel (again, including a judge who would sit on the *Little Thunder* panel in 1975) held in *Feather v. Erickson* that twenty-two tribal members who had been convicted of crimes in state court and sent to state prison had been beyond state jurisdiction because they were Indians living on the Sisseton-Wahpeton Reservation, which was still legally Indian country, despite the opening of its "surplus" land to homesteading.[36] The twenty-two men were released from state prison as a result of the holding.[37]

The Eighth Circuit judges thus *knew very well* that Todd County, which had never been opened to homesteading, was Indian country. They knew the district court holding in *Kneip,* and they entertained the very question of the boundaries of Rosebud Reservation in the *Kneip* appeal, just a few weeks after the *Feather v. Erickson* decision, affirming the district court's holding that Rosebud Reservation had been diminished by the county opening acts, so that *Todd County remained as intact Rosebud Reservation, or Indian country.*[38] The judges on the appeals panel knew even better than most people—and most local people knew this quite well—that neither the state nor any of its subdivisions had any jurisdiction over Indians in Todd County. The Todd County sheriff, for example, who was provided by Tripp County in the attachment arrangement, had no official dealings with Indians, save responsibility for seizing tax-delinquent or foreclosed fee-patented lands (which, after 1934, would have been relatively unusual). One cannot but wonder why the court felt compelled to underline the right of the individual to vote for those who govern her/him while not recognizing the glaring complication that Indians in Todd were simply *not governed* by Tripp County officials. The court no doubt found it impossible to "balance" the (in this case) bodies of law that had been brought into conflict by the *Little Thunder* suit—the rights of Indians and their tribal governments under federal Indian law, and those of citizens under the Constitution.

The best way to understand this is that rather than try to balance the two bodies of law, the appeals court rhetorically "purified" the question before it by excluding the complicating body of law—Indian law—and the complicating body of inescapable and observable facts on the ground about rights and political space. Or, rather than purification, we might usefully call this process disentanglement—disentangling a legal question from the concrete context of interests that generated the suit to begin with. Like economics and markets, legal work and lawsuits perform "disentanglements."[39] This is the process of "framing," as described by Michel Callon, which "puts the outside world in brackets," and hence my reference to treaty rights and voting rights as *apparatuses.*[40] Both attorneys and judges seek rhetorically to narrow legal questions by framing them in such a way that only some points of law and only some aspects of the "fact situation" are "before the court." For judges, this framing is necessary to make a case *decidable,* and attorneys comply by making narrow arguments in pursuit of offering the judge the option of easily deciding a case—what we colloquially call a "no-brainer." Bright lines in decisions require that the question be disentangled from its concrete context. If context matters—and, of course, it always does—most legal discourse and court decisions are inevitably legal fiction.

Such framing may be necessary for both markets and lawsuits, but it is inevitably accompanied, Callon tells us, by the overflowing of what was consigned to the "outside" world of "externalities." In this case, if the appellate court judges were silent about Indian country and jurisdiction while championing the rights of people to vote for the officials who "govern" them, non-Indians in Tripp County were incited to speak publicly in ways that "overflowed" the court decision. They were far more than a little cognizant of two inescapable entanglements of the legal question in the case. First, they understood that it was the reservation status of Todd County that had made the attachment practical at the time it was instituted and at the time of the *Little Thunder* suit—which was externalized by the appeals court. Second, they were deeply concerned about the entanglement of the plaintiffs' goal in *Little Thunder* and the larger context of reservation boundary and jurisdiction cases, something also absent from the court's decision. As mentioned, non-Indians in Tripp County must have seen the suit as an attempt to challenge the existing relationship between the Rosebud Sioux Tribe and Tripp County. The tribe had attempted through the *Kneip* case to get Indians out from state jurisdiction in Tripp County and get the non-Indians there under an expanded, activist tribal jurisdiction.[41] While they had not succeeded so far in extending tribal jurisdiction over non-Indians in Tripp County, they had now won the right to vote for officials in an "off-reservation" county.

In April 1976, the U.S. District Court in Pierre, acting on the remand from the federal appeals court in *Little Thunder,* held an evidentiary hearing followed by a six-hour conference of the attorneys representing the two sides.[42] According to a local newspaper account, one of the issues discussed was the complexities raised by the fact that substantial numbers of the voters in the unorganized counties were Indians living on Indian reservations. An attorney representing Tripp County told the paper this meant that "elected county officials have no jurisdiction over the majority of the voters who would be influencing the decisions and the running of organized county government." His point was that Indian voters had less—or, perhaps, no—substantial interest in the elections for officials in the organized counties, that officials in the organized counties could not accurately be said to "govern" Indians in the unorganized counties, and that it therefore made no sense to let Indians vote in the elections in question.[43] The judge issued his order a few days after the hearing, and concluded that the hearing and conference had not yielded, and could not, a road map for "equitable relief," as ordered by the Eighth Circuit appeals court. Furthermore, "[b]ecause the legislature created the organized–unorganized situation, and because the legislature has special resources necessary to gather all the relevant facts and effectively deal with the total situation, it is the responsibility of the legislature to solve the problems that have arisen therefrom." In the meantime, the judge held that "qualified voters of the unorganized county" must receive ballots listing "the names of candidates for county officers in the organized county" at "every future" election.[44] Clearly, the judge recognized that this was an unfair and unsustainable result, but he had no choice but to reach it, and to delegate a sustainable correction to the legislature. The resentment toward Indian people was made clear in a legal brief for Tripp County: "Never before, in a country where the attainment of rights carries with it the acceptance of obligations, has it been possible for so many to give so little to attain so much[45] (Figure 6.1, box 5).

As was the case in Tripp County's position in *Little Thunder,* the attorneys, commissioners, and some citizens invoked Indian treaty rights as a *fact.* But this did not mean, of course, that these actors viewed treaty rights favorably. It was more an "unfortunate" fact in their mind. The Tripp County commissioners adopted a resolution clearly characterizing Indian treaty rights as rooted in what they saw as unfair racial privileges and recommending that "the United States Congress enact legislation to bring all of South Dakota, including Indian reservations under State law," and that Congress also "pass legislation that essential services, such as social and health programs, provided on reservations with Federal monies be made available to Indians and non-Indians alike." Furthermore,

the commissioners called for "a congressional inquiry and investigation . . . into discriminatory practices of Federal agencies in administering grants and loans to Indian individuals and tribes, and non-Indian
individuals and units of local government, and that steps be taken to correct such discriminatory practices." Finally, the state legislature should
"investigate in depth the conditions in reservation counties in South
Dakota and . . . recommend legislation to preserve and strengthen county
government."[46] This inevitably alarmed tribal officials and confirmed the
fears of Indian people about the import of organizing Todd County on
Rosebud Reservation, the "last remaining" part of the reservation (one
month later, the Supreme Court would affirm the appeals court *Kneip*
holding that the exterior boundaries of Rosebud Reservation had been
implicitly redrawn by the opening of the reservation to homesteading,
which had diminished the reservation to Todd County only). The tribal
council quickly adopted a counterresolution that deemed the actions
sought by the Tripp County commissioners' resolution as "*a direct attack
on the sovereignty of the Rosebud Sioux Tribe.*" The "federal government
[should] refuse to take the actions requested of them for the reason that
such actions would be a violation of the treaties, laws, and trust responsibilities of the United States." Finally, "the Rosebud Sioux Tribe would
look upon any study conducted into reservation conditions by the State
of South Dakota's action [as] beyond South Dakota's authority and jurisdiction."[47] *Voting rights and treaty rights—as they actually existed and were
being played out on the ground—had come into stark conflict for Indian
people in Todd County.*

Tripp County proceeded to distribute ballots for the upcoming election for county commissioner to *all voters in Todd County and to one district in Tripp County*—as required by the *Little Thunder* order on remand.
But Tripp County also sued the state of South Dakota over the attachment law in state circuit court, hoping to compel the legislature to remedy the situation in a way that guaranteed the voting rights of Todd
County residents at the core of *Little Thunder* while also being fair to
Tripp County voters. A state legislative resolution along these lines was
precisely what the federal judge had called for in his decision on *Little
Thunder* on remand. Among other arguments in *Tripp County v. South
Dakota,* the county pointed out that, as things stood after the order on

remand in *Little Thunder*, Todd County voters would actually have voting rights *superior* to those of Tripp County voters in elections for Tripp County commissioners. Tripp County was divided into three districts for representation on the board of county commissioners, and the terms of the commissioners were staggered so that only one district voted in any given election for commissioners, with the other two districts waiting to vote until the term of their commissioner was expiring. Because the order on remand in *Little Thunder* required the provision of ballots for Tripp County elections to Todd County voters in *all* future elections, Todd County would vote for Tripp County officials annually, while Tripp County voters would vote only once every three years. Thus, in every election, Tripp County voters in two districts would be, relative to Todd County voters, "disenfranchised and excluded from participation in the election for commissioner." These excluded voters would be denied "their right to free and equal election" and "their right to equal protection under the law" without any "compelling State interest." What is more, those Tripp County residents in the county voting district whose turn it was to vote for commissioners would have their votes "diminished by being counted with" the votes of Todd County residents (a much higher number of voters than found in each Tripp County district), denying the former "their right to free and equal election . . . and their right to equal protection of the laws." Although it was not put in these terms by Tripp County, it does seem that the arrangements resulting from the *Little Thunder* order on remand were at least as outrageous, if not more so, as the denial of equal protection that *Little Thunder* was meant to remedy. Tripp County sought "severing Todd County . . . and allowing Tripp County to cease the performance of the administrative and governmental function of Todd County."[48]

The state circuit court rejected Tripp County's equal-protection argument that the attachment legislation was unconstitutional and referred Tripp County to the state legislature rather than offer any judicial remedy that might undermine the voting-rights holding of the Eighth Circuit Court of Appeals in *Little Thunder*. The court ordered the Tripp County auditor to certify the election of a Democratic candidate—the candidate who was elected via the inclusion of the Todd County votes (tribal members were most commonly Democrats)—as commissioner.[49] Tripp County appealed the decision to the South Dakota Supreme Court, which, in March 1978, upheld the circuit court's rejection of the equal-protection argument against the attachment legislation (Figure 6.1, box 6).[50]

The Conflict Deepens:
County Severance and the Justice Department

In the face of the apparent disenfranchisement of Tripp County voters in elections for their own county officials (in the wake of the *Little Thunder* order on remand) and the state court system's refusal to sever Todd from Tripp, political support for legislative "severance" began to build. "Severance" was proposed as a solution not only for Tripp County, but also for Fall River County (to which Shannon County of Pine Ridge Reservation was attached) and Jackson County (to which Pine Ridge's Washabaugh County was attached). Legislative severance would get *around* the direct consequences of the *Little Thunder* decision—which seemed not only unfair but irrational to most non-Indians—by bringing about the formal legal organization of the unorganized counties as freestanding and autonomous subdivisions of state government. The South Dakota Association of County Commissioners advocated that the unorganized counties be organized under state law or, if that was not possible because of insufficient tax revenue, administered by the state, to free the adjacent organized counties from the relationship and, of course, the court-ordered voting rights.[51]

The *political* issue was broader—and more potentially "racial"—than the formal legal issue. While Tripp County argued in *Tripp County v. South Dakota* that its grievance was the superior voting rights the order on remand in *Little Thunder* gave to Todd County residents, the South Dakota Supreme Court retorted that the solution was simple: redistricting the two attached counties under House Bill 908 adopted by the legislature in 1977, requiring each pair of organized and attached unorganized counties to reapportion commissioner districts "by treating the organized and unorganized county as a single unit and allocating county commissioner districts within the two counties according to population."[52] House Bill 908 was introduced by a Republican from Murdo, in Jones County, just north of Mellette County in the Rosebud country.[53] This bill was preferred by Todd County voters over an alternative that was also passed in 1977 (over the governor's veto), and that had been preferred by voters in Tripp County. Introduced by Republican representatives from Gregory County in the Rosebud country and Fall River County, House Bill 797 provided for severance if a plurality of voters in either an unorganized county or in the organized county to which it was attached voted in favor.[54] The organized counties' opposition to treating each pair of unorganized and organized counties as a single unit, and redistricting on the basis of total population or registered voter counts, was not satisfactory to Tripp County or the other organized counties. The *Todd County Tribune* succinctly reported the rationale: "Taxpayers receive services from their county officers; they pay money in the form of taxes so the bills can be paid. Non-taxpayers, however, contribute no money but also need license plates, deeds recorded, welfare and food stamps, bridges . . . county graded roads, birth, marriages and deaths recorded and a Sheriff to protect and preserve their rights." The *clear* implication was that non-taxpayers— Indians—had less (or no) right to vote in the election of the officials in the organized county that provided these services.[55]

South Dakota's Local Government Study Commission, composed of legislators and other citizens, discussed the problem at its meeting in October 1975; mostly non-Indians from Tripp, Todd, and other affected counties attended and gave testimony. The state's attorney for Jackson County—who happened to be an Oglala Sioux tribal member but who represented the organized county's official position—told the commission that the organized counties were worried that "unorganized counties with less taxable land could conceivably control an election because of a larger population." He opined that "the judges did not make a good decision" because "the court exaggerated the situation when it ruled that the people had a large interest in the elected officials." This was not the case, he said, because "the [Indian] people complaining were non-taxpayers." This was an argument that would not likely have convinced any court, but it indicates the entanglement of the strictly legal question with resentments regarding the legal status of Indians. The state's attorney from Tripp County reported the desire of the board of county commissioners that Todd be detached from Tripp. He urged a plan by which the existing Todd County highway board (which was appointed at the time) could be reorganized as an elective body and vested with the authority to enter into contracts for "governmental services" (essentially the same arrangement as that in place between the two counties at the time, except that Todd County voters would elect the board in general elections, in theory resolving the central issue in *Little Thunder*). A Fall River County commissioner "questioned why people in organized counties could not vote in tribal government election as long as people in unorganized counties were allowed to vote in election of the organized county."[56]

Because there were political and legal difficulties with house bills 797 and 908, the South Dakota legislature enacted a severance bill in 1979. The Unorganized Counties Act (House Bill 1197) repealed the existing attachment legislation, provided for the governor to appoint an interim board of five county commissioners for Todd County and Shannon County on Pine Ridge Reservation that would have the power to contract government services with an adjoining county. The interim commissioners were to redistrict their soon-to-be-organized counties in preparation for elections of county officers in 1980, which would replace the interim boards on January 1, 1981. Annual tax rates in the newly organized counties would be limited to 105 percent of the previous year's tax bill to allay the fears of non-Indians in the reservation counties that their tax bills would become exorbitant upon organizing (Figure 6.1, box 10).[57]

The Rosebud Sioux Tribal Council was quite understandably alarmed by the new severance bill, which they saw as a direct violation of treaty rights and a direct threat to tribal sovereignty. As the tribal chairman told the council representatives, organizing Todd County under state law meant "the recognition of another government within the boundaries of the Rosebud. [Y]ou are recognizing the state's jurisdiction within the boundaries." One council representative moved to "inform the Justice department [and the] B.I.A. to exercise the trusteeship for Rosebud Reservation and stop the State from organizing Todd County." The motion passed, and another council representative expressed what was likely the opinion of all when she proposed a resolution to "state that we are the governing authority in this area called Rosebud Reservation."[58] Another council member, a well-known advocate of treaty rights, insisted that under the 1868 treaty, Todd County could not be organized without a three-fourths majority vote and demanded the presence of the BIA superintendent.[59] The council passed a resolution declaring that

South Dakota and Tripp County have pursued and undertaken a concerted effort to circumvent the ruling in Little Thunder and abrogate the right of Indian people to exercise their constitutional right to vote, among other conduct: 1) instituting actions in state court to negate the Little Thunder decision, 2) refusing to follow the mandate of the Eighth Circuit requiring implementation of its decision, 3) refusing to follow the mandate of the South Dakota Supreme and Circuit Court requiring redistricting of county commissioner districts, 4) introducing bills in the South Dakota Legislature to overrule the decisions of the South Dakota Supreme Court and the Eighth Circuit Court of Appeals, 5) appealing to racist and bigoted attitudes and attempting to pass legislation emphasizing that Indians would ruin the government of Todd and Tripp County unless the Little Thunder decision and the effects thereof were overturned, 6) amending voter registration laws to make it more difficult for Indian people to vote.

House Bill 1197 would "organize . . . Todd County as a political subdivision of the state of South Dakota" coterminous with "the exterior boundaries of a portion of the Rosebud Sioux Indian Reservation." This would force upon the tribe "recognition of another government within [its] exterior boundaries . . . and . . . recognition of the jurisdiction of the State of South Dakota within the exterior boundaries." The resolution reiterated the tribe's "rights and existence as established by the 1868 Treaty, the 1934 Indian Reorganization Act, the 1968 Civil Rights Act, and the case of *Rosebud Sioux Tribe v. Kneip* which establishes that the boundaries of that land area referred to as Todd County are the exterior boundaries of" the reservation. "[O]nly Federal legislation, with the concurrence of the Rosebud Sioux Tribe can change the existing scheme with the boundaries" (Figure 6.1, box 11).[60]

While the tribal government was certainly not opposed to the voting rights gained by Indian people through the *Little Thunder* decision, and probably would have been amenable to redistricting of the two counties under House Bill 908, such that Todd County residents had voting rights equal to those of Tripp County, it was much more concerned with tribal sovereignty under federal Indian law, going back to the Fort Laramie Treaty. There is little doubt that if expansion of voting rights might undermine treaty rights—as the situation was tending—the priority for Indian people would be treaty rights. The tribal council could not envision the coexistence of a county government and the tribal government in the same territory. Even a tribal member who was not known for his commitment to tribal sovereignty, and who came subsequently to serve for many years on the Todd County Board of Commissioners, "said [at an open meeting on voting rights in 1975] he doubt[ed] that Todd County can be organized unless and until it is determined whether or not [the Rosebud Sioux Tribe] is a sovereign nation."[61] The question was how a state subdivision could be organized on a reservation when the state had no jurisdiction (at least over Indians) on the reservation, and the worry was that the situation might create a foothold for the extension of state jurisdiction over Indians or Indian country. It should also be noted that at the time, the tribe was eager to assert both criminal and civil/regulatory jurisdiction over non-Indians in Todd County, so many Indian people not only could see *no practical need* for a Todd County Board of Commissioners, but saw it as a potential competitor.[62]

The BIA superintendent, who was also a tribal member, forwarded the tribal resolution quoted above to the BIA area office in Aberdeen, South Dakota, urging its "careful attention" (Figure 6.1, box 12). Regarding the Unorganized Counties Act, the superintendent wrote, "[t]he entire manner in which this bill was introduced and its apparent genesis being the Little Thunder decision, one has to draw the inescapable conclusion that it is simply a bill to prevent Indian voters from exercising their right to vote for officers who govern them." It should have had Justice Department approval under the terms of the Voting Rights Act prior to enactment. The superintendent continued:

[H]ad Bill 1197 originated from the legislative halls of any southern state in the 1960s when blacks [began] exercising their right to vote guaranteed to them under the federal voting rights acts, it would have been met with outrage by the citizenry and government of the United States. Our trust responsibility to the Rosebud Sioux Tribe and its good people requires us to act in no less magnitude and with no less vigor. The entire history of this bill, and other related legislation, including but not limited to the change in the voter registration laws, which was also a backlash to Indian voter participation in the last election cannot go ignored.[63]

The Justice Department was already alert to changes in voting laws in South Dakota that might negatively affect Indian voting rights and was in contact with the Rosebud Sioux Tribe.[64] Even if attorneys in the voting-rights section of the department's civil-rights division had not seen the tribal resolutions or the BIA superintendent's letter—although, they probably did—they would have intervened in South Dakota's enactment of the Unorganized Counties Act.

Before continuing, we must briefly examine the history and provisions of the Voting Rights Act (VRA), enacted in 1965 in the wake of the voter-registration drives of "Freedom Summer" and the 1964 murder of voting-rights activists in Mississippi and other violence against African Americans.[65] Among its key provisions was that certain states, with histories of racial discrimination in voting, were required to seek approval from the Justice Department or the U.S. District Court in Washington, D.C., before implementing any changes in voting practices. The jurisdictions in question would be those that "the Attorney General determines maintained on November 1, 1964, any test or device, and . . . [where] the Director of the Census determines that less than 50 per centum of the persons of voting age residing therein were registered on November 1, 1964, or that less than 50 per centum of such persons voted in the presidential election of November 1964." The tests or devices at issue were those "for the purpose or with the effect of denying or abridging the right to vote on account of race or color."[66] The initial list of what became known as "covered jurisdictions" included Georgia, Louisiana, Mississippi, South Carolina, and Virginia, as well as twenty-five counties in North Carolina.[67]

Section 5 of the VRA provided that whenever any covered jurisdiction "shall enact or seek to administer any voting qualification or prerequisite to voting or standard, practice, or procedure with respect to voting different from that in force or effect on November 1, 1964," it must, before enforcement, "institute an action in the United States District Court for the District of Columbia for a declaratory judgment that such qualification, prerequisite, standard, practice, or procedure does not have the purpose and will not have the effect of denying or abridging the right to vote on account of race or color." Alternatively, the covered jurisdiction could obtain what became known as preclearance from the Justice

Department.[68] As the 1978 edition of the *Code of Federal Regulations* described the standard for section 5 administrative decisions by Justice, "the burden of proof [is] on the submitting authority [and] is the same in submitting changes to the Attorney General as it would be in submitting changes to the District Court of Columbia. . . . If the evidence as to the purpose or effect of the change is conflicting . . . [the Attorney General] shall, consistent with the above-described burden of proof applicable in the District Court, enter an objection."[69] The covered jurisdiction would thus need to *prove that the proposed changes were not motivated by, and would not incidentally cause, racial discrimination in the right to vote.* The VRA thus added a stringent regulatory process that went well beyond constitutional equal protection (which had been the issue in *Little Thunder*) to target for special scrutiny laws that *might* be racially discriminatory.

None of this initially applied to South Dakota, which did not have a "southern" history of voting discrimination. But in 1975, Congress amended the VRA to include "language minorities" as an additional target of racial discrimination in voting. The category of language minorities included "persons who are American Indian, Asian American, Alaskan Natives, or of Spanish heritage," and the VRA's list of prohibited tests and devices was expanded to include "[a]ny practice or requirement by which any State or political subdivision provided any registration or voting notices, forms, instructions, assistance, or other materials or information relating to the electoral process, including ballots only in the English language, where the Director of the Census determines that more than five per centum of the citizens of voting age residing in such State or political subdivision are members of a single language minority."[70] The determination that Todd County (and Shannon County) met these criteria was published in the *Federal Register* by the attorney general in January 1976. Todd County was subject to preclearance under section 5 of the VRA until section 5 was struck down by the U.S. Supreme Court in its 2013 *Shelby v. Holder* decision.[71]

Returning to the Unorganized Counties Act (House Bill 1197) that would sever the reservation counties from their attached organized counties, the assistant attorney general in charge of the Justice Department's civil-rights division wrote to the South Dakota attorney general in April

1979 advising that the legislation was subject to the preclearance require-
ments of section 5 of the VRA (Figure 6.1, box 13).[72] Justice's voting-rights
section believed that South Dakota was purposely delaying submission
of the statute for preclearance, and was in fact implementing it without
preclearance, because the governor appointed interim boards of county
commissioners for Todd and Shannon counties, pursuant to the Unorganized Counties Act (in Todd County, the appointed board included three
Indians and two non-Indians).[73] The South Dakota attorney general's
office attributed the delay to its being the office's "first experience with a
section 5 submission" (it is likely that this statement was also meant to
imply that South Dakota did not have a history of racial discrimination
in voting, and that the whole process was a bureaucratic waste of time).[74]
It was only after the Justice Department brought action in U.S. District
Court for the District of South Dakota to enjoin implementation of the
law that South Dakota submitted it for administrative preclearance by
the Voting Rights Section (Figure 6.1, box 14).

The Justice Department's suit is worth examining because it allows
us to address the question of whether the state legislature's severance law
was simply a practical solution to an unforeseen problem—just as was
the original "attachment"—or an intended or unintended form of racial
discrimination against Indian voting. In the suit, the district court had
no authority to consider the substantive question of racial discrimination in the state law but it could, and had been asked by the Justice
Department to, adjudicate the question of whether the Unorganized
Counties Act was in fact subject to section 5 preclearance because it was
a change in voting in a covered jurisdiction. South Dakota challenged
the Justice Department's charge that the Unorganized Counties Act was
so subject, because it did not amount to "a voting qualification or prerequisite to voting, or standard, practice or procedure with respect to voting
that was different from that in force or effected in Todd or Shannon
counties on November 1, 1972." In fact, the act was in "direct compliance
with the mandate set forth in *Little Thunder*," and Indians had strong
representation on the boards appointed by the governor. It was also
pointed out that the South Dakota attorney general had "requested help
from the Department of Justice in determining if Section 5 of the Voting
Rights Act applies to the Unorganized Counties Act and in what way, if

any, and what steps should be taken by the State to comply with that Act and all requests for help [have] been refused."[75] Of course, the default assumption in the VRA regulatory process was that any change in voting law was presumed to have discriminatory intent and/or effect until the jurisdiction proved otherwise, either to the Justice Department or the U.S. district court in Washington, D.C.

Justice submitted its trial brief to the South Dakota federal district court in August, arguing that the Unorganized Counties Act "creates a multitude of electoral changes and alters election law in Todd and Shannon Counties in a very dramatic way."[76] The South Dakota attorney general's office responded that the Supreme Court had held in *Dougherty County Board of Education v. White* that "in determining if an enactment triggered section 5 scrutiny, the question is whether the status change has the potential for discrimination."[77] But the Unorganized Counties Act provided Indian people with precisely "what the 8th Circuit ordered in *Little Thunder . . .* , the rights to vote for their own county officials." The Unorganized Counties Act merely corrected a problem inadvertently created by *Little Thunder,* because "it cannot be argued that the non-Indian has any less rights as to voting than any other citizen of the states, as all other citizens of the state only get to vote for the county officials in the county in which they live. Therefore there is no potential for discrimination by the passage of H.B. 1197."[78] The Justice Department challenged South Dakota's reading of *Dougherty County* as well as its contention that the act had no potential for discriminatory purpose or effect. *Little Thunder* created a situation in which Tripp County citizens (90 percent of whom were white) and Todd County citizens (70 percent of whom were Indian) "voted for the same county officials. By creating separately elected officials for the unorganized counties this Act dramatically changes the racial composition of the electorate." It *could* be the case that this change was

> beneficial to the racial minority because it could assure them control of the selection of county officials in . . . Todd Count[y]. However, it is also possible that this Act was passed for *racial reasons.* The legislature may have responded to white opposition to Indian participation in the selection of county officials who, prior to *Little Thunder,* were elected by an

almost totally white electorate. Thus, when viewed in this historical context, the Unorganized Counties Act may have been adopted for *racial purposes*. If the court with jurisdiction to determine the issue, namely the District Court for the District of Columbia, decides that this enactment was adopted in part for racial reasons, even though the effect of this legislation is arguably ameliorative, it violated Section 5 and cannot be enforced.[79]

Let us unpack the term "Indian" in order to understand how race does and does not matter when the word is used, and how the word relates to the Justice Department's focus on impermissible "racial reasons" behind voting laws. There is little question that non-Indians is Tripp County were concerned about Indians in Todd County voting for Tripp County officials as a result of *Little Thunder*, and that the Unorganized Counties Act was a reaction to *Little Thunder*. The question is whether this is accurately described as "racial" in the sense intended by the Justice Department. It will be recalled that Tripp County and the state forthrightly raised the matter of *Indians* in their defense in *Little Thunder*: they were at pains to point out that the plaintiffs were "members of either the Rosebud or Oglala Sioux Tribe and . . . owe their allegiance to the Oglala Sioux Tribe and the Rosebud Sioux Tribe." But it is critical here to realize that the organized counties cannot be fairly said to have been trying to exclude Indians in any sense that clearly coincides with racial discrimination. After all, Indians who *lived in the organized counties*—and many did—were able to vote for county officers, just as were their non-Indian neighbors, and this even if they lived on trust land and did not pay property taxes and were not subject to state (or county) jurisdiction (this was not, however, raised as a defense either in the *Little Thunder* case or later in litigation under the Voting Rights Act). Tripp County avowedly used the terms "tribal member" and "Indian" *in the same way the federal government uses those terms* in federal Indian law. When non-Indian employees of the BIA challenged the "Indian preference" clause of the Indian Reorganization Act (1934) as having been implicitly repealed by the 1972 Equal Employment Opportunity Act that barred racial discrimination in employment practices, for example, the Supreme Court held in 1974 in *Morton v. Mancari* that there was *no racial discrimination* involved; this is a central touchstone in federal Indian law. Indians are regularly and systematically treated differently from non-Indians because of "the unique legal relationship between the Federal Government and tribal Indians."[80] "Literally every piece of legislation dealing with Indian tribes and reservations . . . single out for special treatment a constituency of tribal Indians living on or near reservations. If these laws, derived from historical relationship and explicitly designed to help only Indians, were deemed individual racial discrimination, an entire Title of the United States Code (25 U.S.C. ["Indians"]) would be effectively erased."[81] Critically, giving Indians an employment preference "does not constitute 'racial discrimination.' Indeed, it is not even a 'racial' preference. . . . The preference, as applied, is granted to Indians not as a discrete racial group, but, rather as members of quasi-sovereign tribal entities."[82] This is the meaning of "Indian" used by Tripp County, and in the core logic of the Unorganized Counties Act.

We do need to recognize, however, that while the terms "Indian" and "tribal member" can be, and no doubt often are, used by non-Indians in an innocuous, even respectful (of sovereignty and treaty rights), way to refer to political and legal status rather than reflective of racist imaginaries driving discrimination and bias, the slippage between the two different meanings of the terms—a classic example of what linguists call code switching—is easy and probably common, even in a single utterance. In other words, mention of the term "Indian" can intentionally mean and be clearly understood as implying both the special status of Indians (even if it is resented by non-Indians) and the racist denigration of Indian people as less civilized or otherwise as less respectable than whites. Alternatively, the term "Indian" can signal both respect for Native legal and political status and concern for their simultaneous *racial* oppression in the U.S. racial formation. Such slippage in meaning is a core component of settler colonialism in the United States, not something limited to the Rosebud country. In the case at hand, the slippage was perhaps even motivated by the resentment on the part of non-Indians over the special legal and political status of Indians, so that the two ideas of "Indian" were opposite sides of the same coin. Thus, it is no surprise that the *Todd County Tribune* could invoke the issue of Indian exemption from property taxes (a matter that concerned the—resented, but "nonracial"—meaning of Indians in *Morton v. Mancari*) with the racial stereotype of "people without training or qualifications" in the same paragraph. Put bluntly, in addition to being members of a "nonracial" political category based on a special relationship with the U.S. government (the sense of "Indian" in the treaty rights apparatus), Indians are at the same time a nonwhite racial minority subjected to racial bias and racial discrimination (the sense of "Indian" in the voting-rights apparatus). The struggle over parsing these two understandings was the central legal question in the conflict examined here.

South Dakota eventually submitted its Unorganized Counties Act to the Justice Department for preclearance, remarking that it "obviously does not have the effect of denying or abridging the right to vote on account of race or color."[83] Nevertheless, the voting rights section concluded that "the information sent [by South Dakota] is insufficient to enable the Attorney General to determine that the proposed changes do not have the purpose and will not have the effect of abridging the right to vote on account of race."[84] After additional material was submitted, the chief of the civil-rights division wrote to the South Dakota attorney general in October 1979, ignoring the political status of Indians in Indian country, and characterizing Indians as a racial minority:

> Our analysis reveals that the proposed change finds its impetus in *Little Thunder.* . . . For many years prior to this decision the predominantly Indian residents of unorganized Todd and Shannon Counties were not permitted to vote for the officials of organized and predominantly White Tripp and Fall River Counties, who provided them with governmental services. The *Little Thunder* decision invalidated this restriction on the basis of the Equal Protection Clause of the Fourteenth Amendment. In response to this decision, which provided Todd and Shannon Counties with political access to county government for the first time, residents of Tripp and Fall River Counties and others began a process which resulted in the passage of House Bill 1197 in 1979. The preponderance of evidence suggests that one of the reasons for the passage of House Bill 1197 is to nullify the effect of the *Little Thunder* decision.[85]

The Justice Department thus insisted that it was the *racial* meaning of "Indian"—Indians as a minority and victims of discrimination, not the political-legal status of Indians—that was at work in the Unorganized

Counties Act, while Tripp County and the state would have insisted that it was *precisely* the legal-political status that was their rationale: Indian people in Todd County were not subject to state or county jurisdiction and Indians did not in general pay property taxes. Thus, the only fair implementation of the holding in *Little Thunder,* the severance argument went, was *to give people in Todd County their own county government to elect.*

The Justice Department proceeded to act administratively on the submission of the Unorganized Counties Act by South Dakota. While it was true, Justice reasoned, that citizens in Todd and Shannon counties would be able to organize "their own [county] government bodies, those bodies would be severely and uniquely limited in their ability to carry out governmental functions" because of insufficient revenue owing to the trust land within the counties (note the lack of attention to what the organization of the counties would mean for the sovereignty of the Rosebud and Oglala Sioux tribes). The newly organized counties would still need to contract with other counties—Indian tribal governments were omitted from the law as allowable contracting bodies (and the Justice Department did not go into the jurisdictional rationale for this exclusion)—for provision of basic county government services, and this is precisely what the interim boards of commissioners, appointed by the governor, of the newly organized counties had done. The effect of the Unorganized Counties Act was, thus, "to return Todd and Shannon Counties to a position of dependence on Tripp and Fall River Counties for governmental services, without electoral participation in either of those counties. . . . The right of access won in *Little Thunder* would thus be negated." South Dakota had not met its burden under section 5 "of proving that [the] submitted change has no discriminatory purpose or effect," and the Justice Department therefore formally objected to the proposed change. The Unorganized Counties Act was thereby "legally unenforceable" unless or until Justice withdrew its objection or the U.S. District Court for the District of Columbia declared that the proposed changes "have neither the purpose nor will have the effect of denying or abridging the right to vote on account of race, color, or membership in a language minority group."[86]

The South Dakota attorney general responded in an adversarial tone by requesting copies of all materials used by the Justice Department in arriving at its determination, insisting that the objection had been made "on sociological rather than legal grounds" (by which he no doubt meant defining Indians as a *race* rather than as *members of a special political-legal class*), and explaining that the information requested was necessary in order to decide whether to resubmit the statute, or go to the U.S. District Court in Washington, D.C. The state had "been kept absolutely ignorant of who was to decide this matter and based upon what evidence," throughout the entire process. "I do not deny," the attorney general wrote, "that I seriously question whether the Voting Rights Act should even apply to this particular instance [again, clearly thinking of Indian political-legal *status* as opposed to an Indian *race*], and there is no doubt that the state was reluctant to even submit in this instance." He insisted that "an independent Todd County board of commissioners gives Todd County residents a greater access to county government providing them with an opportunity to make suggestions for improvements and changes in the way county services are provided. [T]erminating the administrative attachment of Tripp and Todd counties will eliminate resentment on the part of certain Todd County residents by allowing these residents to elect commissioners whom they feel will be more representative and responsive to their wishes." This was because Todd County votes would not be diluted, as would be the case if they voted with Tripp County residents for Tripp County officials. He also wrote that the tax base in Todd County was sufficient to support an organized county government. The Justice Department did not comply with the request for information.[87]

The South Dakota attorney general and the attorney representing Tripp County met with Justice Department officials in March 1980 "to discuss possible approaches for a voluntary resolution which would bring the State into compliance with federal law." Among the matters discussed were "modifications" of the Unorganized Counties Act that would improve the state's chances of success in Justice's reconsideration of the law. The meeting had been set up by South Dakota's congressional delegation.[88] According to the attorneys representing the state and the organized counties, the Justice Department's specific objections related to provisions in the Unorganized Counties Act limiting the rate of increase in property taxes in the unorganized counties, and the requirement that Todd and Shannon counties could only contract for governmental services with bordering counties (there was no suggestion that the tribes should be included as possible contractors for provision of services, and the Justice Department apparently accepted the presumption that this was impossible because the state had no legal jurisdiction over tribal government as it did over county government).[89] Justice agreed, according to the South Dakota attorneys, that the objection would be withdrawn and the 1980 elections would go forward on the basis of modification of the specific provisions, as well as submission of evidence by the state that the newly organized counties would be fiscally viable.[90] *These potential arrangements did not reflect the concerns of Indians about organized counties popping up within the reservation boundaries.* They did not have a seat at the table in these negotiations, and the Justice Department must have either been unaware of the severity of the threat from the point of view of the Rosebud Sioux Tribe or decided to diminish its weight in favor of protecting, as Justice saw it, Indian voting rights.

Even after apparent progress toward an agreement, the Justice Department declined to remove its objection to the Unorganized Counties Act in May 1980 and instructed its staff to resume action seeking an injunction to prevent the 1980 primary elections, "[f]or reasons unknown to the Defendants," who described themselves as surprised by the Justice Department response in light of the meeting in March.[91] The *Todd County Tribune* described the view of the attorney representing Tripp County as the Justice Department not acting in good faith to negotiate with the state and Tripp County—which were eager to compromise—to resolve the matter without going to trial. Furthermore, "although the Justice Department takes the position of protecting minority voting rights, their action is seeking to deprive each voter of Todd and Shannon Counties of their right to elect their own county officials under state legislation would also deprive the citizens of Tripp and Fall River of the same right."[92] South Dakota's congressional delegation wrote to the assistant attorney general in charge of the civil-rights division that "we were under the impression that the state was willing to concede or modify provisions of the 1979 law . . . to which your Department had objected. We understood you and your representatives were agreeable to negotiating those objections."[93]

While the administrative preclearance process was in play, a special three-judge panel disposed of the suit filed in the U.S. district court for

South Dakota by the Justice Department against South Dakota and the organized counties (concerning the applicability of section 5, not the substantive question of discriminatory intent or effect). The Unorganized Counties Act was determined to indeed fall under the provisions of section 5 and would not be valid until precleared by the Justice Department or found not to be discriminatory in intent or effect by the district court for the District of Columbia. The appointment of the interim boards of county commissioners was thus "unlawful" and "null and void," as was the election of county officials in the unorganized counties.[94] The *Todd County Tribune* reported that the "South Dakota Attorney General . . . commented that it was unfortunate the Justice Department singled out South Dakota for this kind of bureaucratic treatment." The attorney general complained that the Justice Department would not cooperate with the state by explaining what would be necessary to obtain clearance, and he clearly did not understand, or refused to acknowledge, the hands-off, adversarial position that was required on the part of the voting-rights section. Tripp County commissioners asked citizens to contact their federal legislators.[95]

Before moving on to describe the organizing of Todd County, we need to add one more element of complexity to the assemblage: "personalities." This assemblage involved not just a complex circuitry but also a great deal of affect: resentment and adversarial heat between actors at an interpersonal level. My focus here is not the resentment and heat over racial matters described above, although that was also a fundamental part of the assemblage. Here I am concerned with the "quirks" of individual actors. As we have seen, the South Dakota attorney general and the lawyers representing the nonreservation counties were not hesitant to express their frustration with the Justice Department. An official opinion published by the attorney general in 1977 is even more telling about idiosyncratic individuals in this assemblage. He brought out in his opinion what he called the "facial absurdity" of section 5's applicability to South Dakota on the basis of the fact that it had historically offered ballots and election materials to Indian voters only in English. "The 'omnipotent' Federal Government has apparently seen fit to impose upon the states an unworkable solution to a nonexistent problem," he said regarding the triggered Justice Department gaze in search of racial discrimination in the state, and concluded, "I cannot in good faith recommend that [the secretary of state] and the State Board of Elections be unnecessarily subjected to the bureaucratic agony of obtaining immediate preclearance of all voting legislation and regulations passed or promulgated since November 1, 1972."[96]

This was, of course, a direct challenge to the authority of the civil-rights division, and the Justice Department had eminently good reason to suspect that the South Dakota attorney general was resisting complying with its intervention on the severance bill. This attorney general lived on in infamy among advocates of voting rights. In the 2011 VRA case of *Shelby County, Alabama v. Eric Holder,* the U.S. District Court for the District of Columbia cited him as an exemplar of racial discrimination in voting: "Historically, the most 'defiant' of all the covered jurisdictions has been South Dakota, where [a] former South Dakota Attorney General . . . notoriously described the preclearance requirement as a 'facial absurdity.' . . . In accordance with [the South Dakota attorney general's] advice, South Dakota sought preclearance for less than five of the more than 600 voting changes that it enacted between 1976 and 2002."[97] No one who knew of his record doubts that the attorney general was an outspoken, combative figure (even prior to his time as attorney general, when he was an attorney at legal aid in Mission fighting for Indian rights, and after it, when he was governor). The point is that we need to factor in this strong personality in making sense of the final outcome of voting rights in Todd County. This personality made a difference in ways that are difficult to assess but that must have been significant nonetheless. Perhaps the Justice Department staff dug in its heels more than it might have because of a combative personality; perhaps there was discussion about making an example of such a recalcitrant attorney general. Perhaps Tripp County obtained a better outcome, and Todd a worse outcome, than would have been the case if the South Dakota attorney general had taken a less adversarial stance. That we cannot answer these questions does not mean that we can ignore the role of personalities in the assemblage, in the game as it was played.

As we have already seen, the Justice Department also came in for criticism. In 1993, I interviewed someone who was privy to communication between the South Dakota attorney general's office and the civil-rights division at Justice during the conflict over House Bill 1197. This interviewee described the federal attorneys as "typical career bureaucrats," "rude," "inconsiderate," and acting with "total arrogance": "They were a government unto themselves." "I was offended personally that our whole state was branded bigots, and [by the implication] that we wanted to do it [discriminate against Indians]." Furthermore, "the idea of innocent until proven guilty didn't apply." Some of this animosity may have simply flowed from South Dakotans *resenting* the legal fact that under the Code of Federal Regulations the burden of proof lay with it in the section 5 preclearance process. While it is difficult to believe that the legal staff in Pierre *did not understand* this legal fact, they (and the state congressional delegation) clearly expected the civil-rights division to give constructive feedback on how to modify House Bill 1197 for preclearance. This was not the procedure followed in Washington, and the civil-rights division took what we might call an officially adversarial position toward jurisdictions applying for preclearance (how more "aloof" or "bureaucratic" they may have become *as a result of* the attorney general's statements and actions, we cannot know). What is clear is that in all this heat surrounding legal, political, and personal details, the concrete concerns of the tribal government and Lakota people in Todd County were not heard.

Organizing Todd County

With the applicability of section 5 now determined, and the green light thus given to the civil-rights division to pursue its objection, South Dakota and the organized counties decided to "bail out" of section 5 applicability, as it was called in VRA procedures, by obtaining a decision in the U.S. District Court for the District of Columbia that the Unorganized Counties Act was not racially discriminatory. As provided for in the VRA, they sought a declaratory judgment that the Unorganized Counties Act "does not have the purpose and will not have the effect of denying or abridging the right to vote on account of race or color."[98] The suit, filed in August 1980, achieved what had not been possible in the administrative back-and-forth between the state and the voting-rights section—a negotiated agreement between the Justice Department and South Dakota officials. In December 1981, a consent decree was reached in which South Dakota agreed that it would "permanently desist and refrain from implementing the property tax and contracting-out limitations imposed by the Unorganized Counties Act," which the Justice Department believed would have impaired the ability of organized Todd County to deliver services. Under the settlement, severance would proceed and Todd County would be organized *without* a vote of its residents.[99] None of this was preordained, and there were alternatives that Todd County citizens would have much preferred, but those alternatives were not under the direct control of the Justice Department or state authorities, or perhaps were simply not thinkable given the legal and political context of the time. One alternative would have been for organized Todd County to contract with the Rosebud Sioux Tribe for government services, which was advocated by the tribal government, and which might seem in hindsight—with a much different political zeitgeist in the present—to have been the best option. The presumption at the time was that this was not possible because the tribe was not subject to state jurisdiction, but we now could ask why state oversight rather than a simple intergovernmental contract for service delivery (such contracts have proliferated in the United States since the 1990s) would not have been workable. And rather than removing protections for Todd County (mostly white) property taxpayers, alternative sources of revenue might have been found. The chair of the American Indian Policy Review Commission, a Democratic senator from South Dakota who was born on Rosebud Reservation (in Wood, in Mellette County), introduced a bill in 1977 to expand the federal program of "payment in lieu of taxes," by which the federal government compensates local governments for the reduction in property-tax revenues owing to federal land ownership, to include Indian trust land. As the *Todd County Tribune* explained, "Indian lands provide an unfair tax burden on local governments the same way National Parks or Forest Service lands do. Since the federal government does not pay any local taxes on Indian land, it means higher taxes for the nearby private property owners."[100] Although this was a smart move on the part of the senator, the proposed legislation was never enacted by Congress (although Indian lands have been included since 1950 in federal aid to school districts under the Impact Aid Program).

A meeting was called in Todd County at which the legal situation was explained by the state's attorney from Tripp County, who had been

one of the attorneys involved in the consent decree. A "ranch wife"—
a property-tax payer—predictably asked about the cost of contracting
for government services. Just as predictably, a Lakota man well known
locally for standing on treaty rights brought up the Fort Laramie Treaty
of 1868 as the supreme law of the land, and another Lakota man, said,
"we have a tribal government that says 'we are the law'; the Supreme
Court says 'OK' and then the state comes in and says 'wait a minute,
you aren't and appoints commissioners for us. [N]ow we're confused." A
tribal member who had served previously as tribal chairman and who
was well known as an activist on tribal sovereignty rejected the visiting
states attorney's insistence that "Indians aren't affected [harmed] by this
decree. We KNOW better," and he demanded a referendum vote on organizing Todd County (everyone knew there would be a landslide against
organizing it in any such referendum). Another Lakota man, married
to a white woman, urged that Indians and whites sit down together to
work out the problems.[101] The *Todd County Tribune* must have spoken
for most Todd County residents, both Indian and white, when it editorialized, "[l]egality does not guarantee justice in either courts of law or in
governmental decrees."[102] The editor clearly felt that a bad situation had
been foisted on citizens of Todd County, white and Indian: "As a citizen
I want to know what is being done to me. I believe I am responsible
enough to have a choice in the process; I believe, as well, there are thousands of other citizens in Todd County and Rosebud Reservation who
have valid questions and opinions that should be expressed, heard and
perhaps heeded . . . even if an election is delayed."[103]

The *Tribune* blamed "the federal government's obvious double-
mindedness in its acknowledgement of citizens in Todd County and
Rosebud Reservation. The U.S Department of the Interior calls this a
reservation; the U.S. Justice Department calls this a county."[104] Certainly,
non-Indian citizens saw the arrangement as unnecessarily convoluted
and even absurd. Rosebud tribal officials and Indian opinion leaders saw
it as an attack on their treaty rights. While relations between the Todd
County Board of Commissioners and the Rosebud Sioux Tribe have
not been completely hostile, there have been points tension in the last
decades. The tribe was understandably concerned when the commissioners committed some of its supposedly hard-to-come-by tax revenue

in 1988 to join in a friend-of-the-court brief in the Supreme Court case of *Brendale v. Yakima Indian Nation* (1989), which limited the reach of tribal jurisdiction over non-Indians living in "open" or "integrated" reservation areas, as local non-Indians argued Todd County was.[105] And after pressure from the tribe, the Justice Department—the Indian resources section, not the voting-rights section—sued South Dakota and Todd County in 1990 over its taxation of fee land owned by tribal members within the county.[106] The legal argument was that even though the practice had been to tax Indian land once the trust status had been removed, federal case law was controlling, and it prohibited state jurisdiction *of any kind* over Indians in Indian country. The case was closed when the Supreme Court held in 1992 in *Yakima v. Confederated Tribes*[107] that the removal of trust status pursuant to the General Allotment Act of 1887[108] permitted states to tax the deeded land of Indians within Indian country. The tribe has sought over the years to elect at least one tribal member to serve as county commissioner in order to monitor, and if necessary, influence or challenge, the activities of the board as they pertain to tribal members and to the tribal government.

One cannot look at Figure 6.1 and not get the impression of a Rube Goldberg contraption. Besides the simple conclusion that an assemblage is complex and hybrid, what lesson should we draw about the social-justice machine that this assemblage was recognized, or expected, to be by the actors engaged by it? One lesson is that the outcome is not best described as "just," "balanced," or thoughtful, nor directly sought by any actor in the process. Was this a case of *bad governance?* We might call it "democracy" and "the rule of law," and people in Tripp County perhaps said of the outcome, "The system works." No doubt we could also say—as many most certainly do—that what happened to people in Todd County and to the Rosebud Sioux Tribe, and the overall time, energy, money, and anxiety spent on this prolonged conflict, are simply the inevitable "price of democracy." Some would also suggest that the case represents the necessary limits on governance when it is subjected to constitutional and other democratic checks (after all, who has the right to decide on their own what "good governance" is for everyone else?).

From the perspective of governmentality, the two legal-political apparatuses at the heart of the assemblage were not inherently antagonistic, but they came into conflict as a result of the historical and unfolding arrangements and the serious political divergence of interests between Indian and non-Indian people in the context of those arrangements. No one actor, or even one set of actors, was truly sovereign in this history, and in this sense a *macro*-theory such as that of settler colonialism or racial formation misses how government works in its actual practices. All actors here were limited by history (or path dependency) and by the weight of politics during a period of heightened racial tension in the United States and South Dakota, of Native activism of various kinds in South Dakota and fear or resentment of it by non-Indians, and of struggle between tribes and the state of South Dakota over a rising movement for tribal sovereignty. Treaty rights and civil rights were in conflict, but *all heads had been cut off*, as Foucault might have put it, so that no one party or institution (much less "the state") was in the driver's seat. To be caught up in an assemblage, or even to have a powerful capacity for action within it, is not to shape outcomes just as one pleases. Indeed, such an outcome seems highly improbable.

On the other hand, it does not come as a complete surprise that both Indian people and non-Indian people in Todd County lost this conflict. Their interests were shunted aside in the rights game depicted in Figure 6.1 by groups of actors that could *afford to ignore them*, or to *act in their "interest" without actually having to account to them*. Nothing—not the law, not political pressure, not professional or other forms of ethics— required any actor or agency to see that the Rosebud Sioux Tribe or the non-Indians in Todd County were not harmed *in net effect*; they had, in the end, only themselves to secure their own interests. And while harming them was not necessary in order to resolve the conflict—options were available, and some even advocated; history might well have unfolded differently here—in the end they had the least capacity to protect themselves. This, of course, is a pattern of inequality we have seen in each case examined in this book.

CONCLUSION

When Stories about the Countryside Have Power

Historian William Cronon published an article a quarter-century ago titled "A Place for Stories" that traced the history of narratives of the Great Plains, including works by scholars. He found that the narratives fell into two broad, diametrically opposed categories, which he described as "the upward or downward sweep of the plot."[1] The former—written by the likes of Frederick Jackson Turner and the newspaper editors and boomers on the plains—partake of "a world-historical plot, Darwinian in shape, that encompasses the entire sweep of human history," what we might fairly call Progress. The latter represent the "'declensionist' or 'tragic' Great Plains history," so obvious in New Deal stories about historical "miscalculation," and clearly implied in stories devaluing the plains while making the area suitable for a buffalo commons, or ICBM silos.[2]

One of Cronon's conclusions is that the two kinds of stories are more inventive and imaginary—fictional—and held together by interpretive communities than they are realist readings of the environment and human history. I made a parallel argument here about the knowledges of "problems" that have informed "solutions" through specific practices of governing. The point is that some stories are never merely "narration" or "text," because some stories are brought into and are inseparable from powerful, if not necessarily successful, practices of governing. This is especially true of prevailing master narratives about the Great Plains in general, and rural South Dakota in particular.

Foucault never directly addressed the question of whether there might be something "out there," in the materially social world, that might have consequences for how problems emerge that seem to demand solutions. He writes at times—especially about discipline—in an instrumentalist vein suggesting that some problems are "real" challenges in specific historical contexts that authorities respond to in pragmatic and effective ways.[3] At other times—in writing about Nazi genocide, for example—he makes it clear that mentalities of governing are better understood as relatively autonomous mutations or involutions of thought than as pragmatic or realist solutions to external or objective problems.[4] My own sense is that the former is the weak version of Foucault, and the latter is the strong and more interesting (and critical) version.

But the fact that discourse has a fictional (as in a legal fiction) or artificial (as in the artifice of money) quality is not the end of the matter. Foucault was at pains to insist that speech and writing are never far from practice and action—in fact, that language and acting are opposite sides of the same coin—to the extent that he meant by the term "discourse" not just inert talk, but talk that has power effects in the social (and even the physical) world.[5] Robert J. C. Young makes this clear in his unpacking of what Foucault meant by stating or the statement (enunciation): "The statement . . . constitutes a specific material event, a performative act or function, an historical eruption that impinges on and makes an incision into circumstance."[6] Discourse, for Foucault, included both language and its material consequences. This is, hopefully, clear to my readers from the cases of governing we have examined where theory and practice have been closely bound to each other.

Why have the discursive apparatuses of governing—with the aim of progress or improvement—found South Dakota such an obvious target? I suspect the answer is that South Dakota was *available* for "improvement" precisely because of its rural character. I mean by this the material and concrete social arrangements that are commonly called *uneven development* by critical geographers and that make it difficult for rural people to have as much control over their regions or the national public sphere as do metropolitan centers. Andre Gunder Frank described this spatial inequality well in his depiction of "satellites" within the picture he drew of the global, multiscalar, metropolis-satellite structure of power in capitalism. Although Frank's use of the theory as a general explanation for global inequality has been criticized, his account of the empirical fact of the spatially uneven distribution of development and power is useful for my purposes here. For Frank, wherever one looks on the planet, and at whatever scale one focuses on, political and economic power is hierarchically (and spatially) organized into a pyramidal arrangement of a more-powerful metropolis tied to less-powerful, dependent satellites. Joseph G. Jorgensen has applied this model compellingly to the U.S. case, the rural West, and Native Americans in particular.[7] The metropolis as a position in the pyramid is a space of concentrated political and economic power. In the United States, this generally takes the form of higher population and voter densities; elected representatives with more resources and power in legislatures; local economies rooted in more value-added processing and services, and thus higher wages and profits; more "agglomeration" of business and infrastructure, and high "multipliers" of wealth; denser concentrations of built environment (or investment in fixed capital); concentration of financial institutions and financial power; greater control of mass media; and concentration of valued institutions in high demand such as hospitals and medical centers, and colleges and universities (along with the credentialed graduates who command higher incomes and who work in, or lead, the more powerful organizations in metropolises). On each measure of power, rural satellites are characterized by the relative lack of political and economic resources in comparison to metropoles. Of course, ultimately the landscape of uneven development is not *only* or *necessarily* based on an urban–rural divide. There has always been plenty of inequality within metropolitan areas, and Saskia Sassen argues that there is an intensifying "[n]ew geography of centrality and marginalization" within global cities.[8] The countryside can also be heavily stratified by class and race, and some rural areas are becoming gentrified in ways that complicate a simple rural–urban divide in terms of power.

But for the purposes of recognizing structural power in the context of the Rosebud country and western South Dakota, rurality is a useful concept for understanding the difficulties people and their governments have in protecting themselves against both prevailing stories and invasive forms of governmentality. Books or editorials on "what's wrong with

California" do not get written by rural people, but "What's wrong with South Dakota?" has been a perennial question posed by relatively powerful people who never lived there (and some who did). One does not have to employ sophisticated theory to see this rural–urban inequality; it is common knowledge in the United States. Although the Populist Party may not have been first to recognize it, it is gospel in agrarian and much populist (with a lower-case "p") thinking in the country today. The metropolitan/cosmopolitan beneficiaries of the rural–urban distribution of political and economic power ("the elites") are also more than a little aware of the fact of its existence, though are more apt to explain it in "evolutionary" terms rather than in terms of uneven development (which is an inherently critical concept). While I was writing this book, David Brooks published an op-ed piece in the *New York Times* titled "The Great Migration" in which he describes how the U.S. "system of higher education . . . is like a giant vacuum cleaner that sucks up some of the smartest people from across the country and concentrates them in a few privileged places. Smart high school students from [and here Brooks names some satellites] rural Nebraska, small-town Ohio and urban Newark get to go to good universities." These students are in for "culture shock," because they are used to "an atmosphere of social equality, and they now find themselves in a culture that emphasizes the relentless quest for distinction—to be more accomplished, more enlightened and more cutting edge." Regardless of the shock, Brooks explains, "the system works. In the dorms, classrooms, summer internships and early jobs they learn how to behave the way successful people do in the highly educated hubs [he has in mind Washington, Boston, San Jose, Raleigh–Durham and San Francisco]. There's no economic reason to return home, and maybe it's not even socially possible anymore." "[T]he magnet places"—and he doesn't mean Sioux Falls or Rapid City—"have positive ecologies that multiply innovation, creativity and wealth. The abandoned places have negative ecologies and fall further behind." This "sorting is self-reinforcing," and apparently natural and for the best, in Brooks's view—indeed, he calls it *meritocracy*—and attempting to "mitigate the inequality" of this geography is "like shooting a water gun at a waterfall." "Pumping a few [government] dollars into" one of the "abandoned places" may be humane "but it won't alter the dynamic."[9] While this is clearly a declensionist story of the rural heartland, it is also a realistic portrait of the process of uneven development as it affects many rural places. What needs to be added is simply that such uneven development was not preordained or inevitable but the product of specific political and economic policies—something I am sure many people I know in South Dakota would be happy to tell Mr. Brooks along with the rest of us who live on the coasts.

The material reality of the relative powerlessness of rural satellites is the context that enabled metropolitan improvers to try their stories and schemes on rural South Dakotans. Again, I do not question their sincerity or goodwill. I do not assume that the schemes for improvement described in this book were either designed or implemented to be self-serving for those who designed and implemented them, nor do I assume that they were all harmful in all ways. This has not been a book about villains and victims. The question I have ended with is why some places and some people get to try to improve other places and other people. The answer is political-economic power organized on the basis of uneven development across space. In the end, who gets to be an improver, and who gets defined as a problem, is already decided by the mosaic of the nation's political-economic landscape. In this arrangement, Indian and white people in rural South Dakota have immensely more in common, relative to the rest of us, than they have differences between them.

ACKNOWLEDGMENTS

I am deeply indebted to the people of the Rosebud country. I have been visiting this part of the heartland for three decades and have always felt welcomed, and even appreciated, for my scholarly interest (how many scholars are *that* blessed?), by both Indian and non-Indian people there. Beyond the warmth and goodwill of the people of the area, I want to single out a few who helped me in very direct ways. In particular, I thank Gerri Night Pipe, who was the secretary of the Rosebud Sioux Tribe at the time I collected some of the archival material for this book, and Linda Marshall who is presently secretary. I also thank Marcella Cash, archivist and director of the Sicangu Heritage Center, Sinte Gleska University; Crystal Gamradt, archivist at Archives and Special Collections, South Dakota State University; Virginia Hansen, Matthew Reitzel, and Ken Stewart at the Archives of the South Dakota State Historical Society; Laurie Langland, archivist at Dakota Wesleyan University; Bonnie Olson, archivist for the Karl E. Mundt Foundation at Dakota State University; Doris Peterson, archivist at the Archives and Special Collections, University of South Dakota. Thanks also to Terry Pechota. Beyond South Dakota, I am indebted to Lori Cox-Paul, archivist at the National Archives in Kansas City, Missouri, and Steven Pevar of the American Civil Liberties Union.

In my immediate academic village, I thank Alicia Cowart of the Berkeley geography department, who expertly drew the maps for this book.

Thanks also to graduate students Tria Blu Wakpa, John Dougherty, and Tasha Hauff, whose discussions made a difference in my thinking on this book, as well as on other matters. David Nugent of Emory University has been listening to me for four decades, and he heard a lot about this book over the fifteen years it took to finish it. He has always given me engaging advice and encouraging support. Nelson Maldonado-Torres, of Rutgers University, and his work inspired me while he was here at Berkeley to read in philosophy, admittedly as a dabbler (but hopefully not a dilettante), in ways that fundamentally changed how I approach intellectual questions during the second half of my career. Nelson taught me a sophisticated vision of what ethnic studies can be, an important lesson for this aging anthropologist. Paulla Ebron of Stanford University is not only a close friend but has, for twenty years, generously shared her feedback on my ideas and set an example for me through her own ethnography and scholarship. Beth Piatote and Shari Huhndorf, who teach Native American studies with me at Berkeley, have read my hopelessly dense chapters—which deadened the senses with overwhelming detail and no apparent point—and helped me to make them better. But far more important than their very talented editorial critique, they have influenced me intellectually in innumerable ways by their own remarkable scholarly work (and teaching) and by our conversations. I always enjoy working with them and feel extremely privileged to have them as close and trusted colleagues. Finally, I have learned so much from and been inspired so often by Carla Hesse, dean of the College of Letters and Science, that it is difficult to imagine anything that I have done in the past eight years without her administrative and intellectual presence and the example it sets.

Anyone who lives with cats knows perfectly well that "all cats are *wakaŋ* [sacred or mysterious]," but it is useful that it has been so precisely stated by at least one Lakota philosopher.[1] I could not have finished this book without my four-legged relatives. Chibby-chan saw me through a good chunk of the research and writing, not to mention most of my stint as department chair. Blaze and Mimi lived with me through the completion of the book, and spent a good deal of time not far from my desk; Blaze regularly spends his days sleeping next to my laptop as I wrap up this book. It's not just animal comfort that I get from them but also their lessons for us clueless two-leggeds. *Mitakuye oyasiŋ,* indeed.

I have known Rose Cordier, my *huŋka* sister, for more than thirty years. I could not have possibly done the work that I have, or led the scholarly life that I do, without Rose's help. She took an immediate interest in my research when I met her as a graduate student in May 1985, and she has facilitated it ever since. It is not just her generosity in introducing me to the right people to talk to but also her own insights into tribal history and government (a tradition she has carried on from her statesman father, Leo Cordier) that have made such a difference to my thinking and research. She has always welcomed me and my family to her home in Antelope. I dedicate this book to her with love and admiration.

I also dedicate this book to my son, Noah. I started working on this book just before he was born. Fifteen years later, I learn from discussions with him all the time. That he also loves South Dakota, Rosebud Reservation, and Rose and her family means the world to me.

Finally, how could I possibly find the words to properly thank my spouse, Miyako Inoue? Her abiding intellectual influence on me is evident on every page of this book. To live with a scholar one admires has to be the best intellectual community one can ever hope to have. Miyako has made me think harder and in more interesting ways than I thought possible of myself. There could be no book without her.

NOTES

Introduction

1. Nikolas Rose and Peter Miller, "Political Power beyond the State: Problematics of Government," *British Journal of Sociology* 43:2 (1992): 173–205.

2. Cf. James C. Scott, *Seeing like a State: How Certain Schemes to Improve the Human Condition Have Failed* (New Haven: Yale University Press, 1998).

3. Michel Foucault, *Security, Territory Population: Lectures at the Collège de France, 1977–1978*, ed. Michel Senellart, trans. Graham Burchell (New York: Picador 2007 [2004]), 24. Foucault was quoting from Guillaume de la Perrière's *Le miroir politique* (1555). A condensed form of Foucault's lecture, widely consulted, is Michel Foucault, "Governmentality," in *The Foucault Effect: Studies in Governmentality*, ed. Graham Burchell, Colin Gordon, and Peter Miller (Chicago: University of Chicago Press, 1991), 87–104.

4. Mitchell Dean and Barry Hindess, "Introduction: Government, Liberalism, Society," in *Governing Australia: Studies in Contemporary Rationalities of Government* (New York: Cambridge University Press, 1998), 8. See also Mitchell Dean, *Governmentality: Power and Rule in Modern Society*, 2d ed. (Los Angeles: Sage, 2010 [1999]).

5. Peter Miller and Nikolas Rose, "Governing Economic Life," *Economy and Society* 19:1 (1990): 10.

6. Michel Foucault, *Discipline and Punish: The Birth of the Prison*, trans. Alan Sheridan (New York: Vintage Books, 1979 [1975]), 264–82. See also James Ferguson, *The Anti-Politics Machine: "Development," Depoliticization and Bureaucratic Power in Lesotho* (New York: Cambridge University Press, 1990), 254.

7. Dean, *Governmentality*, 25; emphasis added.

8. Tanya Murray Li, *The Will to Improve: Governmentality, Development, and the Practice of Politics* (Durham, N.C.: Duke University Press, 2007), 9; Ferguson, *The Anti-Politics Machine*.

9. Nikolas Rose, *Powers of Freedom: Reframing Political Thought* (New York: Cambridge University Press, 1999), 74.

10. Michel Foucault, *"Society Must Be Defended: Lectures at the Collège de France, 1975–1976,* ed. Mauro Bertani and Alessandro Fontana; trans. David Macey (New York: Palgrave MacMillan, 2003 [1997]), 246.

11. Ibid., 247.

12. Michel Foucault, "The Subject and Power," in Hubert Dreyfus and Paul Rabinow, *Michel Foucault: Beyond Structuralism and Hermeneutics,* 2d ed. (Chicago: University of Chicago Press, 1983), 212.

13. My first two books were *Organizing the Lakota: The Political Economy of the New Deal on Pine Ridge and Rosebud Reservations* (Tucson: University of Arizona Press, 1992) and *Deadliest Enemies: Law and Race Relations on and off Rosebud Reservation* (Minneapolis: University of Minnesota Press, 2007 [2001]).

14. Lakota terms are written in the orthography adopted by the Rosebud Sioux Tribe in 2012; see Sicangu Lakota Orthography, electronic document, http://www .rst-education-department.com/sicangu-lakota-orthography/.

15. See Royal B. Hassrick, *The Sioux: Life and Customs of a Warrior Society* (Norman: University of Oklahoma Press, 1972 [1964]); James R. Walker, *Lakota Society,* ed. Raymond J. DeMallie (Lincoln: University of Nebraska Press, 1992 [1982]).

16. 11 Stat. 749, article 5; available at http://digital.library.okstate.edu/Kappler/.

17. 15 Stat. 635; available at http://digital.library.okstate.edu/Kappler/.

18. 25 Stat., 94; available at http://digital.library.okstate.edu/Kappler/.

19. QuickFact, U.S. Census Bureau, http://census.gov.

20. On problematization, see both items cited in note 4.

1. The Birth of Liberalism on the Prairie, or How Not to Govern Too Much

1. John Locke, *Two Treatises of Government,* student edition, ed. Peter Laslett (Cambridge, U.K.: Cambridge University Press, 1988 [1698]), 332, 331; emphasis in original.

2. Frederick Jackson Turner, *The Significance of the Frontier in American History,* ed. Harold P. Simpson (New York: Frederick Ungar, 1985 [1893]), 51.

3. Ibid.

4. Michel Foucault, *The Birth of Biopolitics: Lectures at the Collège de France, 1978–1979,* trans. Graham Burchel, ed. Michael Senellart (New York: Palgrave MacMillan, 2008 [2004]), 13, 1. Foucault's paradigmatic case of the birth of liberalism in the history of (Western) power is the eighteenth-century French Physiocrats who rejected the idea of centralized state control of grain prices and instead sought to harness the "natural" economic force of the market via freedom of commerce. By this technique a scarcity of grain would constitute its own solution through the self-regulating market (33–40).

5. Ibid., 24n10.

6. Ibid., 217. Foucault also argues that this is the case with the postwar German state where, because "History had said no to the [Nazi] state," the 1948 Federal

Republic of Germany had no source of its claim to sovereignty other than to guarantee economic freedom (86).

7. Ibid., 82.

8. Ibid., 218.

9. 15 Stat. 635; available at http://digital.library.okstate.edu/Kappler/.

10. Stopping their off-reservation movements actually awaited more systematic control not accomplished until the later 1870s. See Matthew G. Hannah, "Space and Social Control in the Administration of the Oglala Lakota ('Sioux'), 1871–1879," *Journal of Historical Geography* 19 (1993): 412–32.

11. 15 Stat. 635, at 637, 640.

12. U.S. Congress, Senate, *Message from the President of the United States*, 51st Cong., 1st Sess., Exec. Doc. 51 (1890). See also Thomas Biolsi, *Organizing the Lakota: The Political Economy of the New Deal on Pine Ridge and Rosebud Reservations* (Tucson: University of Arizona Press, 1992), 39–44.

13. Crow Creek Reservation was also established, but east of the Missouri River, outside of the original Great Sioux Reservation.

14. 25 Stat. 888, at 890; available at http://digital.library.okstate.edu/kappler/.

15. Allotment sizes were doubled in the case of lands that supported grazing but not crop farming.

16. Theodore Roosevelt, First Annual Message, 1901, electronic document accessed December 31, 2013, http://www.presidency.ucsb.edu/ws/?pid=29542.

17. 25 Stat. 888, at 896.

18. See Thomas Biolsi, *Deadliest Enemies: Law and Race Relations on and off Rosebud Reservation* (Minneapolis: University of Minnesota Press, 2007 [2001]), 23–27.

19. Karl Marx, *Capital: A Critique of Political Economy*, vol. 1, trans. Ben Fowkes (New York: Penguin Putnam, 1990 [1976, 1867]), chapter 28; available at http://marxists.org/archive/marx/works/1867-c1/index.htm.

20. David Harvey, *The New Imperialism* (New York: Oxford University Press, 2003), chapter 4.

21. 19 Stat. 254, available at http://digital.library.okstate.edu/kappler/; *United States v. Sioux Nation of Indians* (1980), 448 U.S. 371.

22. In accordance with the provision of article 12 of the Fort Laramie Treaty of 1868, no land cession could take place without the consent of three-fourths of the adult males (15 Stat. 635, at 639). For analysis of the "three-fourths-majority rule," see Biolsi, *Organizing the Lakota*, 39–46.

23. U.S. Congress, Senate, *Message from the President of the United States Transmitting Reports Relative to the Proposed Division of the Great Sioux Reservation, and Recommending Certain Legislation*, 51st Cong., 1st Sess., Exec. Doc. 51 (1890), 59.

24. See Biolsi, *Organizing the Lakota*, chapter 1.

25. *Report of the Commissioner of Indian Affairs, October 1, 1891*, in *Report of the Secretary of the Interior*, 1892, 52d Cong., 1st Sess., H. Exec. Doc. 1, pt. 5, vol. 2, 133.

26. *Message from the President of the United States*, 61, 52.

27. *Report of the Commissioner of Indian Affairs, October 1, 1891,* 133.

28. Ibid., 411.

29. Ibid., 412.

30. Ibid.; emphasis added.

31. U.S. Congress, Senate, 1904, *Rosebud Indians of South Dakota,* Exec. Doc. 158, 58th Cong., 2d Sess.

32. 34 Stat. 182, at 183.

33. Declaration of Policy in the Administration of Indian Affairs, April 17, 1917, Ordinances and Resolutions. Records of the Rosebud Agency, Records of the Bureau of Indian Affairs (Kansas City, Mo.: National Archives and Records Administration).

34. Janet A. McDonnell, *The Dispossession of the American Indian, 1887–1934* (Bloomington and Indianapolis: Indiana University Press, 1991); Department of Indian Studies, University of South Dakota, *A Report on the Bureau of Indian Affairs Fee Patenting and Canceling Policies, 1900–1942* (Aberdeen, S.Dak.: U.S. Bureau of Indian Affairs).

35. David Blomley, "Law, Property, and the Geography of Violence: The Frontier, the Survey, and the Grid," *Annals of the Association of American Geographers* 93:1 (2003): 129. See also Robert David Sack, *Human Territoriality: Its Theory and History* (New York: Cambridge University Press, 1986), 33, 143; David Delaney, *Territory: A Short Introduction* (Malden, Mass.: Blackwell Publishing, 2005).

36. Henri Lefebvre, *The Production of Space,* trans. Donaldson Nicholson-Smith (Malden, Mass.: Blackwell Publishing, 1991 [1974]), 15, 13.

37. On the doctrine of discovery, see Vine Deloria, *Behind the Trail of Broken Treaties: An Indian Declaration of Independence* (Austin: University of Texas Press, 1985 [1974]), chapter 5; Robert A. Williams Jr., *The American Indian in Western Legal Thought: The Discourses of Conquest* (New York: Oxford University Press, 1990), and *Like a Loaded Weapon: The Rehnquist Court, Indian Rights, and the Legal History of Racism in America* (Minneapolis: University of Minnesota Press, 2005), chapter 3.

38. The open range, before allotments were fenced, is described by the Rosebud Superintendent, Annual Narrative Report, *Superintendents' Annual Narrative and Statistical Reports from Field Jurisdictions of the Bureau of Indian Affairs, 1907–1938,* Microfilm Publication M1070, Records of the Bureau of Indian Affairs (Washington, D.C.: National Archives and Records Administration, 1914); and by Mabelle Stewart Worsley, "Homesteading on the Rosebud: The Reminiscence of Mabelle Stewart Worsley," *South Dakota History* 35:3 (2005): 231.

39. David Harvey, *The Condition of Postmodernity: An Enquiry into the Origins of Cultural Change* (Cambridge, Mass.: Basil Blackwell, 1989), 254.

40. See Lefebvre, *The Production of Space;* Sack, *Human Territoriality,* chapter 5; Harvey, *The Condition of Postmodernity,* chapter 15; William Cronon, *Nature's Metropolis: Chicago and the Great West* (New York: Norton, 1991), 51–52; David Harvey, *Justice, Nature and the Geography of Difference* (Malden, Mass.: Blackwell

Publishing, 1996), 238–42; James C. Scott, *Seeing like a State: How Certain Schemes to Improve the Human Condition Have Failed* (New Haven: Yale University Press, 1998), chapter 1 and passim.

41. Matthew H. Edney, *Mapping an Empire: The Geographical Construction of British India, 1765–1843* (Chicago: University of Chicago Press, 1997 [1990]), 24–25.

42. John G. Ruggie, *Constructing the World Polity: Essays on Internationalization* (New York: Routledge, 1998), 185–86; see also Scott, *Seeing like a State*, chapters 1, 2.

43. Michel Foucault, *Security, Territory, Population: Lectures at the Collège de France, 1977–1978*, ed. Michel Senellart, trans. Graham Burchell (New York: Palgrave MacMillan, 2007 [2004]), 16, 15.

44. Bruno Latour, "Visualization and Cognition: Thinking with Eyes and Hands," *Knowledge and Society* 6 (1986): 32.

45. Quoted in Richard A. Bartlett, *The New Country: A Social History of the American Frontier, 1776–1890* (New York: Oxford University Press, 1974), 69. See also William D. Pattison, "Reflections on the American Rectangular Land Survey System," in *Pattern and Process: Research in Historical Geography*, ed. R. E. Enrenberg (Washington, D.C.: Howard University Press, 1975), 133.

46. Tony Bennett, *The Birth of the Museum: History, Theory, Politics* (New York: Routledge, 1995), 51, 52.

47. Mary Poovey, *Making a Social Body: British Cultural Formation, 1830–1864* (Chicago: University of Chicago Press, 1995), 28.

48. Walter Benjamin, *Illuminations*, ed. Hannah Arendt, trans. Harry Zohn (New York: Schocken Books, 1968 [1950]), 261; Benedict Anderson, *Imagined Communities: Reflections on the Origin and Spread of Nationalism*, rev. ed. (New York: Verso, 1991 [1983]), 24–26.

49. The allotting agent on Rosebud Reservation reported in 1902 that even those who resisted allotment were familiar with the plat: Winder to Commissioner of Indian Affairs, January 7, 1902, File 1899–1907, Rosebud. Special Cases 147 [Allotment]. Records of the Bureau of Indian Affairs (Washington, D.C.: National Archives and Records Administration). Louise Liffengren Hullinger recalls her aunt, who settled with her parents in Lyman County (just north of the Rosebud country), telling her that "Papa pored over plats of the land, and Mama studied them as much as he did," before they arrived in South Dakota (Louise Liffengren Hullinger, *Next Year Country: Stories of Drought-Stricken South Dakota in the 1930s* [Deerfield, Ill.: Lake Shore Publishing, 2000], 9).

50. Jason Weems, "Images, Technology, and History: Interpreting the 1930 Aerial Survey Photograph: The Artfulness of Technological Images," *History and Technology* 27:2 (2011): 227. See also Jason Weems, *Barnstorming the Prairies: How Aerial Vision Shaped the Midwest* (Minneapolis: University of Minnesota Press, 2015).

51. See Dan Thu Nguyen, "The Spatialization of Metric Time: The Conquest of Land and Labor in Europe and the United States," *Time and Society* 1:1 (1992): 37.

52. Ordinance of April 23, 1784, electronic document accessed January 3, 2014, http://memory.loc.gov/ammem/collections/continental/index.html. See also Thomas Jefferson, *The Papers of Thomas Jefferson, vol. 6*, ed. Julian P. Boyd (Princeton, N.J.: Princeton University Press, 1952), 581–617; Hildegard Binder Johnson, *Order upon the Landscape: The U.S. Rectangular Land Survey and the Upper Mississippi Country* (New York: Oxford University Press, 1976), 40–46.

53. See Delaney, *Territory,* 31.

54. An Ordinance for the Government of the Territory of the United States, North-west of the River Ohio, July 13, 1787, electronic document accessed January 3, 2014, http://memory.loc.gov/ammem/collections/continental/index.html.

55. Bartlett, *The New Country,* 81, 82. See also Pattison, "Reflections on the American Rectangular Land Survey System," 132; Johnson, *Order upon the Landscape,* chapter 3.

56. See Henry Nash Smith, *Virgin Land: The American West as Symbol and Myth* (Cambridge: Harvard University Press, 1970 [1950]), 140; Alexis de Tocqueville, *Democracy in America,* vol. 1, trans. Henry Reeve (New York: Vintage Books, 1959 [1835]), 62–71.

57. Smith, *Virgin Land,* 170; Pattison, "Reflections on the American Rectangular Land Survey System," 132; Helen M. Ingram and Mary G. Wallace, "An 'Empire of Liberty': Thomas Jefferson and Governing Natural Resources in the West," in *Thomas Jefferson and the Changing West: From Conquest to Conservation,* ed. J. P. Ronda (Albuquerque: University of New Mexico Press, 1997), 95; Steven Silvern, "Scales of Justice: Law, American Indian Treaty Rights and the Political Constructions of Scale," *Political Geography* 18 (1999): 647.

58. This crisis-generating tendency is, ironically, an effect of the technical progress driven by competition. While innovation and the ensuing rise in labor productivity increase the rate of profit for a firm in the short term—it can produce the same goods more cheaply, and thus undersell competitors and reap higher rates of profit (until competitors adopt the same innovations)—in the long term (and counterintuitively), innovation reduces the rate of profit for all firms in an industry, and (because capital is fungible and can be shifted between industries) across industries. This happens because, driven by competition, a progressively smaller component of capital is invested in labor (what Marx called variable capital) relative to that invested in machinery and technology (what Marx called constant capital). Because variable capital—capital invested in labor—is the *only* source of surplus value and, thus, of profit, capitalism's technological progress results in the undermining of profits in the long-term functioning of the system as a whole. See Karl Marx, *Capital,* vol. 3, chapter 13, ed. Friedrich Engels (1894), electronic document accessed January 3, 2014, http://marxists.org/archive/marx/works/1894-c3/index.htm; Paul M. Sweezy, *The Theory of Capitalist Development: Principles of Marxian Political Economy* (New York: Monthly Review Press, 1970 [1942]), chapter 9; Ernest Mandel, *Marxist Economic Theory,* vol. 1 (New York:

Monthly Review Press, 1970 [1962]), 166–70; Eric R. Wolf, *Europe and the People without History* (Berkeley and Los Angeles: University of California Press, 2010 [1982]), chapter 10; David Harvey, *The Limits to Capital* (New York: Verso, 2006 [1982]), 176–78; David Harvey, "The Geopolitics of Capitalism," in *Spaces of Capital: Towards a Critical Geography* (New York: Routledge, 2001 [1985]), 312–44; Harvey, *The Condition of Postmodernity,* 180–81.

59. Harvey, *The New Imperialism,* 115, 119. See also David Harvey, "'The Spatial Fix': Hegel, Von Thunen, and Marx," *Antipode* 13:2 (1981): 1–12; Neil Smith, *Uneven Development: Nature, Capital, and the Production of Space,* 3d ed. (Athens: University of Georgia Press, 2008 [1984]); Harvey, "The Geopolitics of Capitalism"; Harvey, *The Condition of Postmodernity,* 182–84; Bob Jessop, "Spatial Fixes, Temporal Fixes, and Spatio-Temporal Fixes," in *David Harvey: A Critical Reader,* ed. Noel Castree and Derek Gregory (Malden, Mass.: Blackwell Publishing, 2006), 142–66.

60. Smith, *Uneven Development,* 116–17.

61. Martin Kenney, Linda M. Lobao, James Curry, and W. Richard Goe, "Midwestern Agriculture in US Fordism: From the New Deal to Economic Restructuring," *Sociological Ruralis* 29:2 (2006): 135.

62. Anonymous, "More Farms for Uncle Sam," *Wall Street Journal,* August 20, 1908, 1. This was front-page news because the *Journal's* readers were interested in the investment potential of commodities futures and railroads.

63. Opie Chambers, "The Early History of the Rosebud Country," in *A Rosebud Review* (Gregory, S.Dak.: *Gregory Times-Advocate,* 1984 [1913]), 5–9; F. H. Jackson, "Homesteading on the Rosebud," in Chambers, *A Rosebud Review,* 17–19; Charles Lowell Green, "The Administration of the Public domain in South Dakota," *South Dakota Historical Collections,* 1940: 167–73.

64. Edith Kohl, *Land of the Burnt Thigh: A Lively Story of Women Homesteaders on the South Dakota Frontier* (St. Paul: Minnesota Historical Society Press, 1986 [1938]), 145–46. The *New York Times* also reported on the opening of Tripp County in 1908: Anonymous, "Rush for 5,000 Farms," October 5, 18; Robert Baker, "Rosebud Reservation," October 7, 8; Anonymous, "Land Worth Twenty Millions to Be Given Away," October 18, Sunday magazine, 3.

65. Anonymous, "Winner," In *A Rosebud Review* (Gregory, S.Dak.: *Gregory Times-Advocate,* 1984 [1913]), 101.

66. State of South Dakota, *Fourth Census of the State of South Dakota,* 1925.

67. Anonymous, "White River," in *A Rosebud Review* (Gregory, S.Dak.: *Gregory Times-Advocate,* 1984 [1913]), 81.

68. State of South Dakota, *Fourth Census of the State of South Dakota.*

69. Joy M. Hackler, "Finances and Financial Institutions," in *A Rosebud Review* (Gregory, S.Dak.: *Gregory Times-Advocate,* 1984 [1913]), 30.

70. Indeed, if empty space cannot be expected to absorb capital and labor at a profit, there is no incentive to impose the forms of power and emptying out that make it substantively empty to begin with.

71. David Harvey, *Spaces of Global Capitalism: Towards a Theory of Uneven Geographical Development* (New York: Verso, 2006), 103.

72. Don H. Foster, "Climate and Rain Fall," in *A Rosebud Review* (Gregory, S.Dak.: *Gregory Times-Advocate,* 1984 [1913]), 27.

73. W. H. Lynn, "Corn Growing in the Rosebud," in *A Rosebud Review* (Gregory, S.Dak.: *Gregory Times-Advocate,* 1984 [1913]), 32.

74. Dallas Real Estate Co. (advertisement), in *A Rosebud Review* (Gregory, S.Dak.: *Gregory Times-Advocate,* 1984 [1913], 1.

75. Anonymous, "Todd County," *Todd County Tribune,* June 30, 1921.

76. Anonymous, "Come to Todd County, S.D.: The Heart of the Rosebud," *Todd County Tribune,* May 5, 1921.

77. Anonymous, "Our County's Showing," *Todd County Tribune,* September 29, 1921.

78. South Dakota Commissioner of Immigration, *First Biennial Report,* 1912, 10. See also reports for 1914, 1916, 1918.

79. Kohl, *Land of the Burnt Thigh,* 1.

80. Ibid., 57.

81. Ibid., 12, 57, 167.

82. Ibid., 12.

83. Locke, *Two Treatises of Government,* 301; see also Williams, *The American Indian in Western Legal Thought.*

84. Locke, *Two Treatises of Government,* 293.

85. *Johnson v. McIntosh* (U.S. Sup. Ct., 1823), 21 U.S. 543, at 590.

86. Kohl, *Land of the Burnt Thigh,* 167–68.

87. Ibid., 200.

88. Ibid., 68, 103.

89. Oscar Micheaux, *The Conquest: The Story of a Negro Pioneer* (New York: Washington Square Press, 2003 [1913]), 50. See also Dan Moos, "Reclaiming the Frontier: Oscar Micheaux as Black Turnerian," *African American Review* 36:3 (2002): 357–81.

90. Frieda Knobloch, *The Culture of Wilderness: Agriculture as Colonization in the American West* (Chapel Hill: University of North Carolina Press, 1996), 3.

91. Ibid., 57.

92. Quoted in Turner, *The Significance of the Frontier in American History,* 42–43.

93. Ibid., 34.

94. Rudolf Freund, "Turner's Theory of Social Evolution," *Agricultural History* 19:2 (1945): 85.

95. Paula M. Nelson, *The Prairie Winnows out Its Own: The West River Country of South Dakota in the Years of Depression and Dust* (Iowa City: University of Iowa Press, 1996), 189.

96. Faye C. Lewis, *Nothing to Make a Shadow* (Ames: Iowa State University Press, 1971), 19.

97. After long controversy and complaints by Indian people, the mural was finally walled over by Governor William Janklow in 1997. For a history of the Blashfield mural, see "South Dakota State Capitol: The Decorated Capitol," electronic document accessed August 21, 2014, https://boa.sd.gov/divisions/capitol/CapitolTour/blashfield.htm.

98. *South Dakota Historical Collections,* 1910, 245.

99. U.S. Census Bureau, *Census of Agriculture,* 1940.

100. Turner, *The Significance of the Frontier in American History,* 51.

101. Jon K. Lauck, *Prairie Republic: The Political Culture of Dakota Territory, 1879–1889* (Norman: University of Oklahoma Press, 2010), 25, 45.

2. Discipline and Governmentality

1. Tania Murray Li, *The Will to Improve: Governmentality, Development, and the Practice of Politics* (Durham, N.C.: Duke University Press, 2007).

2. Ibid., 4–5.

3. Ibid., 9.

4. See especially Tanya Murray Li, *Land's End: Capitalist Relations on an Indigenous Frontier* (Durham, N.C.: Duke University Press, 2014); "To Make Live or Let Die? Rural Dispossession and the Protection of Surplus Populations," *Antipode* 41:S1 (2009): 66–93; "Indigeneity, Capitalism, and the Management of Dispossession," *Current Anthropology* 51:3 (2011): 385–414.

5. Michel Foucault, *Discipline and Punish: The Birth of the Prison,* trans. Alan Sheridan (New York: Vintage Books, 1979 [1975]).

6. Ibid.; Michel Foucault, *The History of Sexuality, Volume I: An Introduction,* trans. Robert Hurley (New York: Vintage Books, 1980 [1976]).

7. Paul Rabinow, "Introduction," in *The Foucault Reader,* ed. Paul Rabinow (New York: Pantheon Books, 1984), 21.

8. See Thomas Biolsi, "The Birth of the Reservation: Making the Modern Individual among the Lakota," *American Ethnologist* 22:1 (1995): 30–34.

9. *Annual Report of the Commissioner of Indian Affairs to the Secretary of the Interior for the Fiscal Year Ended June 30, 1921* (Washington, D.C.: U.S. Government Printing Office, 1921), 25; available at https://uwdc.library.wisc.edu/collections/History/.

10. Rosebud Superintendent, Narrative Report, 1914, *Superintendents' Annual Narrative and Statistical Reports*; Marian Berry Edwards, *Looking Back from the Top of Cedar Butte: Memories of Homestead Days* (Fort Collins, Colo.: Lone Pine Productions, 2003), 29.

11. Berry Edwards, *Looking Back from the Top of Cedar Butte,* 75.

12. Rosebud Superintendent, Narrative Report, 1917, *Superintendents' Annual Narrative and Statistical Reports.*

13. Winder to Commissioner of Indian Affairs, November 7, 1900; Winder to Commissioner of Indian Affairs, September 26, 1901, File 1899–1907, Rosebud,

Special Cases 147 (Allotment), Records of the Bureau of Indian Affairs (Washington, D.C.: National Archives and Records Administration).

14. 25 Stat. 888, at 895; available at http://digital.library.okstate.edu/kappler/.

15. Winder to Commissioner of Indian Affairs, November 7, 1900, File 1899–1907, Rosebud, Special Cases 147, Records of the Bureau of Indian Affairs.

16. Wright to Commissioner of Indian Affairs, April 19, 1893, Special Cases 147, File 1891–98, Rosebud. Records of the Bureau of Indian Affairs; [English Translation of Petition], under cover of Craeger to Commission of Indian Affairs, September 10, 1894, in ibid.

17. Gunderson to Commissioner of Indian Affairs, January 10, 1905, File 1899–1907, Rosebud, Special Cases 147, Records of the Bureau of Indian Affairs.

18. Winder to Jones, March 1, 1903, File 1899–1907, Rosebud, Special Cases 147, Records of the Bureau of Indian Affairs.

19. Winder to Commissioner of Indian Affairs, July 22, 1901; Winder to Commissioner of Indian Affairs, September 26, 1901, File 1899–1907, Rosebud. Special Cases 147, Records of the Bureau of Indian Affairs.

20. Rosebud Superintendent, Narrative Reports, 1911–21, *Superintendents' Annual Narrative and Statistical Reports.*

21. Ibid., 1920.

22. The term "farmers" refers to BIA agency staff whose primary job was to act as the equivalent of extension agents for Indians, but who also acted in effect as assistant agency superintendents.

23. Rosebud Superintendent, 1911, *Superintendents' Annual Narrative and Statistical Reports.*

24. Rosebud Superintendent, 1916, *Superintendents' Annual Narrative and Statistical Reports.*

25. This is an interesting example that contrasts with the way that rent is usually understood in Marxist political economy, as a form of surplus extraction from the primary producers by a privileged class of landowners (see, for example, David Harvey, *The Limits to Capital*, rev. ed. [London and New York: Verso, 2006 (1982)], chapter 11). In this case it is the landowners/rentiers who are disadvantaged—at least in terms of income—relative to the primary producers.

26. Rosebud Superintendent, 1914, *Superintendents' Annual Narrative and Statistical Reports.*

27. See Francis Paul Prucha, ed., *Americanizing the American Indians: Writings of the "Friends of the Indian," 1880–1900* (London and Lincoln: University of Nebraska Press, 1973); Francis Paul Prucha, *American Indian Policy in Crisis: Christian Reformers and the Indian, 1865–1900,* reissue edition (London and Lincoln: University of Nebraska Press, 1976 [1975]); Frederick E. Hoxie, *A Final Promise: The Campaign to Assimilate the Indians, 1880–1920* (London and Lincoln: University of Nebraska Press, 2001 [1984]); Francis Paul Prucha, *The Great Father: The United States Government and American Indians,* vols. 1 and 2, unabridged (Lincoln and

London: University of Nebraska Press, 1995 [1984]), vol. 2, chapters 24–34; William T. Hagan, *The Indian Rights Association: The Herbert Welsh Years, 1882–1904* (Tucson: University of Arizona Press, 1985); William T. Hagan, *Theodore Roosevelt and Six Friends of the Indian* (Norman: University of Oklahoma Press, 1997); Tom Hall, *The Great Confusion in Indian Affairs: Native Americans and Whites in the Progressive Era* (Austin: University of Texas Press, 2005); Margaret Jacobs, *White Mothers to a Dark Race: Settler Colonialism, Maternalism, and the Removal of Indigenous Children in the American West and Australia, 1880–1940* (London and Lincoln: University of Nebraska Press, 2011).

28. See Philip Mirowski, "Postface," in *The Road from Mont Pèlerin: The Making of a Neoliberal Thought Collective,* ed. Philip Mirowski and Dieter Plehwe (Cambridge: Harvard University Press, 2015 [2009]), 428; Mitchell Dean, "Rethinking Neoliberalism," *Journal of Sociology* 50:2 (2014 [2012]): 150–63.

29. *Annual Reports of the Department of the Interior for the Fiscal Year Ended June 30, 1901,* Indian Affairs, Part I, Report of the Commissioner (Washington, D.C.: U.S. Government Printing Office, 1902), 1; available at https://uwdc.library.wisc.edu/collections/History/. See also *Issuing or Withholding Rations from Indians,* 1902, Letter from the Secretary of the Interior, House Document No. 391, 57th Cong., 1st Sess.

30. *Annual Reports of the Department of the Interior for the Fiscal Year Ended June 30, 1901,* 4-5, 6; available at https://uwdc.library.wisc.edu/collections/History/.

31. *Annual Reports of the Department of the Interior for the Fiscal Year Ended June 30, 1905,* Indian Affairs, Part I, Report of the Commissioner (Washington, D.C.: U.S. Government Printing Office, 1906), 6–7; available at https://uwdc.library.wisc.edu/collections/History/.

32. Mitchell Dean, *Governmentality: Power and Rule in Modern Society,* 2d ed. (Los Angeles: Sage, 2010 [1999]), 134.

33. It should be added here that Lakota people did not consider rations, and do not consider "food stamps" or "welfare" in the present, as "free," because rations were provided for in the 1877 "Black Hills Treaty," which ceded the Black Hills to the United States. In return for the cession, the United States agreed, among other things, "to provide the said Indians with subsistence consisting of a ration for each individual of a pound and a half of beef, (or in lieu thereof, one half pound of bacon,) one-half pound of flour, and one-half pound of corn; and for every one hundred rations, four pounds of coffee, eight pounds of sugar, and three pounds of beans, or in lieu of said articles the equivalent thereof, in the discretion of the Commissioner of Indian Affairs. Such rations, or so much thereof as may be necessary, shall be continued until the Indians are able to support themselves" (15 Stat. 635; available at http://digital.library.okstate.edu/kappler/). See also Frances Fox Piven and Richard Cloward, *Regulating the Poor: The Functions of Public Welfare,* 2d ed. (New York: Vintage Books, 1993 [1971]).

34. Inspector to Commissioner of Indian Affairs (December 7, 1926), File 79560–1925–150, Rosebud, Central Classified Files of the Bureau of Indians Affairs

(Washington, D.C.: National Archives and Records Administration). Lakota people at the time called inspectors cats *(igmu)* or big cats *(igmu taŋka)*, no doubt because of the curiosity of cats.

35. Inspection Report (June 16, 1930), File 32661–1930–150, Rosebud, Central Classified Files of the Bureau of Indians Affairs.

36. Foucault, *Discipline and Punish*, 178–79.

37. *Report of the Secretary of the Interior for the Fiscal Year Ending June 30, 1883*, vol. 1 (Washington, D.C.: U.S. Government Printing Office, 1906), x–xiii.

38. U.S. Department of the Interior, *Regulations of the Indian Office* (Washington, D.C.: U.S. Government Printing Office, 1904), 3.

39. Ibid., §584, 102–3.

40. *United States v. Clapox,* 35 Fed. 1st 575 (U.S. District Court for the District of Oregon, 1888), 577.

41. Rosebud Agent to Cut Meat Farmer (July 14, 1910); Cut Meat Farmer to Rosebud Agent (July 20, 1910); Rosebud Agent to Cut Meat Farmer (July 26, 1910); Entry 30, Rosebud Agency Records, Records of the Bureau of Indian Affairs (Kansas City, Mo.: National Archives and Records Administration).

42. Commissioner of Indian Affairs, *Annual Report*, 1901, 4.

43. See Luther H. Martin, Huck Gutman, and Patrick H. Hutton, eds., *Technologies of the Self: A Seminar with Michel Foucault* (Amherst: University of Massachusetts Press, 1988).

44. Graham Burchell, "Liberal Government and Techniques of the Self," in *Foucault and Political Reason: Liberalism, Neo-Liberalism, and Rationalities of Government,* ed. Andrew Barry, Thomas Osborne, and Nokolas Rose (Chicago: University of Chicago Press, 1996), 26.

45. For a thorough analysis of regulation of Indian dancing by the BIA, see John W. Troutman, *Indian Blues: American Indians and the Politics of Music, 1879–1934* (Norman: University of Oklahoma Press, 2009).

46. Clark Wissler, "General Discussion of Shamanistic and Dancing Societies," *Anthropological Papers of the American Museum of Natural History* 11:2 (1916): 853–76.

47. Copy of Missionary to Bishop, February 4, 1913, File 20057–13–063, General Service. Central Classified Files, Records of the Bureau of Indian Affairs (Washington, D.C.: National Archives and Records Administration).

48. The Code of Indian Offenses was an administrative code (not a legislative act) promulgated by the commissioner of Indian affairs in 1883. *Report of the Secretary of the Interior, 1883,* x–xiii. The code criminalized, among other things, traditional dances (although not specifically the Omaha dance), polygynous marriages, cohabitation of legally unmarried couples, the practices of medicine men, and other acts (*Regulations of the Indian Office,* 101–5). On the application of the code, see Thomas Biolsi, *Organizing the Lakota: The Political Economy of the New Deal on Pine Ridge and Rosebud Reservations* (Tucson: University of Arizona Press, 1992), 7–11.

49. Burke to Superintendents, April 26, 1921, Circular 1665, File 10429–1922–063, General Service, Central Classified Files of the Records of the Bureau of Indian Affairs.

50. Rosebud Superintendent, Narrative Report, 1924, *Superintendents' Annual Narrative and Statistical Reports*.

51. Investigation into the Practices of the Sioux Indians on the Dakota Reservations, Transcript, File 10429–1922–063, General Service, Central Classified Files of the Records of the Bureau of Indian Affairs.

52. Ibid., 17, 60. This imputed rationality of the giveaway is almost certainly off base. See the discussion of sharing among the Lakota later in this chapter.

53. Commissioner Burke had in mind here not only Omaha dances and fairs, but, perhaps ironically, religious convocations sponsored by Catholic and Protestant missionaries.

54. Burke to Superintendents, February 14, 1923, Supplement to Circular 1665, File 10429–1922–063, General Service, Central Classified Files of the Records of the Bureau of Indian Affairs.

55. Ibid.

56. Burke to All Indians, April 12, 1923, File 10429–1922–063, General Service, Central Classified Files, of the Records of the Bureau of Indian Affairs.

57. Rosebud Superintendent, Narrative Report, 1925, *Superintendents' Annual Narrative and Statistical Reports*.

58. Criteria Used in Surveying Lakota Men, 1907. Adapted from Report of Visits to Home of Patrons (Men) of the Whirlwind Soldier Day School, 1907, Rosebud Agency Records, Records of the Bureau of Indian Affairs (Kansas City, Mo.: National Archives and Records Administration, 1907).

59. Investigation into the Practices of the Sioux Indians on the Dakota Reservations with Particular Reference to the Indian Dance, Transcript of Proceedings, October 24, 1922, 20, File 10429–22–063, General Service, Central Classified Files of the Bureau of Indian Affairs.

60. Rosebud Superintendent, 1914, *Superintendents' Annual Narrative and Statistical Reports*.

61. Circular, March 17, 1923, Reports of Industrial Surveys, Rosebud, Records of the Bureau of Indian Affairs (Washington, D.C.: National Archives and Records Administration).

62. Narrative Report of Agricultural Extension Agent, Records of the Division of Extension and Industry, Records of the Bureau of Indian Affairs (Washington, D.C.: National Archives and Records Administration, 1931).

63. Criteria Used in Surveying Lakota Women, 1907. Adapted from Report of Visits to Home of Patrons (Women) of the Corn Creek Day School, 1907, Rosebud Agency Records, Records of the Bureau of Indian Affairs (Kansas City, Mo.: National Archives and Records Administration).

64. Rosebud Superintendent to Chief Supervisor, March 6, 1911, File 15326–1911–917.1, General Service, Central Classified Files of the Bureau of Indian Affairs.

65. Day School Physician to All Female Industrial Teacher, March 6, 1911, Circular No. 26, Rosebud Reservation, File 15326–1911–917.1, General Service, Central Classified Files of the Records of the Bureau of Indian Affairs.

66. Copy of Winner Chair to State Chair, Indian Welfare, General Federation of Women's Clubs (December 16, 1932), File 46696–31–917, General Service, Part 1-C; "Home Extension Work with Indian Women," presented by A. C. Cooley to the Board Meeting of the General Federation of Women's Clubs, 1932, File 46696–31–917, General Service, Part 1-D; Plans for the Year 1932 (Home Demonstration Agent), March 10, 1932, File 46696–31–917, General Service, Part 1-C; all in Records of the Bureau of Indian Affairs.

67. *Indian Home Care* (General Federation of Women's Clubs), May 1932, File 46696–31–917, General Service, Part 1-C. Records of the Bureau of Indian Affairs.

68. Circular 2305, April 1, 1927, *Procedural Issuances: Orders and Circulars, 1854–1955*, Records of the Bureau of Indian Affairs, Microfilm publication M1121 (Washington, D.C.: National Archives and Records Administration).

69. Karl Marx, *Capital: A Critique of Political Economy*, vol. 1 (London and New York: Penguin Books, 1976 [1867]), 899. Marx was writing specifically of wage workers under capitalism, "who have nothing to sell but their labor-power," but the compulsion entailed applies in a parallel way to family farmers as petty commodity producers.

70. Haviland Scudder Mekeel, "The Economy of a Modern Teton Dakota Community," *Yale Publications in Anthropology* 6 (1936): 11. See this article also for a concrete snapshot of family reproduction in the face of poverty.

71. Foucault, *Discipline and Punish.*

72. *Report of the Country Life Commission*, Senate Doc. 705, 60th Cong., 2d Sess., 1909, 22. Subsequent references are given in the text.

73. The commission also raised the issues of lack of credit "on fair terms," lack of good roads, labor shortages (compounded by intemperance), the provision of parcel post and a postal savings bank, and the general need to consider the farmer's standpoint in national and state policy. Particular attention was paid to the problems of cotton monocropping and tenant farming or sharecropping in the South (15).

74. William L. Bowers, "Country-Life Reform, 1900–1920: A Neglected Aspect of Progressive Era History," *Agricultural History* 45:3 (1971): 212.

75. Ibid., 218–19.

76. I. B. Johnson, *The County Farm Bureau and County Agent in South Dakota*, Extension Circular No. 1 (1917), 8.

77. M. R. Benedict and H. D. McCullough, *Farm Record Keeping and the Application of Business Principles to Farming*, Extension Circular No. 39 (1922), 1, 2.

78. *Annual Report of the Extension Division*, Circular No. 17 (1918), 71.

79. *Annual Report of the Extension Division*, Circular No. 37 (1920), 71.

80. Deborah Fitzgerald, *Every Farm a Factory: The Industrial Ideal in American Agriculture* (New Haven: Yale University Press, 2003), 47. See generally her analysis of teaching farmers "to think quantitatively" (ibid.) in chapter 3.

81. Benedict and McCullough, *Farm Record Keeping and the Application of Business Principles to Farming,* 3–4, 7.

82. Ibid., 8.

83. Ibid.

84. Nikolas Rose and Peter Miller, "Political Power beyond the State: Problematics of Government," *British Journal of Sociology* 43:3 (1992): 187. See also Peter Miller and Ted O'Leary, "Accounting and the Construction of the Governable Person," *Accounting, Organizations and Society* 12:3 (1987): 235–65; Peter Miller, "Governing by Numbers: Why Calculative Practices Matter," *Social Research* 68:2 (2001): 379–96.

85. Benedict and McCullough, *Farm Record Keeping and the Application of Business Principles to Farming,* 3.

86. Ibid., 10–11.

87. This summary definition is based on the (no less complex and abstract) textual explanation in ibid., 12.

88. Ward A. Ostander, *Farming as a Business,* Circular 10, 30.

89. Fitzgerald, *Every Farm a Factory,* 50.

90. Johnson, *The County Farm Bureau and County Agent in South Dakota,* 7.

91. Ibid., 8.

92. *Annual Report of the Extension Division,* Extension Circular No. 17 (1918), 7, 34, 49, 57. Todd County was lumped into a multicounty extension district that shared an agent. There were, of course, fewer non-Indian farmers in Todd and other reservation counties, and Indian farmers received their "extension" from the BIA farmers described earlier. The emergency demonstration agents focused on organizing local farm bureaus, improving crop and livestock production (especially preventing animal diseases), and facilitating the provision of hired labor for farmers. Hog production was particularly at stake: "Bacon and lard constitute two important foods for our armies. They are concentrated and nonperishable. Considerable of the emergency money was set aside to stimulate increased pork production in South Dakota which is one of the leading hog producing states" (89, 7, 34, 49, 57).

93. Ibid., 62.

94. *Report of Chief of Bureau of Agricultural Economics* (Washington, D.C.: Department of Agriculture, 1923), 5; Kenneth H. Parsons, "Foreword," in Henry C. Taylor, *A Farm Economist in Washington, 1919–1925* (Madison: Department of Agricultural Economics, University of Wisconsin—Madison, 1992 [1926]), viii.

95. Taylor, *A Farm Economist in Washington,* 83, 84.

96. *The Agricultural Outlook for 1924,* Miscellaneous Circular No. 23, United States Department of Agriculture (Washington, D.C.: U.S. Government Printing Office, 1924), 1.

97. Taylor, *A Farm Economist in Washington,* 85.

98. In addition to providing guidance for production decisions, the Outlook Program also advised farmers on when to market supplies of commodities held on

farms. *South Dakota's Agricultural Outlook for 1930* published in January, for example, suggested that farmers could get a good price for wheat supplies held on the farms through February, because of demand in importing countries, but that prices might become more volatile in March as contingencies in weather and the commodity market could intervene (South Dakota Extension Service, *South Dakota's Agricultural Outlook for 1930* [Brookings: South Dakota State College, 1930]).

99. Ibid., 1928.

100. "Prices of several major crops are relatively high by reason of poor yields and this coincides with an upward trend in livestock prices. . . . In so far as they merely serve to beckon producers into a still heavier acreage of wheat cotton, corn, potatoes, along with more hogs, cattle and sheep for 1926, they represent a dubious substitution of the promise for the fulfillment," South Dakota Extension Service, *South Dakota Monthly Farm Outlook,* 1 September 15, 1925 (Brookings: South Dakota State College).

101. Extension Service, *The South Dakota Farm Outlook,* February 15, 1930 (Brookings: South Dakota State College). The Great Plains Committee appointed by Franklin Roosevelt wrote in 1936 that when the price farmers received for wheat "collapsed during the post-[World War I] period Great Plains farmers continued to plant large wheat acreages in a desperate endeavor to get money with which to pay debt charges, taxes, and other unavoidable expenses. They had no choice in the matter" (Great Plains Committee, *The Future of the Great Plains: Report of the Great Plains Committee* [Washington, D.C.: U.S. Government Printing Office, 1936], 4). USDA economist Don Paarlberg reported in 1956 that "[t]here is a belief, held by considerable numbers of people, that if prices fall, farmers generally will increase their production in order to maintain their incomes." Paarlberg rejected that idea ("Shortcomings in Current Explanations of National Farm Surpluses," *Journal of Farm Economics* 38:5 (1956): 1710.

102. H. R. Tolley, "The History and Objectives of Outlook Work," *Journal of Farm Economics* 13 (1931): 524.

3. New Deal Practices

1. Michel Foucault, *Security, Territory, Population: Lectures at the Collège de France, 1977–1978,* ed. Michel Senellart, trans. Graham Burchell (New York: Palgrave MacMillan, 2007 [2004]), 347.

2. Michel Foucault, *"Society Must Be Defended": Lectures as the Collège de France, 1975–1976,* ed. Mauro Bertani and Alessandro Fontana, trans. David Macey (New York: St. Martin's Press, 2003 [1997]), 244.

3. Ibid., 245. For more on the subject matter of biopolitics/security/governmentality, see Mitchell Dean, *Governmentality: Power and Rule in Modern Society,* 2d ed. (Thousand Oaks, Calif.: Sage Publications, 2010 [1999]), 118–19.

4. Michel Foucault, *The History of Sexuality, Volume I: An Introduction,* trans. Robert Hurley (New York: Random House, 1980 [1976]), 139–43; Foucault, *"Society*

Must Be Defended," 241–53; Foucault, *The Birth of Biopolitics: Lectures at the Collège de France, 1978–1979,* ed. Michel Senellart, trans. Graham Burchell (New York: Palgrave MacMillan, 2008 [2004]).

5. Foucault, *Security, Territory, Population.*

6. Michel Foucault, "Governmentality," in *The Foucault Effect: Studies in Governmentality,* ed. Graham Burchell, Colin Gordin, and Peter Miller (Chicago: University of Chicago Press, 1991 [1978]), 87–104.

7. Pat O'Malley, *Risk, Uncertainty and Government* (Portland, Ore.: Glass House Press, 2004), 38, 41. See also Dean, *Governmentality,* 133.

8. Foucault, *The Birth of Biopolitics,* 2.

9. Roberto Esposito, *Bíos: Biopolitics and Philosophy,* trans. Timothy Campbell (Minneapolis: University of Minnesota Press, 2008), 74.

10. See Elizabeth Sanders, *Roots of Reform: Farmers, Workers, and the American State, 1877–1917* (Chicago: University of Chicago Press, 1999).

11. Louise Liffengren Hullinger, *Next Year Country: Stories of Drought-Stricken South Dakota in the 1930s* (Deerfield, Ill.: Lake Shore Publishing, 2000).

12. Emergency Agricultural Assistant, Tripp County, *Annual Report, 1935* (Winner, S.Dak.: Extension Service, Tripp County Courthouse).

13. "Proclamation of Mayor," (March 28, 1935), *Winner Advocate,* 1.

14. Mabelle Stewart Worsley, "Homesteading the Rosebud: The Reminiscence of Mabelle Stewart Worsley," ed. James J. Balakier, *South Dakota History* 35:3 (2005): 248. Worsley's niece recorded a series of interviews in December 1973 through January 1974.

15. Ollie Napesni, *Salt Camp, Her Story: Lakota Living Treasure,* recorded, transcribed, and edited by Dianna Torson (Victoria, B.C.: Trafford Publishing, 2003), 106.

16. Emergency Agricultural Assistant, Tripp County, *Annual Report,* 1934 (Winner, S.Dak.: Extension Service, Tripp County Courthouse), 14.

17. Emergency Agricultural Agent, Mellette and Todd Counties, *Annual Report,* 1940, Agricultural Extension Service Annual Reports, 1909–1968, Microfilm publication T888 (Washington, D.C.: National Archives and Records Administration).

18. Worsley, "Homesteading the Rosebud," 247.

19. Franklin D. Roosevelt, Inaugural Address, March 4, 1933, electronic document accessed October 12, 2012, http://www.archives.gov/education/lessons/fdr-inaugural/.

20. Rexford G. Tugwell located the birth of the critique in the conservation movement at the turn of the twentieth century when a "few questioners began to ask whether the use of land solely in the interest of each individual holder was the only possible way to proceed," "The place of Government in a National Land Program," *Journal of Farm Economics* 16 (1934): 57. See also National Conference on Land Utilization, *Proceedings of the National Conference on Land Utilization* (Washington, D.C.: U.S. Government Printing Office, 1932), 240, 244; Theodore

Saloutos and John D. Hicks, *Agricultural Discontent in the Middle West, 1900–1939* (Madison: University of Wisconsin Press, 1951); John A. Crampton, *The National Farmers Union: Ideology of the Pressure Group* (Lincoln: University of Nebraska Press, 1965); Elizabeth Sander, *The Roots of Reform: Farmers, Workers, and the American State, 1877–1917* (Chicago: University of Chicago Press, 1999). On South Dakota specifically, see Herbert S. Schell, *History of South Dakota*, 4th ed., ed. John E. Miller (Pierre: South Dakota State Historical Society Press, 2004 [1961]); Lynwood E. Oyos, *The Family Farmers' Advocate: South Dakota Farmers Union, 1914–2000* (Sioux Falls, S.Dak.: Center for Western Studies, Augustana College, 2000).

21. Tugwell, "The Place of Government in a National Land Program," 58.

22. Rexford G. Tugwell, "Farm Relief and a Permanent Agriculture," *Annals of the America Academy of Political and Social Science* 142 (1929): 280, 281.

23. Great Plains Committee, *The Future of the Great Plains: Report of the Great Plains Committee* (Washington, D.C.: U.S. Government Printing Office, 1936), 4.

24. Ibid., 7.

25. Ibid., 6, 63.

26. Ellis W. Hawley, *The New Deal and the Problem of Monopoly: A Study in Economic Ambivalence* (New York: Fordham University Press, 1995 [1966]); Theodore Rosenof, "New Deal *Pragmatism* and Economic *Systems*: Concepts and Meanings," *The Historian* 49:3 (1987): 368–82; William J. Barber, *Designs within Disorder: Franklin D. Roosevelt, the Economists, and the Shaping of American Economic Policy, 1933–1945* (New York: Cambridge University Press, 1996); Theodore Rosenof, *Economics in the Long Run: New Deal Theorists and Their Legacies, 1933–1993* (Chapel Hill: University of North Carolina Press, 1997).

27. Gardiner C. Means, "The Growth in the Relative Importance of the Large Corporation in American Economic Life," *American Economic Review* 21:1 (1931): 37.

28. Adolf A. Berle Jr. and Gardiner C. Means, *The Modern Corporation and Private Property* (New York: MacMillan, 1933), 1.

29. Gardiner C. Means, "The Separation of Ownership and Control in American Industry," *Quarterly Journal of Economics.* 46:1 (1931): 97; emphasis added.

30. Gardiner C. Means, "Business Combinations and Agriculture," *Journal of Agricultural Economics* 20:2 (1938): 54.

31. Ibid., 53.

32. Ibid. See also Gardiner C. Means, "The N.R.A., A.A.A., and the Making of Industrial Policy," Letter from the Secretary of Agriculture in Response to Senate Resolution No. 17, A Report Relating to the Subject of Industrial Prices and their Relative Inflexibility, Senate Doc. 14, 74th Cong., 1st Sess. (Washington, D.C.: U.S. Government Printing Office, 1935); Frederic S. Lee and Warren J. Samuels, *The Heterodox Economics of Gardiner C. Means* (Armonk, N.Y.: M. E. Sharpe, 1992).

33. Henry A. Wallace, "For a Domestic 'Ever-Normal Granary,'" in *Agricultural Thought in the Twentieth Century*, ed. George McGovern (New York: Bobbs-Merrill, 1967 [1938]), 235.

34. Rexford G. Tugwell, "Reflections of Farm Relief," *Political Science Quarterly* 43:4 (1928): 493.

35. See Foucault, *Security, Territory, Population,* 104.

36. Means, "The N.R.A., A.A.A., and the Making of Industrial Policy," 20.

37. Foucault, *Security, Territory, Population,* 353.

38. See Foucault, *"Society Must Be Defended."*

39. Foucault, *Security, Territory, Population,* 118.

40. Ibid., 46–47.

41. Ibid., 352–53.

42. On global mobile technologies, see Aihwa Ong and Stephen J. Collier, eds., *Global Assemblages: Technology, Politics, and Ethics as Anthropological Problems* (Malden, Mass.: Blackwell Publishers, 2005); Aihwa Ong, "Neoliberalism as a Mobile Technology," *Transactions of the Institute of British Geogpraphers* 32:1 (2007): 3–8.

43. Arthur M. Schlesinger Jr., *The Coming of the New Deal* (Boston: Houghton Mifflin, 2003 [1958]), 179.

44. Means, "N.R.A., A.A.A., and the Making of Industrial Policy," 9.

45. Rosenof, *Economics in the Long Run,* 24, 31.

46. Hawley, *The New Deal and the Problem of Monopoly,* 187.

47. Rexford G. Tugwell, "The Principle of Planning and the Institution of Laissez Faire," *American Economic Review* 22:1 (1932): 89. Tugwell, an internationalist, believed that "often, not even" the federal government would be coextensive with industry, and implied that transnational or even world government would ultimately be necessary for rational political-economic planning.

48. Ibid., 88.

49. Rexford G. Tugwell, "The Planned Use of the Land," *Today* 1:13 (1934): 6.

50. Adolf Berle, "The Social Economics of the New Deal," *New York Times,* Sunday magazine, October 29, 1933, 5.

51. Mordecai Ezekiel and Louis H. Bean, *The Economic Bases for the Agricultural Adjustment Act* (Washington, D.C.: U.S. Department of Agriculture, 1933), 40.

52. See William D. Rowley, *M. L. Wilson and the Campaign for Domestic Allotment* (Lincoln: University of Nebraska Press, 1970), 32–61.

53. Tugwell, "Reflections on Farm Relief," 490. Tugwell imagined that enforcement would be based on government "denial of the use of railways and warehouses to produce grown on unauthorized acreage" (ibid.). He also imagined that the higher prices that urban consumers paid for farm prices would be offset by the general increase in industrial production (and workers' wages) that would result from increased consumption of manufactured goods by farmers, as well as by the long-term decline of prices for farm products as the industry became more efficient (which could, of course, only happen if it became a *profitable* industry) (492–93).

54. John D. Black, *Agricultural Reform in the United States* (New York: McGraw-Hill, 1929), chapter 10.

55. Richard S. Kirkendall, *Social Scientists and Farm Politics in the Age of Roosevelt* (Columbia: University of Missouri Press, 1966), 27, 28, 24, 26.

56. Rowley, *M. L. Wilson and the Campaign for Domestic Allotment*, 131–32.

57. Elizabeth Evenson Williams, *Free to Speak His Mind: W. R. Ronald, Prairie Editor and an AAA Architect* (Freeman, S.Dak.: Pine Hill Press, 1999), 45; and Rowley, *M. L. Wilson and the Campaign for Domestic Allotment*, 132.

58. Kirkendall, *Social Scientists and Farm Politics in the Age of Roosevelt*, 31–32; Rowley, *M. L. Wilson and the Campaign for Domestic Allotment*, 135; Williams, *Free to Speak His Mind*, 45–46.

59. Peter Norbeck, "The Voluntary Allotment," *Farm Journal* 56 (1932): 5–6; Williams, *Free to Speak His Mind*, 50.

60. Rowley, *M. L. Wilson and the Campaign for Domestic Allotment*, 143.

61. "W. R. Roland Submits Allotment Aid Bill to Senate," *Evening Republican*, February 7, 1933, 1, 8.

62. The term "cooperators" predates the New Deal and was used by agricultural experts in the 1920s. See Deborah Fitzgerald, *Every Farm a Factory: The Industrial Ideal in American Agriculture* (New Haven: Yale University Press, 2003), 51.

63. Means, "N.R.A., A.A.A., and the Making of Industrial Policy," 15, 17.

64. "Mark Wheat Contract Acres without Cost," *Todd County Tribune*, October 5, 1933; "Local Wheat Men Soon to Get Cash Benefits," *Todd County Tribune*, July 20, 1933; "Answers Questions on Wheat Adjustment Plan," *Todd County Tribune*, August 3, 1933; "District Supervisor Here on Wheat Allotment Plan," *Gregory Times-Advocate*, August 10, 1933; "Wheat Program Committee Named," *Todd County Tribune*, August 24, 1933; "Wheat Plan on Farms with No 1933 Crop," *Todd County Tribune*, August 31, 1933; "Wheat Plan Lowers Usual Risk in Crop," *Gregory Times-Advocate*, September 7, 1933; "13,912 Acres Signed up in County on Wheat Allotment Plan," *Todd County Tribune*, October 19, 1933; "Corn-Hog Control Plan Offers Big Grower Benefits," *Todd County Tribune*, November 2, 1933; "News of Wheat and Corn-Hog Programs," *Winner Advocate*, January 11, 1934; "Lists High Points of Corn-Hog Contracts," *Todd County Tribune*, January 25, 1934; "Insurance Feature in Corn-Hog Program," *Todd County Tribune*, February 9, 1934.

65. *United States v. Butler* (1936), 297 U.S. 1, at 9.

66. Ibid., 16.

67. 49 Stat. 163.

68. 49 Stat. 1148. The act also specified that funding would be distributed through state agricultural conservation committees, and that state plans for agricultural conservation were required in order to receive the payments.

69. Ibid., 1150.

70. Kirkendall, *Social Scientists and Farm Politics in the Age of Roosevelt*, 144–46.

71. Foucault, *Security, Territory, Population*, 118.

72. "News of Interest to Farmers of County," *Winner Advocate*, April 16, 1936.

73. "New Soil Conservation Practices Get Approval," *Todd County Tribune*, May 14, 1936; "Drought Modifications Made in Farm Program," *Todd County Tribune*,

July 23, 1936; "Practices Applicable only to Range Lands," *Todd County Tribune,* January 28, 1937; "Procedure for Election of Range Area Examiners," *Todd County Tribune,* February 14, 1937; "33 Counties Join in Triple A Range Program," *Todd County Tribune,* June 10, 1937; Extension Agent, Annual Report, 1937, Mellette and Todd Counties, Agricultural Extension Service Annual Reports, 1909–1968, Records of the Agricultural Extension Service, Microfilm publication T888 (Washington, D.C.: National Archives and Records Administration); "News of Interest to Farmers," *Todd County Tribune,* February 24, 1938.

74. 48 Stat. 984, at 984, 985.

75. Ibid., 987, 988.

76. It was not the case that there was no "tribal" organization prior to the ratification of the IRA constitution in 1935. A tribal council existed on the reservation, and in fact the Lakota and their linguistic neighbors living on eight different reservations had a Black Hills, or Great Sioux Nation, Treaty Council, composed of representatives of the bands and tribes that had been signatories of the Fort Laramie Treaty of 1868. But these entities met at the pleasure of the BIA superintendent and were largely powerless except for agenda items that might be approved by the superintendent. See Thomas Biolsi, *Organizing the Lakota: The Political Economy of the New Deal on Pine Ridge and Rosebud Reservations* (Tucson: University of Arizona Press, 1992), chapter 2.

77. This would, of course, require some ongoing tutelage for inexperienced tribal officials, and this job of education in tribal administration was handed over to the Organization Division of the BIA (see ibid., chapters 4 and 6).

78. Transcript in Vine Deloria Jr., ed., *The Indian Reorganization Act: Congresses and Bills* (Norman: University of Oklahoma Press, 2002), 31.

79. Rider to Temporary Assignment and Occupancy Permit, n.d., Rosebud Housing Development Records, Records of the Bureau of Indian Affairs (Kansas City, Mo.: National Archives and Records Administration); "Grass Mountain Colony," *Indians at Work,* June 1939, 28–29.

80. Memorandum of Hearing (January 27, 1939), Rosebud Housing Development Records, Records of the Bureau of Indian Affairs (Kansas City, Mo.: National Archives).

81. Rosebud Superintendent to Collier, May 4, 1940, and Two Kettle Project, 1940 Extension and Credit File, Rosebud Reservation Records, Archives and Special Collections, I. D. Weeks Library (Vermillion: University of South Dakota).

82. Stock Certificate Plan, July 14, 1941, Washington Office Circulars File, Subject Correspondence Files, Rosebud Agency Records, Records of the Bureau of Indian Affairs (Kansas City, Mo.: National Archives). See Richmond Lee Clow, "The Rosebud Sioux Tribe and the Creation of the TLE, 1943–1955: A Case Tribal Heirship Land Management," in *Trusteeship in Change: Toward Tribal Autonomy in Resource Management,* ed. Richmond Lee Clow and Imre Sutton (Boulder: University Press of Colorado, 2002), 145–64.

83. By-Laws, Tribal Land Enterprise. Rosebud, S.Dak.: Rosebud Sioux Tribe, Purpose, paragraph 6.

84. When the original draft of what was to become the IRA was being prepared in 1933, the assistant solicitors in the Interior Department sent a confidential memo to the commissioner of Indian affairs outlining the powers of the chartered Indian community. These included "provisions authorizing the lease, sale or exchange of individual lands to the community" as a mechanism for correcting the land problems produced by the allotment policy. The assistant solicitors were concerned to find a way to eliminate inequality in landownership among individual Indian people: "Plainly, such inequality must be eliminated as quickly as possible, if every member of the community is to be granted some opportunity to wrest a livelihood from the limited resources of the community." One mechanism would be a non-stock membership corporation "from which members of the community will be entitled to receive a fair share [not a prorated share based on existing equities] of community income and the use of a fair share of the community assets." "To state these objectives in statutory terms," the memo warned, "is perhaps politically inadvisable and at all events legally unnecessary, since consent of the Indians to such a system will have to be secured by reasoning and bargaining," Assistant Solicitors to Collier ("Confidential"), December 28, 1933, File 3395–1934–066, General Service, Central Classified Files, Records of the Bureau of Indian Affairs (Washington, D.C.: National Archives and Records Administration).

85. 48 Stat. 984, at 985.

86. "Excerpt from an Address by Ward Shepard, Indian Office Land Policy Specialist, to the Conference on Minorities of the Women's International League for Peace and Freedom, Chicago, 28 May 1934," *Indians at Work*, June 15, 1934, 7.

87. The predecessor of the SCS was the Soil Erosion Service in the Department of the Interior.

88. Hugh H. Bennett, "Soil Conservation: Farm by Farm, and Field by Field," *Soil Conservation* 4:1 (July 1938): 8, 9. In 1890, John Wesley Powell described "a hydrographic basin" as "a unit of country well defined in nature." He went on: "such a district of country is a commonwealth by itself. The people who live therein are interdependent in all their industries. Every man is interested in the conservation and management of the water supply," John Wesley Powell, "Institutions for the Arid Lands," *Century Illustrated Magazine* 40:1 (1890): 113–14. See also Donald Wooster, "A River Running West: Reflections of John Wesley Powell," *Journal of Cultural Geography* 26:2 (2009): 113–26.

89. Hugh H. Bennett, "Developing Enlightened Public Opinion in Conservation," Address before the Assembly on Use of Human and Natural Resources in Education, National Education Association (July 2, 1940) (Washington, D.C.: U.S. Government Printing Office, 1940), 5; emphasis added.

90. Ibid., 9.

91. This is likely because it was easier to steer a horse-drawn plow or a tractor-drawn plow up or down a slope, rather that sideways on a slope.

92. Bennett, "Developing Enlightened Public Opinion in Conservation," 5.

93. 1939 Evaluation Survey Report, Winner–Dixon Project, Folder 101.6, Reports, 1940, Records of the Natural Resources Conservation Service (Kansas City, Mo.: National Archives and Records Administration).

94. Acting Project Manager to Acting Regional Conservator (May 12, 1938), Folder 101, Administration, Winner, S.Dak., January–June, 1938, Box 23, Records of the Natural Resources Conservation Service (Kansas City, Mo.: National Archives and Records Administration).

95. Nikolas Rose, *Powers of Freedom: Reframing Political Thought* (New York: Cambridge University Press, 1999), 36.

96. On the role of aesthetic choice in the history of science, see Thomas S. Kuhn, *The Structure of Scientific Revolutions,* 2d ed. (Chicago: University of Chicago Press (1970 [1962]), 157–58 (on the intellectually revolutionary effects of aesthetic choice); and James W. McAllister, "Scientists' Aesthetic Preferences among Theories: Conservative Factors in Revolutionary Crises," in *The Elusive Synthesis: Aesthetics and Science,* ed. Alfred I. Tauber (Dordrecht, the Netherlands: Kluwer Academic Publishers (1997 [1996]), 169–87 (on the role of aesthetics in intellectual stability).

97. This was a common New Deal policy throughout the arid West.

98. Rosebud Superintendent, Narrative Report, 1932, *Superintendents' Annual Narrative and Statistical Reports,* Microfilm Publication M1011 (Washington, D.C.: National Archives and Records Administration). Sustained-yield management originated in forestry in the 1890s; it was developed for range management in the Department of Agriculture at the opening of the twentieth century. See Samuel P. Hays, *Conservation and the Gospel of Efficiency: The Progressive Conservation Movement, 1890–1920* (Pittsburgh: Pittsburgh University Press, 1999 [1959]), 28, 52–53.

99. 48 Stat. 984, at 986.

100. Truman C. Anderson memorandum to A. E. McClymonds (June 26, 1937), Folder 101, Administration, General, S.Dak., January–June 1938, Box 23, Records of the Natural Resources Conservation Service (Kansas City, Mo.: National Archives and Records Administration).

101. R. F. Humphrey memorandum to P. B. Lister (September 9, 1937), Folder 101, Administration, General, S.Dak., January–June 1938, Box 23, Records of the Natural Resources Conservation Service.

102. F. DeWitt Abbott, Range Management Plan Report for the Rosebud Indian Reservation, First Rough Draft (May 1939), Box 212, Records of the Natural Resources Conservation Service.

103. "Powers of Indian Tribes" (October 25, 1934), Opinion of the Solicitor, U.S. Department of the Interior; emphasis in original; electronic document accessed December 18, 2015, http://digital.library.okstate.edu/kappler/vol5/html_files/v5p0 778.html, 780.

104. 163 U.S. 376, at 384.

105. Partha Chatterjee, "The Nation in Heterogeneous Time," *Futures* 37 (2005): 925–42.

106. "Powers of Indian Tribes," 19.

107. Rosebud Superintendent to Collier, April 25, 1934, File 20707-1934-066, Rosebud, Central Classified Files, Records of the Bureau of Indian Affairs (Washington, D.C.: National Archives and Records Administration).

108. Felix S. Cohen, *On the Drafting of Tribal Constitutions*, ed. David E. Wilkins (Norman: University of Oklahoma Press, 2006 [1934]), 25–27.

109. See Thomas Biolsi, *Organizing the Lakota: The Political Economy of the New Deal on Pine Ridge and Rosebud Reservations* (Tucson: University of Arizona Press, 1992), 104–8.

110. Group Organization, Circular No. 3095 (August 8, 1936), *Procedural Issuances: Orders and Circulars, 1854–1955*, Microfilm Publication M1121, Records of the Bureau of Indian Affairs (Washington, D.C.: National Archives and Records Administration).

111. Lewis Meriam, *The Problem of Indian Administration*, Institute for Government Research, Studies in Administration (New York: Johnson Reprint Corporation, 1971 [1928]), 471.

112. National Resources Board, *Indian Land Tenure, Economic Status, and Population Trends*, Part X of the Report on Land Planning (Washington, D.C.: U.S. Government Printing Office, 1935), 16.

113. Ibid., 17.

114. National Planning Board, December 11, 1933, Federal Assistance for Planning, Fifth Circular Letter (Washington, D.C.: Federal Emergency Administration of Public Works). See also Patrick D. Reagan, *Designing a New America: The Origin of New Deal Planning, 1890–1943* (Amherst: University of Massachusetts Press, 1999), 186; Alan Brinkley, "The National Resources Planning Board and the Reconstruction of Planning," in *The American Planning Tradition: Culture and Policy*, ed. Robert Fishman (Washington, D.C.: Woodrow Wilson Center Press, 2000), 174–75.

115. Franklin D. Roosevelt, June 30, 1934, Executive Order 6777, Establishing the National Resources Board, electronic document accessed December 6, 2012, http://www.presidency.ucsb.edu.

116. National Resources Board, *A Report on National Planning and Public Works in Relation to Natural Resources and Including Land Use and Water Resources with Findings and Recommendations* (Washington, D.C.: U.S. Government Printing Office, December 1, 1934), 83, 84.

117. Ibid., 83; emphasis added.

118. Michel Foucault, *Discipline and Punish: The Birth of the Prison*, trans. Alan Sheridan (New York: Vintage Books, 1979 [1977]), 176–77.

119. National Resources Board, *A Report on National Planning and Public Works in Relation to Natural Resources and Including Land Use and Water Resources with Findings and Recommendations*, 83, 84.

120. On the history of the South Dakota State Planning Board, see Thomas Biolsi, "New Deal Visions of an Agrarian Commonwealth: The South Dakota Planning Board, 1934–1939," in *Political Culture of South Dakota*, ed. Jon K. Lauck, John E. Miller, and Donald C. Simmons Jr. (Pierre: South Dakota State Historical Society Press, 2014), 77–102. On W. R. Ronald, see Williams, *Free to Speak His Mind*.

121. South Dakota Planning Board, 1935, "The Planning Movement," County and Regional Notes and Reports File, Records of the State Planning Board; emphasis added.

122. Minutes of the First Regional Meeting of the County Planning Boards (June 18, 1935), Box 7423C, Records of the State Planning Board.

123. South Dakota State Planning Board, *Progress Report* 1:30 (November 9, 1935): 2.

124. South Dakota Planning Board, 1936, *First Biennial Report of the South Dakota State Planning Board* (Pierre: South Dakota State Historical Society), 125, 126, 128.

125. South Dakota State Planning Board, *Progress Report* 6 (June 22, 1935): 3.

126. Outline for Preparation of Reports by County Planning Boards, [1935], County Planning Board Minutes File, Records of the South Dakota Planning Board.

127. Memorandum: Suggestions for Consideration by the Executive Committee and the Committee on Agricultural Resources and Development of the South Dakota State Planning Board in Connection with the Emergency Drouth Problem in South Dakota (1936), I. D. Weeks Papers, Presidents Series, USD Archives, Archives and Special Collections, I. D. Week Library (Vermillion: University of South Dakota).

128. Kirkendall, *Social Scientists and Farm Politics in the Age of Roosevelt*, 172ff.; Mary W. M. Hargreaves, *Dry Farming in the Northern Great Plains: Years of Readjustment, 1920–1990* (Lawrence: University Press of Kansas, 1993), 150.

129. Ellery A. Foster and Harold A. Vogel, "Cooperative Land Use Planning—A New Development in Democracy," in *Farmers in a Changing World*, The Yearbook of Agriculture, U.S. Department of Agriculture (Washington, D.C.: U.S. Government Printing Office, 1940), 1138.

130. Tripp County Extension Agent, Annual Report, 1940, South Dakota Cooperative Extension Service (Winner, S.Dak.: Tripp County Courthouse).

131. S. W. Jones, "County Land Use Planning is Democracy in Action," *Farm-Home News* (April 1941) (Brookings: South Dakota Extension Service).

132. Ibid., 1.

133. "Farmers to Designate Type of Farming Area," *Todd County Tribune*, April 20, 1939.

134. Tripp County Land Use Planning Committee, 1941, *Land Use Planning in Tripp County, South Dakota*, 1.

135. County Land Use Planning, Work Outline Number 1, October 1938, File 101.3, County Land Use Planning, 1938–39, Box 459, Records of the Natural Resources Conservation Service.

136. *Land Use Planning in Tripp County,* Tripp County Land Use Planning Committee (1941), 24, 25.

137. County Land Use Planning, Work Outline Number 1.

4. Making New Deal Subjects

1. Rexford G. Tugwell, *The Diary of Rexford G. Tugwell: The New Deal, 1932–1935,* ed. Michael V. Namorato (New York: Greenwood Press, 1992), 52–53.

2. Chester C. Davis, "The Program of Agricultural Adjustment," *Journal of Farm Economics* 16:1 (1934): 92.

3. Henry A. Wallace, "The Farmer and Social Discipline," *Journal of Farm Economics* 16:1 (1934): 7, 8; emphasis added.

4. Ralph E. Hansen to Dan E. Cass, August 21, 1939, File 101.6, Report, 1940, Records of the Natural Resources Conservation Service (Kansas City, Mo.: National Archives and Records Administration).

5. Bringing the Plains Back, Filmstrip Lecture, Rapid City, South Dakota, October 12, 1936, File S.D. Press and Radio Releases (2 of 6), Box 303, Records of the Natural Resources Conservation Service (Kansas City, Mo.: National Archives and Records Administration).

6. B. R. Fenn, "Thinks Contour Strip Farming Profitable," *Winner Advocate,* December 10, 1936. 1.

7. B. R. Fenn, "Farmers Urged to Try Soil Saving Methods," *Winner Advocate,* December 17, 1936, 1.

8. "Causes and Remedies for Erosion of Soil," *Winner Advocate,* September 26, 1935, 1.

9. Emergency Agricultural Agent, "News of Interest to Farmers of County," *Winner Advocate,* October 31, 1935, 1.

10. Tripp County Extension Agent, *Annual Report, 1941* (Winner, S.Dak.: Tripp County Courthouse), emphasis added.

11. Ralph E. Johnston to M. H. Saunderson, March 2, 1938, File 184–04, Land Use Planning, Research and Studies, Records of the Bureau of Agricultural Economics (Kansas City, Mo.: National Archives and Records Administration).

12. Ralph E. Hansen to Dan E. Cass, August 21, 1939; Dan E. Cass to Ralph Hansen, August 29, 1939, File 101.6, Report, 1940, Records of the Natural Resources Conservation Service (Kansas City, Mo.: National Archives and Records Administration).

13. Report of the Project Planning Committee, Winner, South Dakota, Project SD-2, December 18, 1939, File 101.6, Reports, 1940, Records of the Natural Resources Conservation Service. The plan was for the cooperators themselves to conduct "evaluation survey work by making trials and comparisons of different practices."

14. Dan E. Cass to A. E. McClymonds, May 12, 1938, File 101, Administration, General, S.Dak., January–June, 1938, Box 23; Annual Report, 1938–39, Clearfield

Keyapaha District, File S.D. Winner Dist., Misc. (2 of 2), Box 358, Records of the Natural Resources Conservation Service.

15. Semi-Annual Report, Clearfield–Keyapaha Soil Conservation District, June 30, 1939, File S.D. Winner Dist., Misc. (2 of 2), Box 358, Records of the Natural Resources Conservation Service.

16. L. C. Gray, "The Economic Possibilities of Conservation," *Quarterly Journal of Economics* 27:3 (1913): 503, 514. Gray examined the economic context of conservation in detail and determined that when prices for agricultural commodities are high relative to costs of production, immediate returns outweigh "loss from diminishing [future] returns" and the farmer will opt to "mine" his land. Only when the rate of return on farming is low is "a policy of conservation more profitable to the owner" (506). Gray also pointed out that when land prices are higher, conservation is more likely to be the optimal strategy. Writing in 1913, Gray was witnessing a period of rising prices for agricultural products. See also Richard S. Kirkendall, "L. C. Gray and the Supply of Agricultural Land," *Agricultural History* 37 (1963): 206–13.

17. Gray, "The Economic Possibilities of Conservation," 517.

18. Walter W. Wilcox, "Economic Aspects of Soil Conservation," *Journal of Political Economy* 46:4 (1938): 703, 707, 708. See also E. C. Weitzell, "Economics of Soil Conservation: I., Individual and Social Considerations," *Journal of Land and Public Utility Economics* 19:3 (1943): 339–53.

19. Karl Marx, *Capital: A Critique of Political Economy*, vol. 1 (London and New York: Penguin Books, 1976 [1867]), 899. See Richard Hofstadter, *The Age of Reform: From Bryan to F.D.R.* (New York: Vintage Books, 1955), 43: "What differentiated [American agriculture] . . . from . . . European agriculture [and] . . . from the agrarian myth . . . was not simply that it produced for a market, but that it was so speculative, so mobile, so mechanized, so 'progressive,' so thoroughly imbued with the commercial spirit." See also Harriet Friedmann, "Simple Commodity Production and Wage Labour in the American Plains," *Journal of Peasant Studies* 6:1 (1978): 71–100; Harriet Friedmann, "World Market, State, and Family Farm: Social Bases of Household Production in the Era of Wage Labor," *Comparative Studies in Society and History* 20:4 (1978): 545–86; and Catherine McNickol Stock, *Main Street in Crisis: The Great Depression and the Old Middle Class on the Northern Plains* (Chapel Hill: University of North Carolina Press, 1997), 9.

20. South Dakota State Planning Board, *Land Use Problems in Central South Dakota, 1937* (Brookings: South Dakota State Planning Board, 1939), 11–12.

21. Supplement to the Semi-Annual Report, Clearfield–Keyapaha Soil Conservation District, December 31, 1939, File S.D. Winner Dist., Misc. (2 of 2), Box 358, Records of the Natural Resources Conservation Service. The source of the internal quotation is Gove Hambridge, "Soils and Men—A Summary," in *Yearbook of Agriculture, 1938*, Department of Agriculture (Washington, D.C.: U.S. Government Printing Office, 1939), 3.

22. Henry A. Wallace, "The War at Our Feet," *Survey Graphic* 29:2 (1940): 109; electronic document accessed February 25, 2014, http://newdeal.feri.org/survey/ 40a07.htm; A Statement by Secretary Wallace [internal Department of Agriculture circular], December 15, 1939, File 400.6, Report 2, 1940, Box 466, Records of the Natural Resources Conservation Service.

23. Hugh H. Bennett, "Developing Enlightened Public Opinion in Conservation," (Washington, D.C.: U.S. Soil Conservation Service, 1940), 2, 10, 4.

24. *Dakota Zephyr,* February 7, 1942, 3, File S.D. Agri. College, Records of the Natural Resources Conservation Service.

25. M. L. Wilson, "Society and the Farmer Have Mutual Interests in the Land," *Soil Conservation* 3:5 (1937): 117.

26. L. C. Gray, "Our Major Land Use Problem and Suggested Lines of Action," in *Farmers in a Changing World, The Yearbook of Agriculture,* United States Department of Agriculture (Washington, D.C.: U.S. Government Printing Office, 1940), 401, 402.

27. A Statement by Secretary Wallace, December 15, 1939 (internal Department of Agriculture circular), File 400.6, Report 2, 1940, Box 466, Records of the Natural Resources Conservation Service.

28. Henry A. Wallace, "Spiritual Forces and the State." *Forum and Century* 91:6 (1934): 353, 354, 355, 356.

29. *Dakota Zephyr,* May 1941, 6, File S.D. Agri. College, Box 294, Records of the Natural Resources Conservation Service.

30. Thomas Biolsi, *Organizing the Lakota: The Political Economy of the New Deal on Pine Ridge and Rosebud Reservations* (Tucson: University of Arizona Press, 1992).

31. Ibid., 86–88.

32. Ibid., 88.

33. Ibid., 89–91. When I interviewed one of the BIA field agents in 1984 who had been tasked to work on the constitution and develop tribal government in Lakota country, he said that many Lakota people mistook the English word *tenure* in the constitution (concerning the tenure of trust land) for "ten year." One can easily imagine the difficulties of translation that must have been involved.

34. See ibid., 129–34, on the tribal council's attempt to license dance halls.

35. For the original text adopted in 1935, see "Constitution and By-Laws of the Rosebud Sioux Tribe," electronic document accessed June 14, 2016, https://www .loc.gov/law/help/american-indian . . ./36026264.pdf. For the most current (2007), amended version, see http://www.narf.org/nill/constitutions/rosebudconst/.

36. Required approval meant that the council action in question was not effective until approved by the secretary of the interior. Review meant that the superintendent could approve or veto the action within ten days. An action so approved by the superintendent could still be vetoed by the secretary within ninety days. The tribal council could, by majority vote, refer an action vetoed by the superintendent to the secretary, who might override the veto within ninety days.

37. In this case, the individual liberty at issue derived from an administrative directive issued by Collier in 1934, protecting the Native American Church and other native religions *from the BIA*. See Biolsi, *Organizing the Lakota*, 134–35.

38. Ibid., 136–37. In fact, the U.S. Supreme Court had held in 1896 in *Talton v. Mayes* (163 U.S. 376) that the U.S. Constitution was not applicable to Indian tribal governments in their dealings with their own tribal citizens.

39. See ibid., 102–4.

40. Report of the Great Plains Drought Area Committee, August 27, 1936, electronic document accessed February 27, 2014, http://newdeal.feri.org/hopkins/hop 27.htm.

41. Jon K. Lauck, *Prairie Republic: The Political Culture of Dakota Territory, 1879–1889* (Norman: University of Oklahoma Press, 2010), 25, 45. On the ideology of "petty producerism," see Stock, *Main Street in Crisis*, 9–10.

42. Currin V. Shields, "The American Tradition of Empirical Collectivism," *American Political Science Review* 46:1 (1952): 104. Subsequent references are given in the text.

43. Gilbert C. Fite, *Peter Norbeck: Prairie Statesman* (Pierre: South Dakota State Historical Society Press, 2005 [1948]), 53; Herbert S. Schell, *History of South Dakota*, 3d ed. (Lincoln: University of Nebraska Press, 1975 [1961]), 268.

44. Gilbert C. Fite, "South Dakota's Rural Credit System: A Venture on State Socialism, 1917–1946," *Agricultural History* 21:4 (1947): 239.

45. Ibid., 240, 242.

46. Ibid., 248. I recognize that my colleague Jon Lauck, from whom I have learned a great deal about South Dakota political culture, may not agree with my equation of republicanism and progressive Republican collectivism, and I acknowledge that I may well be, from his point of view, distorting his argument.

47. Series III, Local Unions, 1914–92, Box 1, South Dakota Farmers Union Records, Archives and Special Collections (Brookings: South Dakota State University).

48. "President's Radio Address," *South Dakota Union Farmer*, July 15, 1931, 18.

49. "President's Department," *South Dakota Union Farmer*, July 15, 1931, 18.

50. Everson distinguished such capitalism from the truly free market, which he did not see as "capitalism."

51. "The Power of Organized Group Action, IV," *South Dakota Union Farmer*, December 30, 1931, 3.

52. The similarity to David Ricardo's portrait of Robinson Crusoe emerging naturally as an economic man on his island, a portrait critiqued by Marx, is noteworthy in what follows. See Karl Marx, *Capital: A Critique of Political Economy*, vol. 1, trans. Ben Fowkes (New York: Penguin Putnam, 1990 [1976, 1867]), 169n31; available at http://marxists.org/archive/marx/works/1867-c1/index.htm.

53. J. N. Simkins to Editor, Open Forum, *South Dakota Union Farmer*, July 25, 1931, 2.

54. Ibid.

55. Theodore Saloutos and John D. Hicks, *Agricultural Discontent in the Middle West, 1900–1939* (Madison: University of Wisconsin Press, 1951), 287–78, 290; Jon Lauck, *American Agriculture and the Problem of Monopoly: The Political Economy of Grain Belt Farming, 1953–1980* (Lincoln: University of Nebraska Press, 2000), 111.

56. Lynwood E. Oyos, *The Family Farmers' Advocate: South Dakota Farmers Union, 1914–2000.* (Sioux Falls, S.Dak.: Center for Western Studies, Augustana College, 2000), 32.

57. Saloutos and Hicks, *Agricultural Discontent in the Middle West, 1900–1939*, 304; Oyos, *The Family Farmers' Advocate*, 32.

58. Oyos, *The Family Farmers' Advocate*, 32–33.

59. Ibid., 33, 35.

60. "Farmers Purchase Winner Elevator," *Winner Advocate*, September 7, 1916, 1; *South Dakota Union Farmer*, October 21 and November 4, 1931.

61. Schell, *History of South Dakota*, 265–66.

62. Ibid., 275.

63. Saloutos and Hicks, *Agricultural Discontent in the Middle West, 1900–1939*, 378; "McMaster Speaks to Many Wed," *Todd County Tribune*, October 23, 1924; Fite, *Peter Norbeck*, 107–8.

64. President's Radio Address, *South Dakota Union Farmer*, February 24, 1932, 1.

65. President's Radio Address, *South Dakota Union Farmer*, May 17, 1933, 1.

66. Fourth District Convention at White River. *South Dakota Union Farmer*, June 29, 1932, 2.

67. Paula M. Nelson, *The Prairie Winnows Out Its Own: The West River Country of South Dakota in the Years of Depression and Dust* (Iowa City: University of Iowa Press, 1996), 171–72.

68. C. H. Corey to Norbeck, February 7, 1936, Peter Norbeck Papers (Pierre: South Dakota State Historical Society).

69. Editorial, *Gregory Times-Advocate*, August 3, 1933, 1.

70. Paul H. Landis, "The New Deal and Rural Life," *American Sociological Review* 1:4 (1936): 602.

71. John E. Miller, "Two Visions of the Great Plains: The Plow That Broke the Plains and South Dakotans' Reactions to It," *Upper Midwest History* 11 (1982): 4.

72. Percentage of Farm Land in Tax Delinquency, 1938, South Dakota State Planning Board, *Tax Status of Farm Land in South Dakota, January 1, 1938*, Brookings.

73. T. E. Hayes, "Hayes Sees Things Going in Reverse Gear," *Dakota Farmer*, April 13, 1935, 141. See also T. E. Hayes, "Sub-Marginal Land," *Dakota Farmer*, July 17, 1934, 299.

74. "The American Spirit in South Dakota," *Gregory Times-Advocate*, December 13, 1934, 2.

75. National Resources Board, *A Report on National Planning and Public Works*, 1934, 16.

76. Minutes, December 28, 1934, South Dakota State Planning Board—General Correspondence File, Box 25, I.D. and Virginia Weeks Collection, Archives and Special Collections, I.D. Weeks Library (Vermillion: University of South Dakota).

77. "South Dakota's Dander Up over Federal Scheme," *Gregory Times-Advocate*, January 3, 1937, 2.

78. The full video is available at the Internet Archive, accessed January 28, 2018, https://archive.org/details/plow_that_broke_the_plains.

79. Film script, *The Plow That Broke the Plains*, 1936, electronic document accessed January 28, 2018, http://xroads.virginia.edu/~1930s/film/lorentz/plowscript .html.

80. "AAA Committeemen Are Guests at Rotary Dinner," *Winner Advocate*, February 15, 1940, 1.

81. *Congressional Record*, February 16, 1939, 1522, 1523, 1524.

82. Scott Heidepreim, *A Fair Chance for a Free People: Biography of Karl E. Mundt, United States Senator*, Karl E. Mundt Historical and Educational Foundation (Madison, S.Dak.: Dakota State College, 1988).

83. Miller, "Two Visions of the Great Plains," 10.

84. Editorial, *Gregory Times-Advocate*, April 27, 1939, 2. See also Jon Lauck, "Dorothea Lange and the Limits of the Liberal Narrative: A Review Essay," *Heritage of the Great Plains* 45:1 (2012): 4–37.

85. *The True Story of "The Plow That Broke the Plains" in South Dakota* (Pierre: South Dakota Rural Credit Board, 1936).

86. Quoted in Gilbert C. Fite, "Farmer Opinion and the Agricultural Adjustment Act, 1933," *Mississippi Valley Historical Review* 48 (1962): 665.

87. President's Address, *South Dakota Union Farmer*, July 25, 1931, 1.

88. Letter to the editor, ibid., 2.

89. "Cat Control," *South Dakota Union Farmer*, January 10, 1934 (from the *Chicago Tribune*, December 24, 1933).

90. T. E. Hayes, "Inside the Pasture Fence-Sub-Marginal," *Dakota Farmer*, July 17, 1934, 299.

91. "Individual Problem," *Argus Leader*, December 18, 1934, 6.

92. F. A. Hayek *The Road to Serfdom*, ed. Bruce Caldwell (Chicago: University of Chicago Press, 2007 [1944]).

93. Hayes, "Inside the Pasture Fence-Sub-Marginal," 299.

94. "Whither Are We Drifting?" *Gregory Times-Advocate*, December 14, 1933, 2.

95. "The Threat of Tugwell," *Gregory Times-Advocate*, July 5, 1934, 2.

96. "Socialistic Community Planned for Indians," *Gregory Times-Advocate*, August 16, 1934, 1.

97. Paul Rabinow, "Introduction," in *The Foucault Reader*, ed. Paul Rabinow (New York: Pantheon Books, 1984), 21.

98. Lila Abu-Lughod, "The Romance of Resistance: Tracing Transformations of Power through Bedouin Women," *American Ethnologist* 17:1 (1990): 48, 42.

99. Michel Foucault, "The Subject and Power," in *Michel Foucault: Beyond Structuralism and Hermeneutics,* 2d ed., ed. Hubert L. Dreyfus and Paul Rabinow (Chicago: University of Chicago Press, 1982 [1983]), 212; emphasis added.

100. Ibid.

101. Williams suggests "practical consciousness" as a way of describing the "structures of feeling" or "structures of experience" that entail "meanings and values as they are actively lived and felt" or "thought as felt and feeling as thought" (Raymond Williams, *Marxism and Literature* [Oxford: Oxford University Press, 1977], 132). While it would seem unlikely to anthropologists to mention systems theorist Anthony F. C. Wallace in the same breath as Marxist Raymond Williams, Wallace's concept of mazeway has remarkable overlap: "[I]t includes perceptions of both the maze of physical objects of the environment (internal and external, human and nonhuman) and also of the ways in which this maze can be manipulated by the self and others in order to minimize stress. The mazeway is nature, society, culture, personality, and body image, as seen by one person." It is "organized by the individual's own experience" (Anthony F. C. Wallace, "Revitalization Movements," *American Anthropologist* 58:2 [1956]: 266).

102. Thomas Frank, *What's the Matter with Kansas? How Conservatives Won the Heart of America* (New York: Metropolitan Books, 2004).

5. Planning Who Shall Die So Others May Live

1. Frank J. Popper and Deborah Epstein Popper, "Saving the Plains: The Bison Gambit," *Washington Post,* August 6, 1989, B3. The Poppers had published an article to the same effect in 1987: "The Great Plains: From Dust to Dust," *Planning* 53:12 (1987): 12–18.

2. The representative from Antelope had also come of age during the "termination and relocation" period of federal policy toward Indians when the solution to "the Indian problem" was to encourage tribal members to move to metropolitan areas so that tribes and reservations could be abolished as quickly as possible. See, for example, Donald L. Fixico, *Termination and Relocation: Federal Indian Policy, 1945–1960* (Albuquerque: University of New Mexico Press, 1990).

3. Annual Report, 1938–39, LU-SD, 38–1, Rapid City, Land Utilization Folder 1 (Rapid City, Badlands Project); Analysis and Evaluation Committee Report, Project LU-SD-38–1, Rapid City, 1940, Land Utilization Project File 2; Institutional Adjustments Survey, Badlands–Fall River Land Use Adjustment Project, Lincoln, Nebraska, May 1940, Records of Natural Resources Conservation Service (Kansas City, Mo.: National Archives and Records Administration).

4. Paul H. Landis, "Probable Social Effects of Purchasing Submarginal Land in the Great Plains," *Journal of Farm Economics* 13:3 (1935): 513.

5. Institutional Adjustments Survey, Badlands–Fall River Land Use Adjustment Project, Lincoln, Nebraska, May 1940, Records of Natural Resources Conservation Service.

6. Major General Bernard A. Schriever, "Introduction: The USAF Ballistic Missile Program," in *The United States Air Force Report on the Ballistic Missile: Its Technology, Logistics, and Strategy*, ed. Kenneth F. Gantz (Garden City, N.Y.: Doubleday, 1958), 25–46.

7. ICBM and IRBM [intermediate range ballistic missile] Siting and Deployment, May 16, 1957, Joint Chiefs of Staff, Document NH00577, Digital National Security Archives, electronic document accessed August 30, 2013, http://nsarchive .chadwyck.com/home.do; emphasis added.

8. WSEG Report No. 26, October 23, 1957, Joint Chiefs of Staff Document NH00590 (ibid.).

9. Proposed Preliminary Operational Concept for Minuteman, April 8, 1958, appended to Robert F. Piper, *The Development of the SM-80 Minuteman*, 1962, Historical Office, Deputy Commander for Aerospace Systems. Document NH00024, Digital National Security Archive, electronic document accessed August 30, 2013, http://nsarchive.chadwyck.com/home.do.

10. Air Force Vice Chief of Staff, April 16, 1960, quoted in Piper, *The Development of the SM-80 Minuteman*, 116, electronic document accessed June 7, 2014, http://nsarchive.chadwyck.com/home.do.

11. U.S. Congress, House of Representatives, Subcommittee on Government Operations, 1960, *Civil Defense*, 86th Cong., 2d Sess. (Washington, D.C.: U.S. Government Printing Office, 1960), 138, 137.

12. Gretchen Heefner, *The Missile Next Door: The Minuteman in the American Heartland*. (Cambridge: Harvard University Press, 2012), 32. Heefner's book comprehensively narrates and compellingly analyzes both the history of United States strategic nuclear weapons policy, and the thinking of rural South Dakotans about the presence of the missiles.

13. Subcommittee on Government Operations, *Civil Defense*, 137.

14. E. N. to Case, March 29, 1961, Minuteman Unit, Ellsworth Air Force Base File, Case File 34, Drawer 136 (Old Drawer 140), Box 1, Senator Francis H. Case Collection, Archives, McGovern Library (Mitchell, S.Dak.: Dakota Wesleyan University).

15. The RAND Corporation (the acronym for research and development) began as Project RAND, a nonprofit entity split off from Douglas Aircraft in 1945. It was incorporated in 1948.

16. See, for example, Larry Ceplair, *Anti-Communism in Twentieth-Century America: A Critical History* (Santa Barbara, Calif.: Praeger, 2011).

17. "Long Telegram," Harry S. Truman Library, electronic document accessed June 9, 2014, http://www.trumanlibrary.org/whistlestop/study_collections/coldwar/.

18. Mr. X, "The Sources of Soviet Conduct," *Foreign Affairs* 25:4 (1947): 568. Kennan was less temperate in his telegram to Byrnes, which, of course, was not for public consumption (it was not declassified until 1972). Beyond the idea of containment, he raised the critical Cold War specter of world communist infiltration, arguing that the Communist parties organized in the Comintern were "working

closely together as an underground directorate of world communism, . . . tightly coordinated and directed by Moscow." The "[r]ank and file" of the national Communist parties was "used to penetrate, and to influence or dominate . . . other organizations. . . . A wide variety of national associations or bodies . . . can be dominated or influenced by such penetration. These include: labor unions, youth leagues, women's organizations, racial societies, religious societies, social organizations, cultural groups, liberal magazines, publishing houses, etc."

"It may be expected that component parts of this far-flung apparatus will be utilized . . . as follows: . . . To undermine [the] general political and strategic potential of major western powers. Efforts will be made in such countries to disrupt national self-confidence, to hamstring measures of national defense, to increase social and industrial unrest, to stimulate all forms of disunity. All persons with grievances, whether economic or racial, will be urged to seek redress not in mediation and compromise, but in defiant violent struggle for destruction of other elements of society. Here poor will be set against rich, black against white, young against old, newcomers against established residents, etc."

In a familiar trope, Kennan concluded that "[w]orld communism is like [a] malignant parasite which feeds only on diseased tissue." Such tropes of communist pollution or contagion would soon become common in the United States. See Daryl Ogden, "Cold War Science and the Body Politic: An Immuno/Virological Approach to *Angels in America*," *Literature and Medicine* 19:2 (2000): 241–61; Priscilla Wald, *Contagious: Cultures, Carriers, and the Outbreak Narrative* (Durham, N.C.: Duke University Press, 2008), chapter 4.

19. Mr. X, "The Sources of Soviet Conduct," 570.

20. Ibid., 572.

21. Ibid., 581.

22. Walter LaFeber, *America, Russia, and the Cold War, 1945–2006*, 10th ed. (Boston: McGraw-Hill, 2008 [1967]), 103. For the historical context, see, in addition to LaFeber, Richard Dean Burns and Joseph M. Siracusa, *A Global History of the Nuclear Arms Race: Weapons, Strategy, and Politics*, vol. 1 (Santa Barbara, Calif.: Praeger, 2013), chapter 4.

23. Michael S. Sherry, *The Rise of American Air Power: The Creation of Armageddon* (New Haven: Yale University Press, 1987), 195.

24. A Report to the National Security Council—NSC 68, April 12, 1950, President's Secretary's File, Truman Papers (Independence, Mo.: Harry S. Truman Library), electronic document accessed August 7, 2013, http://www.trumanlibrary .org/whistlestop/study_collections/coldwar/index.php?action=docs. This document is a draft of final policy adopted by Truman and the National Security Council; the final draft has not been declassified.

25. Richard Hofstadter, *The Paranoid Style in American Politics* (New York: Vintage Books, 2008 [1952]), 29–30.

26. Republican Party Platform of 1952, electronic document accessed June 9, 2014, http://www.presidency.ucsb.edu/platforms.php; emphasis added.

27. Andrew Ross, *No Respect: Intellectuals and Popular Culture* (New York: Routledge, 1989), chapter 2; Daryl Ogden, "Cold War Science and the Body Politic: An Immuno/Virological Approach to *Angels in America*," *Literature and Medicine* 19:2 (2000): 241–61; Priscilla Wald, *Contagious: Cultures, Carriers, and the Outbreak Narrative* (Durham, N.C.: Duke University Press, 2008), chapter 4.

28. Tracy G. Davis, *Stages of Emergency: Cold War Nuclear Civil Defense* (Durham, N.C.: Duke University Press, 2007).

29. Joseph Masco, "'Survival Is Your Business': Engineering Ruins and Affect in Nuclear America," *Cultural Anthropology* 23:2 (2008): 366.

30. Sherry, *The Rise of American Air Power*, 54.

31. George H. Quester, *Deterrence before Hiroshima: The Airpower Background of Modern Strategy* (New York: John Wiley and Sons, 1966), 25.

32. Ibid., 150.

33. Ibid., 167.

34. Sherry, *The Rise of American Air Power*, 285, 232, 234–35.

35. Ibid. 285. See also Quester, *Deterrence before Hiroshima*, 167.

36. Sherry, *The Rise of American Air Power*, 231, 245–46, 285. The air force also claimed that domestic piecework in Japanese homes was a critical part of war industries, and therefore a legitimate strategic target. After the war, General Curtis LeMay, who commanded the firebombing of Japan, recalled: "I'll never forget Yokohama. . . . That was what impressed me: drill presses. There they were, like a forest of scorched trees and stumps, growing up throughout that [burned-out] residential area" (quoted in ibid., 285).

37. Ibid., 277, 413n43.

38. Quester, *Deterrence before Hiroshima*, 167.

39. Sherry, *The Rise of American Air Power*, 323.

40. Notes of the Interim Committee Meeting, May 31, 1945 (Independence, Mo.: Harry S. Truman Library), electronic document accessed June 6, 2014, http://www.trumanlibrary.org/whistlestop/study_collections/bomb/large/index.php; emphasis in original.

41. Manhattan Engineer District, U.S. Army Corps of Engineers, *The Atomic Bombing of Hiroshima and Nagasaki* (1946), electronic document accessed July 7, 2016, http://avalon.law.yale.edu/subject_menus/mpmenu.asp.

42. Edward Kaplan, *To Kill Nations: American Strategy in the Air-Atomic Age and the Rise of Mutually Assured Destruction* (Ithaca, N.Y.: Cornell University Press, 2015), 18.

43. David Alan Rosenberg, "The Origins of Overkill: Nuclear Weapons and American Strategy, 1945–1960," *International Security* 7:4 (1983): 15–16.

44. Quoted in ibid., 18.

45. R. D. Little, *The History of Air Force Participation in the Atomic Energy Program, 1943–1953*, 1959, vol. 2, *Foundations of an Atomic Air Force and Operation Sandstone, 1946–1948*, part 1, 265, Document NH00011, Digital National Security

Archives, electronic document accessed June 7, 2014, http://nsarchive.chadwyck
.com/home.do; quoted in Rosenberg, "The Origins of Overkill," 15.

46. David Alan Rosenberg, "'A Smoking Radiating Ruin at the End of Two Hours': Documents on American Plans for Nuclear War with the Soviet Union, 1954–1955," *International Security* 6:3 (1982): 9; emphasis added.

47. Joint Chiefs of Staff, 1954, quoted in "Briefing of WSEG Report No. 12" (July 1954), ed. David Alan Rosenberg, *International Security* 6:3 (1982): 30.

48. Memorandum Op-36c/jm (March 18, 1954), ed. David Alan Rosenberg, *International Security* 6:3 (1982): 25.

49. "Briefing of WSEG Report No. 12" (July 1954), ed. David Alan Rosenberg, *International Security* 6:3 (1982): 30–31.

50. Ibid., 32.

51. *A Report to the National Security Council by Secretary on Basic National Security Policy,* NSC 162/2, October 30, 1953, electronic document accessed August 20, 2013, https://www.fas.org/irp/offdocs/nsc-hst/nsc-162-2.pdf.

52. "Text of Dulles' Statement on Foreign Policy of Eisenhower Administration," *New York Times,* January 13, 1954, 2. On the threat to use nuclear weapons in Korea (and other places), see Daniel Ellsberg, "Introduction: Call to Mutiny," in *Protest and Survive,* ed. E. P. Thompson and Dan Smith (New York: Monthly Review Press, 1981), i–xxviii.

53. Rosenberg, "The Origins of Overkill," 61.

54. Joint Chiefs of Staff, "SIOP-62 Briefing" (1969), ed. Scott D. Sagan, *International Security* 12:1 (1987): 43. For additional details on SIOP-62, see Fred Kaplan *The Wizards of Armageddon* (Stanford, Calif.: Stanford University Press, 1991 [1983]), chapter 18; Rosenberg, "The Origins of Overkill," 61–67; Scott D. Sagan, "SIOP-62: The Nuclear War Briefing to President Kennedy," *International Security* 12:1 (1987): 22–40; William Burr, "The Creation of SIOP-62: More Evidence of Overkill," National Security Archive Electronic Briefing Book No. 130, National Security Archive (Washington, D.C.: George Washington University), electronic document accessed July 13, 2016, http://nsarchive.gwu.edu/NASEBB/NASEBB130/index.htm; John H. Rubel, *Doomsday Delayed: USAF Strategic Weapons and SIOP-62, 1959–1962* (Lanham, Md.: Roman and Littlefield, 2008); Kaplan, *To Kill Nations,* chapter 6.

55. Henry S. Rowen, "Formulating Strategic Doctrine," *Report of the Commission on the Organization of the Government for the Conduct of Foreign Policy,* Appendices, vol. 4 (Washington, D.C.: U.S. Government Printing Office, 1975), 220.

56. Memorandum, Secretary McNamara's Visit to JSTPS [Joint Strategic Target Planning Staffs], February 6, 1961, Document 24 B, National Security Archive Electronic Briefing Book 130, electronic document accessed October 28, 2016, http://nsarchive.gwu.edu/NSAEBB/NSAEBB130/.

57. Albert Wohlstetter, "The Delicate Balance of Terror," *Foreign Affairs* 37:2 (1959): 212, 211, 215.

58. E. J. Barlow, *Is Deterrence Enough or Should We Be Prepared to Fight a General War in the 1960s?* P. 1850 (Santa Monica, Calif.: The RAND Corporation, 1959), 4–5.

59. Paul Nitze, "Atoms, Strategy and Policy," *Foreign Affairs* 34:2 (1956): 90–91.

60. Ibid., 192–93.

61. Ibid., 196–97. See also Barlow, *Is Deterrence Enough or Should We Be Prepared to Fight a General War in the 1960s?* 14–15.

62. Henry A. Kissinger, "Force and Diplomacy in the Nuclear Age," *Foreign Affairs* 34:3 (1956): 360.

63. Herman Kahn, *On Thermonuclear War* (New York: Free Press, 1969 [1960]), 113, 166.

64. Cable from Vice Admiral Parker, Naval Reserve Training Command, Offutt Air Force Base, to CNO [Chief of Naval Operations], February 6, 1961, Document 24A, National Security Archive Electronic Briefing Book 130, electronic document accessed October 28, 2016, http://nsarchive.gwu.edu/NSAEBB/NSAEBB130/.

65. "Memorandum on Review of FY 1961 and FY 1962 Military Programs and Budgets," attached to McNamara to Kennedy, February 20, 1961, Document 17, *Foreign Relations of the United States, 1961–1963, Vol. VIII, National Security Policy,* 38, 41–42, Office of the Historian: United States Department of State, electronic document accessed July 29, 2013, http://history.state.gov/historicaldocuments/frus1961–63v08. President Kennedy was himself briefed on SIOP-62 in September 1961. See Scott D. Sagan, "SIOP-62: The Nuclear War Plan Briefing to President Kennedy," *International Security* 12:1 (1987): 22–40, and the attached edited, original document, "SIOP-62 Briefing," 41–51.

66. "Memorandum on Review of FY 1961 and FY 1962 Military Programs and Budgets," 38, 41–42; "History of the Joint Strategic Target Planning Staff: Preparation of SIOP-63," January 1964, History and Research Division, Headquarters Strategic Air Command, The Nuclear Vault, National Security Archives (Washington, D.C.: George Washington University), electronic document accessed October 7, 2013, http://www2.gwu.edu/~nsarchiv/nukevault/ebb236/index.htm.

67. Editorial note, Document 92, *Foreign Relations of the United States, 1961–1963, Vol. VIII, National Security Policy,* Office of the Historian: United States Department of State, electronic document accessed October 14, 2013, http://history.state.gov/historicaldocuments/frus1961–63v08.

68. Robert S. McNamara, Commencement Address, University of Michigan, June 9, 1962, *Air Force Magazine* 94:6, electronic document accessed October 14, 2013, http://www.airforcemag.com/MagazineArchives/Pages/2011/June2011/0611 keeper.aspx.

69. Draft Memorandum from Secretary of Defense McNamara to President Kennedy, November 21, 1962, Document 112, *Foreign Relations of the United States, 1961–1963, Volume VIII, National Security Policy,* Office of the Historian, U.S. Department of State, electronic document accessed November 18, 2013, http://history .state.gov/historicaldocuments/frus1961–63v08/d96.

70. Kahn, *On Thermonuclear War*, 20.

71. Thomas C. Schelling, *The Strategy of Conflict* (Cambridge: Harvard University Press, 1960), 53, 79.

72. National Intelligence Estimate, July 6, 1962, Document 96, *Foreign Relations of the United States, 1961–1963, Volume VIII, National Security Policy*, Office of the Historian, U.S. Department of State, electronic document accessed November 12, 2013, http://history.state.gove/historicaldocuments/frus1961–63v08/d96.

73. Report of the Net Evaluation Subcommittee, National Security Council, Oral Report, August 27, 1963, "Special Collection: Some Key Documents on Nuclear Policy Issues, 1945–1990," ed. William Burr, The Nuclear Vault, National Security Archive (Washington, D.C.: George Washington University, 1963), electronic document accessed November 18, 2013, http://www2.gwu.edu/~nsarchiv/nukevault/special/index.htm.

74. Hearings on Military Posture and H.R. 2440, Armed Services Committee, U.S. House of Representatives, 309.

75. Draft Memorandum from Secretary of Defense McNamara to President Johnson, December 6, 1963, Document 151, *Foreign Relations of the United States, 1961–1963, Volume VIII, National Security Policy*, Office of the Historian, U.S. Department of State, electronic document accessed November 22, 2013, http://history.state.gov/historicaldocuments/frus1961–63v08/d151.

76. Henry S. Rosen, "Formulating Strategic Doctrine," *Commission on the Organization of the Government for the Conduct of Foreign Affairs* (Washington, D.C.: U.S. Government Printing Office, 1975), vol. 4, appendix k, 230. Political scientist Eric Mlyn has argued that while McNamara may have seemed to return to assured destruction as a declaratory policy, secret operational plans continued to offer counterforce/limited-war options (*The State, Society, and Limited Nuclear War* [Albany: State University of New York Press, 1995] chapter 4).

77. Draft Memorandum from Secretary of Defense McNamara to President Johnson, December 6, 1963.

78. U.S. Strategic Objectives and Force Posture, Executive Summary, January 3, 197, Document 4, "'To Have the Only Option That of Killing 80 Million Peoples Is the Height of Immorality': The Nixon Administration, the SIOP, and the Search for Limited Nuclear Options, 1969–1974," Electronic Briefing Book No. 173, ed. William Burr, National Security Archive (Washington, D.C.: George Washington University), electronic document accessed November 25, 2013, http://www2.gwu.edu/~nsarchiv/NSAEBB/NSAEBB173/; William Burr, "The Nixon Administration, the 'Horror Strategy,' and the Search for Limited Nuclear Options, 1969–1972," *Journal of Cold War Studies* 7:3 (2005): 34–78. By 1971, the president also had the option of "selective release or ad hoc planning if he wants to execute a limited strike with nuclear weapons," but "selective release procedures for . . . strategic nuclear weapons are not [drilled] and, therefore, their responsiveness in a crisis is uncertain" (U.S. Strategic Objectives and Force Posture).

79. "History of the Joint Strategic Target Planning Staff: Preparation of SIOP-63," January 1964, History and Research Division, Headquarters Strategic Air Command, The Nuclear Vault, National Security Archives (Washington, D.C.: George Washington University), 5, 6, electronic document accessed October 7, 2013, http://www2.gwu.edu/~nsarchiv/nukevault/ebb236/index.htm.

80. Richard Nixon, "First Annual Report to the Congress on United States Foreign Policy for the 1970's," February 18, 1970, Document 45, The American Presidency Project, electronic document accessed June 30, 2014, http://www.presidency.ucsb.edu/ws/?pid=2835.

81. Burr, "The Nixon Administration, the 'Horror Strategy,' and the Search for Limited Nuclear Options, 1969–1972," 45.

82. Henry A. Kissinger Memorandum for the President, January 7, 1974, Document 24A, Electronic Briefing Book 173, ed. William Burr, The National Security Archive (Washington, D.C.: George Washington University), electronic document accessed December 2, 2013, http://www2.gwu.edu/~nsarchiv/NSAEBB/NSAEBB 173/.

83. "National Security Decision Memorandum 242," January 17, 1974, Document 24B, Electronic Briefing Book 173, ed. William Burr, The National Security Archive (Washington, D.C.: George Washington University), electronic document accessed December 4, 2013, http://www2.gwu.edu/~nsarchiv/NSAEBB/NSAEBB173/.

84. "Policy Guidance for the Employment of Nuclear Weapons," April 3, 1974, Document 25, Electronic Briefing Book 173, ed. William Burr, The National Security Archive (Washington, D.C.: George Washington University), electronic document accessed December 2, 2013, http://www2.gwu.edu/~nsarchiv/NSAEBB/NSA EBB173/.

85. John W. Finney, "U.S. Retargeting Some Missiles under New Strategic Concept," *New York Times,* January 11, 1974, 6.

86. "Nixon's Nuclear Doctrine," *New York Times,* January 15, 1974, 36.

87. Subcommittee on Arms Control, International Security Agreements, Committee on Foreign Relations, U.S. Senate, *Analyses of Effects of Limited Nuclear Warfare,* 94th Cong., 2d Sess. (Washington, D.C.: U.S. Government Printing Office, 1975), 112. One of the exceptions "involving a relatively close co-location of strategic targets and a major urban population center" was Whiteman Air Force Base, located upwind from St. Louis.

88. For context, see Mlyn, *The State, Society, and Limited Nuclear War,* chapter 6.

89. Presidential Directive 59, July 25, 1980, The Nuclear Vault: Resources from the National Security Archive Nuclear Documentation Project, National Security Archive (Washington, D.C.: George Washington University), electronic document accessed June 23, 2014, http://www2.gwu.edu/~nsarchiv/nukevault/ebb390/.

90. Harold Brown, "The Flexibility of Our Plans: Strategic Nuclear Policy" (August 20, 1980), *Vital Speeches of the Day,* October 1, 1980, 743.

91. National Security Decision Directive 13, Nuclear Weapons Employment Policy, October 19, 1981, Ronald Reagan Presidential Library, electronic document

accessed July 18, 2016, https://www.reaganlibrary.archives.gov/archives/reference/NSDDs.html.

92. Michel Foucault, *The History of Sexuality, Volume I: An Introduction,* trans. Robert Hurley (New York: Vintage Books, 1980 [1976]), 141.

93. Ibid., 136, 138; emphasis in original.

94. Michael Foucault, *"Society Must Be Defended": Lectures at the Collège de France, 1975–1976,* trans. David Macey (New York: Picador, 2003 [1997]), 241; emphasis added. The parallel with Zygmunt Bauman's location of Nazi eugenics in the logic of gardening is noteworthy. See Zygmunt Bauman, *Modernity and the Holocaust* (Ithaca, N.Y.: Cornell University Press, 1989), 65.

95. Foucault, *The History of Sexuality,* 144.

96. Ibid., 139. Foucault asserts that sex became a prime target of biopower because "[i]t was at the pivot of the two axes along which developed the entire political technology of life" (145).

97. Michel Foucault, "Governmentality," in *The Foucault Effect: Studies in Governmentality,* ed. Graham Burchell, Colin Gordon, and Peter Miller (Chicago: University of Chicago Press, 1991 [1978]), 103.

98. See, for example, his comments on the death penalty in *The History of Sexuality,* 138, and his explanation for the appearance of racism in *"Society Must Be Defended,"* 254, 257.

99. See Mitchell Dean, *Governmentality: Power and Rule in Modern Society,* 2d ed. (Los Angeles: Sage, 2010 [1999]), 90–101.

100. Foucault, *The History of Sexuality,* 137; emphasis added.

101. Ibid., 136–37.

102. Ibid., 137.

103. Foucault, *"Society Must Be Defended,"* 254.

104. Ibid., 257.

105. Ibid., 261.

106. Foucault, *The History of Sexuality,* 138. It is also recognized that the whole carceral system that Foucault examined in *Discipline and Punish: The Birth of the Prison* (trans. Alan Sheridan [New York: Random House, 1979 (1975)]) is based on the biologicalization of the delinquent, even if he is sometimes redeemable through correct penal practices.

107. Foucault, *"Society Must Be Defended,"* 261–62.

108. Foucault, *The History of Sexuality,* 137. Although it was "Nazism alone [that] took the play between the sovereign right to kill and the mechanisms of biopower to this paroxysmal point," Foucault asked in one of his lectures on biopower if it was not the case that "this play is in fact inscribed in the workings of all States," "all modern States," or "all capitalist states." While he backed off this generalization in the next sentence in the lecture by answering, "Perhaps not" (*"Society Must Be Defended,"* 259, 260), it is instructive, indeed, that he used nuclear weapons as his example of the paradox into which biopower can mutate, and he raised

nuclear weapons in his lecture before he got to the Nazis and the Final Solution: "We are . . . in a power that has taken control of both the body and life or that has, if you like, taken control of life in general—with the body at one pole and the population as the other. We can therefore immediately identify the paradoxes that appear at the points where the exercise of this biopower reaches its limits. The paradoxes become apparent if we look on the one hand, at atomic power, which is not simply the power to kill, in accordance with the rights that are granted to any sovereign, millions and hundreds of millions of people (after all, that is traditional). . . . The power to manufacture and use the atom bomb represents the deployment of a sovereign power that kills, but it is also the power to kill life itself" (ibid., 253). Again, in an unfortunate wording, "paradox" is probably not the right word to do justice to Foucault's argument. A paradox is not possible, but Foucault's point is that this—only *seemingly* paradoxical—historical surprise is really not surprising. He mentions a better phrase a few sentences below in his lecture to account for the capacity for global thermonuclear war: an *"excess of biopower"* (ibid., 254; emphasis added). Whether we interpret this as biopower folding back on itself, or as biopower reaching the point of transformation of the quantitative into the qualitative, the point is that biopower itself is accountable, in its own internal logic of development, for its turn to murderous splendor.

109. Benedict Anderson, *Imagined Communities: Reflections on the Origin and Spread of Nationalism*, rev. ed. (New York: Verso, 1991 [1983]), 19.

110. Rogers Brubaker, *Citizenship and Nationhood in France and Germany* (Cambridge: Harvard University Press, 1992), 41.

111. William Cronon, *Nature's Metropolis: Chicago and the Great West* (New York: W. W. Norton, 1991), 48–51.

112. Matthew Farish, *The Contours of America's Cold War* (Minneapolis: University of Minnesota Press, 2010), 194.

113. American Institute of Planners, "Defense Consideration in City Planning," *Bulletin of the Atomic Scientists* 9:7 (1953): 268.

114. Tracy B. Augur, "The Dispersal of Cities as a Defense Measure," *Bulletin of the Atomic Scientists* 4:4 (1948): 132, 131.

115. Ibid., 133.

116. Bernard Brodie, "Military Policy and the Atomic Bomb," *American Thought* (1947 [1946]): 287.

117. Ibid., 275, 288.

118. See Davis, *Stages of Emergency*, chapter 5.

119. Farish, *The Contours of America's Cold War*, 232, quoting Federal Civil Defense Administration, *4 Wheels to Survival* (Washington, D.C.: U.S. Government Printing Office, 1947 [1946]), electronic document accessed June 29, 2014, https://sites.google.com/a/elgintime.com/cd/home/4wheels.

120. Barlow, *Is Deterrence Enough?* 10–11.

121. Ibid., 12.

122. Ibid., 14.

123. "Here Comes the Minuteman: EAFB Chosen as Center for Solid Fuel Missile Base," *Rapid City Journal*, January 5, 1961, 1; "Destructive Power to S.D.," *Argus Leader*, January 11, 1961, 8.

124. "Minuteman Promises Economic Lift," *Rapid City Journal*, January 17, 1961, 1.

125. "Missile Moving on S.D. Roads Appears Safe," *Daily Plainsman* (Huron, S.Dak.), June 3, 1962.

126. "Minuteman Will Affect Region's School, Power, Transportation," *Rapid City Journal*, January 10, 1961; "Strange and Unusual Sights Seen in Western South Dakota," *South Dakota High-Liner* (South Dakota Rural Electric Association), August 1962.

127. Cash to Case, October 17, 1960; Case to Cash, October 19, 1960; Air Force Legislative Liaison to Case, November 9, 1960; all in Minuteman Unit, Ellsworth Air Force Base, 8–20–1960, File 34, Drawer 36, Box 1, Senator Francis H. Case Collection, Archives, McGovern Library (Mitchell, S.Dak.: Dakota Wesleyan University).

128. U.S. Army Corps of Engineers, *Facts about Minuteman Land Acquisition*, 1961, Omaha, Minuteman Unit, Ellsworth Air Force Base, 8–20–1960, File 34, Drawer 36, Box 1, Senator Francis H. Case Collection, 8.

129. Ibid., 11.

130. Ibid., 12.

131. Articles of Association, Missile Area Land Owners Association, Minuteman Unit, Ellsworth Air Force Base File, Case File 34, Drawer 136 (Old Drawer 140), Box 1, Senator Francis H. Case Collection.

132. "Missile Site Deals Not Fair—Owners," *Aberdeen American*, March 10, 1961, 12.

133. Vice President of the Missile Area Land Owners of Association to Case, April 21, 1961; Vice President of the Missile Area Land Owners of Association to Case, April 26, 1961; all in Minuteman Unit, Ellsworth Air Force Base File, Case File 34, Drawer 136 (Old Drawer 140), Box 1, Senator Francis H. Case Collection.

134. Vice President of the Missile Area Land Owners of Association to Case, April 21, 1961, in ibid.

135. Eagle Butte Correspondent to Case, March 26, 1962, in ibid. There is no indication that the rancher had consulted with the Cheyenne River Sioux Tribe, or with his neighbors, on the question.

136. "The Inconvenience of Missile Sites," *Argus Leader*, May 16, 1961.

137. Vice President of the Missile Area Land Owners of Association to Case (April 21, 1961).

138. Vice President of the Missile Area Land Owners of Association to Case, April 7, 1961; Elm Springs Rancher to Case, April 19, 1961; Attorney to Corps of Engineers, June 6, 1961; Case to Cottonwood Rancher, November 1, 1961, all in

Minuteman Unit, Ellsworth Air Force Base File, Case File 34, Drawer 136 (Old Drawer 140), Box 1, Senator Francis H. Case Collection.

139. Vice President of the Missile Area Land Owners of Association to Case, April 21, 1961, in ibid.

140. Attorney to Corps of Engineers, June 6, 1961, in ibid.

141. Vice President of the Missile Area Land Owners Association to Case, June 19, 1961, in ibid.

142. Vice President of the Missile Area Land Owners Association, May 15, 1961; Case to Secretary of the Air Force, May 31, 1962; in ibid.

143. "Here Comes the Minuteman," 1.

144. "The Inconvenience of Missile Sites."

145. U.S. Army Corps of Engineers, *Facts about Minuteman Land Acquisition,* 5.

146. Richard Frylund, "Minuteman Silo Sites Stir Pentagon Dispute," *Washington Star,* May 25, 1962; emphasis added.

147. Case to Secretary of the Air Force, May 31, 1962, Minuteman Unit, Ellsworth Air Force Base File, Case File 34, Drawer 136 (Old Drawer 140), Box 1, Senator Francis H. Case Collection.

148. "Case Advocates Preparedness for Survival," *Rapid City Journal,* August 9, 1961.

149. South Dakota "Operational Survival Plan for Civil Defense," August 1963, Survival Plan, Box 46, Archie Gubbrud Papers, Special Collections and Archives, I. D. Week Library (Vermillion: University of South Dakota).

150. Heefner, *The Missile Next Door,* 142.

151. *Civil Defense,* Hearings before a Subcommittee on Government Operations, House of Representatives, 86th Cong., 2d Sess. (Washington, D.C.: U.S. Government Printing Office, 1960), 135; emphasis added.

152. Ibid., 137.

153. Ibid., 138.

154. "Churchill's decision to bomb Berlin almost certainly was a conscious effort to bait Hitler into an immediate shifting of the Luftwaffe attack on to London, away from the RAF [Royal Air Force] Fighter Command bases which were beginning to collapse under the strain" (George H. Quester, *Deterrence before Hiroshima: The Airpower Background of Modern Strategy* [New York: John Wiley and Sons, 1966], 117).

155. Ibid., 139.

156. Ibid., 150–51.

157. Ibid., 229, 230.

158. Another widespread criticism was that limited war/counterforce would lower the threshold to nuclear war, making it more likely rather than enhancing deterrence.

159. Joseph Masco, *The Nuclear Borderlands: The Manhattan Project in Post–Cold War New Mexico* (Princeton, N.J.: Princeton University Press, 2006), 4–5.

160. Subcommittee on Arms Control, International Organizations and Security Agreements of the Committee on Foreign Relations, U.S. Senate, *Analyses of Effects of Limited Nuclear Warfare*, 94th Cong., 1st Sess. (Washington, D.C.: U.S. Government Printing Office, 1975), 112, 113.

161. Leslie H. Gelb, "The Changing Estimates of Nuclear Horror," *New York Times*, October 19, 1975, 195.

162. *Analyses of Effects of Limited Nuclear Warfare*, 48. The new (higher) fatality count was substantiated by Congress's Office of Technology Assessment in 1979 (U.S. Congress, Office of Technology Assessment, 1979, *The Effects of Nuclear War*, 4, 7–8, 10, electronic document accessed June 23, 2014, http://ota.fas.org/reports/7906.pdf). The report also explained that U.S. fatality estimates for Soviet counterforce strikes were significantly "sensitive" to "potential restraint on the part of the Soviets to minimize collateral damage," meaning that there was reason to assume the Soviets might have an incentive to avoid collateral damage to the U.S. population, if this meant that the United States would do the same in retaliation.

163. *Analyses of Effects of Limited Nuclear Warfare*, 52, 53, 74, 91, 98.

164. Kahn, *On Thermonuclear War*, 58–59.

165. National Security Council Meeting (September 17, 1975), Gerald R. Ford Presidential Library and Museum, electronic document accessed July 1, 2014, http://www.fordlibrarymuseum.gov/library/document/0312/750917.pdf.

166. The phrase "coyote nowhere" originates in Jack Kerouac's *On the Road* (New York: Viking Press, 1957) and went viral with the 2000 publication of John Holt's *Coyote Nowhere: In Search of America's Last Frontier* (New York: St. Martin's Press).

167. My son Noah and I clocked the mileage between abandoned silo E4 and Main Street, Kadoka, in the summer of 2015.

Herbert Marcuse famously described what he labelled Orwellian language (from George's Orwell's *1984*) with the example of the "clean bomb," an innovation in the early 1960s that had somewhat lower radiation effects than alternative weapons. Through Orwellian language *a quantitative difference (unspecified) is transformed into a qualitative binary difference*: a less dirty bomb is described as a clean bomb (Marcuse, *One-Dimensional Man* [Boston: Beacon Press, 1964], 72, electronic document accessed July 1, 2014, http://www.marcuse.org/herbert/pubs/64onedim/odmcontents.html).

6. Voting Rights, or How a Regulatory Assemblage Governs

1. Tim Giago, "Notes from Indian Country," *Todd County Tribune*, March 10, 1982.

2. *Rosebud Sioux Tribe v. Kneip*, 430 U.S. 584 (1977).

3. For a short summary of legal tensions between the Rosebud Sioux Tribe and the state of South Dakota and its subdivisions (especially the city of Mission in Todd County), see Thomas Biolsi, "Bringing the Law Back In: Legal Rights and the Regulation of Indian–White Relations on Rosebud Reservation," *Current Anthropology* 36:4 (1995): 543–71.

4. "Smoke Signals," *Todd County Tribune,* July 21, 1982.

5. The phrase "treaty rights" is commonly used by Lakota people to include both tribal sovereignty and other special legal statuses and arrangements for Indian people and tribes under federal Indian law.

6. Michel Foucault, "The Confession of the Flesh," in *Power/Knowledge: Selected Interviews and Other Writings, 1972–1977,* ed. Colin Gordon (New York: Pantheon, 1980 [1977]), 194, 195; emphasis in original. See also Giorgio Agamben, *What Is an Apparatus? and Other Essays* (Stanford, Calif.: Stanford University Press, 2009).

7. See, for example, Aihwa Ong and Stephen J. Collier, eds., *Global Assemblages: Technology, Politics, and Ethics as Anthropological Problems* (Malden, Mass.: Blackwell, 2006); Manuel DeLanda, *A New Philosophy of Society: Assemblage Theory and Social Complexity* (New York: Continuum, 2006); Tania Murray Li, "Practices of Assemblage and Community Forest Management," *Economy and Society* 36:2 (2007): 263–93; Ben Anderson and Colin McFarlane, "On Assemblages and Geography," *Dialogues in Human Geography* 2:2 (2012): 171–89; Michele Actuo and Simon Curtis, eds. *Reassembling International Theory: Assemblage Thinking and International Relations* (New York: Palgrave Macmillan, 2014); Manuel DeLanda, *Assemblage Theory* (Edinburgh: Edinburgh University Press, 2016); Martin Müller and Carolin Schurr, "Assemblage Thinking and Actor-Network Theory: Conjunctions, Disjunctions, Cross-Fertilizations," *Transactions of the Institute of British Geographers* 41 (2016): 217–29.

8. Foucault, "The Confession of the Flesh," 195.

9. John Law, *After Method: Mess in Social Science Research* (New York: Routledge, 2004), 41–42.

10. Non-Indians were subject to federal jurisdiction only in the case of crimes against Indian victims. See "General Scope of Criminal Jurisdiction in Indian Country," electronic document accessed October 7, 2016, http://www.tribal-insti tute.org/lists/jurisdiction.htm.

11. It is likely that non-Indians relied, as a practical matter, on BIA police officers under the authority of the superintendent of the Rosebud Agency until 1993, and after that on the Rosebud Sioux Tribe Law Enforcement Services, for emergencies. It is also likely that non-Indians would go to the Rosebud Hospital, at least for emergencies (indeed, I went to the Rosebud Hospital twice for dog bites and relied on the tribal police to run down the owners of the dogs to confirm their rabies vaccination). When the BIA fights grass fires on Rosebud Reservation, no distinction is made between Indian trust land and deeded land owned by non-Indians.

12. South Dakota Session Laws, 1909, chapter 280, 427–29.

13. South Dakota Session Laws, 1923, chapter 304, 319–20.

14. South Dakota Codified Laws, 1967, §7-17-1.

15. "County Administration Aired at Kadoka, Pierre Meetings," *Todd County Tribune,* October 30, 1975.

16. An earlier case had been filed in 1968 by a non-Indian South Dakota Legal Services attorney and two tribal members in state circuit court "saying they were

denied the right to vote for the Tripp County officials. . . . . The three men contended they have no effective voice in county government either by vote or by running for office." The suit was abandoned before disposition. (". . . Two Sioux Voting Rights," *Rosebud Sioux Herald*, December 16, 1968, 1).

17. Personal e-mail communication from Stephen Pevar, American Civil Liberties Union, August 25, 2016.

18. *Little Thunder v. South Dakota*, Civil Case 74–3033, U.S. District Court for the District of South Dakota, Central Division, Complaint, October 11, 1974, File 002671, National Indian Law Library (Boulder, Colo.: Native American Rights Fund).

19. Ibid., Plaintiff's Memorandum of Law, October 15, 1974, Accession 021–85–0094, Agency Box 4, Federal Records Center (FRC) Locator 45535 (Denver, Colo.: Federal Records Center).

20. Prior to 1924, individual Indians could become citizens through BIA declaration of their competency to manage their own affairs, or though military service in World War I. The Rosebud superintendent reported in 1923: "[l]ast election, several Indians were prevented from voting and one Indian soldier of the World War was denied the right to vote when he presented himself at the proper place." But there is no evidence that this happened from 1924 onward (Annual Narrative Report, Rosebud, 1923, Superintendents' Annual Narrative and Statistical Reports from Field Jurisdiction of the Bureau of Indian Affairs, Record Group 75, Microfilm Publication M1011 [Washington, D.C.: National Archives and Records Administration]).

21. See Richmond L. Clow, "Robert Burnette: A Postwar Lakota Activist," in *The Human Condition in the American West*, ed. Benson Tong and Regan A. Lutz (Wilmington, Del.: Scholarly Resources, 2002), 193–208.

22. Vine Deloria Jr., *Behind the Trail of Broken Treaties: An Indian Declaration of Independence* (Austin: University of Texas Press, 1985 [1974]). On the birth of the sovereignty movement, see also David E. Wilkins, ed., *The Hank Adams Reader: An Exemplary Native Activist and the Unleashing of Indigenous Sovereignty* (Golden, Colo.: Fulcrum, 2011). Deloria actually saw civil rights as potentially in conflict with treaty rights and was at pains to distinguish the Native struggle for tribal sovereignty from the civil-rights struggles of other racial minorities.

23. Ordinance 74–07–30, April 30, 1974, Tribal Secretary's Office (Rosebud: Rosebud Sioux Tribe).

24. 435 U.S. 191; 450 U.S. 544.

25. Personal e-mail communication, September 2, 2016.

26. South Dakota was no less characterized by "attitudes" on the part of civil servants in state and county government than other places in the United States prior to the partial "reinvention" of government as "customer service" in the 1990s. I myself have felt aggrieved in some situations by South Dakota civil servants, though I hasten to add no more so than I have been by California or New York civil servants.

27. Defendants' Brief (October 24, 1974), *Little Thunder v. South Dakota*, 74–3033, U.S. District Court for the District of South Dakota, Central Division, Accession 021-85-0094, Agency Box 4, FRC Locator 45535 (Denver: Federal Records Center).

28. Transcript of Hearing (October 24, 1974), in ibid.

29. Defendants' Brief, *Little Thunder v. South Dakota*, U.S. District Court. The defendant counties and state also challenged the plaintiffs' claim that each pair of attached organized and unorganized counties was in fact functioning as a single county (but with some county residents geographically disenfranchised). The taxes paid in the unorganized county were calculated on a basis different from that for the organized county; both the tax rate for the unorganized counties and the use to which taxes could be put were specially limited by the attachment law. Separate county records were kept. Far from denying citizens the right to vote, the state had merely "established a regulated system for the administration of the unorganized counties who are financially incapable of providing for their own administration"—essentially a fee-for-services arrangement. Furthermore, citizens in unorganized counties were free to organize their own county governments under state law—a remedy for their claimed harm was readily available—but "citizens of the unorganized county realize that it is definitely to their advantage to remain unorganized and attached to the organized counties" because of the lack of sufficient tax base.

30. David Delaney, "The Boundaries of Responsibility: Interpretations of Geography in School Desegregation Cases," *Urban Geography* 15:5 (1995): 481.

31. *Worcester v. Georgia*, 31 U.S. (6 Pet.) 515, 561.

32. *Little Thunder v. South Dakota*, Memorandum Opinion, October 24, 1974.

33. Ibid., 518 F.2d 1253 (1975), at 1255, 1256; emphases in original.

34. Ibid., 1265, 1257.

35. *Condon v. Erickson*, 478 F.2d 684, U.S. Court of Appeals for the Eighth Circuit (1973). The main issue in Condon was whether Cheyenne River Reservation had been diminished. Other "reservation boundary" cases decided by the Eighth Circuit at the time included *Cook v. Parkinson* (Pine Ridge Reservation), 525 F.2d 120 (1975). The *Condon* decision was subsequently overruled by the Supreme Court in *DeCouteau v. District County Court*, 420 U.S. 425 (1975), but, again, this was a decision about *boundaries,* not about the lack of state jurisdiction within reservation boundaries, which was clear.

36. 489 F. 2d 99.

37. 420 U.S. 425. In this case the appeals court was overruled by the Supreme Court in *DeCouteau v. District County Court,* handed down a few months before the *Little Thunder* decision, and which denied the existence of Indian country within the "former" boundaries of the Sisseton-Wahpeton Reservation, and put Indians living there back under state jurisdiction. But this was not a case in opposition to the treaty-rights assemblage; it was, rather, like *Kneip,* a decision that

merely perfected the practical boundaries of Indian country, not the legal import of the concept.

38. 521 F.2d 87. See Thomas Biolsi, *Deadliest Enemies: Law and Race Relations on and off Rosebud Reservation* (Minneapolis: University of Minnesota Press, 2007 [2001]), chapter 2.

39. Michel Callon, "What Does It Mean to Say That Economics Is Performative?" in *Do Economists Make Markets? On the Performativity of Economics,* ed. Donald MacKenzie, Fabian Muniesa, and Lucia Siu (Princeton, N.J.: Princeton University Press, 2007), 345.

40. Michel Callon, "An Essay on Framing and Overflowing: Economic Externalities Revisited by Sociology," in *The Laws of the Markets,* ed. Michel Callon (Malden, Mass.: Blackwell, 1998), 249.

41. See ibid. At this point, it was not a foregone conclusion that the tribe had lost the *Kneip* case, and it filed a petition for a writ of certiorari with the Supreme Court in October 1975.

42. The judge had waited for correction of the situation by the South Dakota legislature, which met early in 1976, but "a complete session of the South Dakota Legislature has come and gone and neither the parties to this action, nor their elected representatives, nor the South Dakota Legislature has taken any serious productive action to deal with the inequities" (*Little Thunder v. South Dakota,* Civil Case 74–3033, U.S. District Court for the District of South Dakota, Central Division, Order, May 6, 1976, Accession 021–85–0094, Agency Box 4, FRC Locator 45535 [Denver, Colo.: Federal Records Center]).

43. "Federal Court Ruling on Voting Rights Hanging," *Todd County Tribune,* May 6, 1976.

44. *Little Thunder v. South Dakota,* Civil Case 74–3033, U.S. District Court for the District of South Dakota, Central Division, Order, May 6, 1976, Accession 021–85–0094, Agency Box 4, FRC Locator 45535 (Denver, Colo.: Federal Records Center).

45. *County of Tripp v. State of South Dakota,* Civil Case 76–43, Memorandum in Support of Interlocutory Injunction, May 14, 1976 (Winner, S.Dak.: Tripp County Courthouse).

46. "Tripp–Todd Commissioners Support Corson County Idea Re State Law on Reservations," *Todd County Tribune,* February 10, 1977.

47. "Rosebud Tribe Answers Commissioners' Resolution," *Todd County Tribune,* March 3, 1977; emphasis added.

48. Complaint, May 10, 1976, *County of Tripp v. State of South Dakota,* Civil Case 76–43.

49. Memorandum Decision, January 18, 1977, in *County of Tripp v. State of South Dakota,* Civil Case 76–43.

50. *County of Tripp v. State of South Dakota* (1978), 264 N.W.2d 213. But the supreme court did find that the election process was unconstitutional, because

citizens in Todd County could vote in all elections for Tripp County commissioners, while Tripp County citizens could vote for a commissioner only when the term for the commissioner of their district was expiring. Neither the Democratic nor the Republican candidate for commissioner could, therefore, be certified.

51. "Resolution Adopted to Organize Todd, Shannon, and Washabaugh Counties," *Todd County Tribune*, October 16, 1975.

52. *County of Tripp v. State of South Dakota* (1978), 264 N.W.2d 213, at 220.

53. Reapportionment of Certain County Commissioners' Districts Required, Chapter 60 (House Bill 908), *South Dakota Session Laws, 1977*, 98–99.

54. *House Journal, 1977*, 1713.

55. "County Administration Aired at Kadoka, Pierre Meetings, *Todd County Tribune*, October 30, 1975.

56. Minutes of the Local Government Study Commission, October 23–24, 1975 (Pierre: South Dakota Legislative Research Council).

57. An Act to Provide for the Organization of the Unorganized Counties, Chapter 45 (House Bill 1197), *South Dakota Session Laws, 1979*.

58. Minutes, Rosebud Sioux Tribal Council, March 20, 1979, Office of the Tribal Secretary (Rosebud, S.Dak.: Rosebud Sioux Tribe).

59. Minutes, Rosebud Sioux Tribal Council, March 22, 1979, Office of the Tribal Secretary (Rosebud, S.Dak.: Rosebud Sioux Tribe). On the three-fourths majority rule in the 1868 treaty, see Thomas Biolsi, *Organizing the Lakota: The Political Economy of the New Deal on Pine Ridge and Rosebud Reservations* (Tucson: University of Arizona Press, 1992), 39–46.

60. Resolution 79–36, March 23, 1979, Office of the Secretary (Rosebud, S.Dak.: Rosebud Sioux Tribe).

61. "County Administration Aired at Kadoka, Pierre Meetings," *Todd County Tribune*, October 30, 1975.

62. See Biolsi, *Deadliest Enemies*, chapter 5.

63. Rosebud Superintendent to Aberdeen Area Office, April 6, 1979. Frank Lapointe Papers, Sicangu Heritage Center (Mission, S.Dak.: Sinte Gleska University).

64. The Justice Department had intervened in the implementation of House Bill 908, which reapportioned the voting districts in Todd and Tripp counties. Commissioner districts had been apportioned on the basis of counts of registered voters in April 1978 so that two districts were in Tripp County and one was composed of all of Todd County. This arrangement was established in a meeting of representatives from both counties and from the Rosebud Sioux Tribe. Todd County would constitute one voting district and elect one commissioner to the Tripp County Board of Commissioners, and each of two districts in Tripp County would elect one commissioner. But the Rosebud Sioux Tribe complained to the Justice Department about this arrangement. The board of commissioners had used tallies of registered voters rather than census figures to establish the districts. If apportionment had been based on population, Todd County would be allocated two

commissioners and Tripp County only one. The tribal member who attended the redistricting meeting may not have recognized this or argued it with sufficient robustness, and the tribe alerted the Justice Department about the arrangement ("Justice Department Still Objecting," *Todd County Tribune*, November 23, 1978; Days to Tripp County Board of Commissioners [November 9, 1978], *U.S. v. Tripp County*, 783–45, files, Civil Rights Division, U.S. Department of Justice, Freedom of Information Act [FOIA] Request 99–0494[4–337]). The chief of the voting-rights section in the civil-rights division of the Justice Department wrote to the Tripp County auditor requesting submission of the redistricting plan for preclearance under the provisions of section 5 of the Voting Rights Act (VRA) (*U.S. v. Tripp County*, U.S. District Court for the District of South Dakota, Western Division, Civil case 78–3045, Consent Order, November 1, 1978, copy in *U.S. v. State of South Dakota*, Civil case 3039, U.S. District Court for the District of South Dakota, Central Division [Denver, Colo.: Federal Records Center], quoting from *Burns v. Richardson*, U.S. Sup. Ct., 1966, 384 U.S. 73, 95; Days to Tripp County Board of Commissioners [November 9, 1978], *U.S. v. Tripp County*, 783–45, files, Civil Rights Division, U.S. Department of Justice, FOIA Request 99–0494[4–337]; Days to Tripp County Auditor [May 3, 1978]; *U.S. v. Tripp County*, 783–45, files, Civil Rights Division, U.S. Department of Justice, FOIA Request 99–0494[4–337]). South Dakota's submission regarding reapportionment of the three districts for Tripp and Todd counties was received in September 1978, and in October, Drew Days III, assistant attorney general in charge of the civil-rights division, interposed an objection: "While we recognize that the Supreme Court has ruled that the use of voter registration statistics in such a reapportionment is not per se unconstitutional, it has also been held that use of this statistical base can constitute a violation of the equal protection clause unless 'it appears that the distribution of registered voters approximates the distribution of state citizens or another permissible population base.'" The latter was not the case in the redistricting plan at issue, where the three districts varied widely in population and "the one district which is predominantly Indian in population . . . is substantially underrepresented whereas the two predominantly white districts are both significantly over represented." The Justice Department was "unable to conclude that the plan under submission does not have the purpose or effect of abridging the right to vote on account of race." The redistricting was "unenforceable" without removal of the objection by Justice or a declaratory judgment by the U.S. District Court for the District of Columbia (Days to Tripp County States Attorney [October 26, 1978], *United States v. Tripp County*, No. 783045, Records of the Civil Rights Division, U.S. Department of Justice, FOIA Request 99–0494[4–337]). The Tripp County commissioners requested a reconsideration one week before the election under the new redistricting plan, explaining that they had "reapportioned the three Tripp County Commissioner districts by making Todd County one of the three districts as well as by substantially shifting the boundaries of the two other commissioner districts. This reapportionment was done by the Tripp County Commissioners after receiving the endorsement of both local Tripp and Todd county Democratic Organizational Representatives and local Tripp and Todd County Republican Organizational Representatives and Representatives of the Rosebud Sioux Tribe in a special public meeting convened for this purpose. The reapportionment was based upon the number of registered voters in both counties as required by Statute for all other South Dakota Counties rather than a 1970 federal census which would have been of limited usefulness for Todd County [because it was known to have undercounted Indians]."

Because there was no time left for resolution, the commissioners asked "that the county officials and your Office enter into a Stipulation permitting the holding of the 1978 general election" in the two counties, with the results not to be certified until resolution (Tripp County Commissioners to Days [October 31, 1931], *U.S. v. Tripp County*, 783–45, files, Civil Rights Division, U.S. Department of Justice, FOIA Request 99–0494[4–337]). The Justice Department responded by filing a complaint in the U.S. District Court in South Dakota alleging that "[n]otwithstanding the Attorney General's objections, the defendants intend to use the reapportionment plan . . . at the November 7, 1978, general election." The Justice Department requested the convening of a three-judge panel to declare the Tripp County commissioners' reapportionment plan in violation of section 5 of the VRA and to enjoin Tripp County from implementing the plan (Complaint, November 1, 1978; Days to Tripp County Board of Commissioners [November 9, 1978], *U.S. v. Tripp County*, 783–45, files, Civil Rights Division, U.S. Department of Justice, FOIA Request 99–0494[4–337]). Tripp County and the Justice Department entered into a consent decree the following day in federal district court. The election would go ahead as planned, but without certification prior to resolution (Consent Order, November 1, 1978, *U.S. v. Tripp County*, 783–45, files, Civil Rights Division, U.S. Department of Justice, FOIA Request 99–0494[4–337]). The Justice Department subsequently responded to the Tripp County request for reconsideration by pointing out that it could not withdraw the objection and rejected the commissioners' argument that the "representative" of the tribe who attended the redistricting meeting in Winner and opposed use of census population figures for redistricting was in fact representative of the tribe's position on the matter (Days to Tripp County Board of Commissioners, November 9, 1978, *U.S. v. Tripp County*, 783–45, files, Civil Rights Division, U.S. Department of Justice, FOIA Request 99–0494[4–337], Civil Rights Division, U.S. Department of Justice). The Tripp County state's attorney contested the Justice Department's question regarding the representativeness of the meeting on reapportionment. He "said that 5 tribal members had testified although the minutes reflect that only two had spoken. He said that [while n]either the tribal council nor the tribal attorney had been asked for or had given an opinion regarding the plan [, . . .] we had no reason to believe that the Indians did not support the original plan" (Record of Telephone Communication, December 4, 1978, *U.S. v. Tripp County*, 783–45, files, Civil Rights Division, U.S. Department of

Justice, FOIA Request 99–0494[4–337]). As the Justice Department explained to Senator George McGovern (Democrat of South Dakota), "The plan deviated 53% from an ideal one-person one-vote standard and underrepresented predominantly Indian Todd County by 40% while overrepresenting the two predominantly white districts in Tripp County by 17% and 23%, respectively" (Days to McGovern, April 11, 1979, *U.S. v. Tripp County*, 783–45, files, Civil Rights Division, U.S. Department of Justice, FOIA Request 99–0494[4–337]). By this simple measure, the discriminatory effect was obvious, whatever the intent had been.

65. 79 Stat., 437.

66. Ibid., 438, 439.

67. Section 5, Covered Jurisdictions, United States Department of Justice, electronic document accessed April 19, 2013, http://www.justice.gov/crt/about/vot/sec_5/covered.php.

68. 79 Stat., 439.

69. 28 Code of Federal Regulations 51.19, 375–76 (1978).

70. 89 Stat. 400, 403, 401–2.

71. 579 U.S. 529. It is worth noting that the Rosebud Sioux Tribe has, since it was established in 1936, issued ballots for tribal elections only in English. The tribe is not subject to the provisions of the VRA.

72. Assistant Attorney General for Civil Rights Division to South Dakota Attorney General, April 2, 1979, *U.S. v. South Dakota, Tripp County, and Fall River County* (Civil Case 79–3039) file (Winner, S.Dak.: John Simpson Law Office).

73. Days to South Dakota Attorney General, May 24, 1979; Days telegram to South Dakota Attorney General, June 22, 1979; Complaint, June 26, 1979, *U.S. v. South Dakota, Tripp County, and Fall River County* (Civil Case 79–3039) file (Denver, Colo.: Federal Records Center); "[Governor] Appoints Board," *Todd County Tribune,* June 28, 1979.

74. Deputy South Dakota Attorney General to Days, June 21, 1979, *U.S. v. South Dakota* file, 79–3039, files, Civil Rights Division, U.S. Department of Justice, FOIA Request 99–0494[4–337].

75. Defendants' Answer, July 3, 1979, *U.S. v. South Dakota, Tripp County, and Fall River County,* Civil Case 79–3039, U.S. District Court for the District of South Dakota, Central Division (Denver, Colo.: Federal Records Center).

76. Brief for Plaintiff, in ibid.

77. 439 U.S. 32 (1978).

78. Brief of the State's on the Issues, August 28, 1979, *U.S. v. South Dakota, Tripp County, and Fall River County* (Denver, Colo.: Federal Records Center).

79. Plaintiff's Reply to Briefs of State and County Defendants, September 27, 1979, *U.S. v. South Dakota, Tripp County, and Fall River County* (Denver, Colo.: Federal Records Center); emphases added (citing *Richmond v. U.S.,* 422 U.S. 358 [1975]).

80. 417 U.S. 535,550.

81. Ibid., 552.

82. Ibid., 553–54. Advocates for Native students in the University of California system have been hoping for some years to make the case to the legislature, or in court, that the state's 1996 constitutional amendment (via referendum) that prohibits, among other things, the university from taking race into account, does not apply to policy directed to Native Americans, whose special situation is based on political status, not race.

It must also be said that the federal government treats Indians differently in ways that are harmful—and many would say, racially discriminatory. Indians in Indian country are subject to federal criminal law, not state law, and it often turns out that federal criminal law has lower bars for conviction and/or is more punitive than state criminal law. In *U.S v. Antelope*, 430 U.S. 631 (1977), for example, two tribal members were convicted in federal court of first-degree murder on Coeur d'Alene Reservation in Idaho. Had they been non-Indians and tried under state law, the prosecution would have had to demonstrate premeditation and deliberation. This was not necessary under federal law. Even though the Ninth Circuit Court of Appeals reversed the convictions as violations of the tribal members' right to equal protection, the Supreme Court sustained the convictions, deciding this was not racial discrimination but simply another case of treating Indians differently as members of a special political-legal category. What Tripp County sought in the severing of Todd County was certainly less harmful to Indian people.

83. *U.S. v. South Dakota, Tripp County, and Fall River County* (Civil Case 79–3039), U.S. District Court for the District of South Dakota, Central Division, Submission of HB 1197, received by the Justice Department June 29, 1979 (Denver, Colo.: Federal Records Center).

84. *U.S. v. South Dakota, Tripp County, and Fall River County* (Civil Case 79–3039), U.S. District Court for the District of South Dakota, Central Division, Assistant Attorney General for Civil Rights to South Dakota Attorney General, July 17, 1979 (Denver, Colo.: Federal Records Center).

85. *U.S. v. South Dakota, Tripp County, and Fall River County* (Civil Case 79–3039), U.S. District Court for the District of South Dakota, Central Division, Chief of Voting Rights Section to South Dakota Attorney General, October 22, 1979 (Denver, Colo.: Federal Records Center).

86. Ibid.

87. Letter quoted in "[Attorney General] Seeks Info on Justice Department Ruling," *Todd County Tribune*, November 29, 1979; "Justice Department Seeks Speedier Decision in Tripp–Todd Case," *Todd County Tribune*, November 15, 1979; "State Suing on Todd–Shannon Counties Issue" (reprinted from *Rapid City Journal*, December 13, 1979).

88. "Justice Department to Reconsider Opposition to Tripp-Todd Ruling," *Todd County Tribune*, March 27, 1980; *U.S. v. South Dakota, Tripp County, and Fall River County* (Civil Case 79–3039), U.S. District Court for the District of South Dakota,

Central Division, Acting Assistant Attorney General for the Civil Rights Division to South Dakota Attorney General, April 10, 1980 (Denver, Colo.: Federal Records Center).

89. Of course, it is not at all clear, given intergovernmental contracts, why a tribal government could not have provided the requisite services, usually provided by county governments, to non-Indians in Todd County. The Rosebud Sioux Tribe had, in fact, proposed precisely this. But the 1970s was a period of heightened political strife between Indians and non-Indians in and around Indian country (see my *Deadliest Enemies*) and such an arrangement must have been simply too threatening to non-Indians.

90. *U.S. v. South Dakota, Tripp County, and Fall River County* (Civil Case 79–3039), U.S. District Court for the District of South Dakota, Central Division, Defendants' Response to Plaintiff's Motion of Immediate Injunctive Relief, May 19, 1980 (Denver, Colo.: Federal Records Center).

91. *U.S. v. South Dakota, Tripp County, and Fall River County* (Civil Case 79–3039), U.S. District Court for the District of South Dakota, Central Division, Assistant Attorney General for Civil Rights Division to South Dakota Attorney General, May 2, 1980; Defendants' Response to Plaintiff's Motion for Immediate Injunctive Relief, May 19, 1980 (Denver, Colo.: Federal Records Center).

92. "Justice Department Seeks to Stop June 3 Primary," *Todd County Tribune*, May 15, 1980.

93. *U.S. v. South Dakota, Tripp County, and Fall River County* (Civil Case 79–3039), U.S. District Court for the District of South Dakota, Central Division, South Dakota Congressional Delegation to Assistant Attorney General, May 16, 1980 (Denver, Colo.: Federal Records Center).

94. *U.S. v. South Dakota, Tripp County, and Fall River County* (Civil Case 79–3039), U.S. District Court for the District of South Dakota, Central Division, Order, May 20, 1980 (Denver, Colo.: Federal Records Center).

95. "Commissioners to Set New Districts Monday," *Todd County Tribune*, May 29, 1980.

96. Official Opinion No. 77–73, Voting Rights Act of 1965, as amended by Public Law 94–73: Bilingual Elections, electronic document accessed October 10, 2016, https://atg.sd.gov/OurOffice/OfficialOpinions/default.aspx. He cited Cato W. Valandra (from Rosebud Reservation), director of the Institute of Indian Studies at the University of South Dakota, that "less than one percent of Indian people of voting age could *read* the native language"; emphasis in original.

97. 811 F. Supp. 2d 424, 479. The court's source on the South Dakota attorney general was the House Judiciary Committee's report on the proposed reauthorization of the Voting Rights Act: "Perhaps the most egregious example of non-compliance received by the Committee occurred in South Dakota" (Fannie Lou Hamer, Rosa Parks, and Coretta Scott King Voting Rights Act Reauthorization and Amendments Act of 2006, Report 109–78, U.S. House of Representatives, 109th

Congress, 2d Sess., 42, electronic document accessed April 18, 2013, http://thomas.loc.gov/cgi-bin/cpquery/R?cp109:FLD010:@1%28hr478%29).

98. Complaint, August 6, 1980, *South Dakota v. U.S.*, 80–1976, U.S. District Court for the District of Columbia. Records for this case have been destroyed and are no longer archived at either the District Court or the Federal Records Center. The author thanks Jennifer Robinson of the Center for Public Policy and Administration at the University of Utah for providing a copy.

99. Consent Decree, December 2, 1981, *South Dakota v. U.S.*, 80–1976, U.S. District Court for the District of Columbia. Records for this case have been destroyed and are no longer archived at either the District Court or the Federal Records Center. The author thanks Jennifer Robinson of the Center for Public Policy and Administration at the University of Utah for providing a copy.

100. "Payment-in-Lieu of Taxes on Indian Lands," *Todd County Tribune*, April 28, 1977.

101. "Most Agree County Situation Needs More Talk," *Todd County Tribune*, January 6, 1982.

102. "Two Sides to Every Story," *Todd County Tribune*, May 5, 1982.

103. "Smoke Signals," *Todd County Tribune*, April 7, 1982.

104. "Smoke Signals," *Todd County Tribune*, July 21, 1982. The editor added: "Since I am not allowed to vote in tribal elections, serve on tribal juries, hold tribal office or in any way contribute to tribal government, I am forced by the denial to pledge allegiance to the only other government located here—the county of Todd. [I am] force[d] to uphold the Constitution of my state and nation simply because the other nation located here won't let me in."

105. 492 U.S. 408.

106. *U.S. v. South Dakota and Todd County*, U.S. District Court for the District of South Dakota, Central Division, 90–3017, 1990.

107. 502 U.S. 251.

108. 24 Stat. 388.

Conclusion

1. William Cronon, "A Place for Stories: Nature, History, Narrative," *Journal of American History* 78:4 (1992): 1347.

2. Ibid.

3. Foucault argued, for example, that discipline replaced slavery as a mode of domination because "it could dispense with [slavery's] costly and violent relation by obtaining effects of utility at least as great," and he cites discipline's functional role in capitalism. See Michel Foucault, *Discipline and Punish: The Birth of the Prison,* trans. Alan Sheridan (New York: Vintage Books, 1979 [1975]), 137, 175, 220–21.

4. See Michel Foucault, *"Society Must Be Defended": Lectures at the Collège de France, 1975–1976,* ed. Mauro Bertani and Alessandro Fontana, trans. David Macey (New York: Picador, 2003 [1997]), 254–60.

5. On the effects of discourse on the social and material world, see Edward W. Said, *Orientalism* (New York: Vintage Books, 1978 [1979]), 94). Here Said raises the important insight that discourses "can create the very reality they appear to describe."

6. Robert J. C. Young, *Postcolonialism: An Historical Introduction* (Malden, Mass.: Blackwell Publishers, 2001), 401–2.

7. Andre Gunder Frank, *Capitalism and Underdevelopment in Latin America: Historical Studies of Chile and Brazil* (New York: Monthly Review Press, 1967); Joseph G. Jorgensen, "Indians and the Metropolis," in *The American Indian in Urban Society,* ed. Jack O. Waddell and O. Michael Watson (Boston: Little Brown, 1971), 67–113; Joseph G. Jorgensen, *The Sundance Religion: Power for the Powerless* (Chicago: University of Chicago Press, 1972); Joseph G. Jorgensen "A Century of Political-Economic Effects on American Indian Society, 1880–1980," *Journal of Ethnic Studies* 6:3 (1978): 1–82.

8. Saskia Sassen, *Cities in a World Economy,* 2d ed. (Thousand Oaks, Calif.: Pine Forge Press, 2000), 140.

9. David Brooks, "The Great Migration," *New York Times,* January 24, 2013, electronic document accessed January 28, 2013, http://www.nytimes.com/2013/01/25/opinion/brooks-the-great-migration.html.

Acknowledgments

1. James R. Walker, *Lakota Belief and Ritual,* ed. Raymond J. DeMallie and Elaine A. Jahner (Lincoln: University of Nebraska Press, 1991 [1980]), 169.

INDEX

THOMAS BIOLSI is professor in the ethnic studies department at the University of California at Berkeley, where he teaches Native American studies and comparative ethnic studies. He has been conducting research on the Rosebud Reservation in South Dakota since 1985. His earlier books include *Organizing the Lakota: The Political Economy of the New Deal on Pine Ridge and Rosebud Reservations* and *Deadliest Enemies: Law and Race Relations on and off Rosebud Reservation* (Minnesota, 2007).